FAIRY TAIL

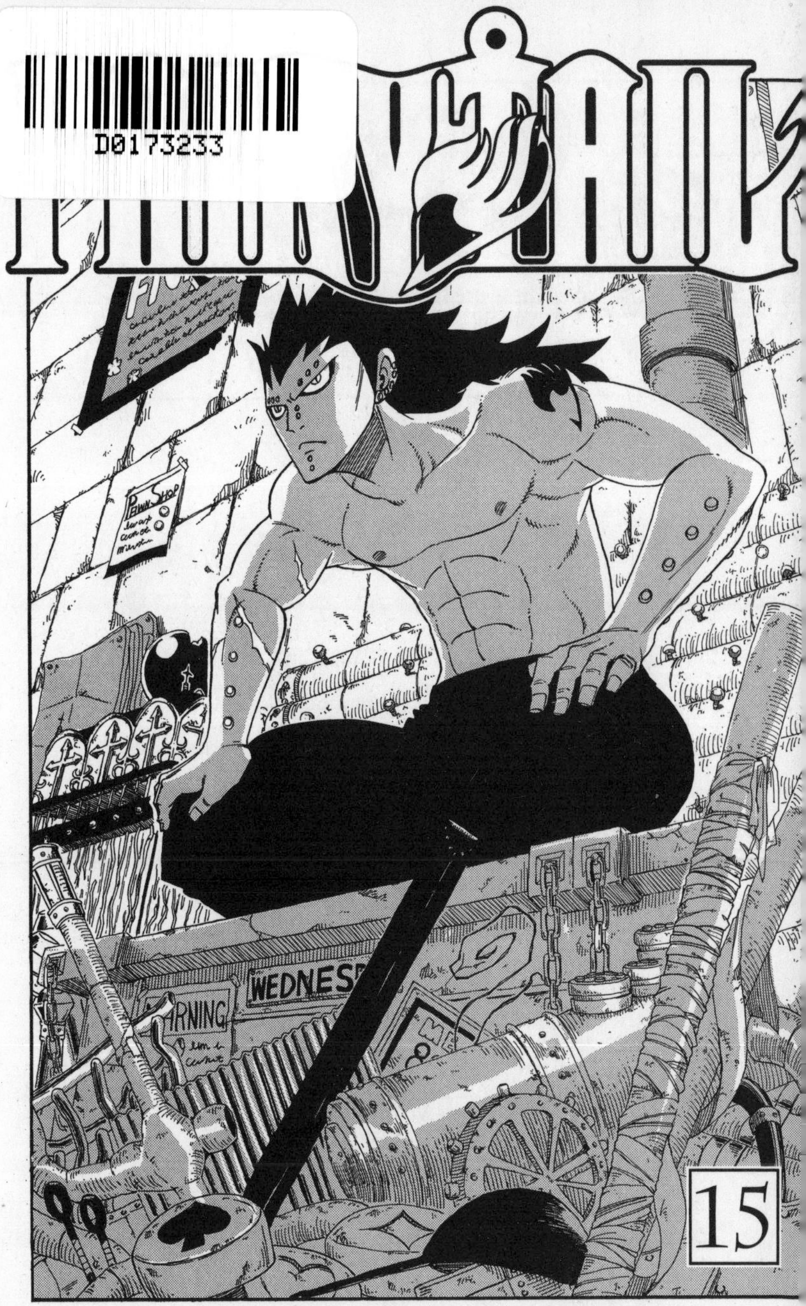
PAWN SHOP
WEDNES
RNING

15

HIRO MASHIMA

FAIRYTAIL CONTENTS

These are the contents for Volume 15!

Chapter 119: Attack! The Great Kardia Cathedral ⋯ 3

Chapter 120: Mystogan ⋯ 23

Chapter 121: My Chance to Take the Top, Right? ⋯ 43

Chapter 122: The Lonely Thunder Clap ⋯ 63

Chapter 123: Double Dragon ⋯ 83

Chapter 124: Triple Dragon ⋯ 103

Chapter 125: Face of a Devil, Heart of an Angel ⋯ 123

Chapter 126: Stand up!!!! ⋯ 143

Side Story X778: Natsu and the Dragon's Egg ⋯ 163

Translation Notes ⋯ 192

Preview of Vol. 16 ⋯ 194

FAIRY TAIL

Chapter 119: Attack! The Great Kardia Cathedral

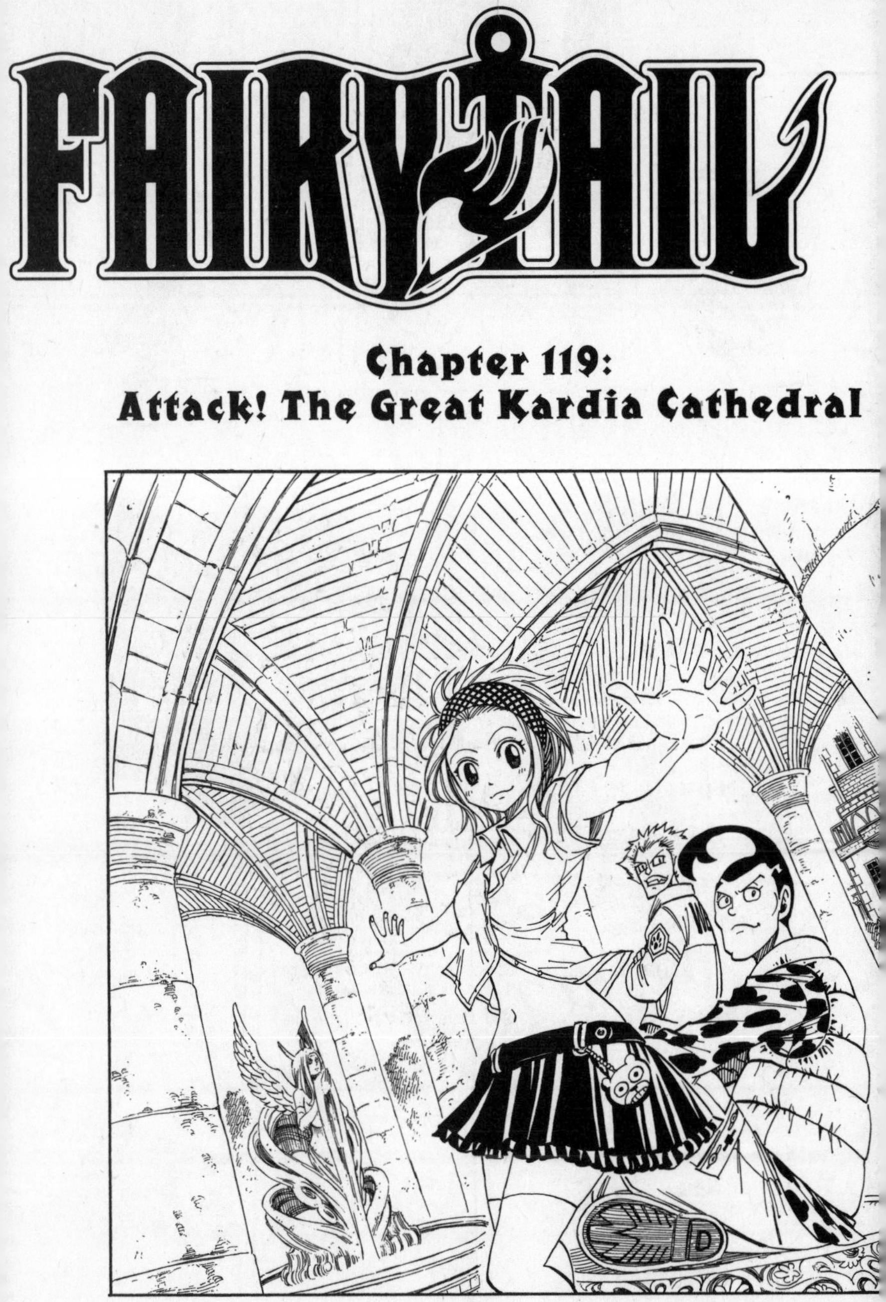

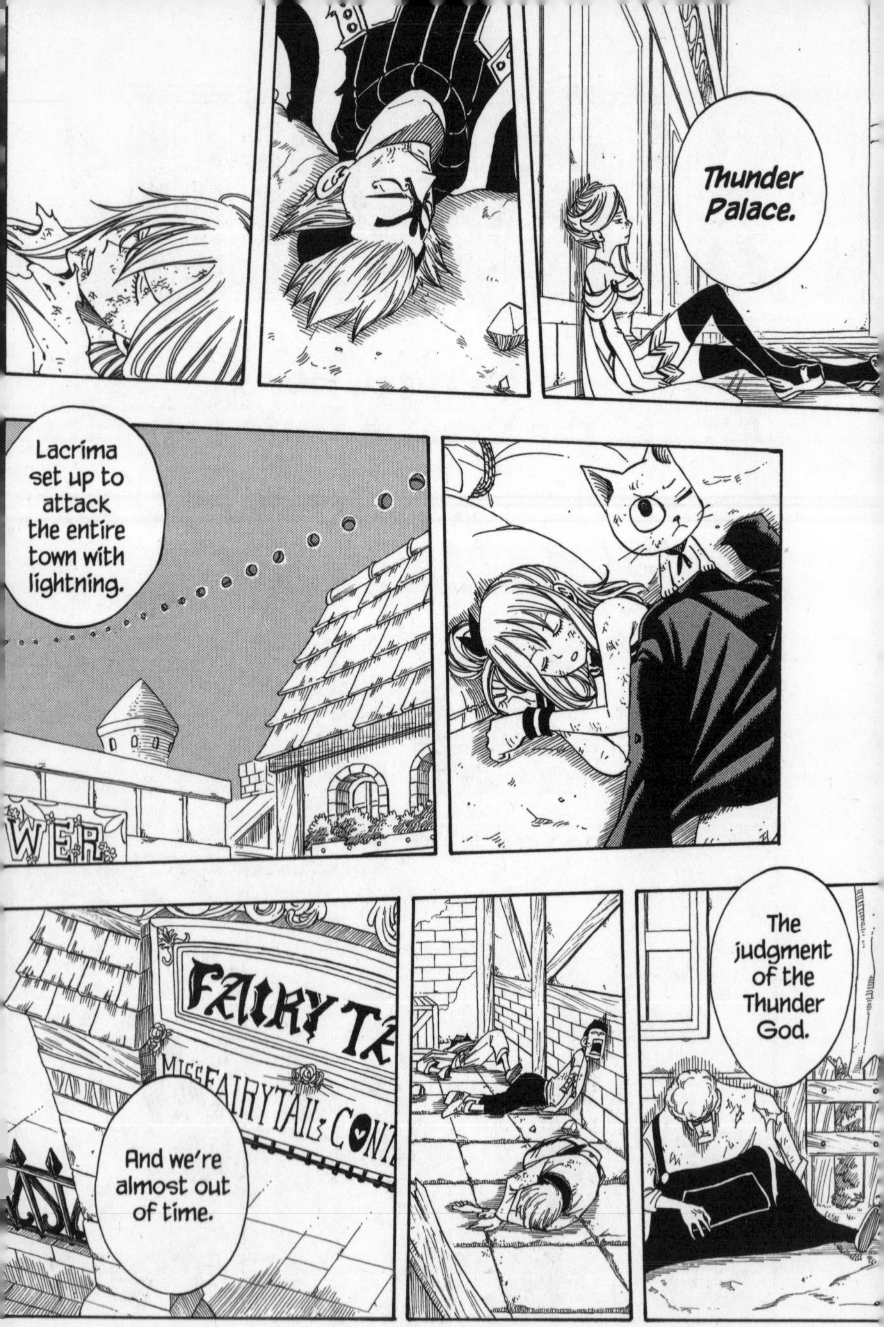
Thunder Palace.
Lacrima set up to attack the entire town with lightning.
The judgment of the Thunder God.
And we're almost out of time.

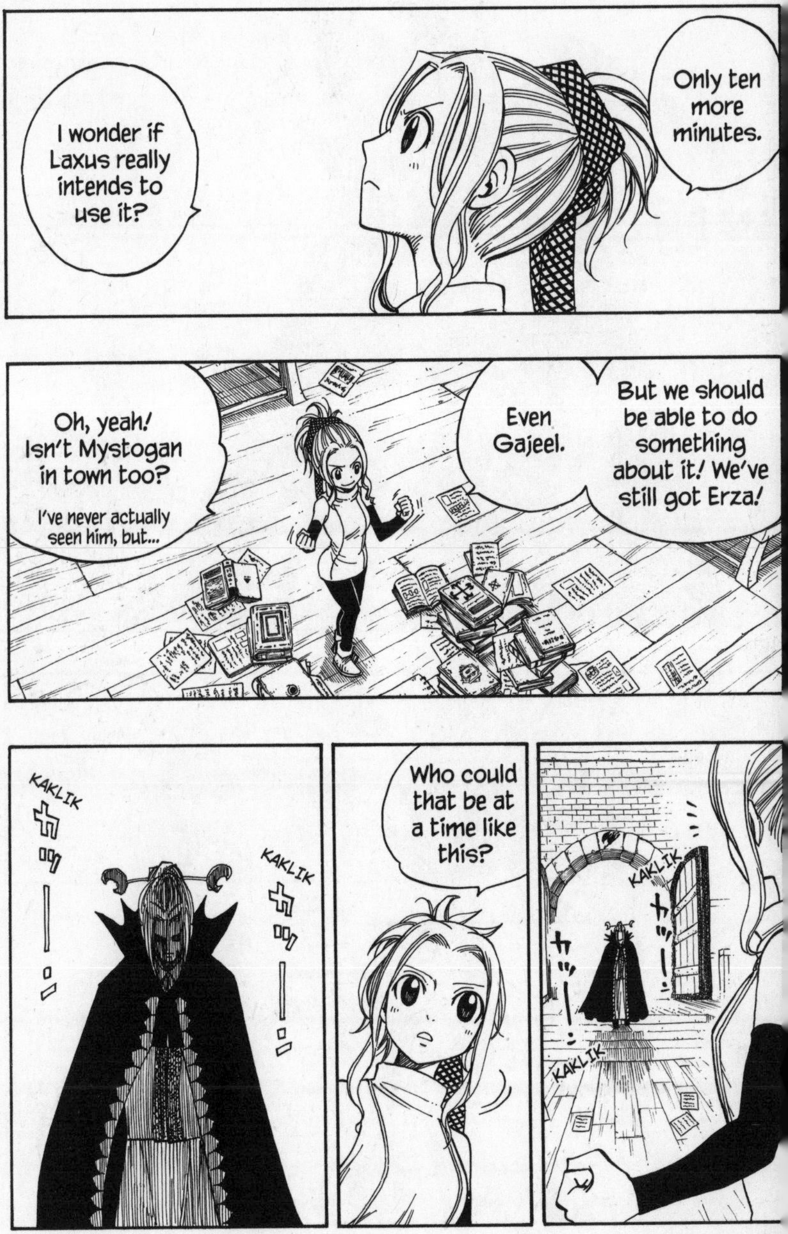
Only ten more minutes.
I wonder if Laxus really intends to use it?
But we should be able to do something about it! We've still got Erza!
Even Gajeel.
Oh, yeah! Isn't Mystogan in town too?
I've never actually seen him, but...
KAKLIK
KAKLIK
Who could that be at a time like this?
KAKLIK
KAKLIK

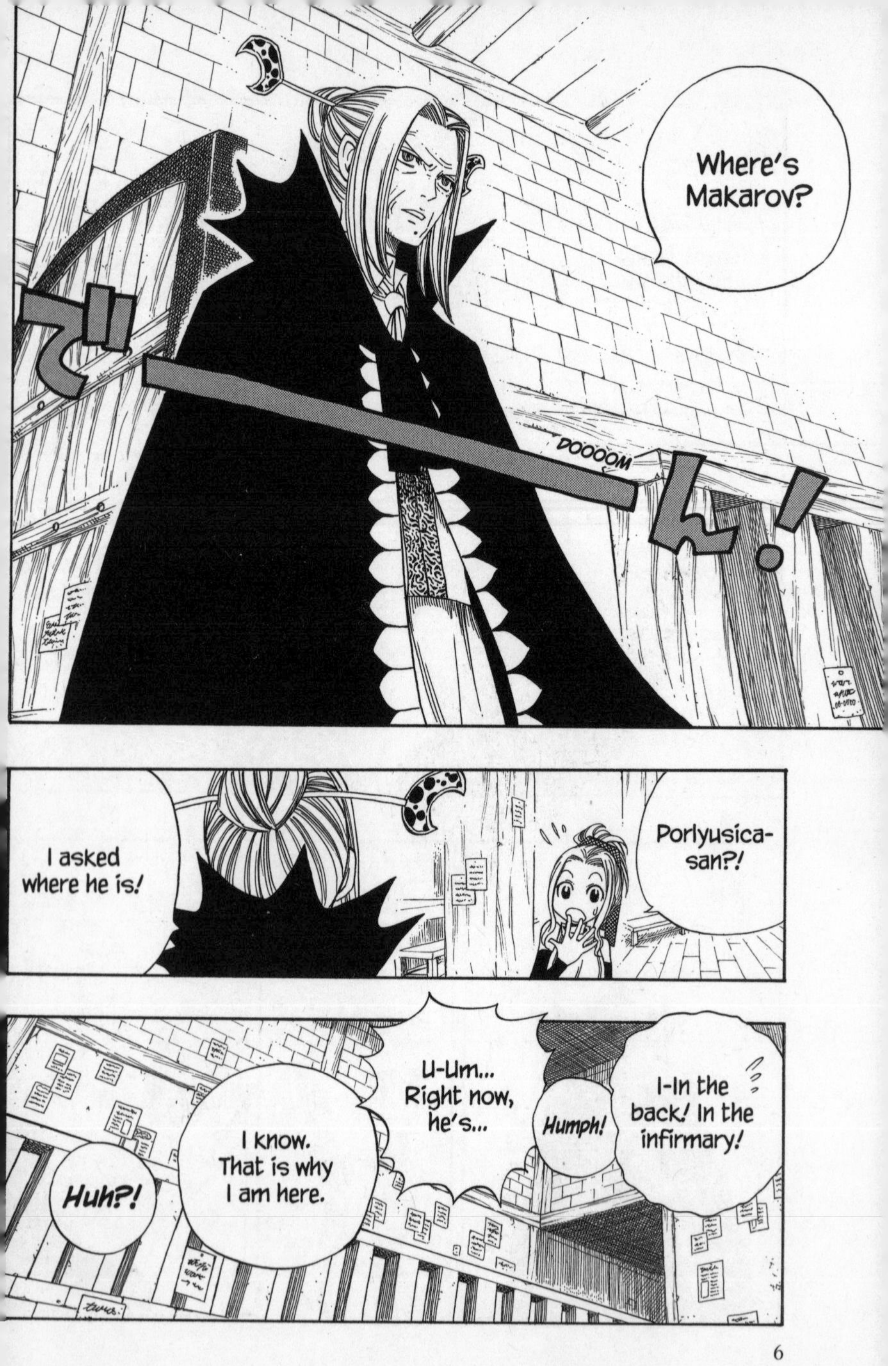
Where's Makarov?
DOOOOM
Porlyusica-san?!
I asked where he is!
I-In the back! In the infirmary!
Humph!
U-Um... Right now, he's...
I know. That is why I am here.
Huh?!

. . . . . .

Then, maybe, you're here to help treat him?!

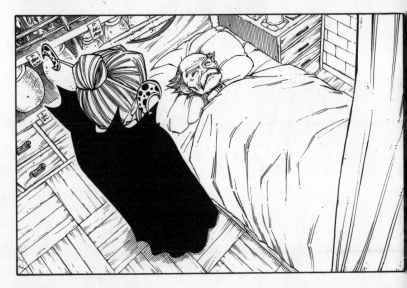

Eh?

Bring Laxus here.

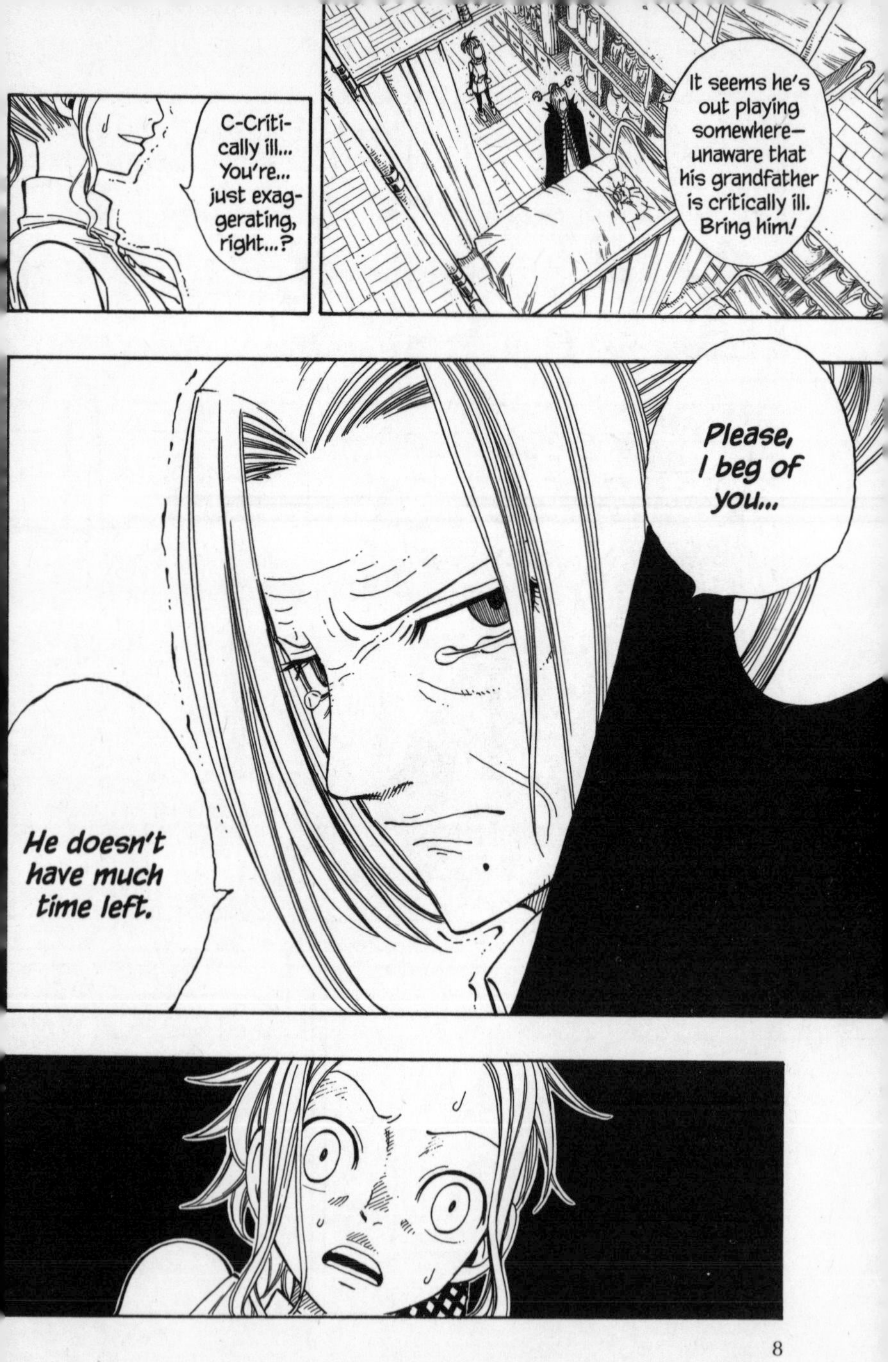
It seems he's out playing somewhere—unaware that his grandfather is critically ill. Bring him!
C-Critically ill... You're... just exaggerating, right...?
Please, I beg of you...
He doesn't have much time left.

Laxus...

Will you
shape up
and help
us with
Fantasia?

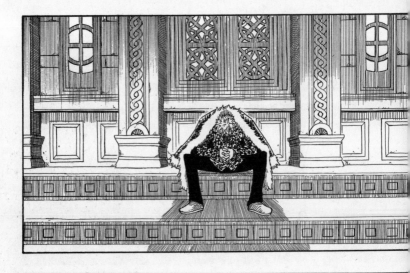

...you have
no right to
talk!

Old man...

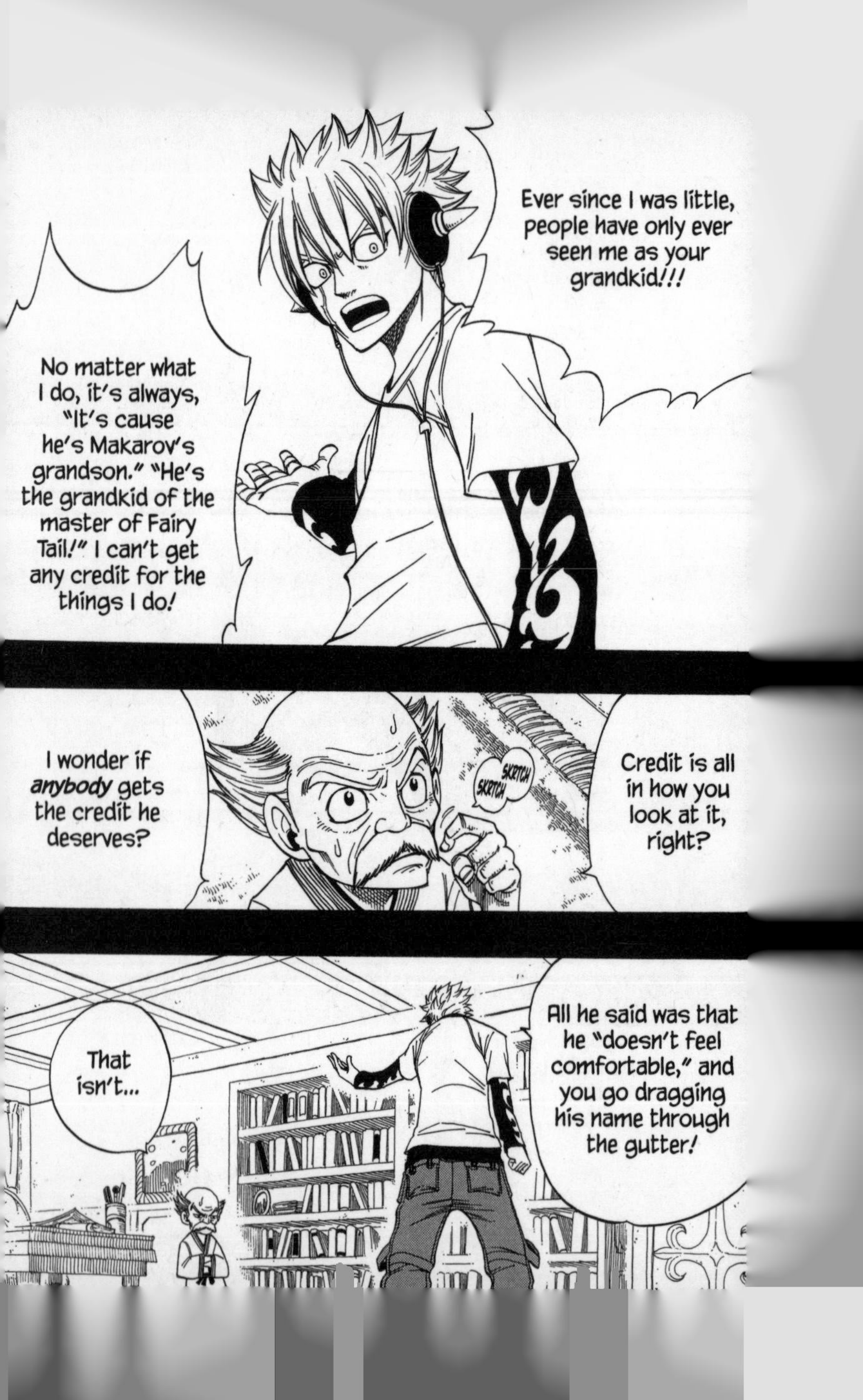
Ever since I was little, people have only ever seen me as your grandkid!!!
No matter what I do, it's always, "It's cause he's Makarov's grandson." "He's the grandkid of the master of Fairy Tail!" I can't get any credit for the things I do!
Credit is all in how you look at it, right?
SKRTCH SKRTCH
I wonder if *anybody* gets the credit he deserves?
All he said was that he "doesn't feel comfortable," and you go dragging his name through the gutter!
That isn't...

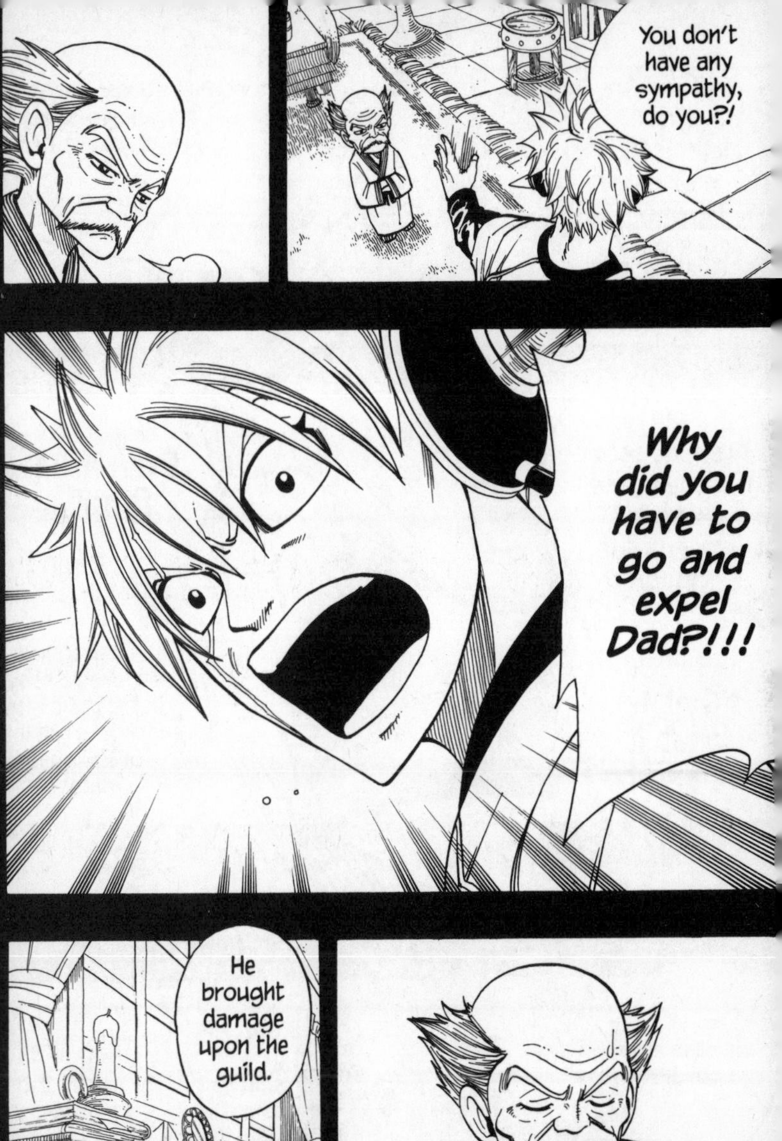
You don't have any sympathy, do you?!
Why did you have to go and expel Dad?!!!
He brought damage upon the guild.

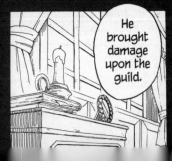

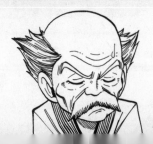

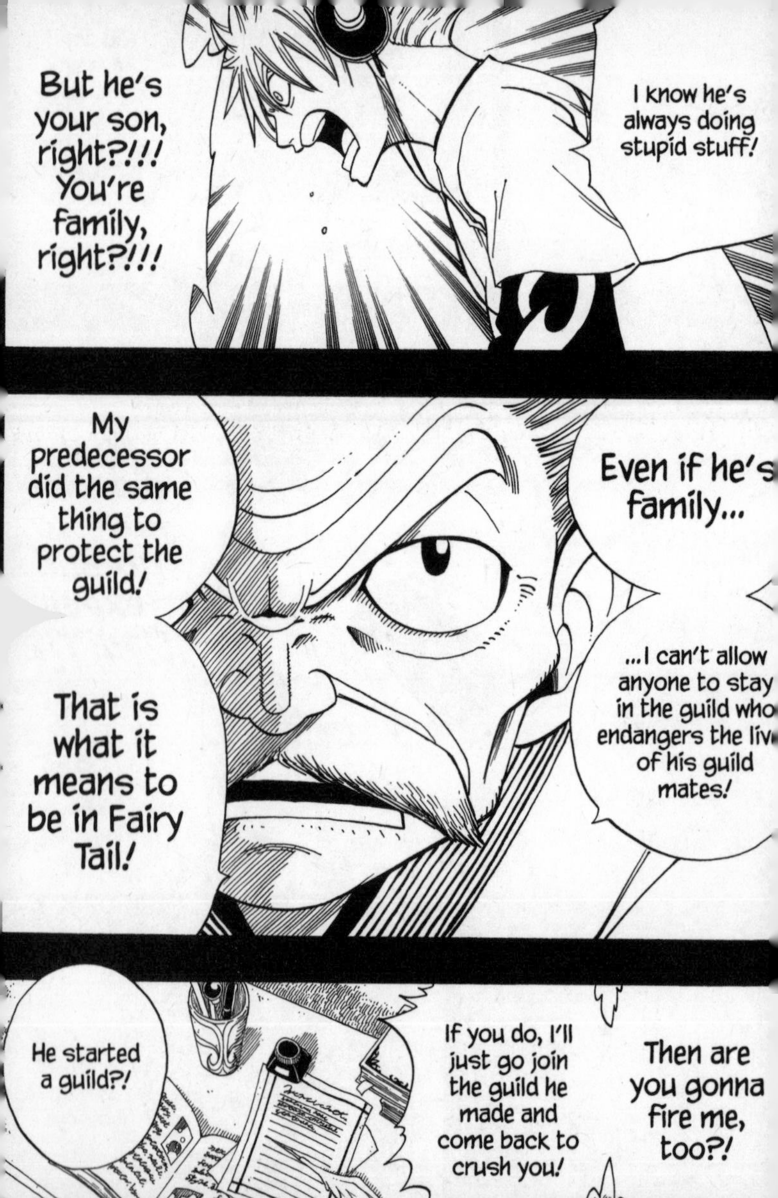
I know he's always doing stupid stuff!
But he's your son, right?!!! You're family, right?!!!
Even if he's family...
...I can't allow anyone to stay in the guild who endangers the liv
of his guild mates!
My predecessor did the same thing to protect the guild!
That is what it means to be in Fairy Tail!
Then are you gonna fire me, too?!
If you do, I'll just go join the guild he made and come back to crush you!
He started a guild?!

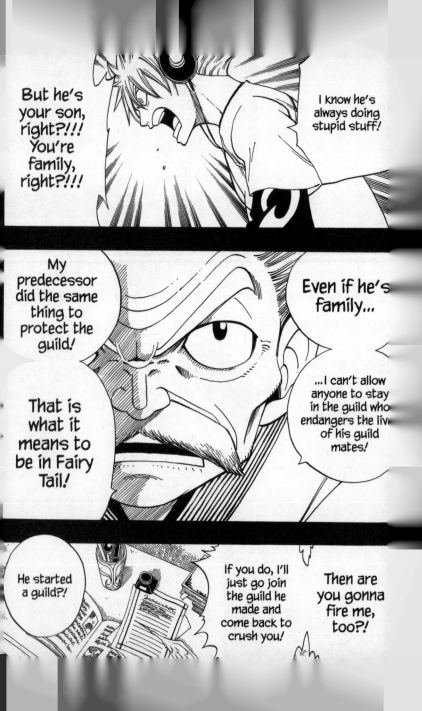

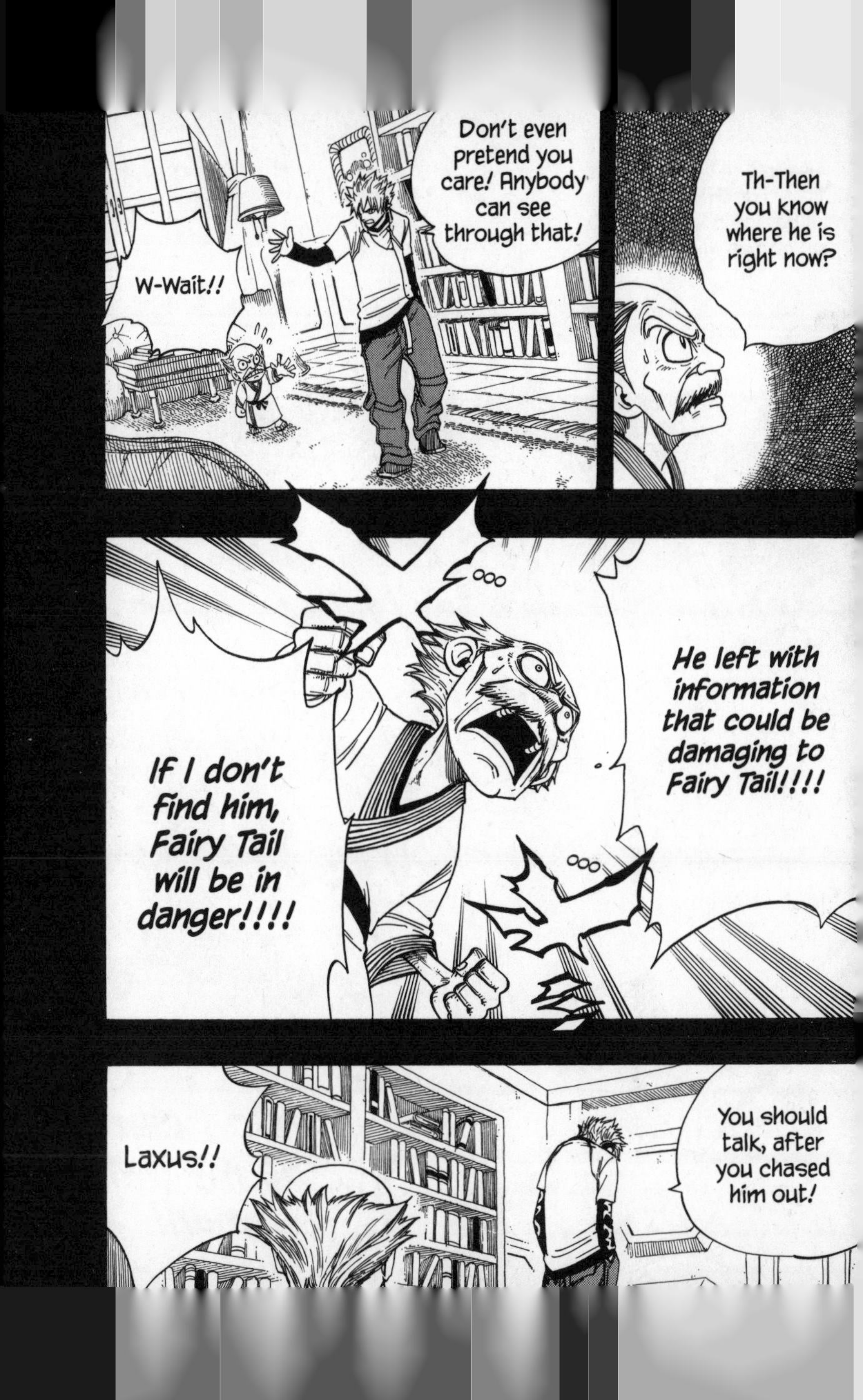
Th-Then you know where he is right now?
Don't even pretend you care! Anybody can see through that!
W-Wait!!
He left with information that could be damaging to Fairy Tail!!!!
If I don't find him, Fairy Tail will be in danger!!!!
You should talk, after you chased him out!
Laxus!!

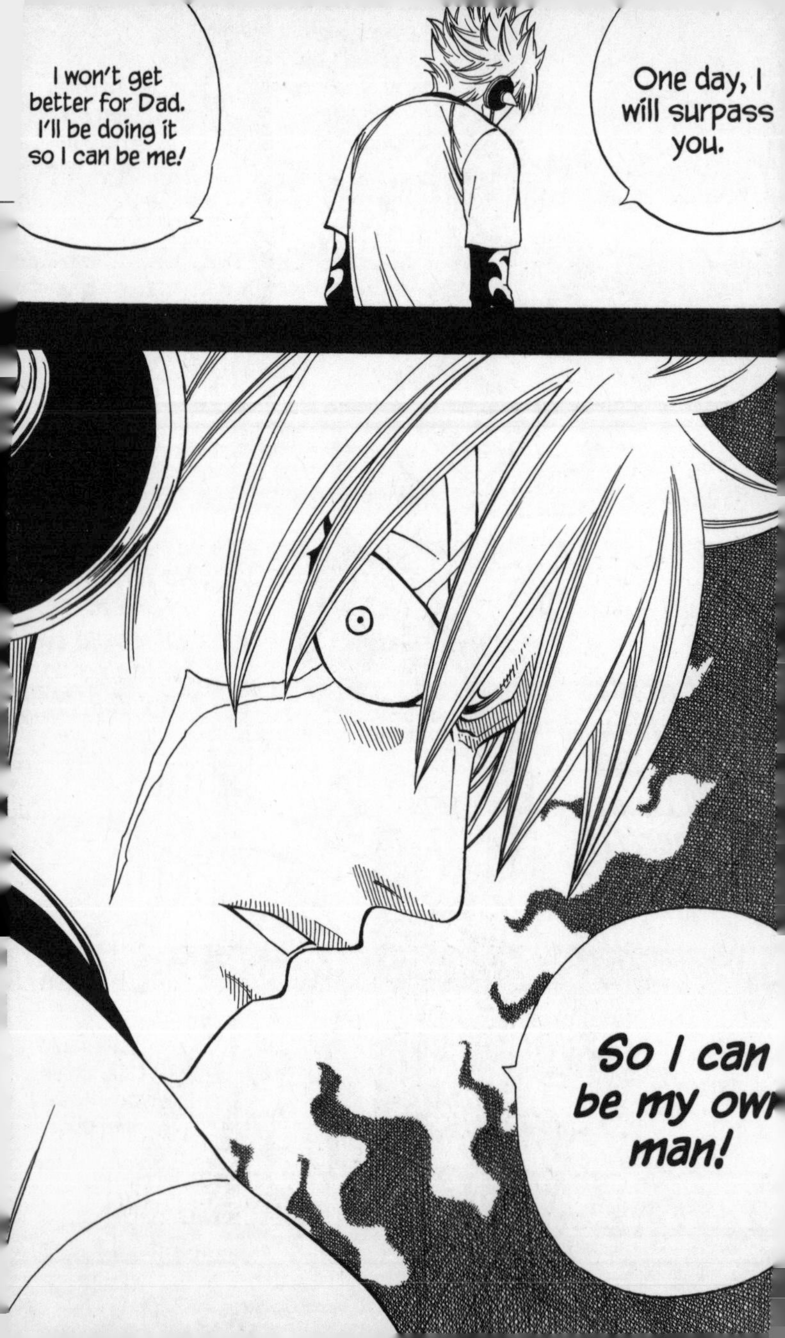
One day, I will surpass you.
I won't get better for Dad. I'll be doing it so I can be me!
So I can be my ow
man!

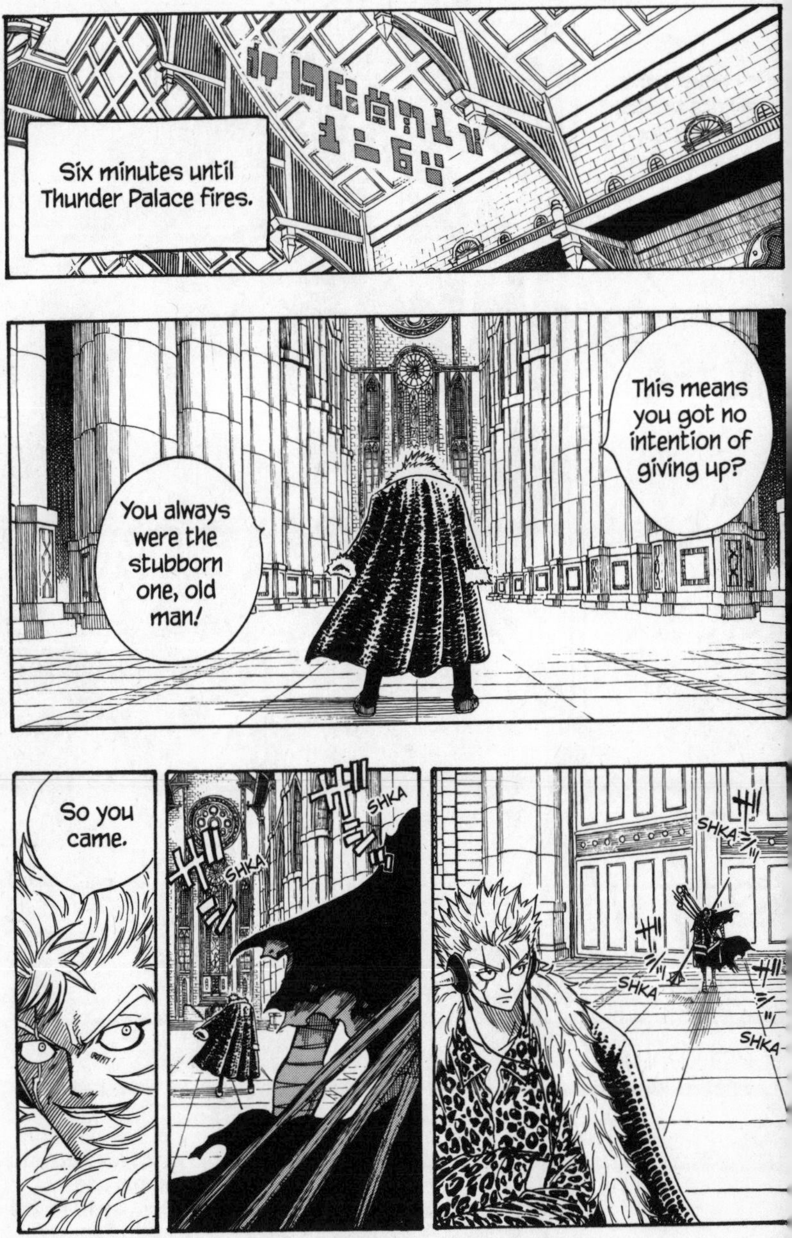
Six minutes until Thunder Palace fires.
This means you got no intention of giving up?
You always were the stubborn one, old man!
SHKA
SHKA
SHKA
SHKA-
SHKA
SHKA
So you came.

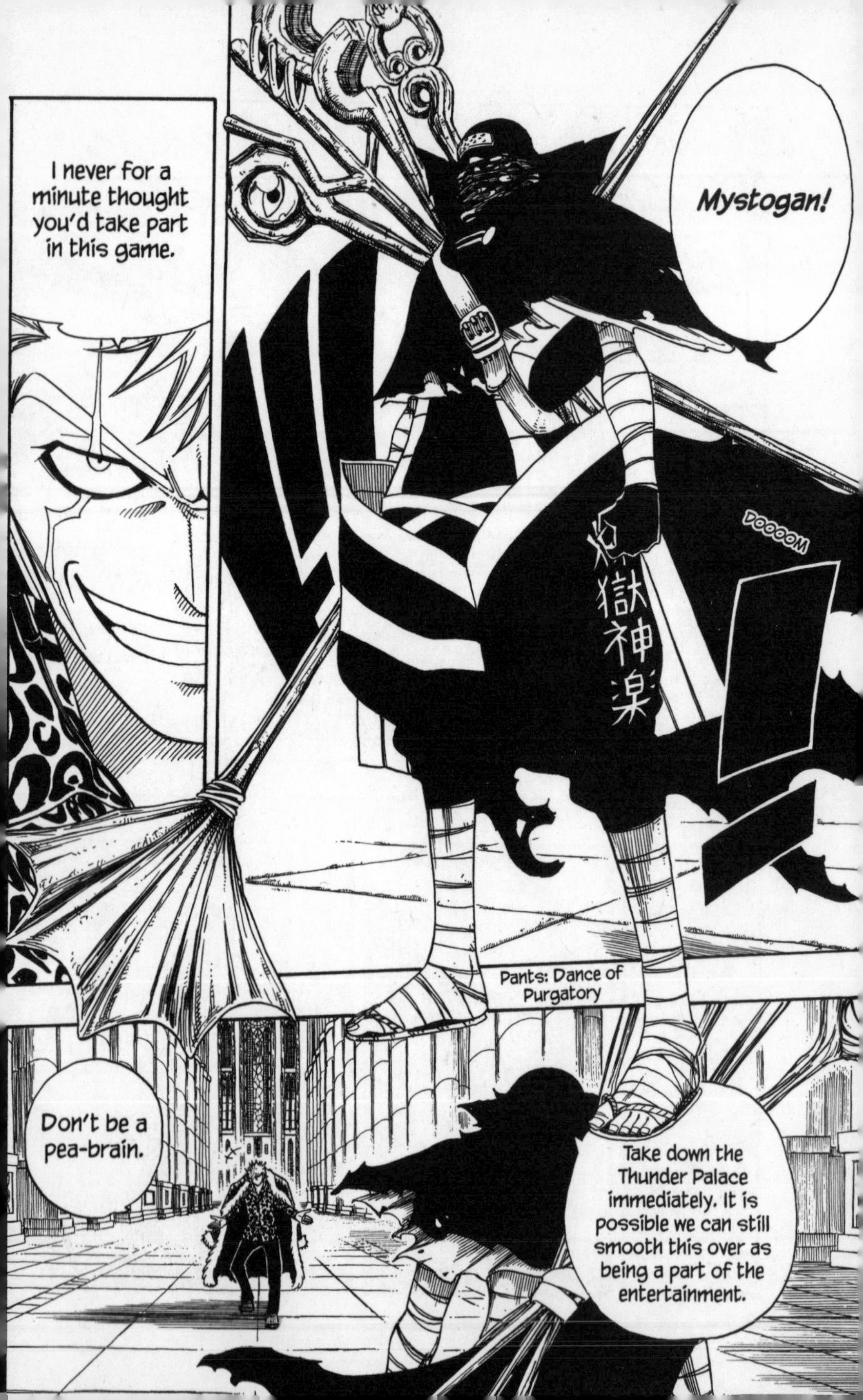
Mystogan!
DOOOOM
Pants: Dance of Purgatory
I never for a minute thought you'd take part in this game.
Don't be a pea-brain.
Take down the Thunder Palace immediately. It is possible we can still smooth this over as being a part of the entertainment.

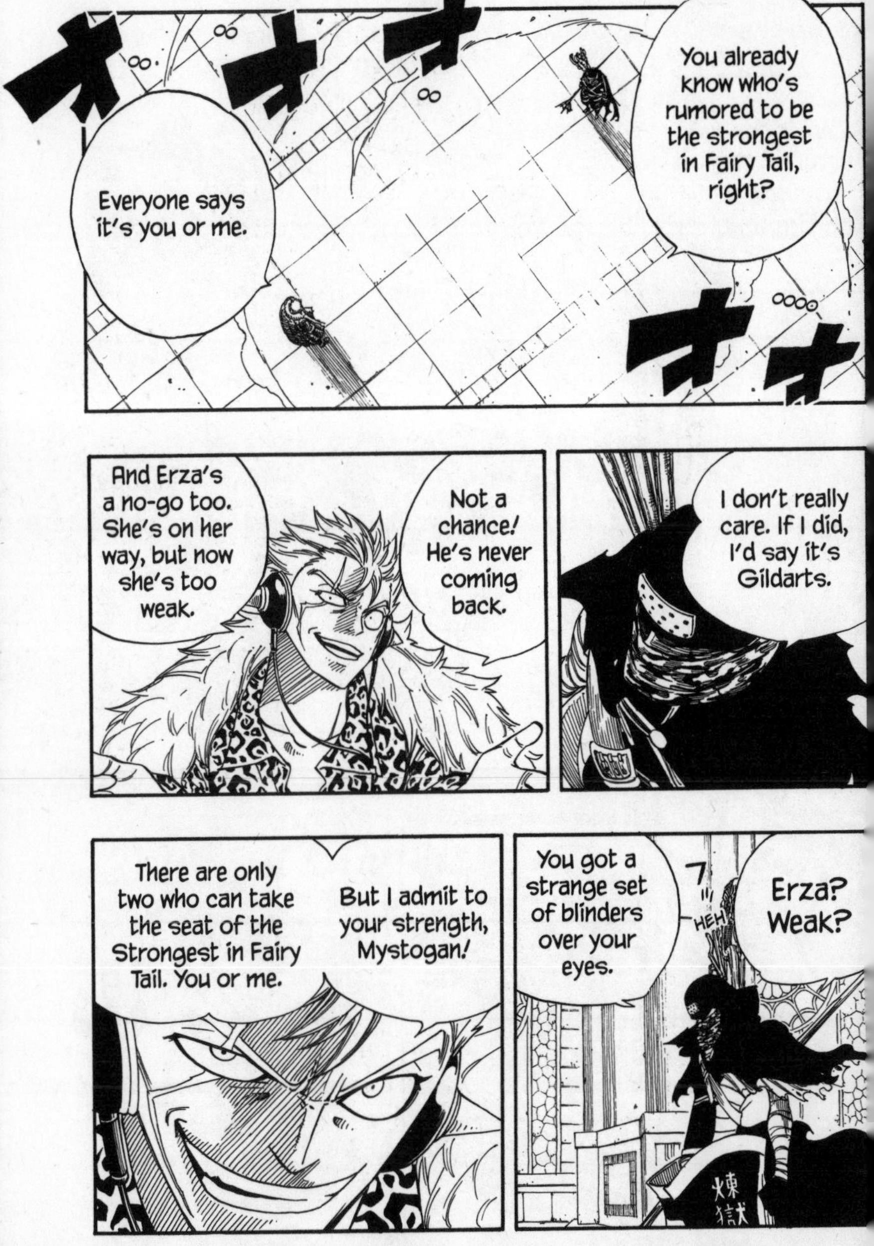

You already know who's rumored to be the strongest in Fairy Tail, right?
オオ
オオオ
Everyone says it's you or me.
I don't really care. If I did, I'd say it's Gildarts.
Not a chance! He's never coming back.
And Erza's a no-go too. She's on her way, but now she's too weak.
Erza? Weak?
HEH
You got a strange set of blinders over your eyes.
煉獄
But I admit to your strength, Mystogan!
There are only two who can take the seat of the Strongest in Fairy Tail. You or me.

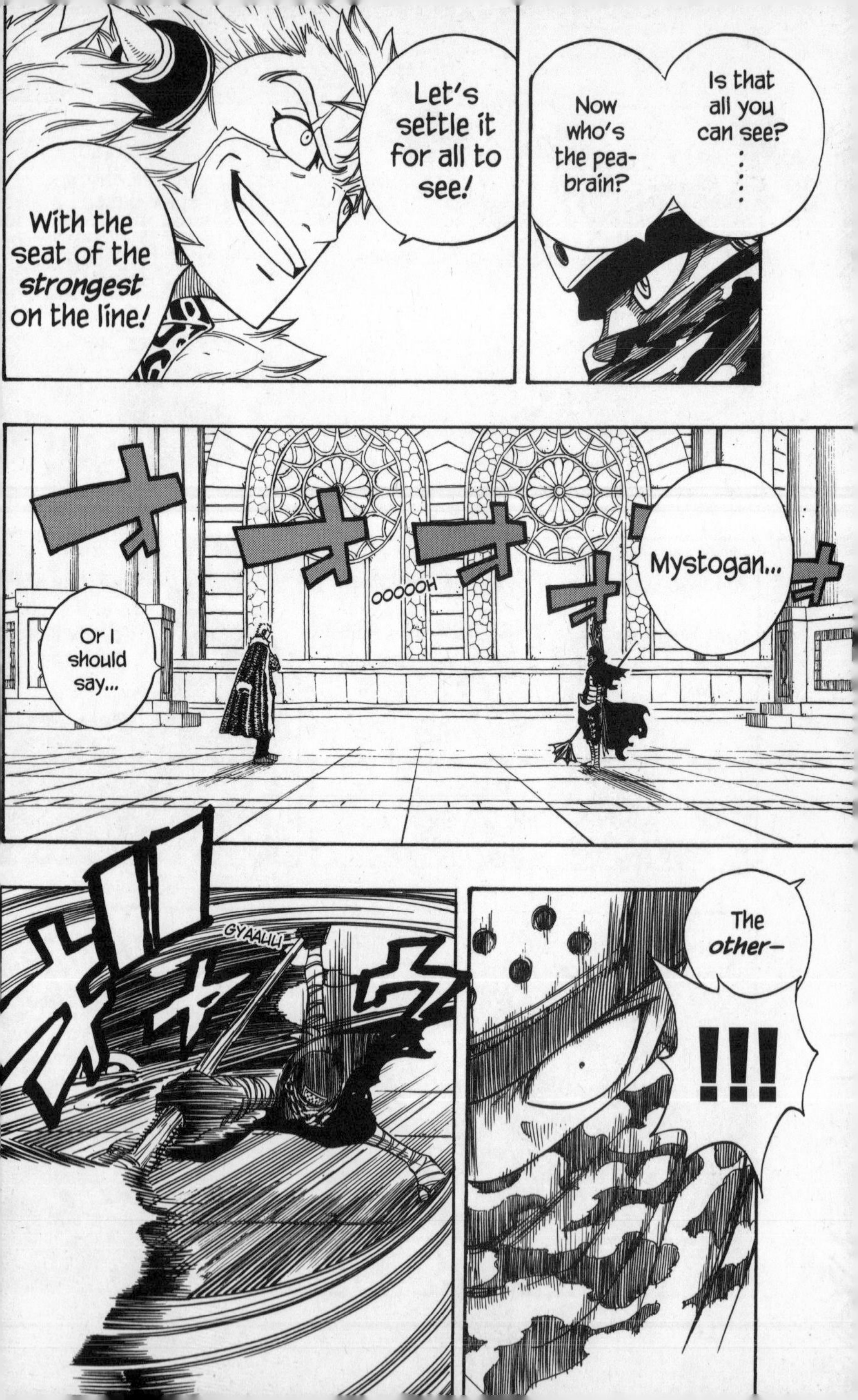
Is that all you can see? ......
Now who's the pea-brain?
Let's settle it for all to see!
With the seat of the *strongest* on the line!
Mystogan...
OOOOOH
Or I should say...
The *other*–
!!!
GYAALLL

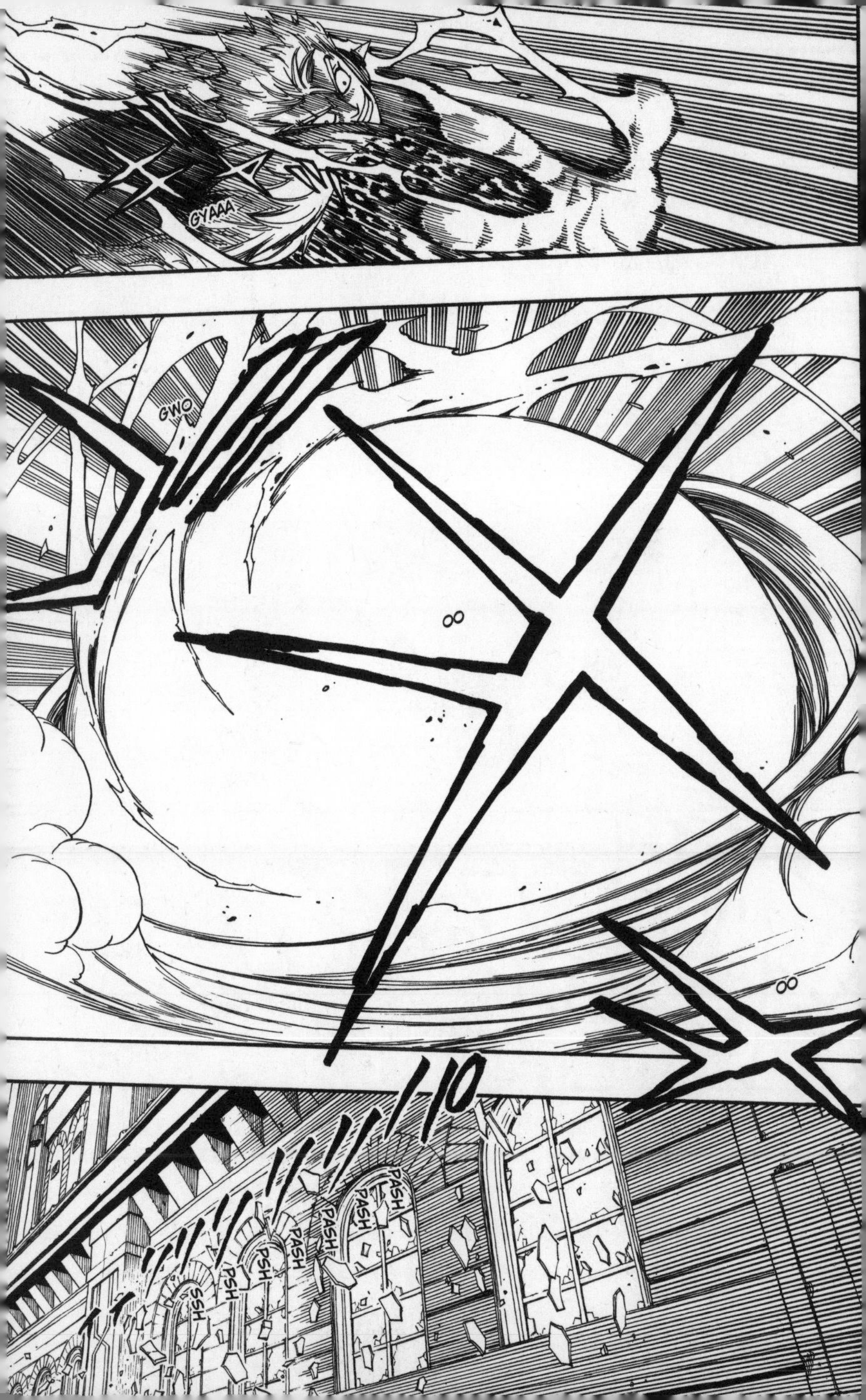
GYAAA
GWO
PASH
PASH
PASH
PASH
PSH
PSH
SSH

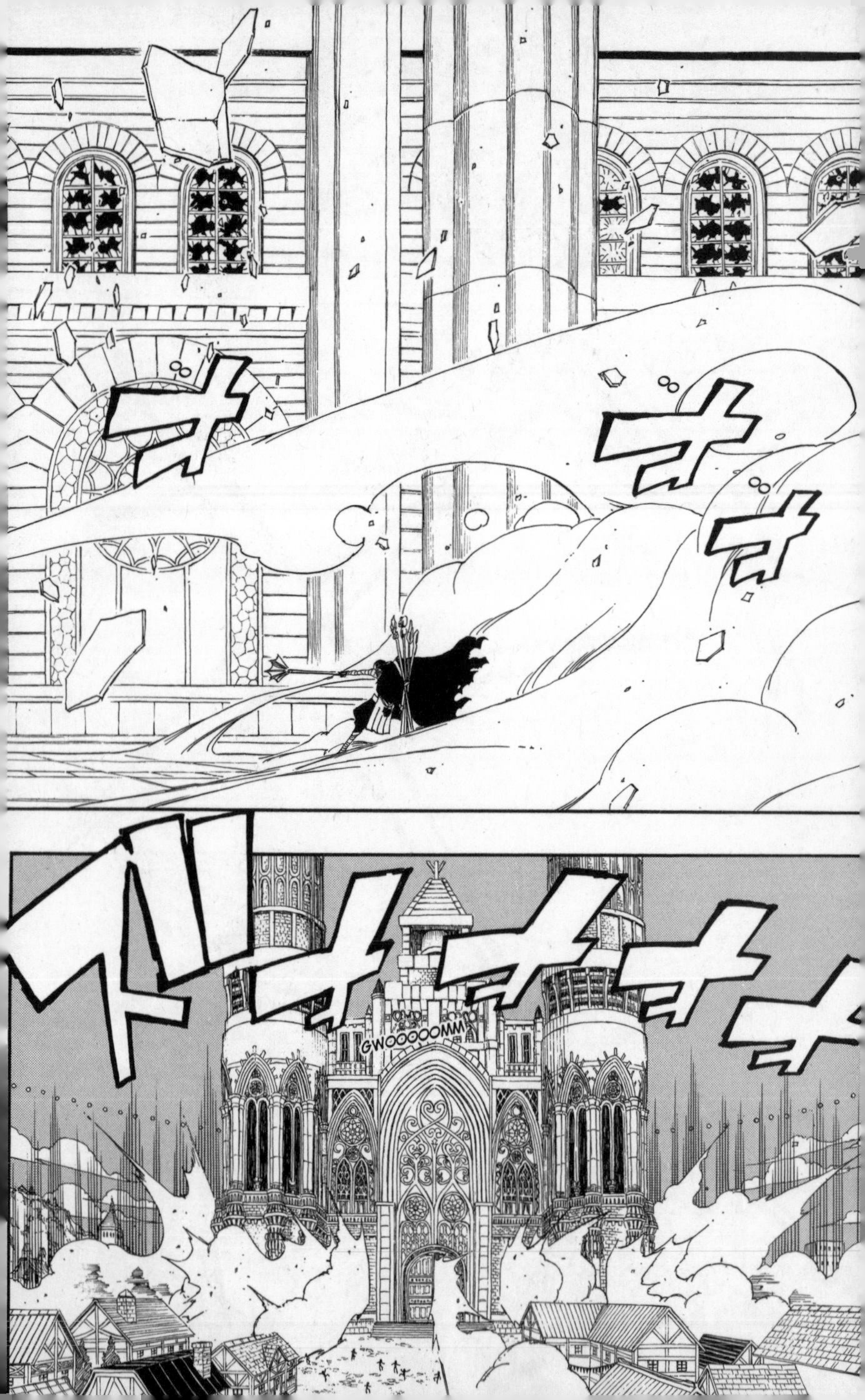
GWOOOOOMM

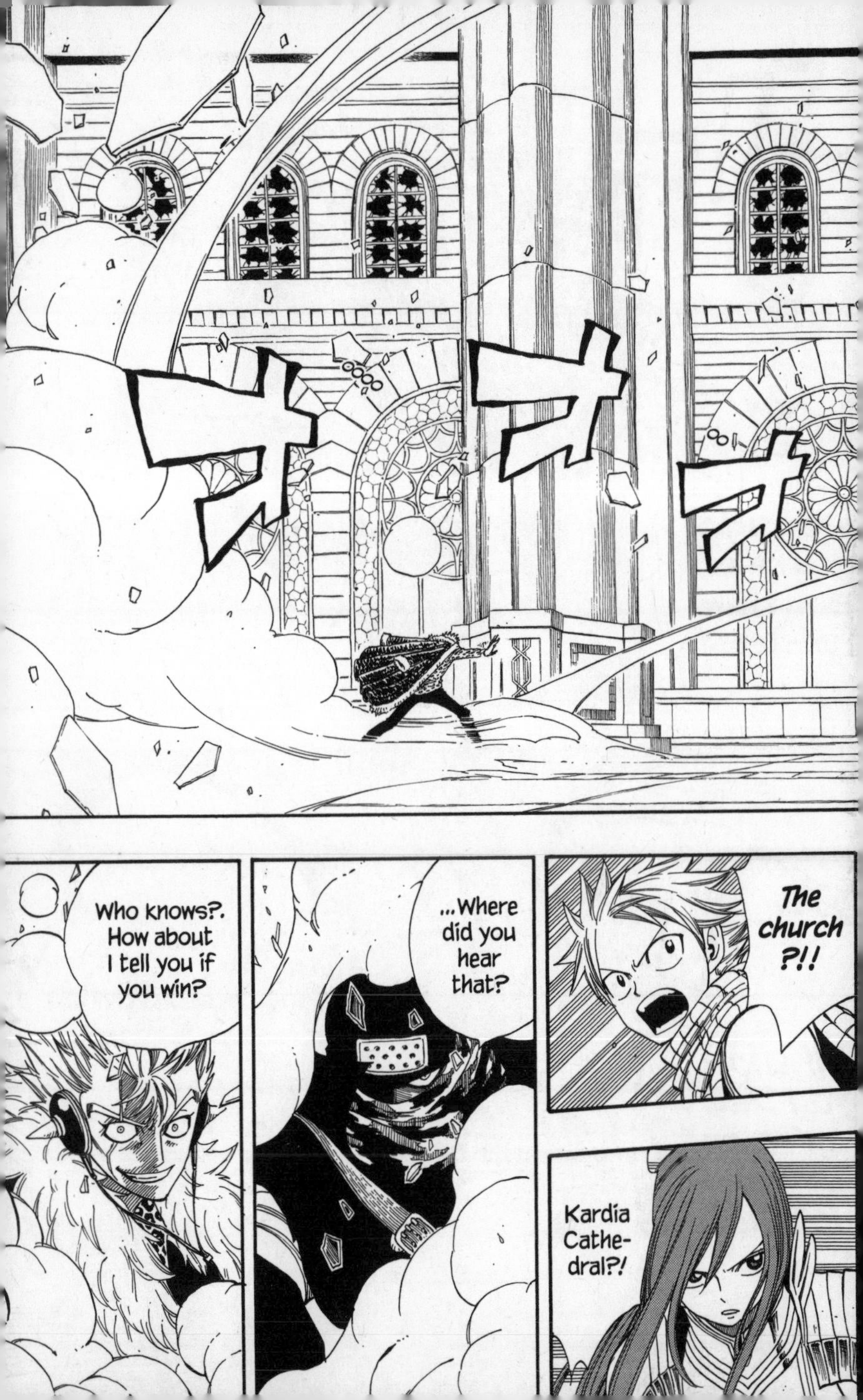
オオオ
The church?!!
Kardia Cathedral?!
...Where did you hear that?
Who knows?. How about I tell you if you win?

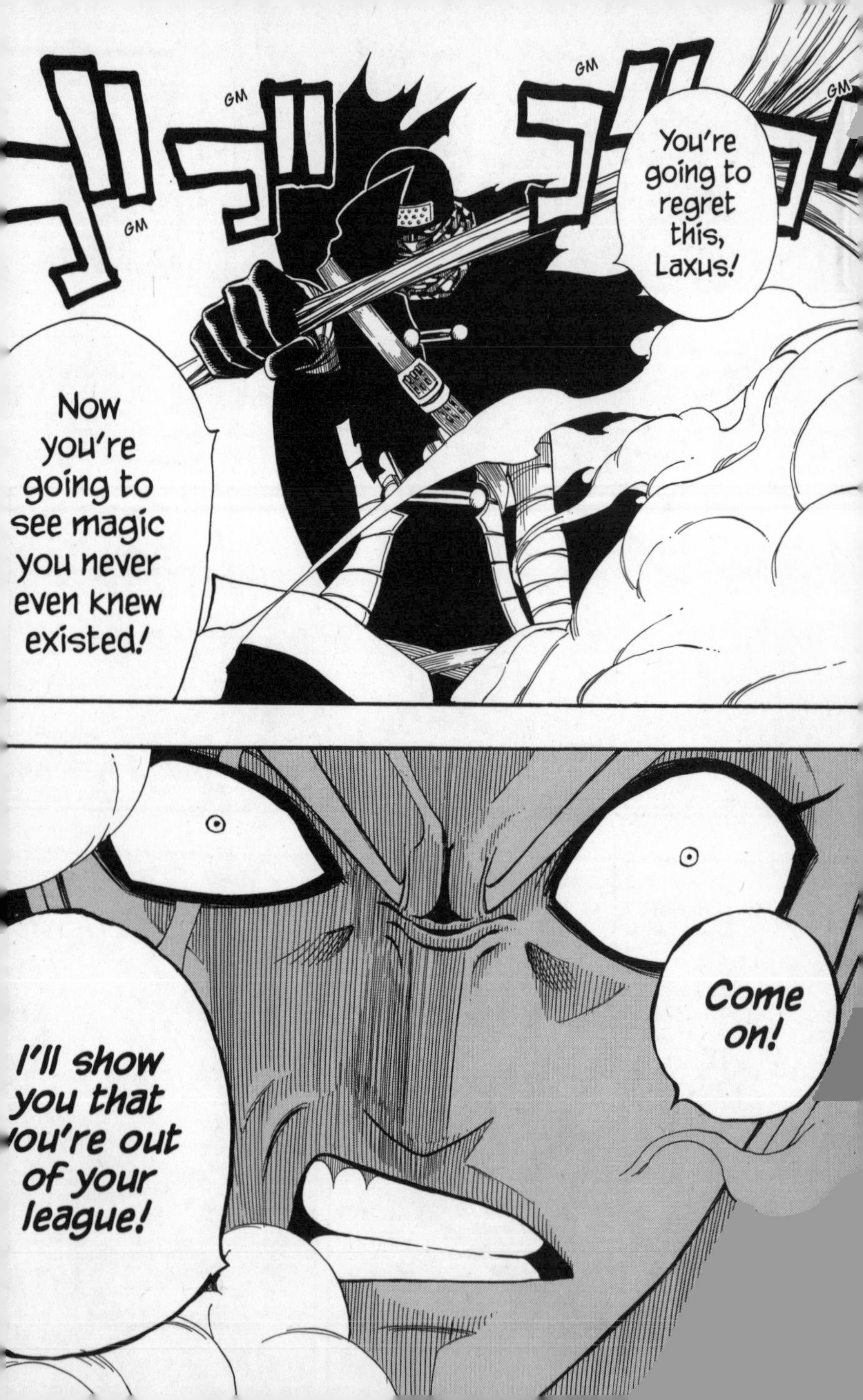
GM GM GM GM
You're going to regret this, Laxus!
Now you're going to see magic you never even knew existed!
Come on!
I'll show you that ou're out of your league!

FAIRY TAIL

Chapter 120: Mystogan

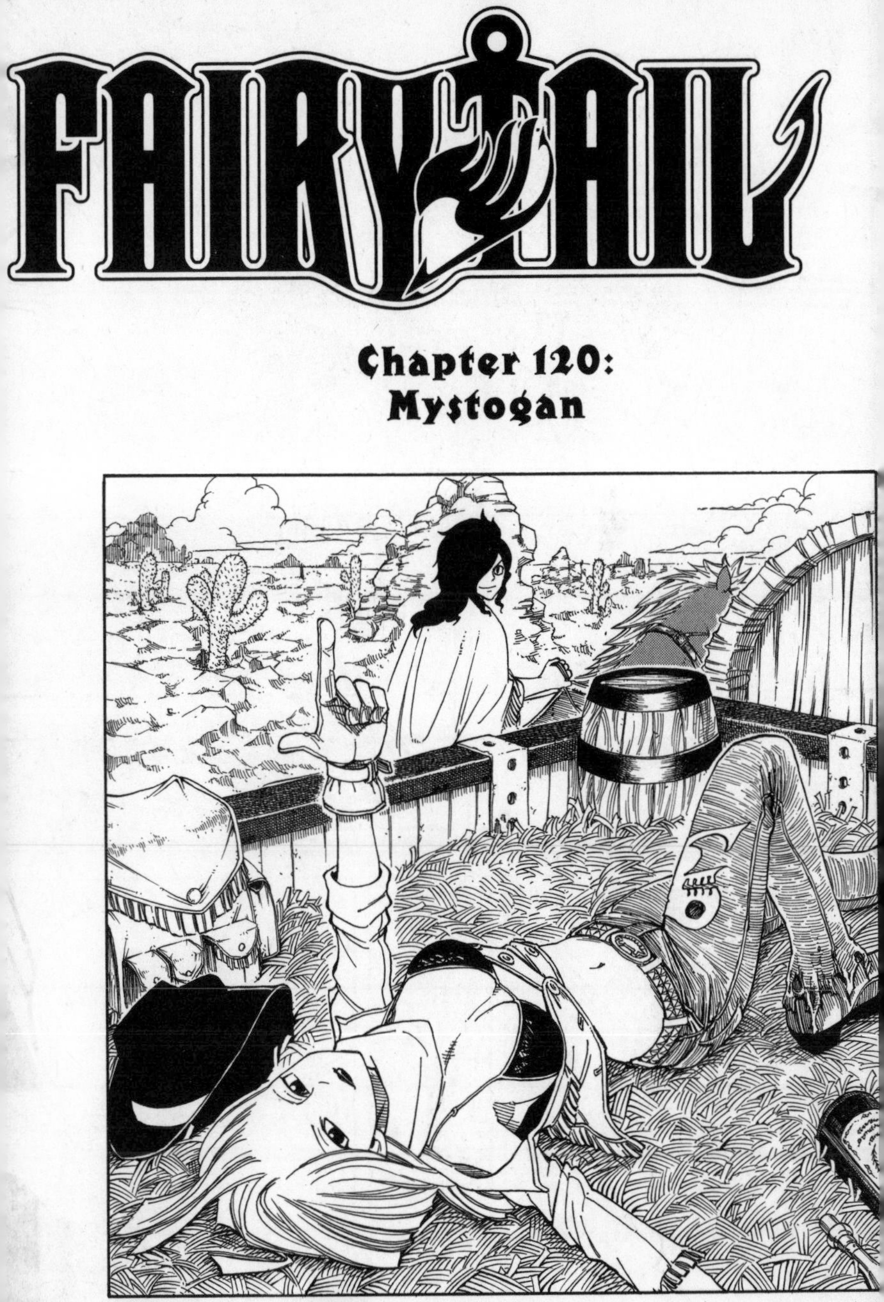

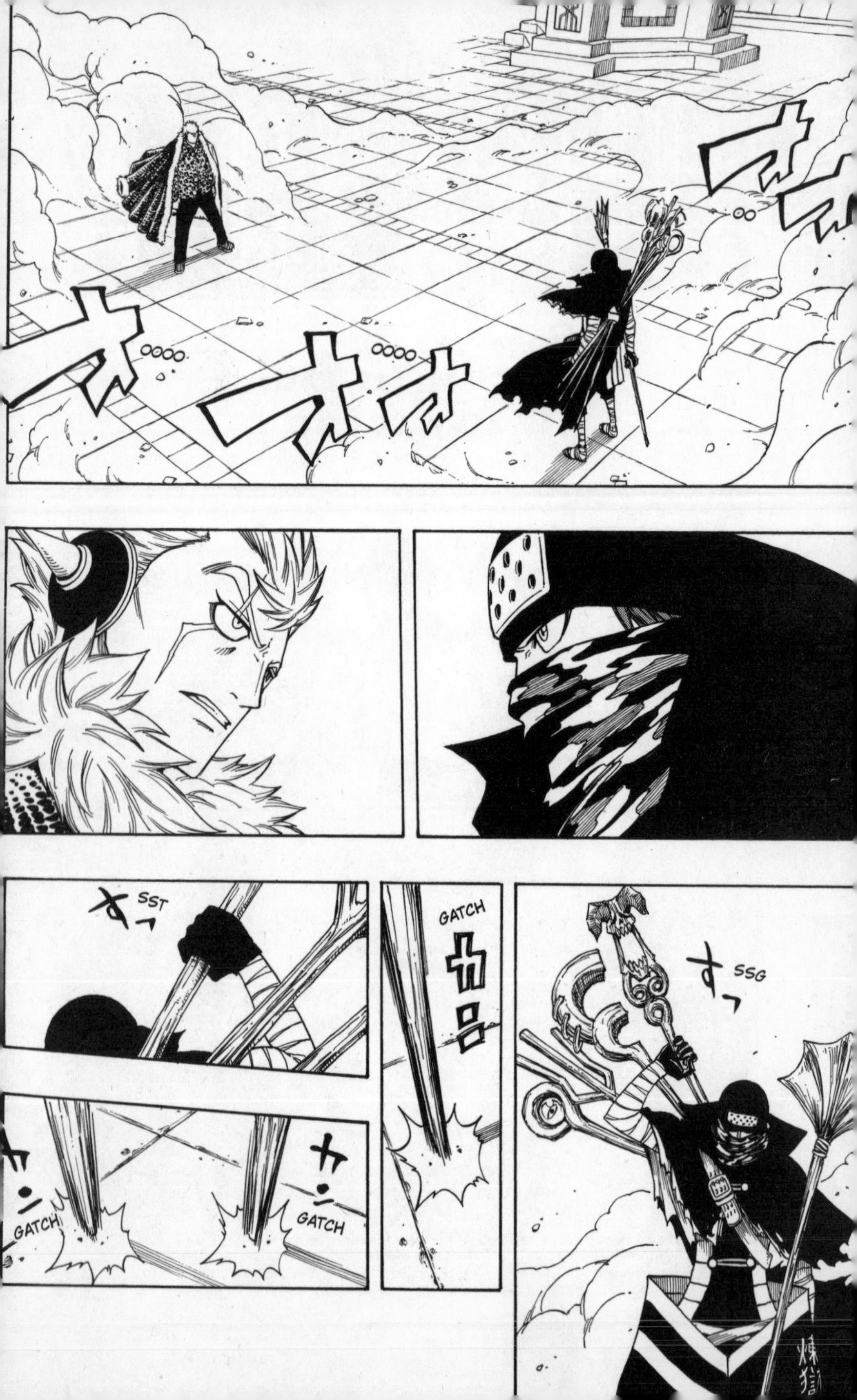

oo
oooo
oooo
SSG
GATCH
SST
GATCH
GATCH

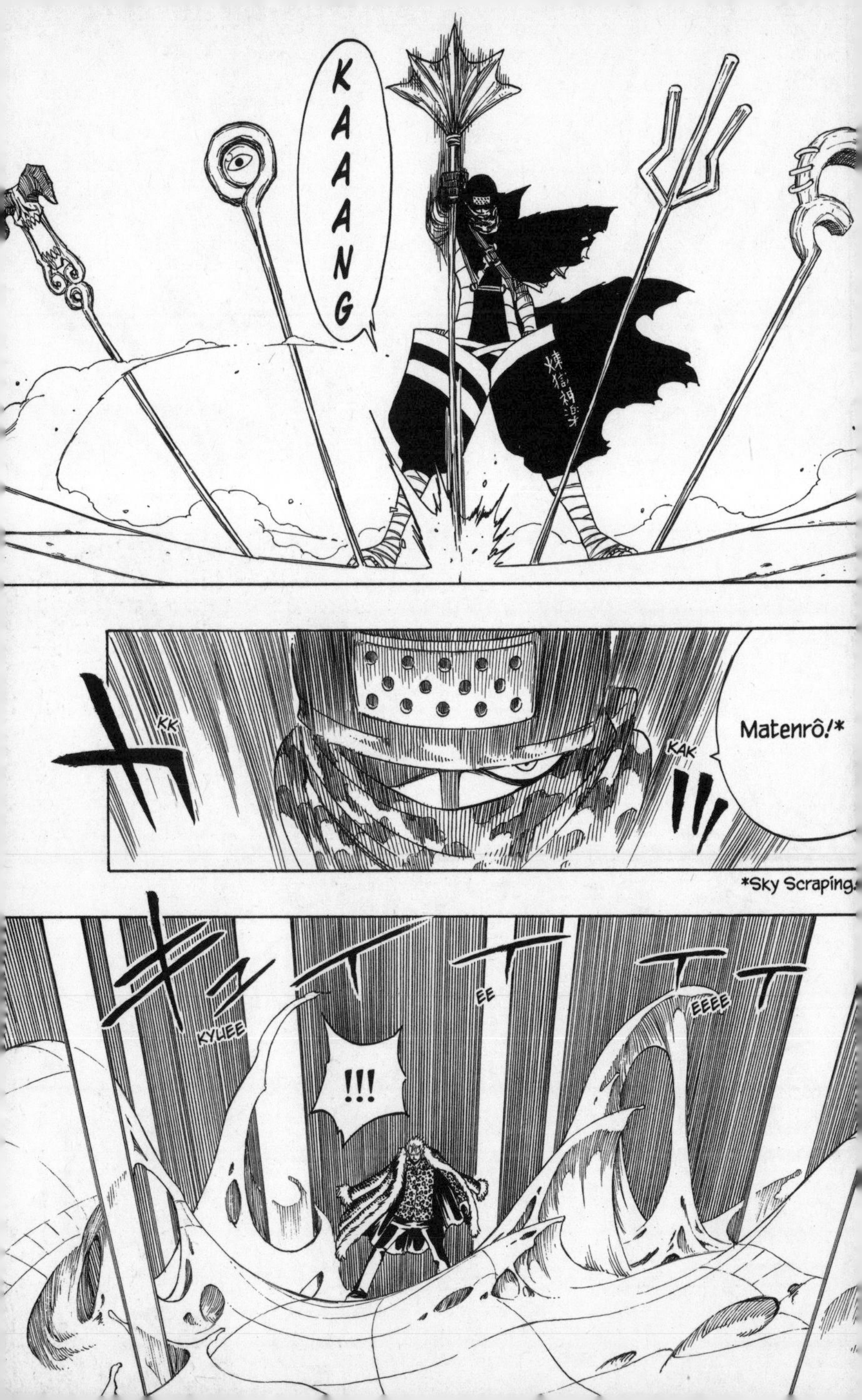
KAAAANG
Matenrô!*
KAK
KK
KYLEE
EE
EEEE
!!!
*Sky Scraping.

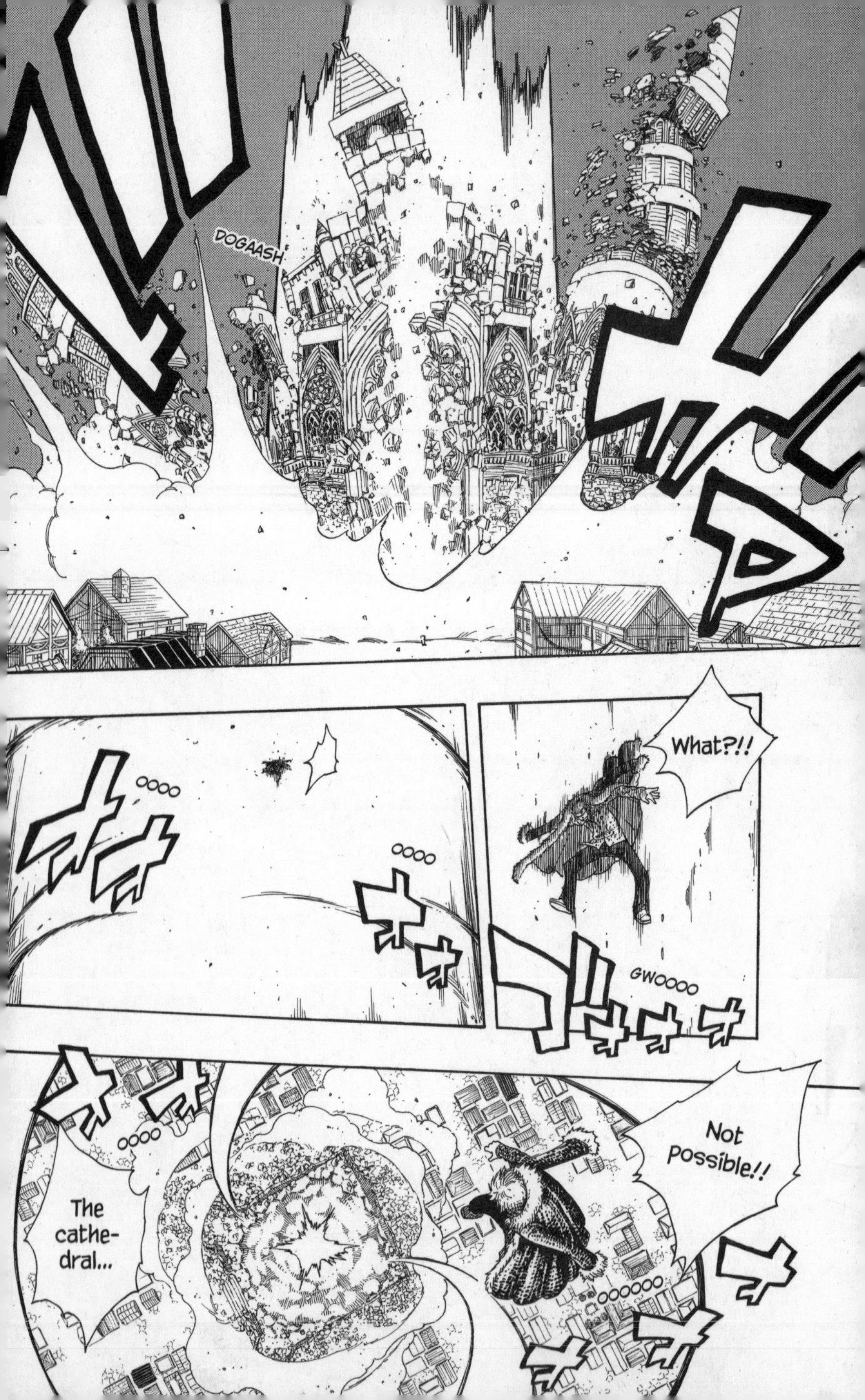
DOGAASH
What?!!
GWOOOO
OOOO
OOOO
Not possible!!
OOOOOO
OOOO
The cathedral...

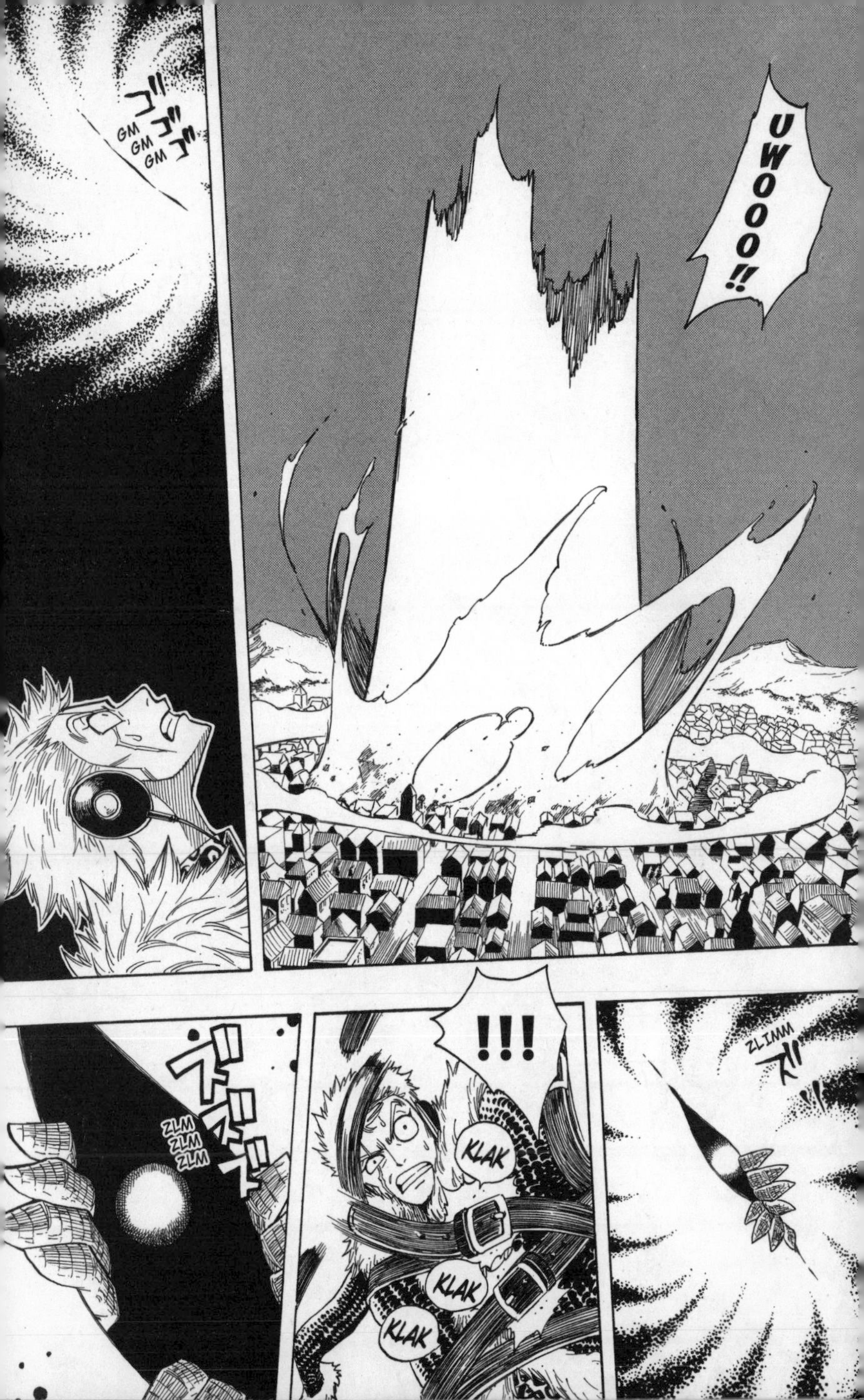
UWOOOO!!
GM GM GM
ゴゴゴ
ZLIMM
ズ!!
!!!
KLAK
KLAK
KLAK
ZLM ZLM ZLM
ズズズ

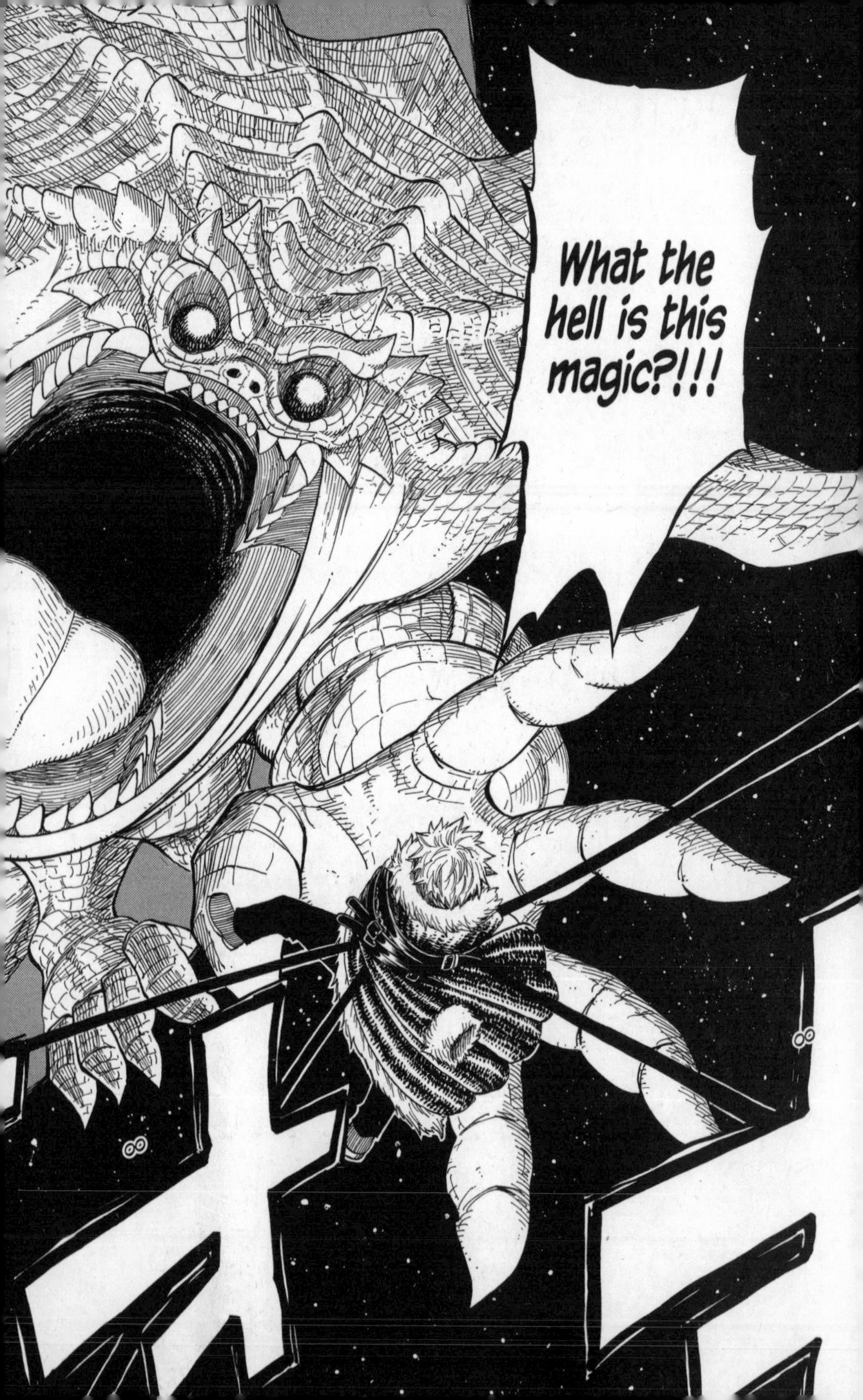
What the hell is this magic?!!!

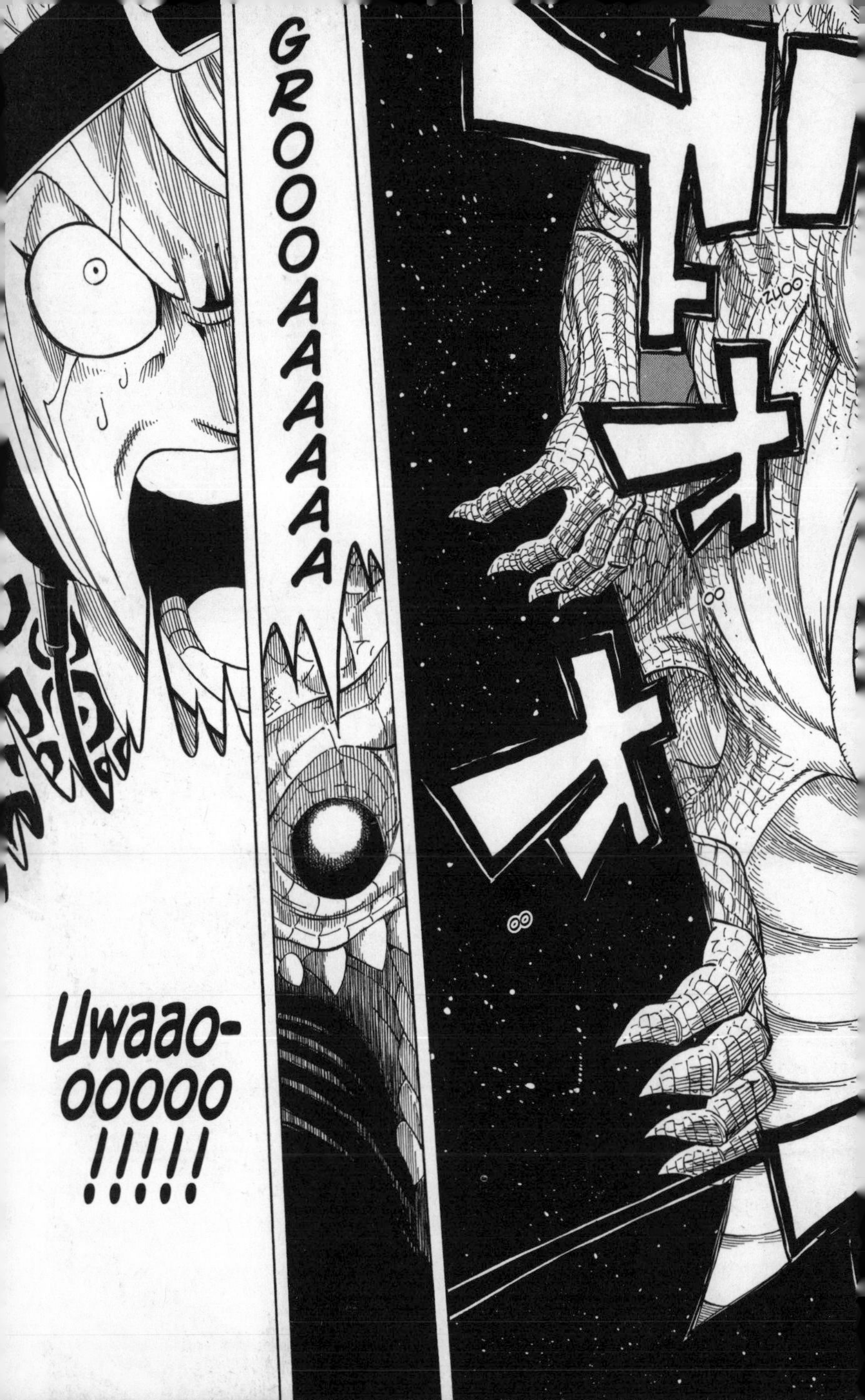
ZUOO
GROOOAAAAAA
Uwaao-ooooo!!!!!

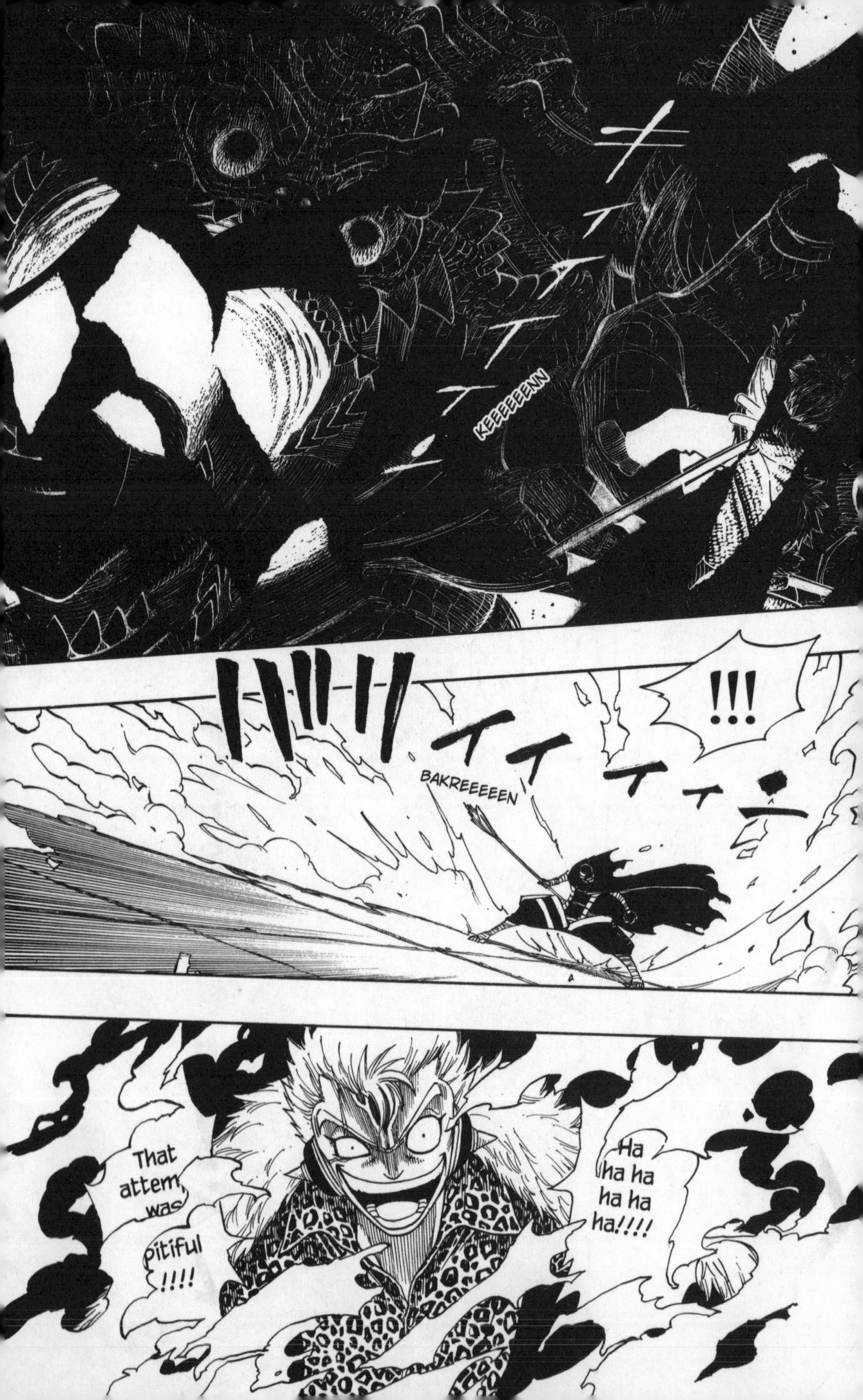
KEEEEEEENN
!!!
BAKREEEEEN
Ha ha ha ha ha ha!!!!
That attem was pitiful !!!!

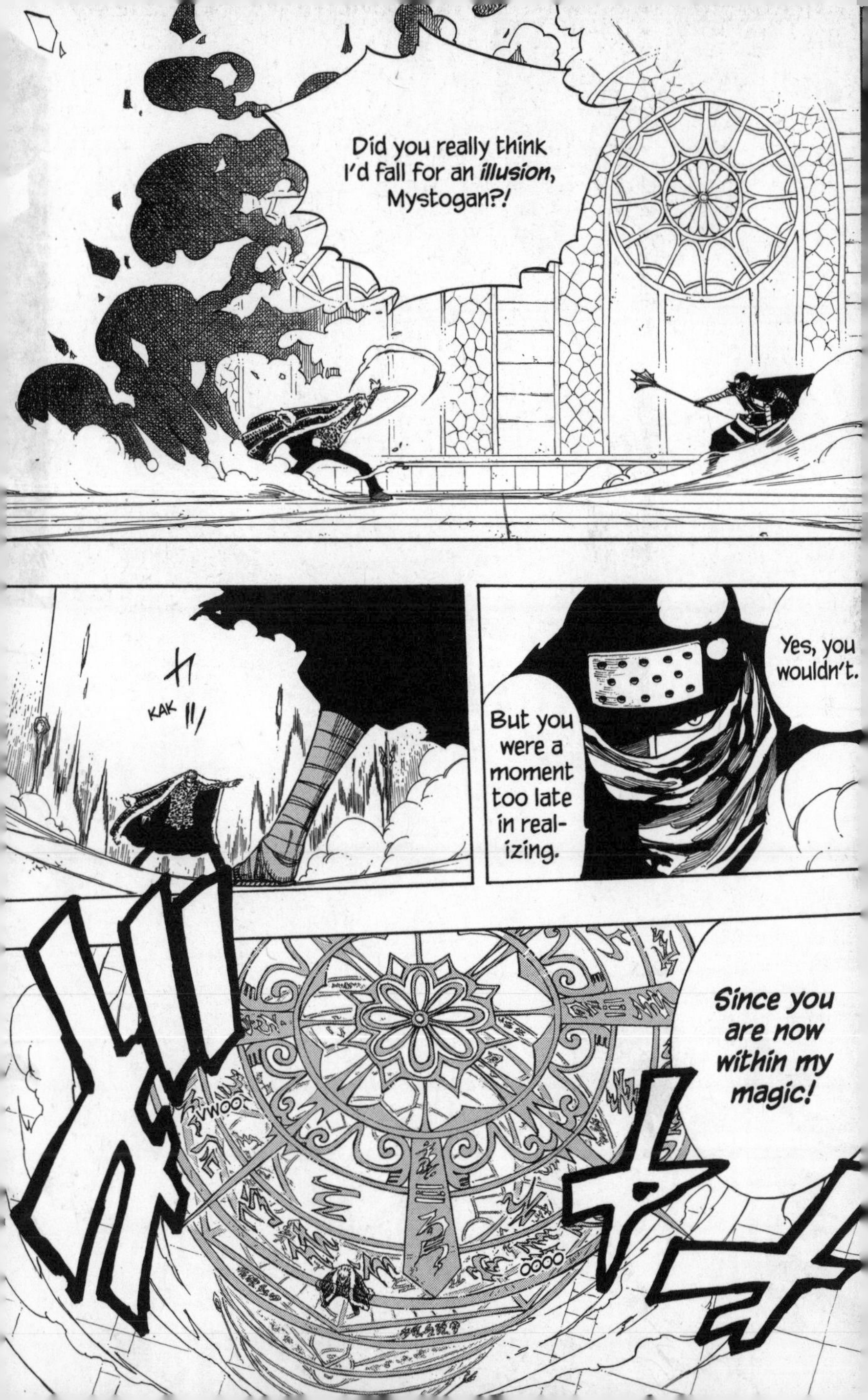
Did you really think I'd fall for an *illusion*, Mystogan?!
Yes, you wouldn't.
But you were a moment too late in real-izing.
KAK
Since you are now within my magic!
VWOO
OOOO

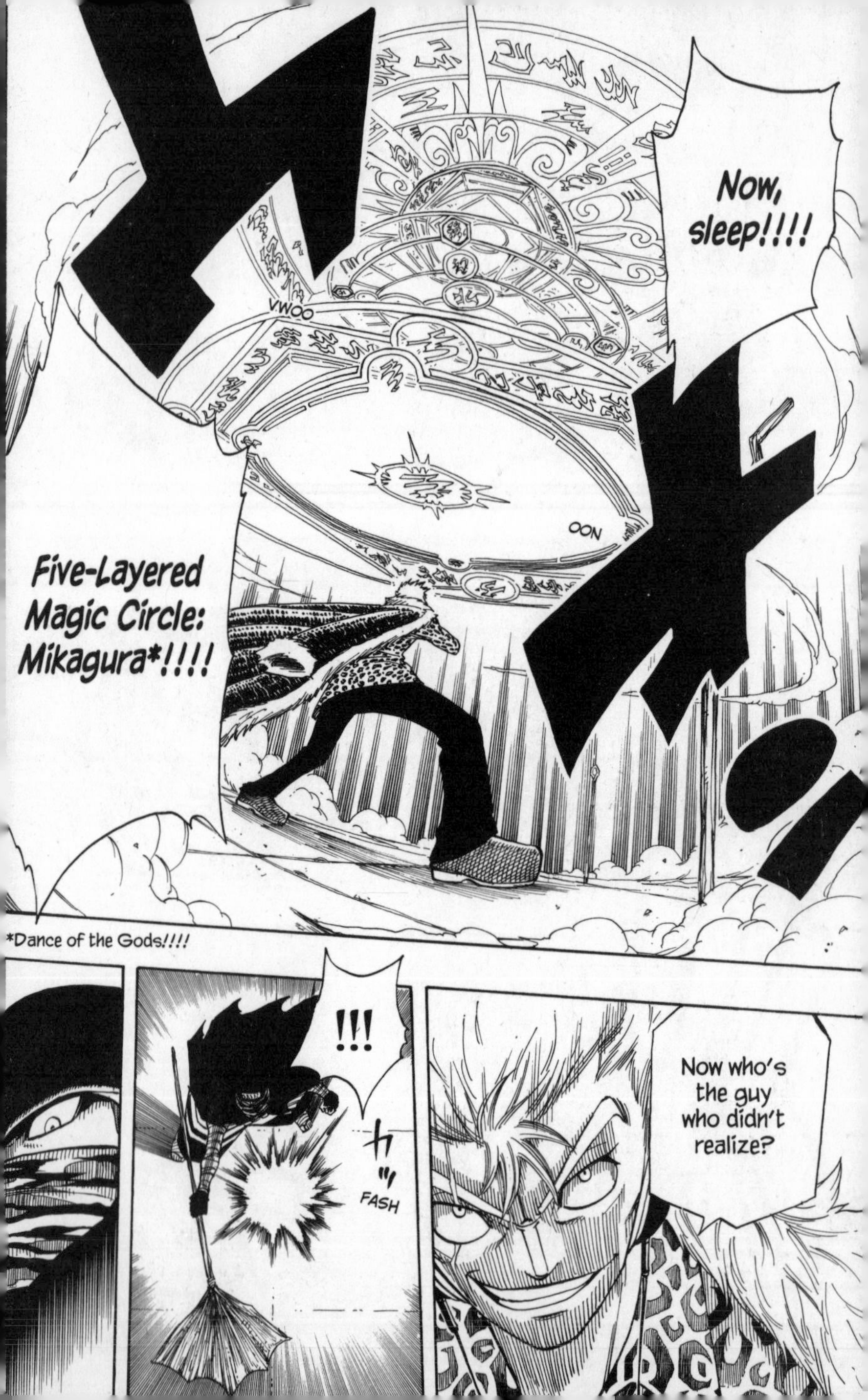
Now, sleep!!!!
VWOO
OON
Five-Layered Magic Circle: Mikagura*!!!!
*Dance of the Gods!!!!
Now who's the guy who didn't realize?
!!!
FASH

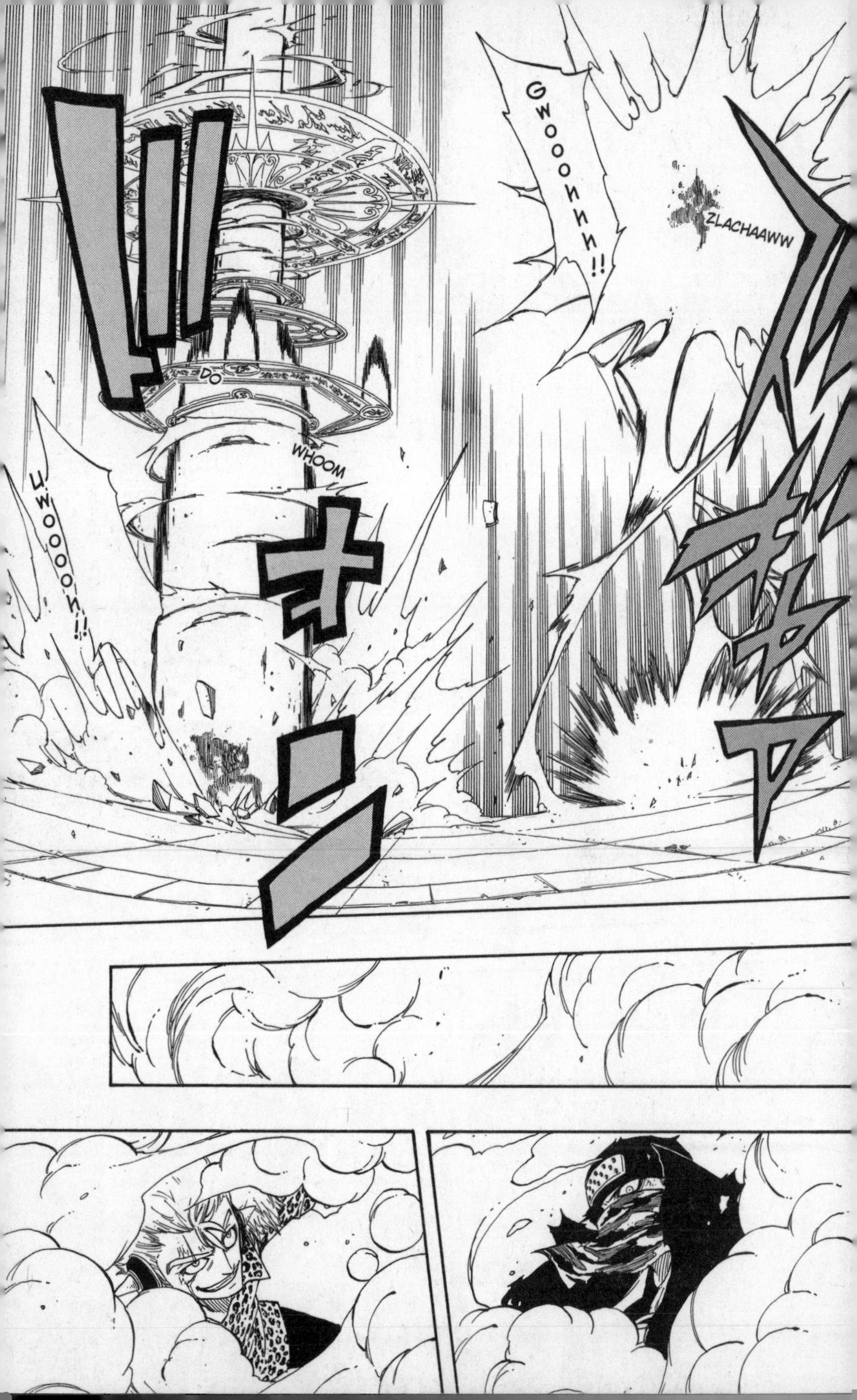
ZLACHAAWW
GWOOOHHH!!
WHOOM
DO
UWOOOOOH!!

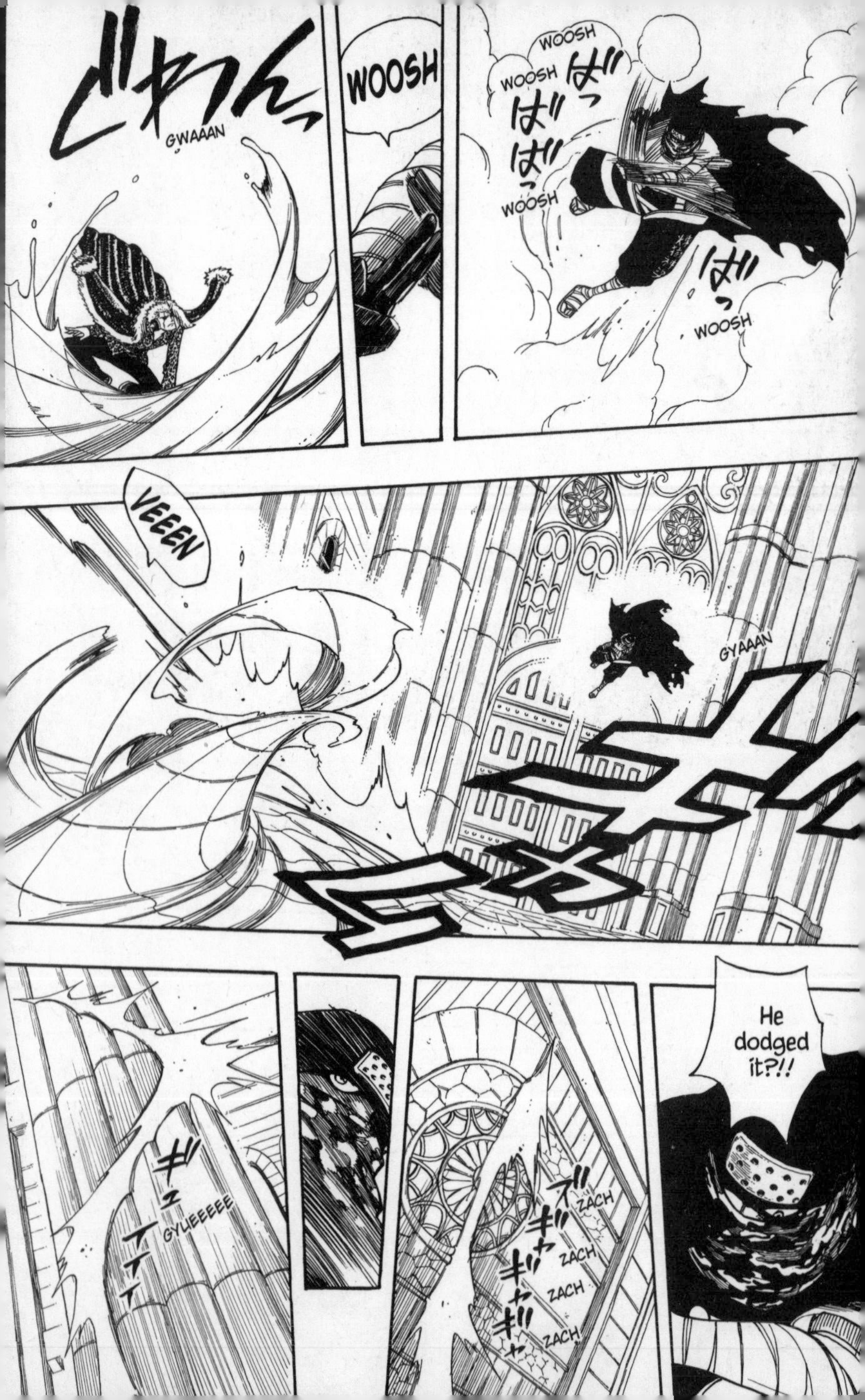
WOOSH
WOOSH
WOOSH
WOOSH
WOOSH
GWAAAN
VEEEN
GYAAAN
He dodged it?!!
ZACH
ZACH
ZACH
ZACH
GYIIEEEEE

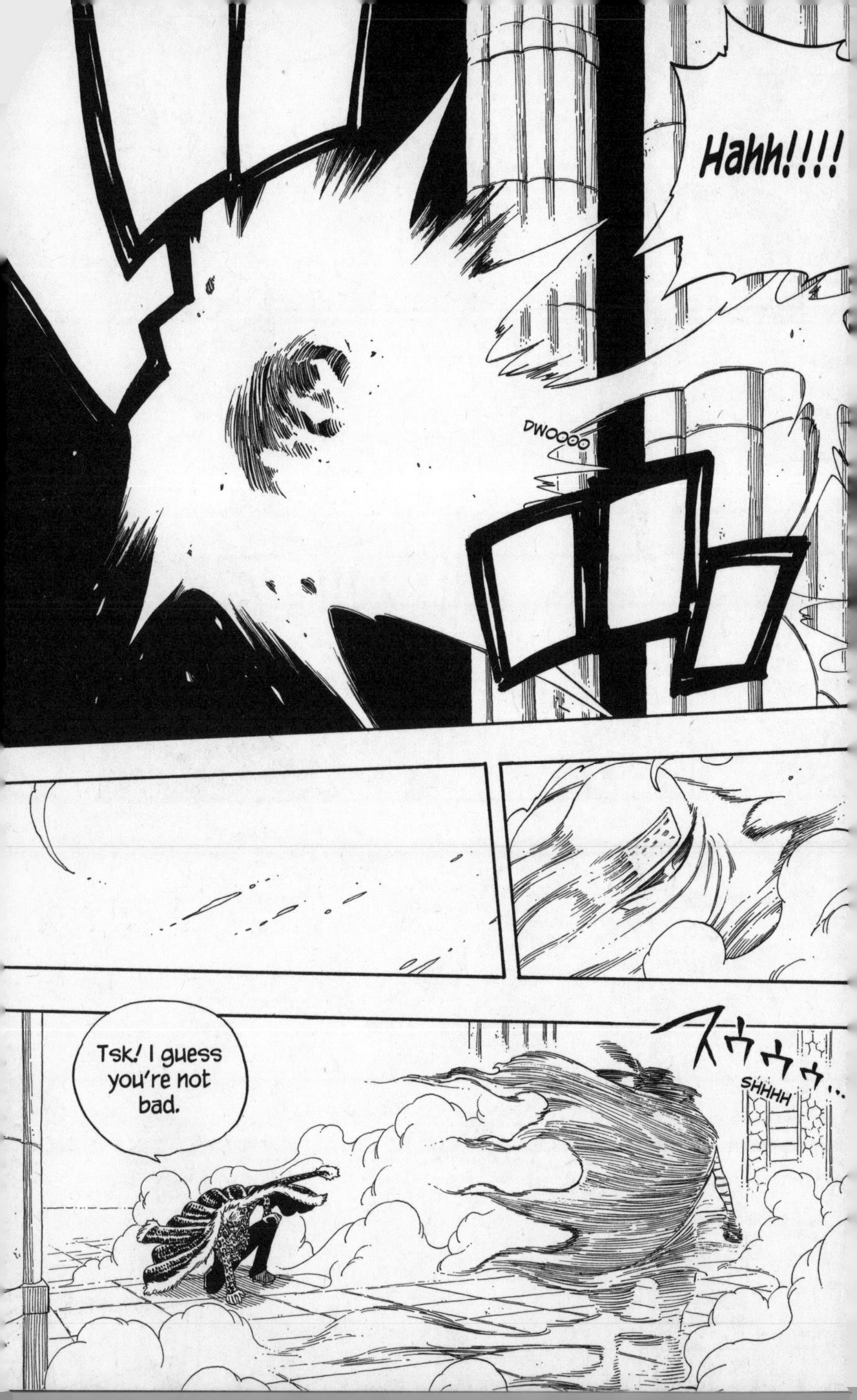
Hahh!!!!
DWOOOO
スウウウ…
SHHHH
Tsk! I guess you're not bad.

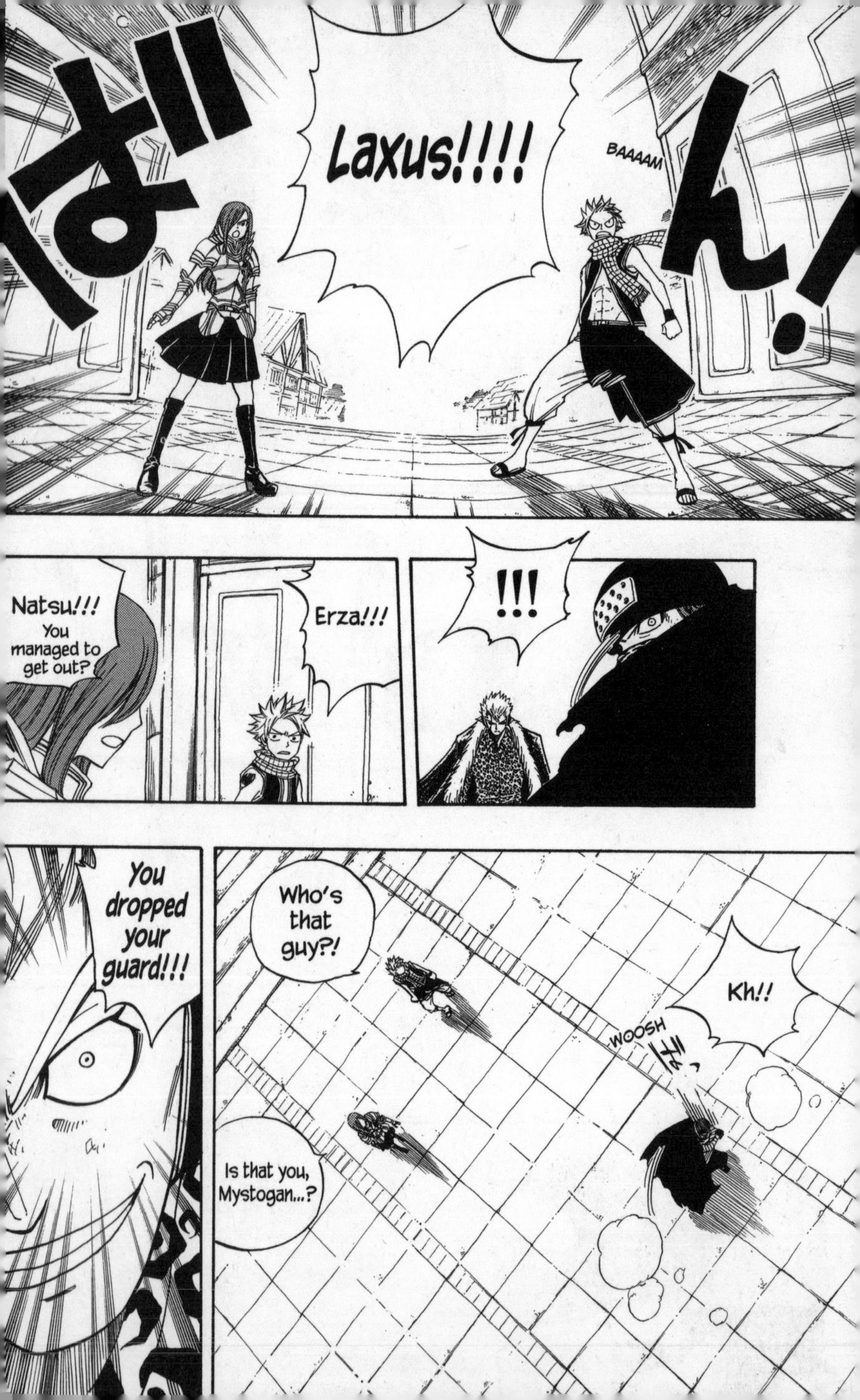
Laxus!!!!
BAAAAM
ば
ん!
!!!
Erza!!!
Natsu!!! You managed to get out?
Kh!!
Who's that guy?!
WOOSH
Is that you, Mystogan...?
You dropped your guard!!!

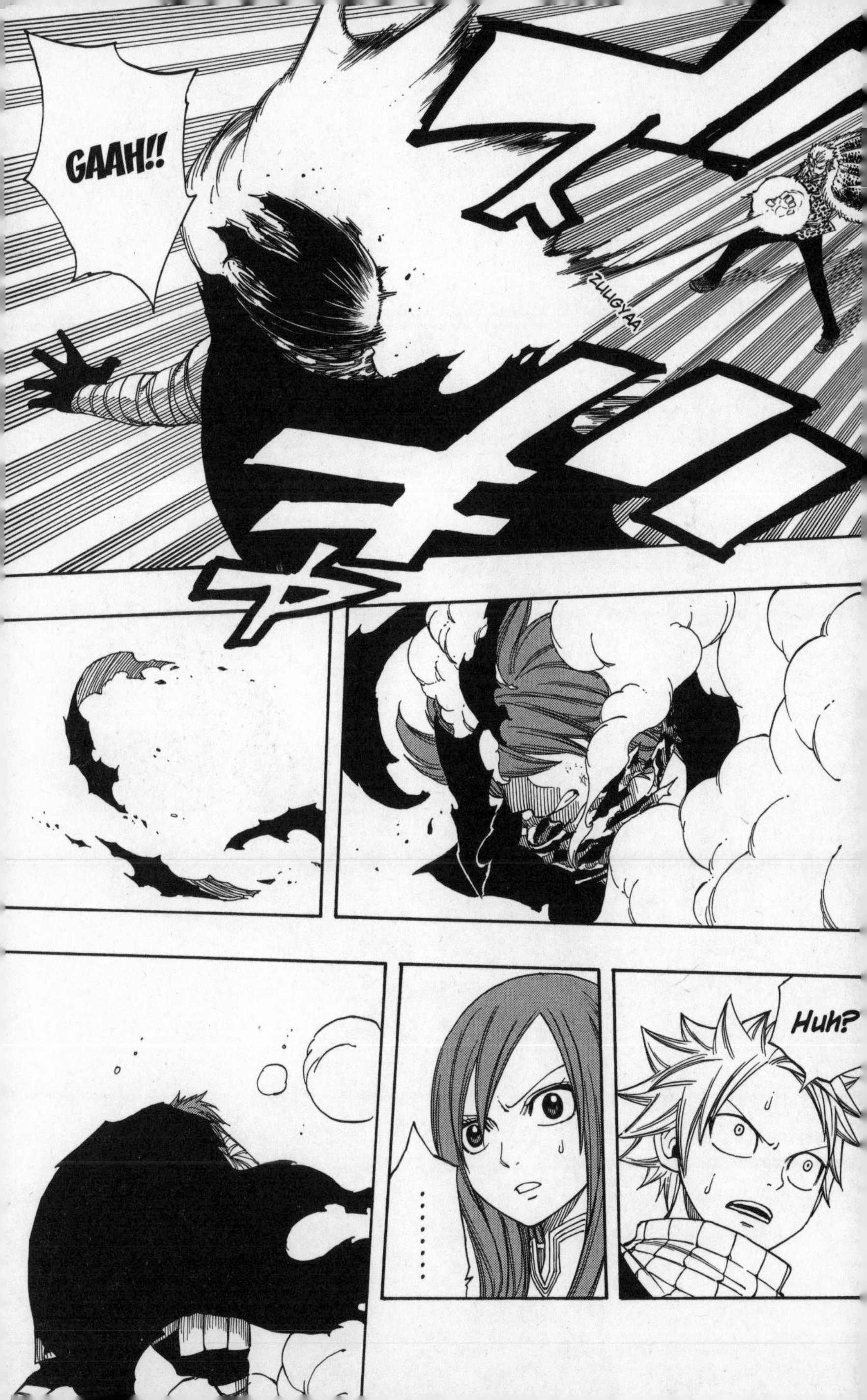

GAAH!!
ZUUGYAA
Huh?
......

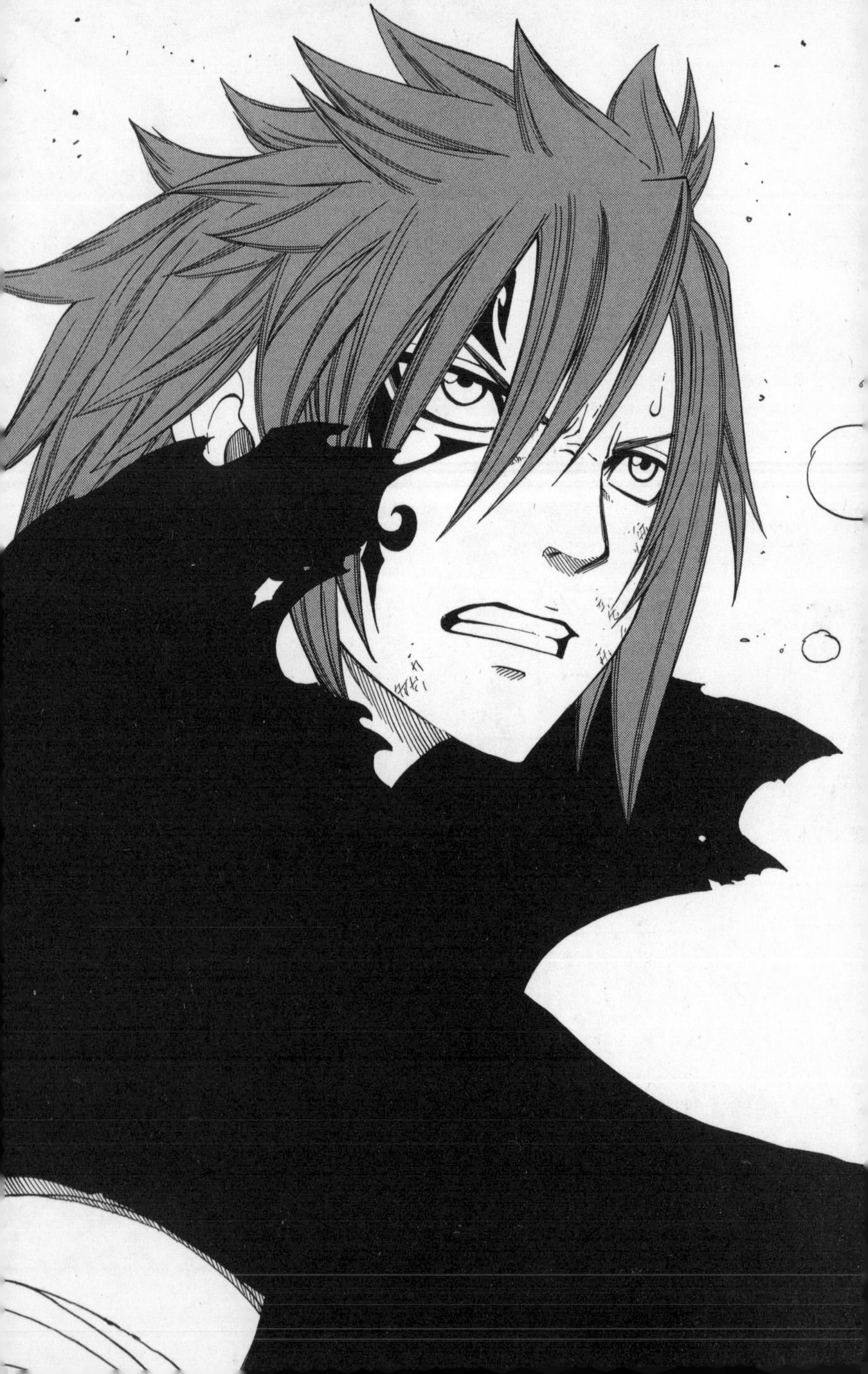

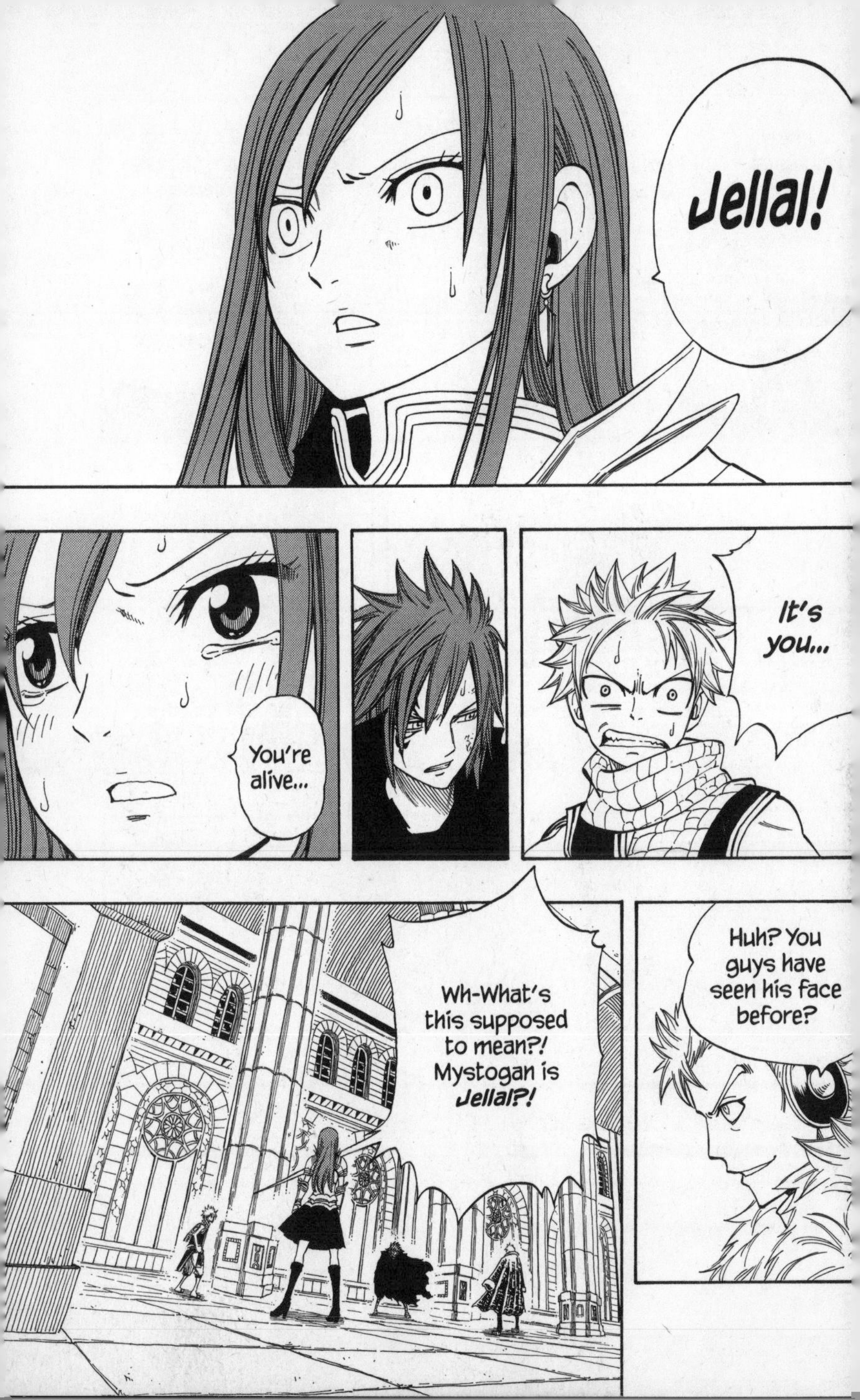
Jellal!
It's you...
You're alive...
Huh? You guys have seen his face before?
Wh-What's this supposed to mean?! Mystogan is Jellal?!

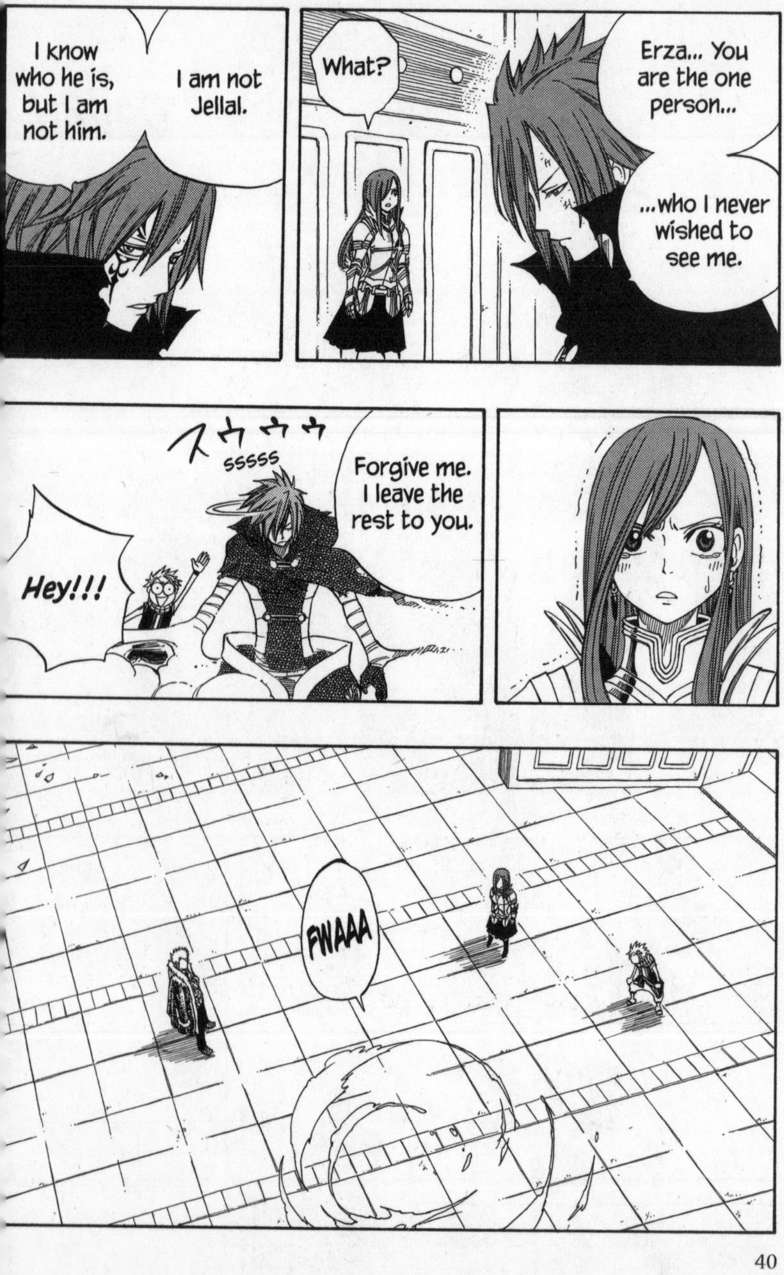
Erza... You are the one person...
...who I never wished to see me.
What?
I am not Jellal.
I know who he is, but I am not him.
Forgive me. I leave the rest to you.
スウウウ
SSSSS
Hey!!!
FWAAA

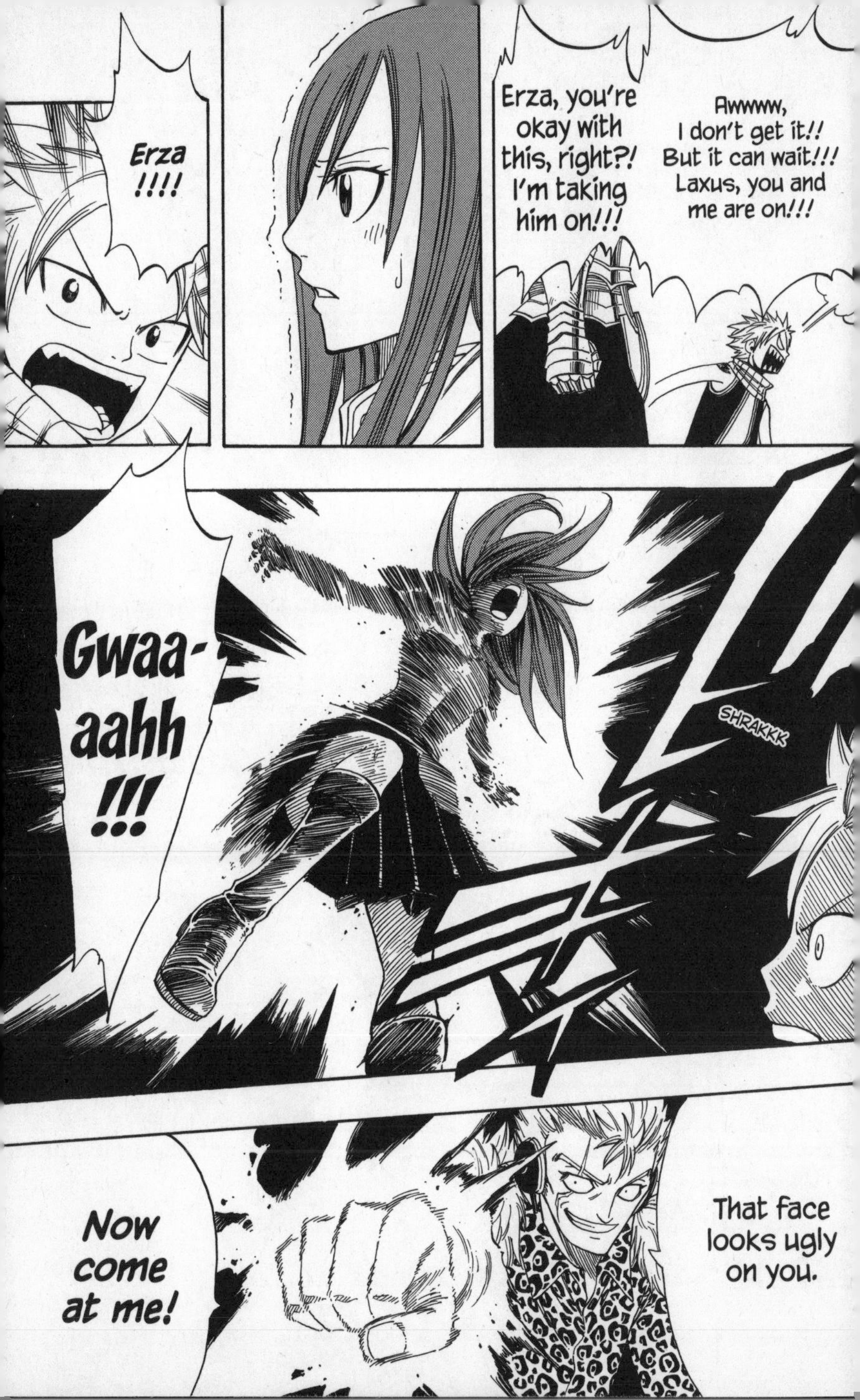
Awwww, I don't get it!! But it can wait!!! Laxus, you and me are on!!!
Erza, you're okay with this, right?! I'm taking him on!!!
Erza !!!!
SHRAKKK
Gwaa-aahh !!!
That face looks ugly on you.
Now come at me!

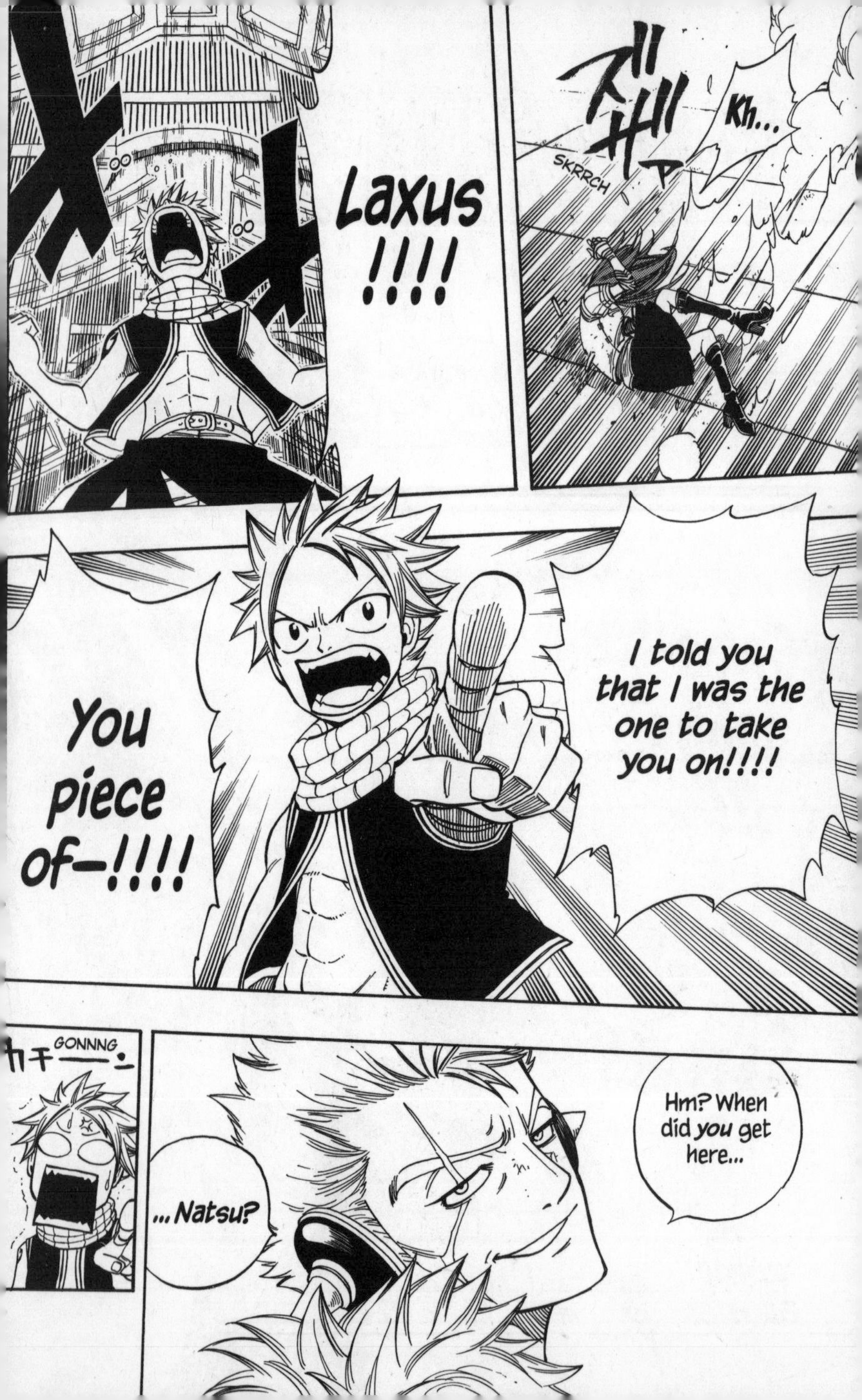
SKRRCH
Kh...
Laxus!!!!
I told you that I was the one to take you on!!!!
You piece of–!!!!
Hm? When did you get here...
...Natsu?
GONNNG

FAIRY TAIL

Chapter 121: My Chance to Take the Top Seat, Right?

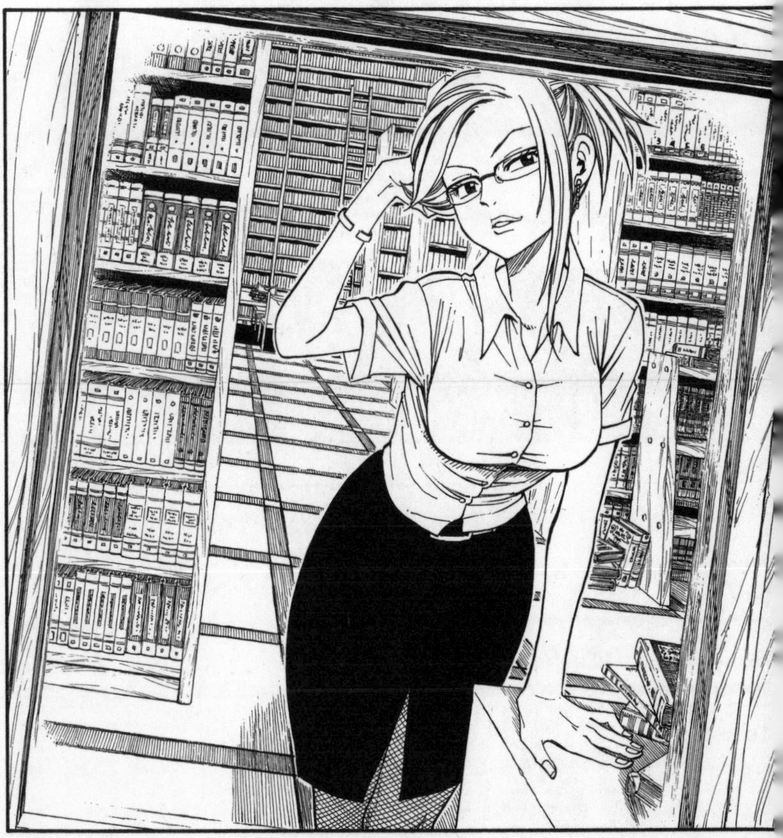

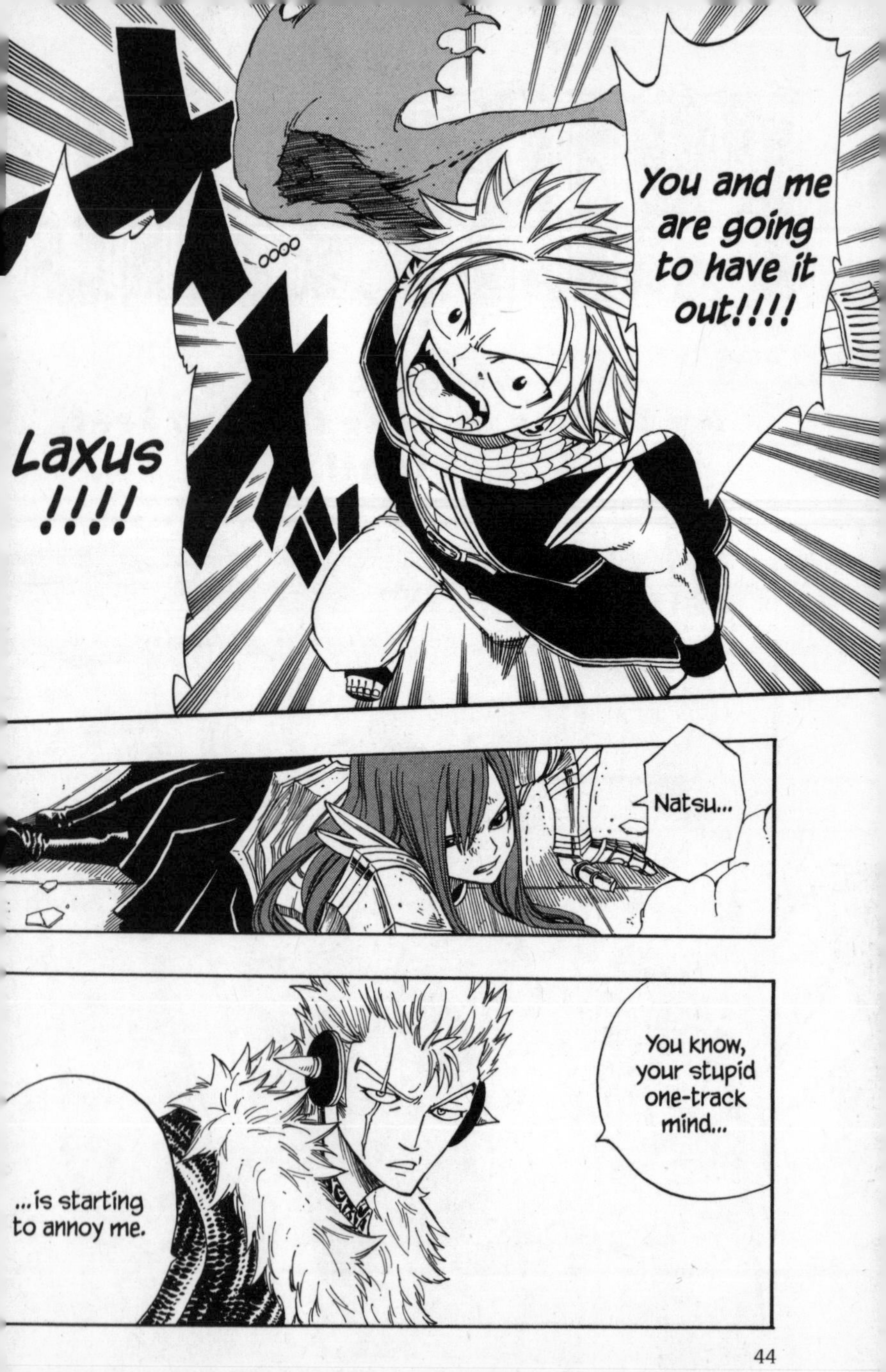
You and me are going to have it out!!!!
Laxus !!!!
Natsu...
You know, your stupid one-track mind...
...is starting to annoy me.

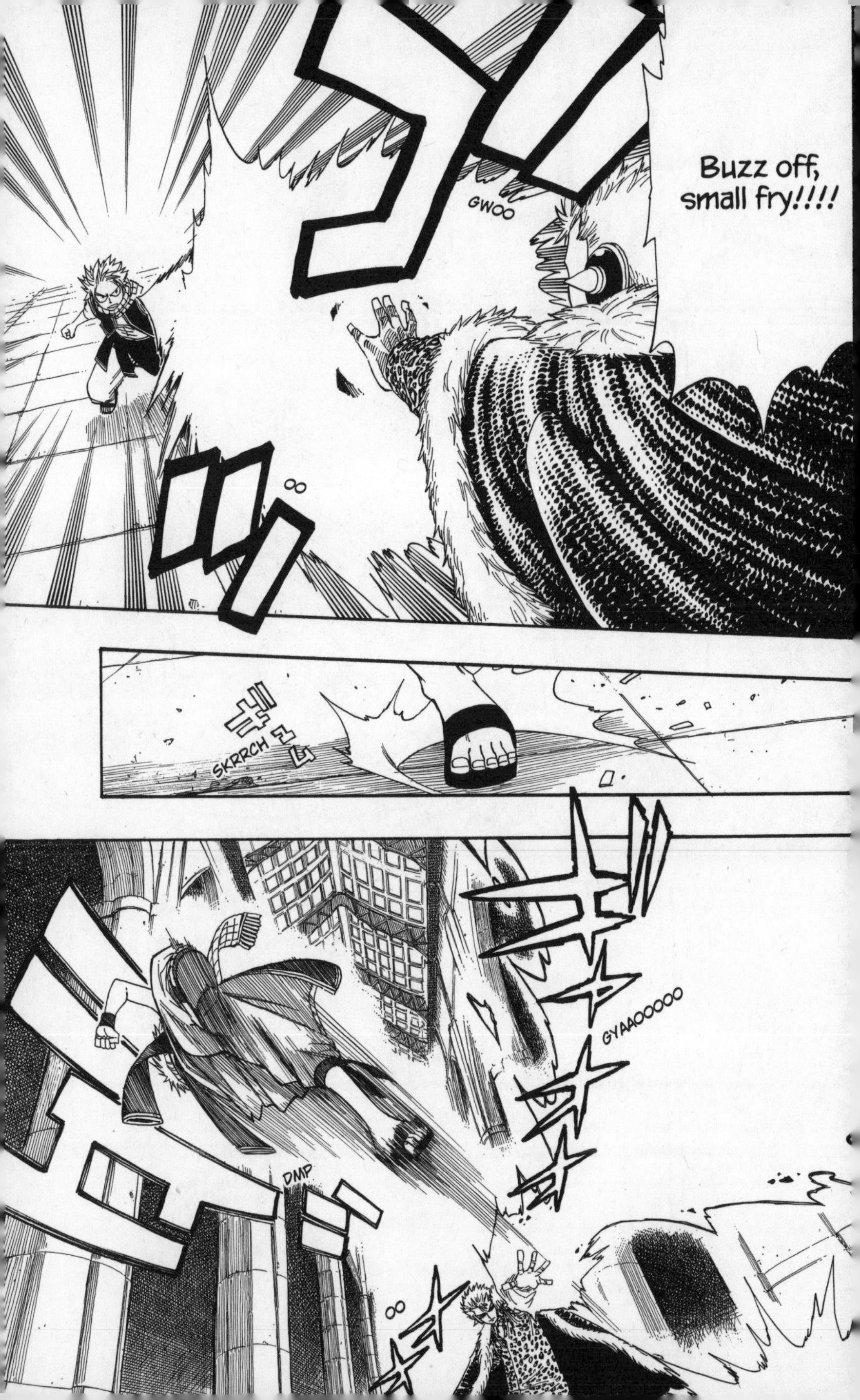
Buzz off, small fry!!!!
GWOO
SKRRCH
GYAAOOOOO
DMP

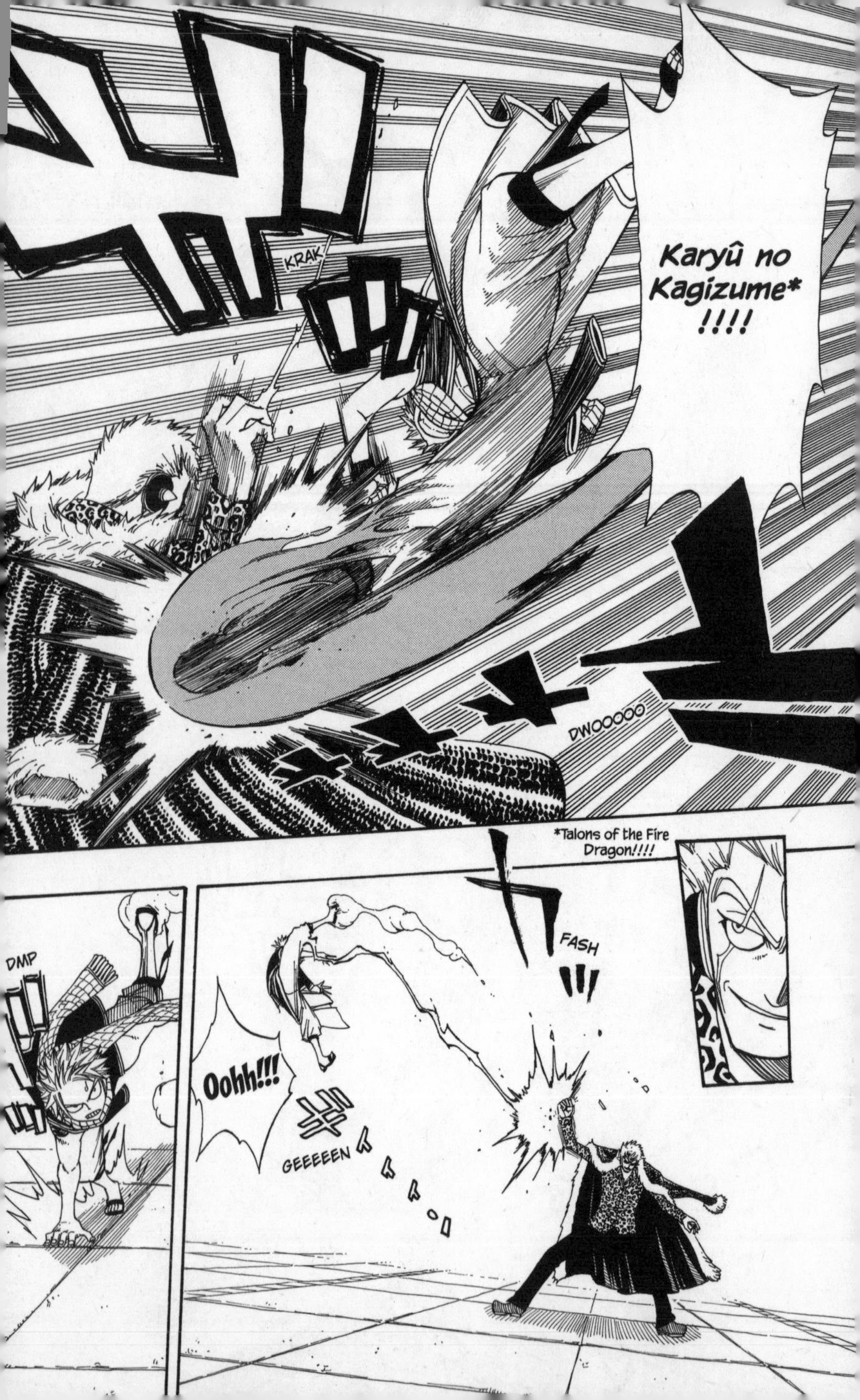
Karyû no Kagizume* !!!!
KRAK
DWOOOOO
*Talons of the Fire Dragon!!!!
FASH
Oohh!!!
GEEEEEN
DMP

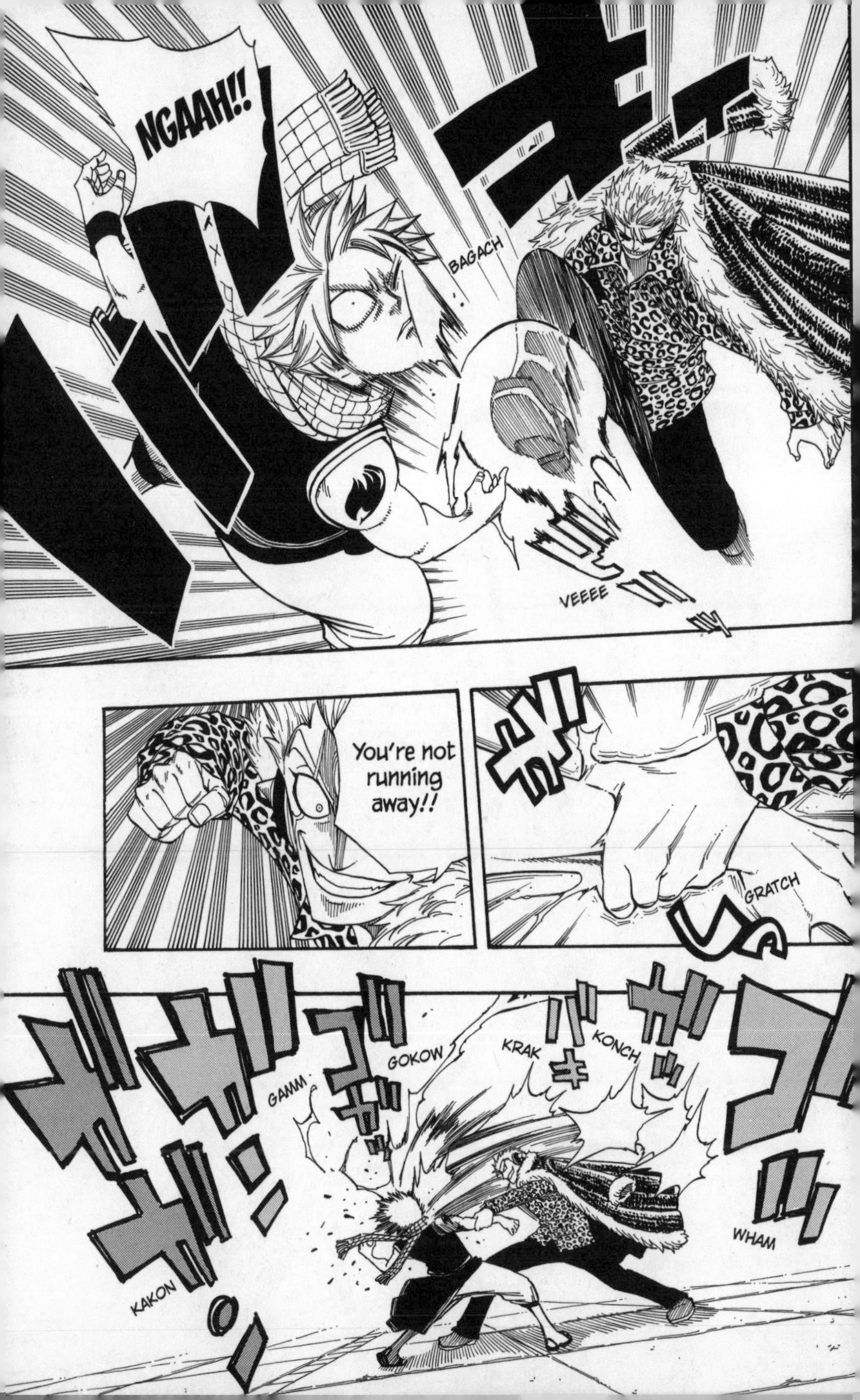
BAGACH
NGAAH!!
VEEEE
GRATCH
You're not running away!!
WHAM
KONCH
KRAK
GOKOW
GANM
KAKON

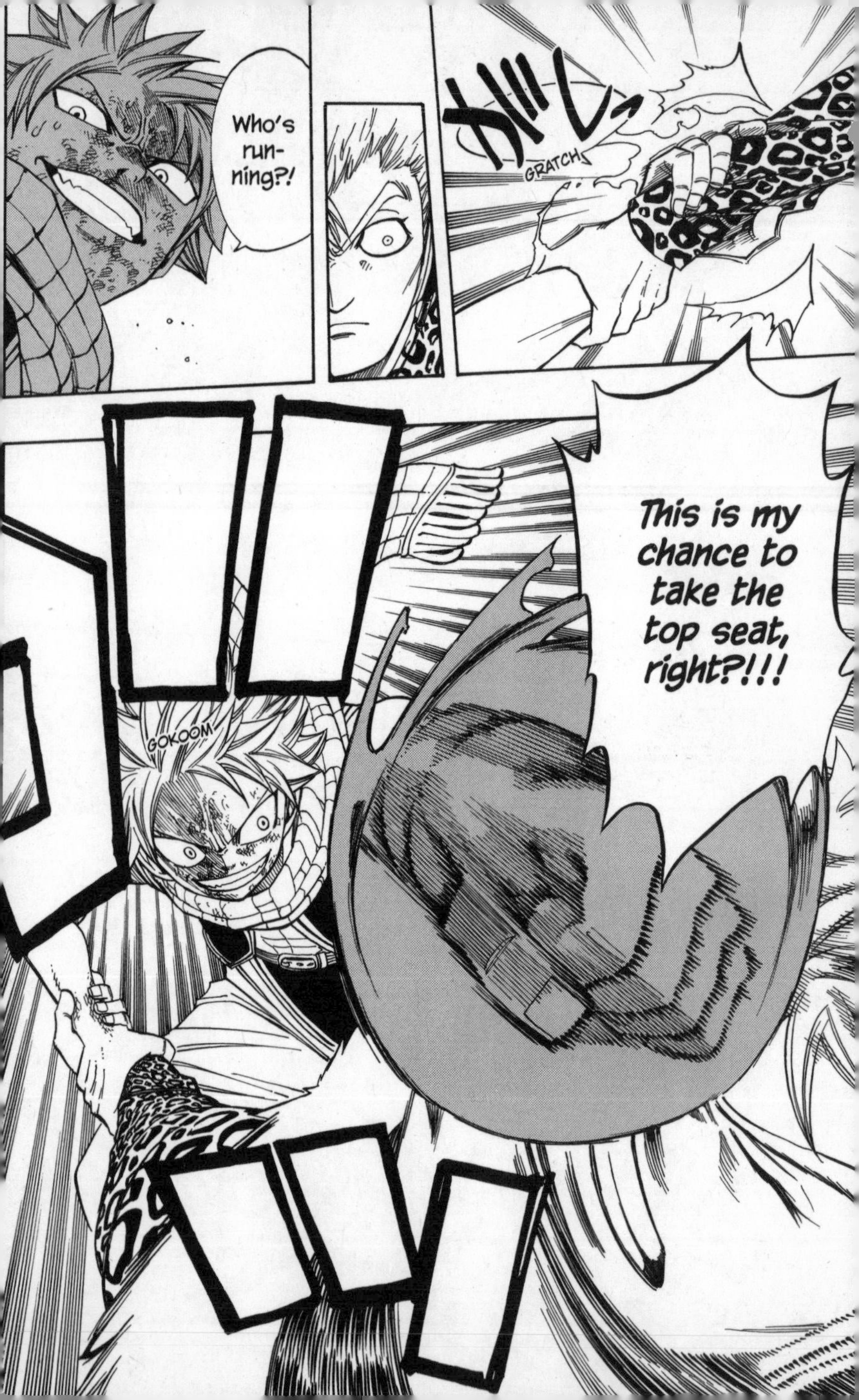
GRATCH
Who's run-ning?!
This is my chance to take the top seat, right?!!!
GOKOOM

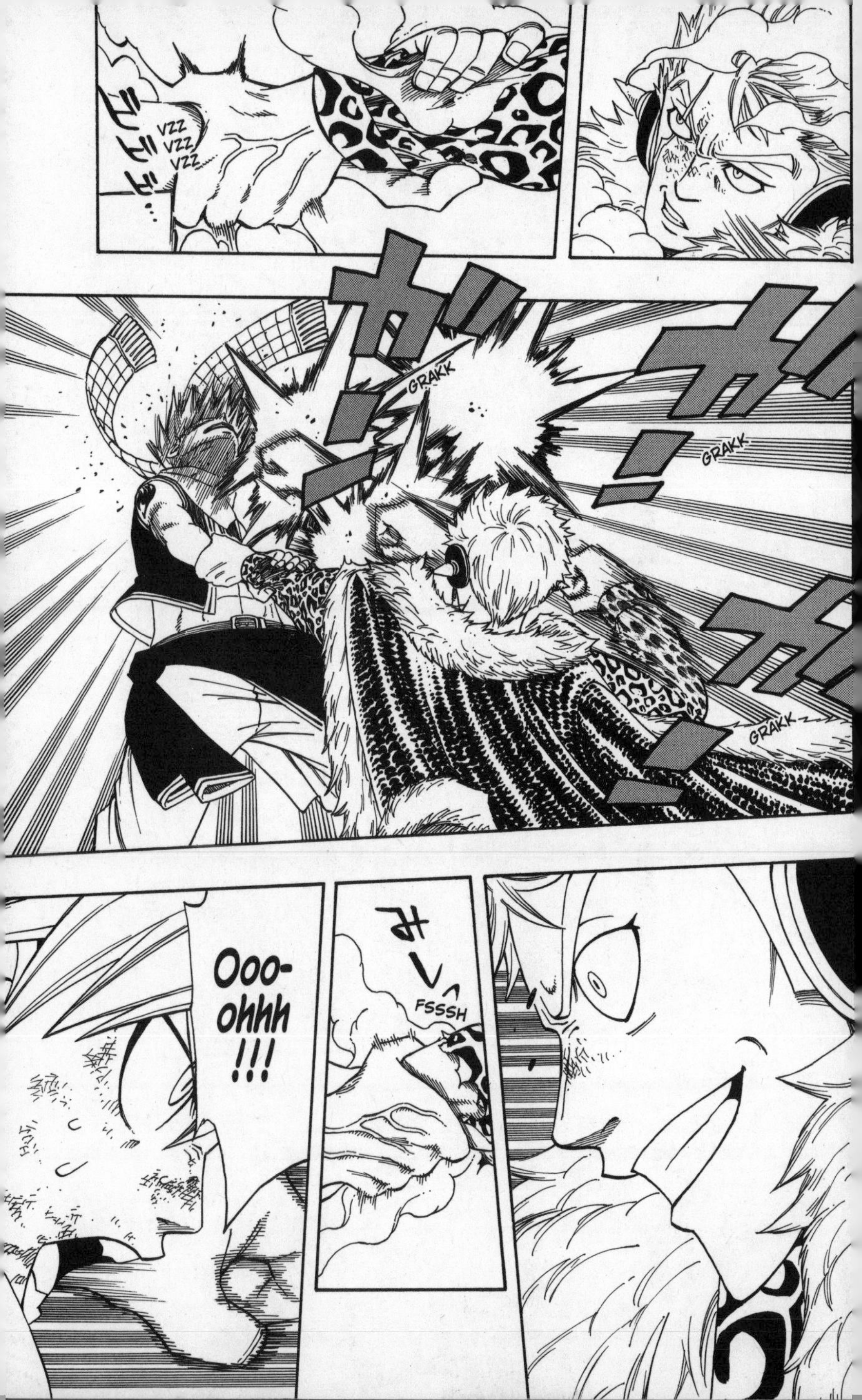
VZZ
VZZ
VZZ
GRAKK
GRAKK
GRAKK
FSSSH
Ooo-ohhh!!!

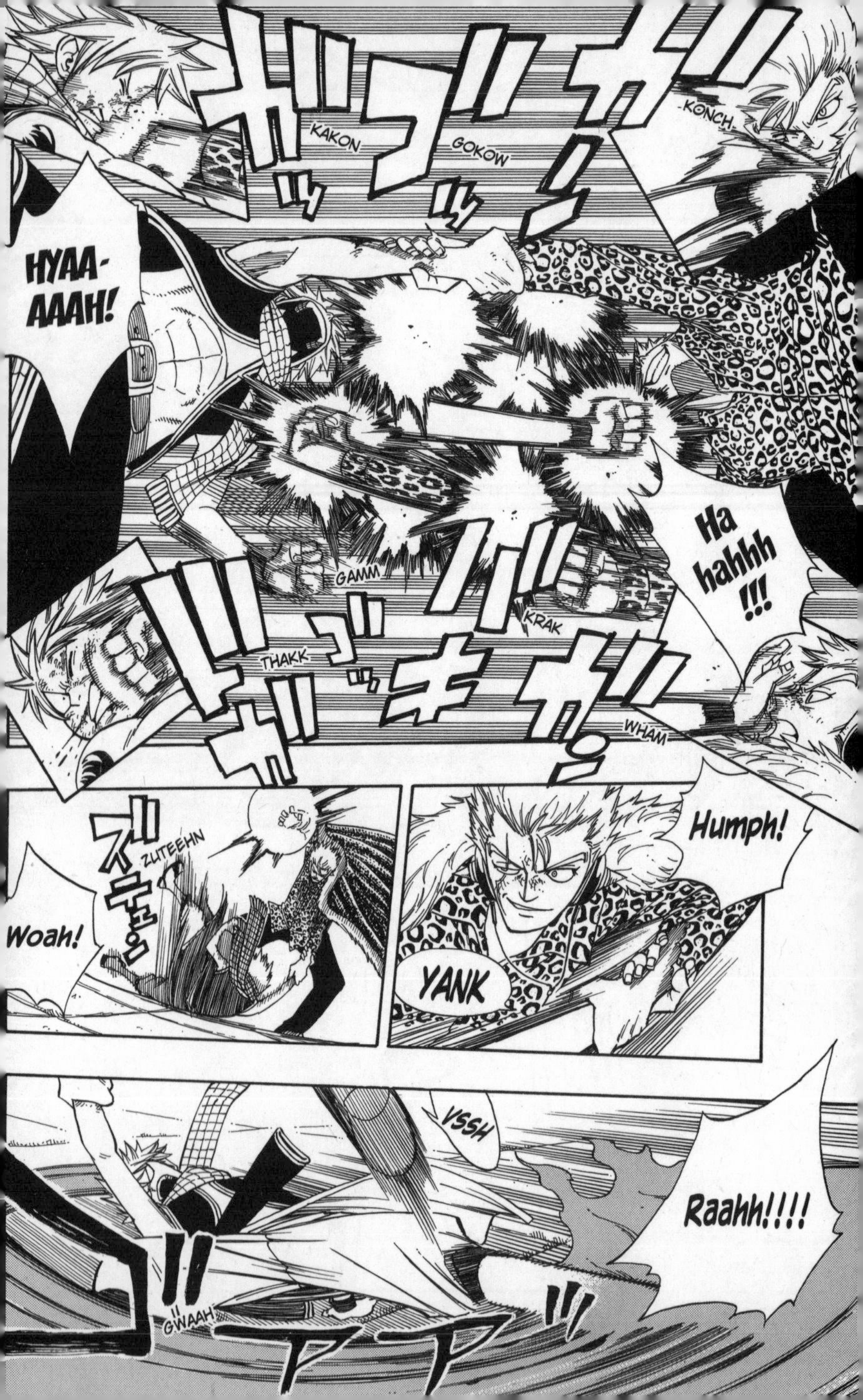

KONCH
GOKOW
KAKON
HYAA-AAAH!
Ha hahhh!!!
GAMM
KRAK
THAKK
WHAM
Humph!
YANK
ZUTEEHN
Woah!
Raahh!!!!
VSSH
GWAAH

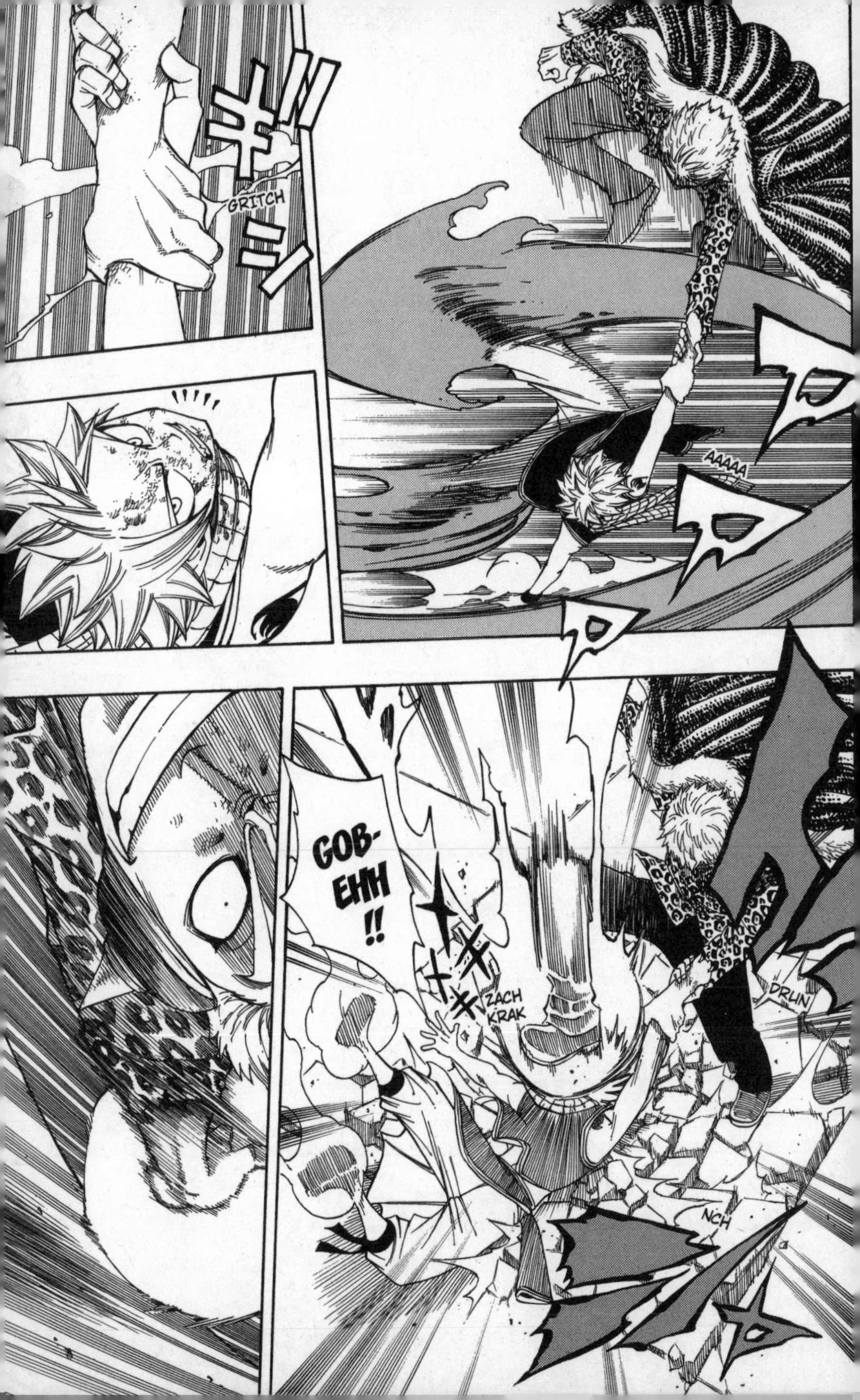
AAAAA
GRITCH
GOB-EHH!!
ZACH KRAK
DRUN
NCH

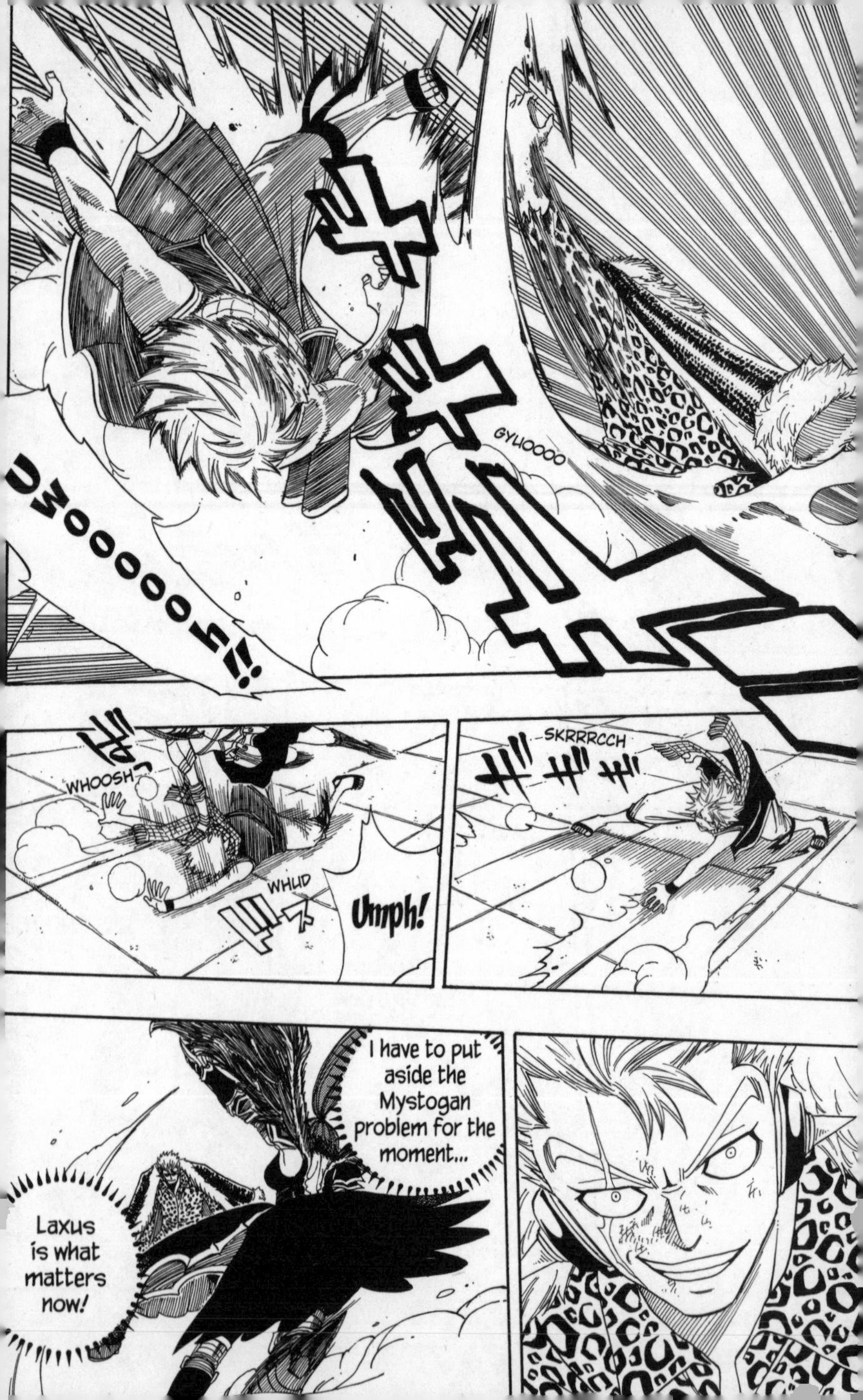
GYUOOOO
Uwoooooh!!
SKRRRCCH
WHOOSH
WHUD
Umph!
I have to put aside the Mystogan problem for the moment...
Laxus is what matters now!

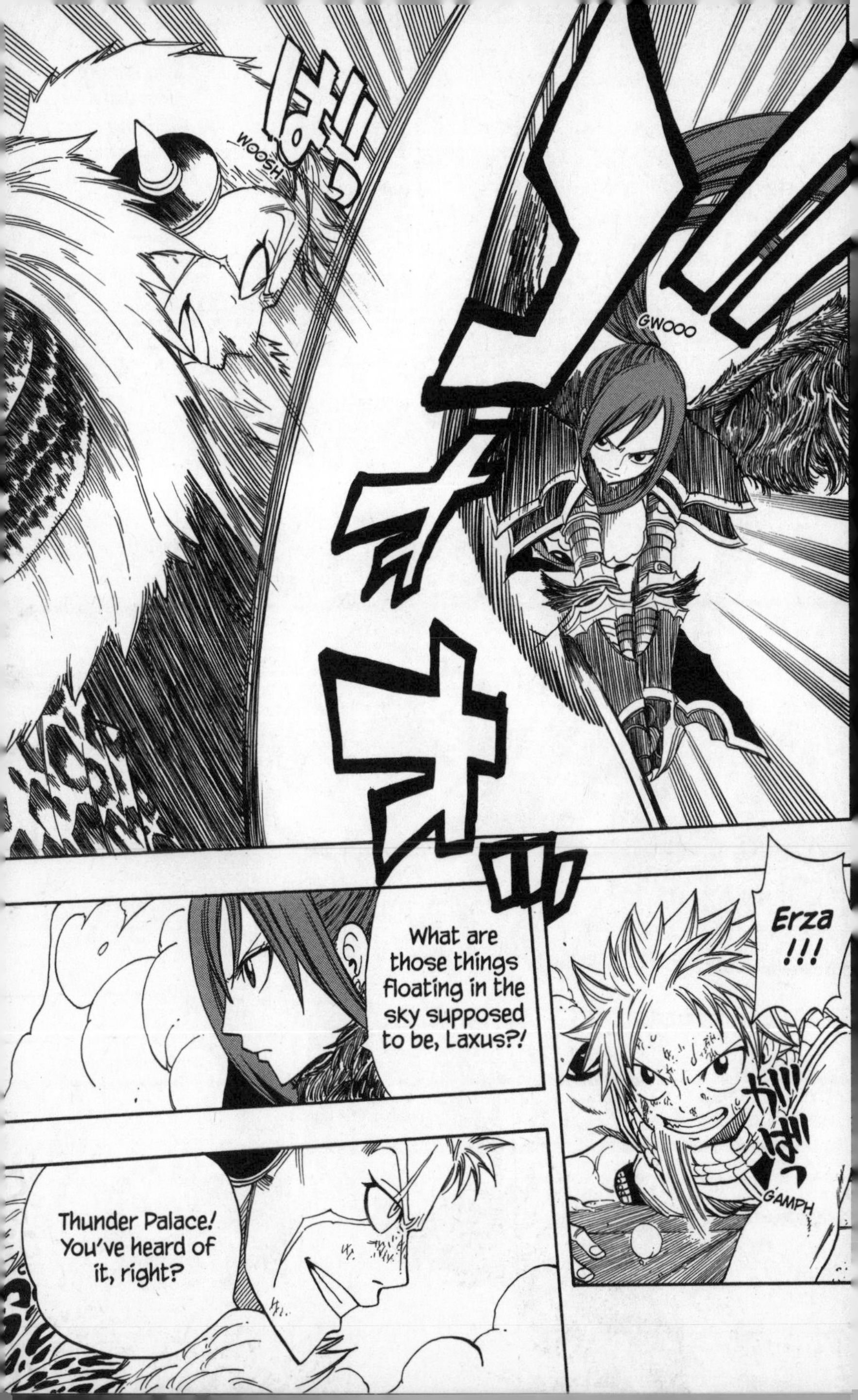

GWOOO
WOOSH
Erza!!!
GAMPH
What are those things floating in the sky supposed to be, Laxus?!
Thunder Palace! You've heard of it, right?

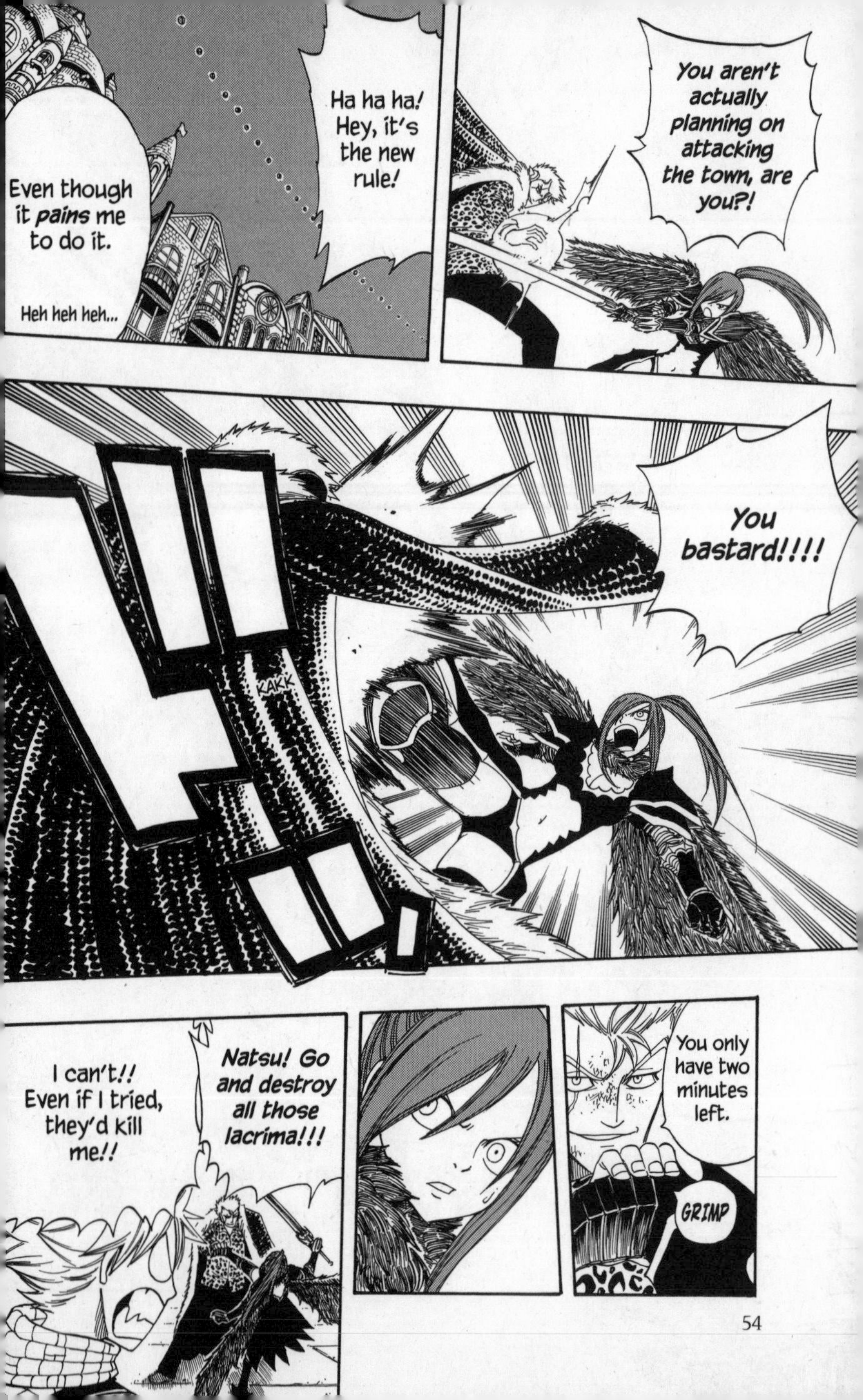
You aren't actually planning on attacking the town, are you?!
Ha ha ha! Hey, it's the new rule!
Even though it *pains* me to do it.
Heh heh heh...
You bastard!!!!
KAKK
You only have two minutes left.
GRIMP
Natsu! Go and destroy all those lacrima!!!
I can't!! Even if I tried, they'd kill me!!

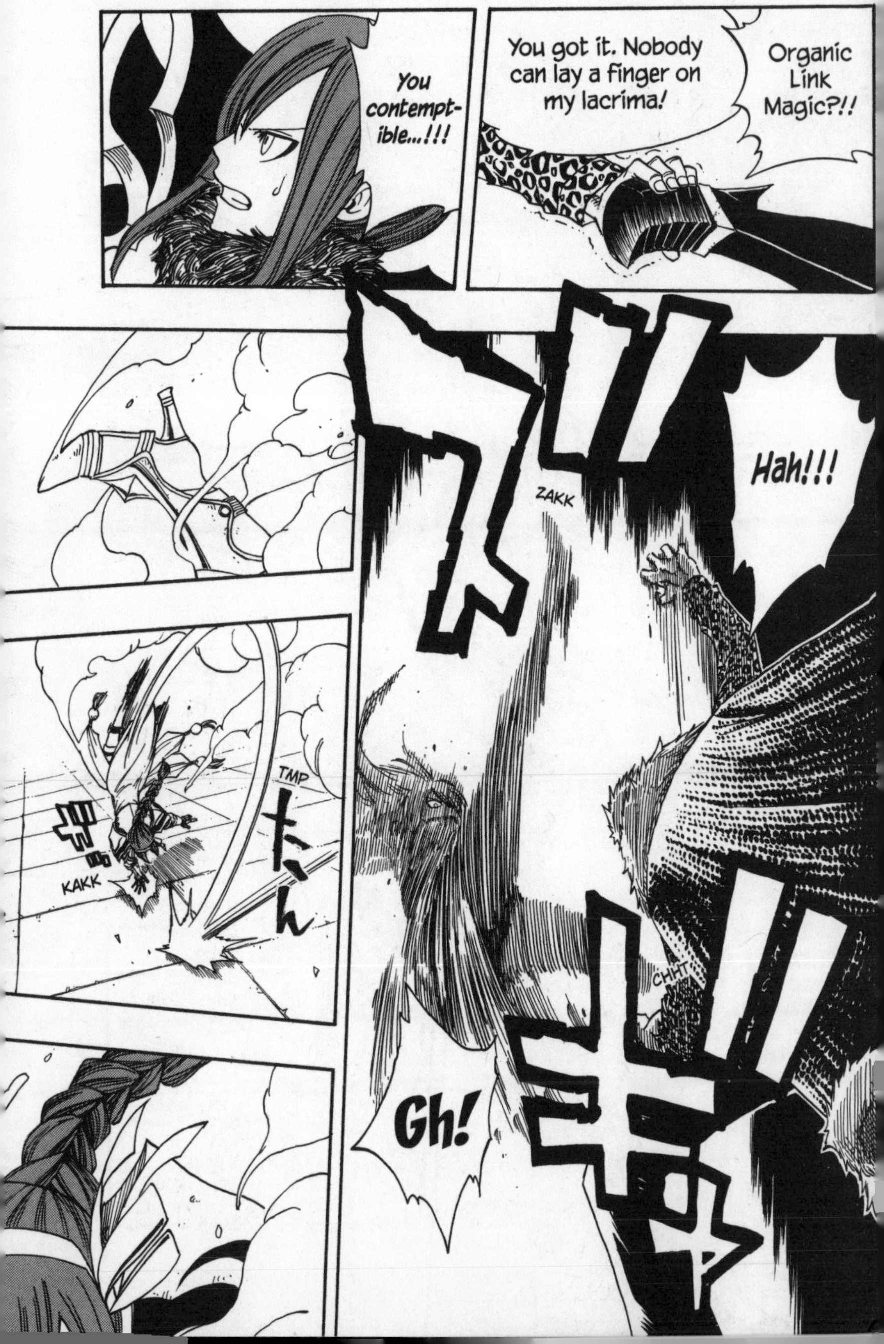
Organic Link Magic?!!
You got it. Nobody can lay a finger on my lacrima!
You contemptible...!!!
Hah!!!
ZAKK
CHHT
Gh!
TMP
たん
KAKK

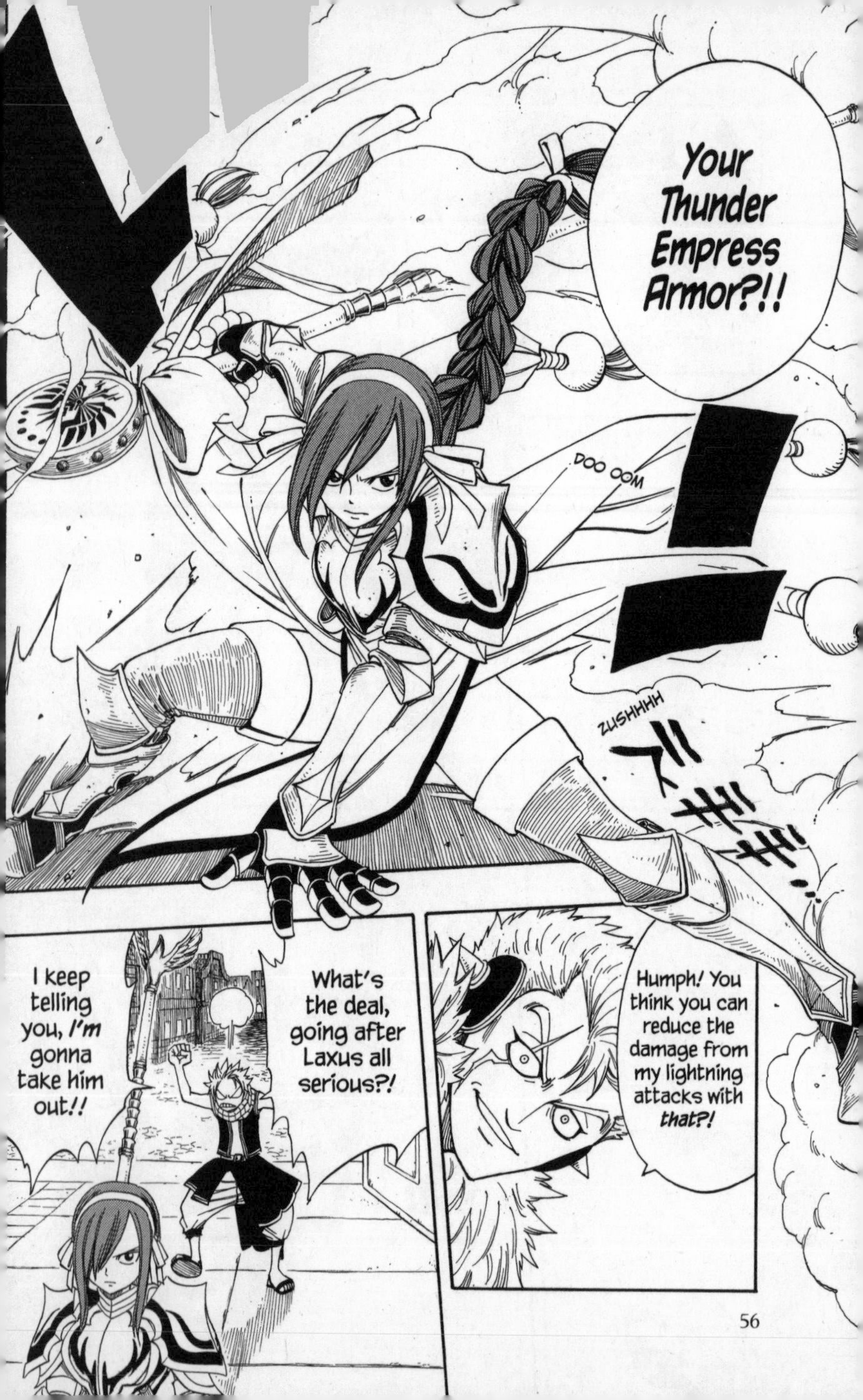
Your Thunder Empress Armor?!!
DOO OOM
ZUSHHHH
Humph! You think you can reduce the damage from my lightning attacks with *that?!*
What's the deal, going after Laxus all serious?!
I keep telling you, *I'm* gonna take him out!!

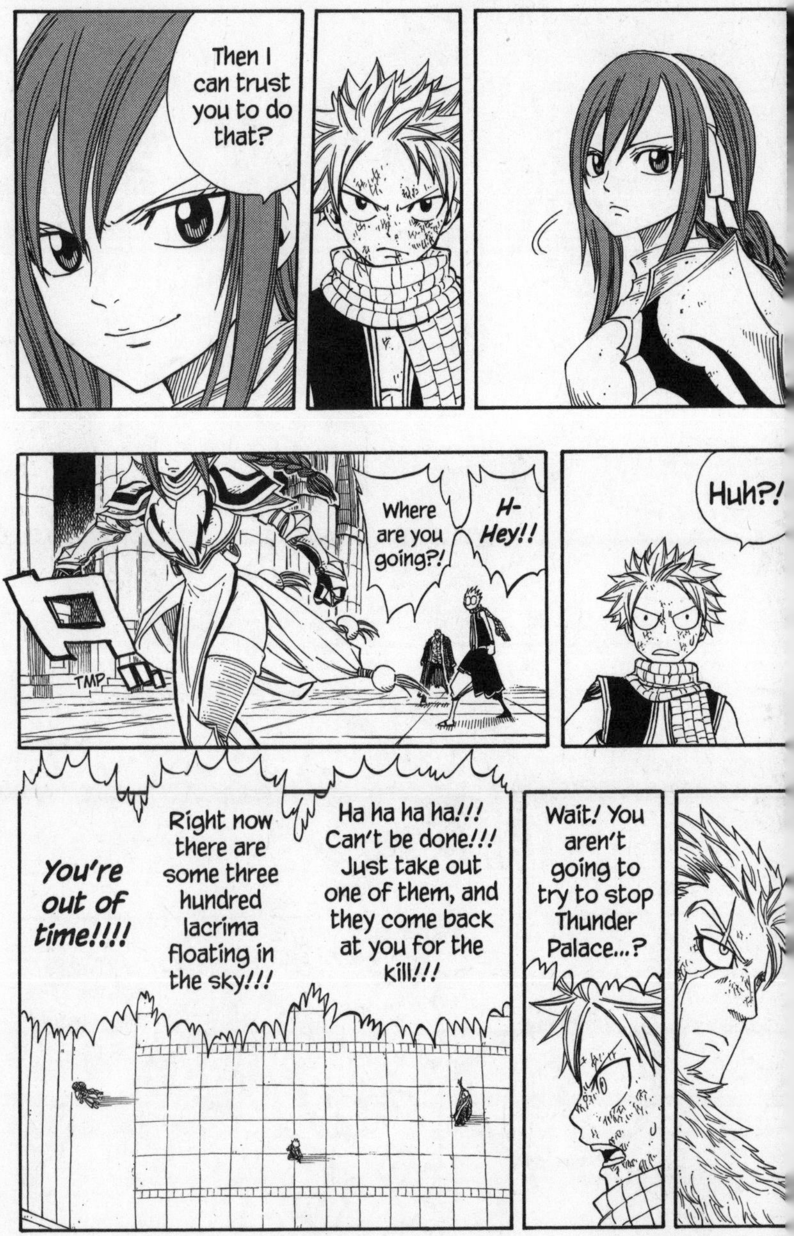
Then I can trust you to do that?
Huh?!
H- Hey!!
Where are you going?!
TMP
Wait! You aren't going to try to stop Thunder Palace...?
Ha ha ha ha!!! Can't be done!!! Just take out one of them, and they come back at you for the kill!!!
Right now there are some three hundred lacrima floating in the sky!!!
You're out of time!!!!

Not if I destroy them all at once!

And even if you could, you wouldn't survive it!!!!

Can't be done!!!!

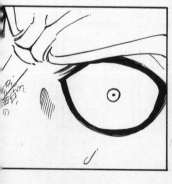

Perhaps not, but the town would be saved!

CHANK

CHANK

CHANK

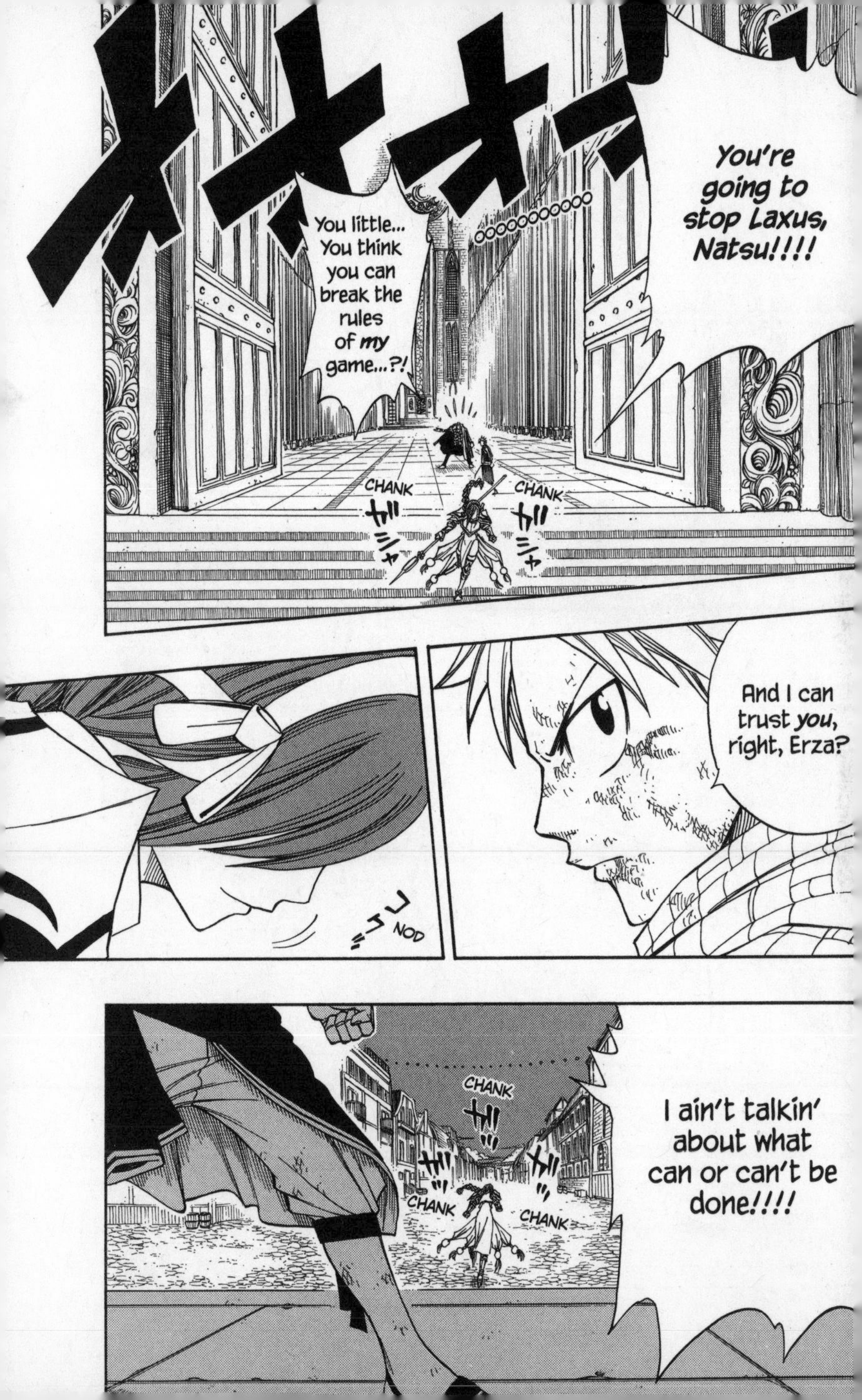
You're going to stop Laxus, Natsu!!!!
You little... You think you can break the rules of my game...?!
CHANK
CHANK
And I can trust you, right, Erza?
NOD
CHANK
CHANK
CHANK
I ain't talkin' about what can or can't be done!!!!

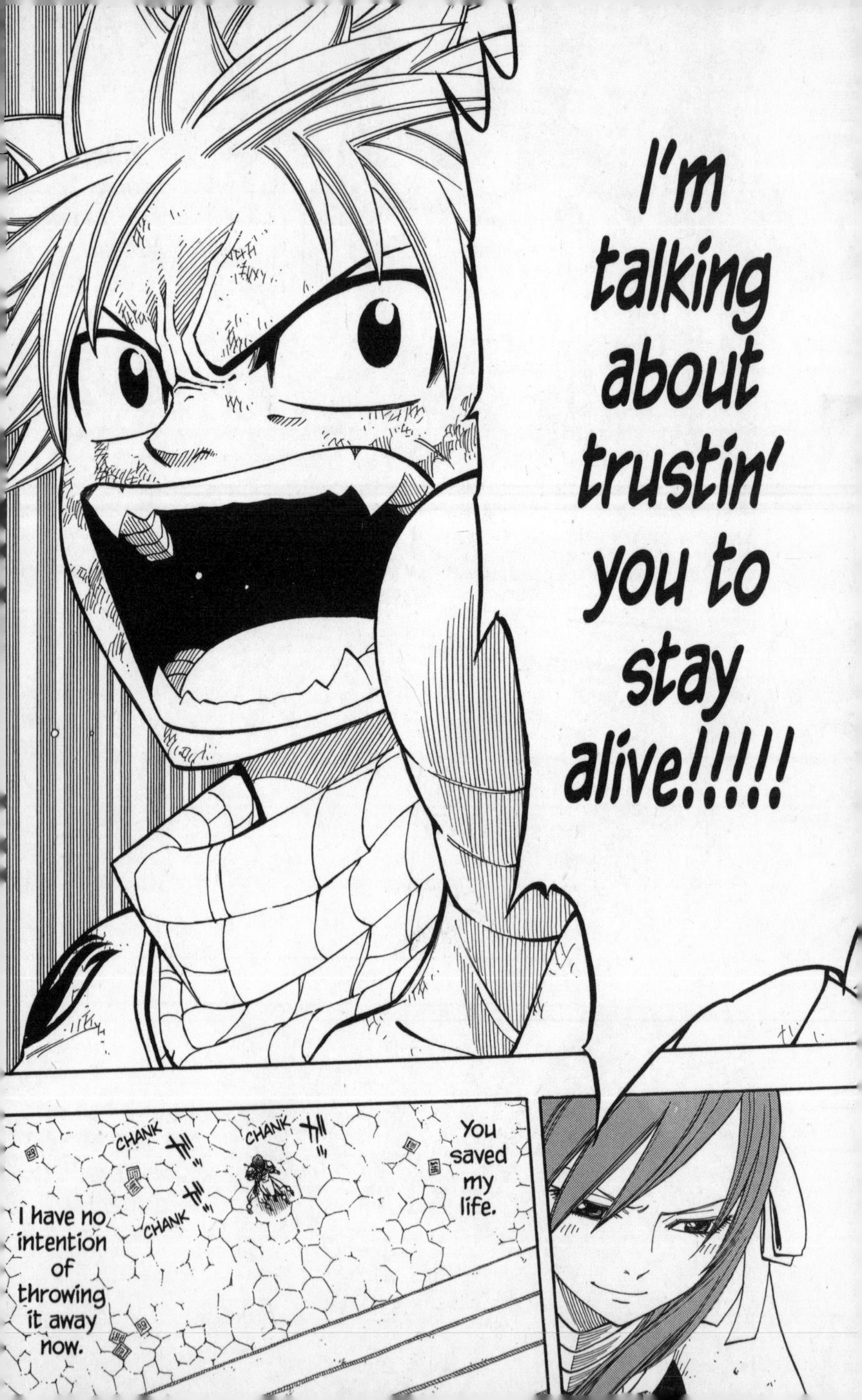
I'm talking about trustin' you to stay alive!!!!!
You saved my life.
CHANK
CHANK
CHANK
I have no intention of throwing it away now.

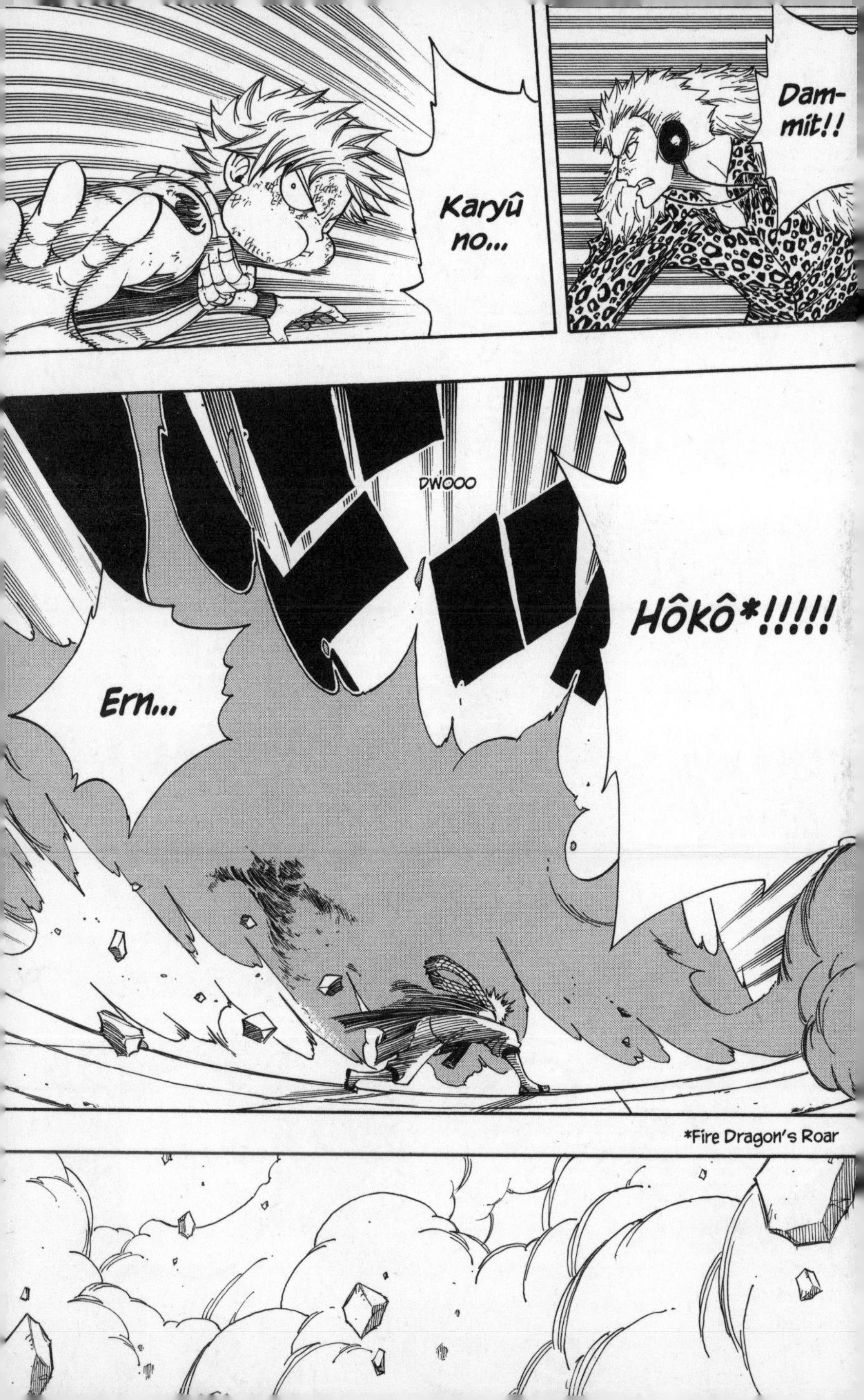
Dam-
mit!!
Karyû
no...
DWOOO
Hôkô*!!!!!
Ern...
*Fire Dragon's Roar

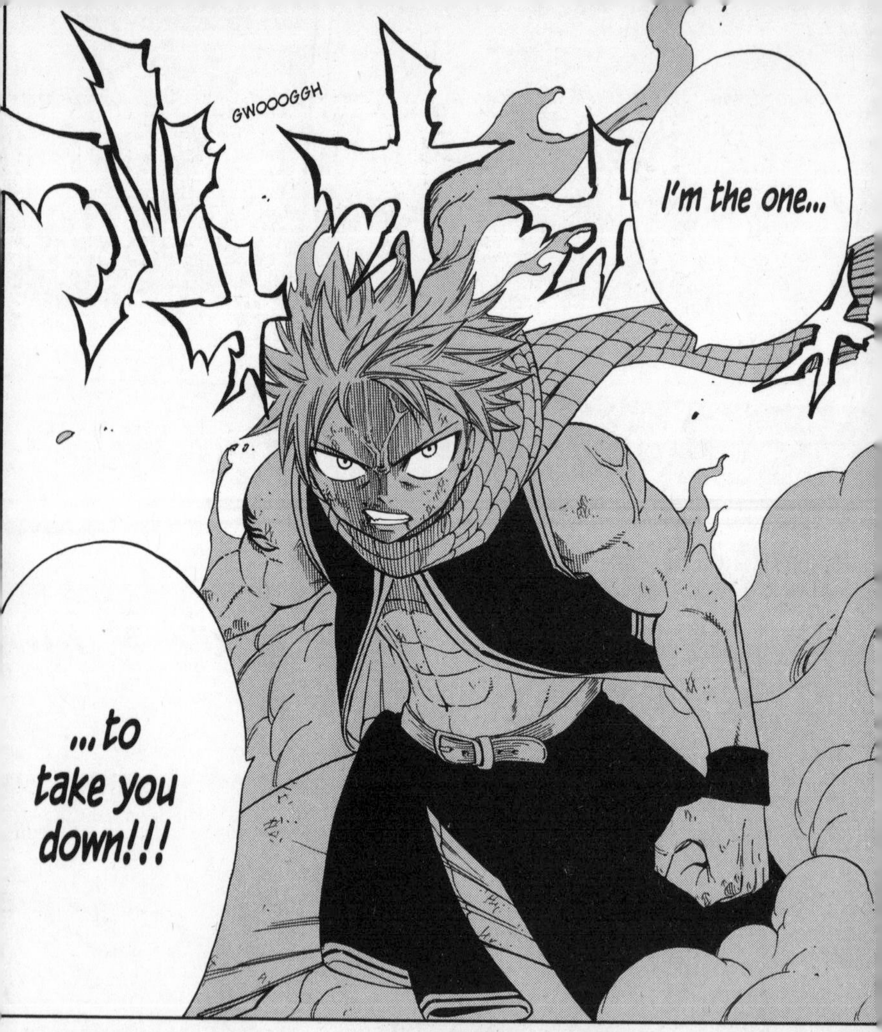
GWOOOGGH
I'm the one...
...to take you down!!!
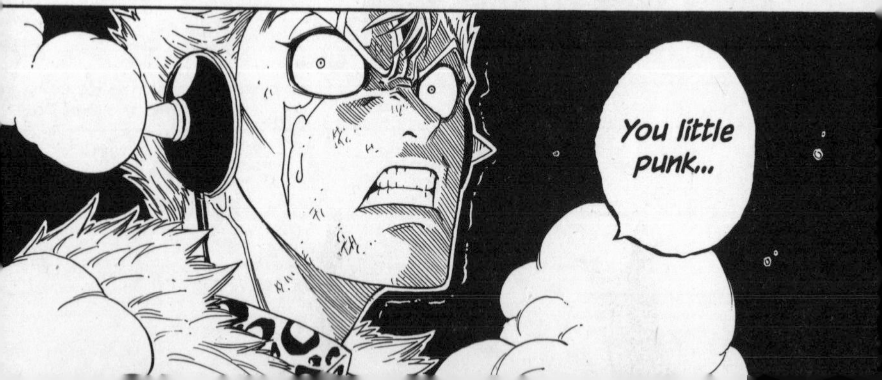
You little punk...

FAIRY TAIL

Chapter 122: The Lonely Thunder Clap

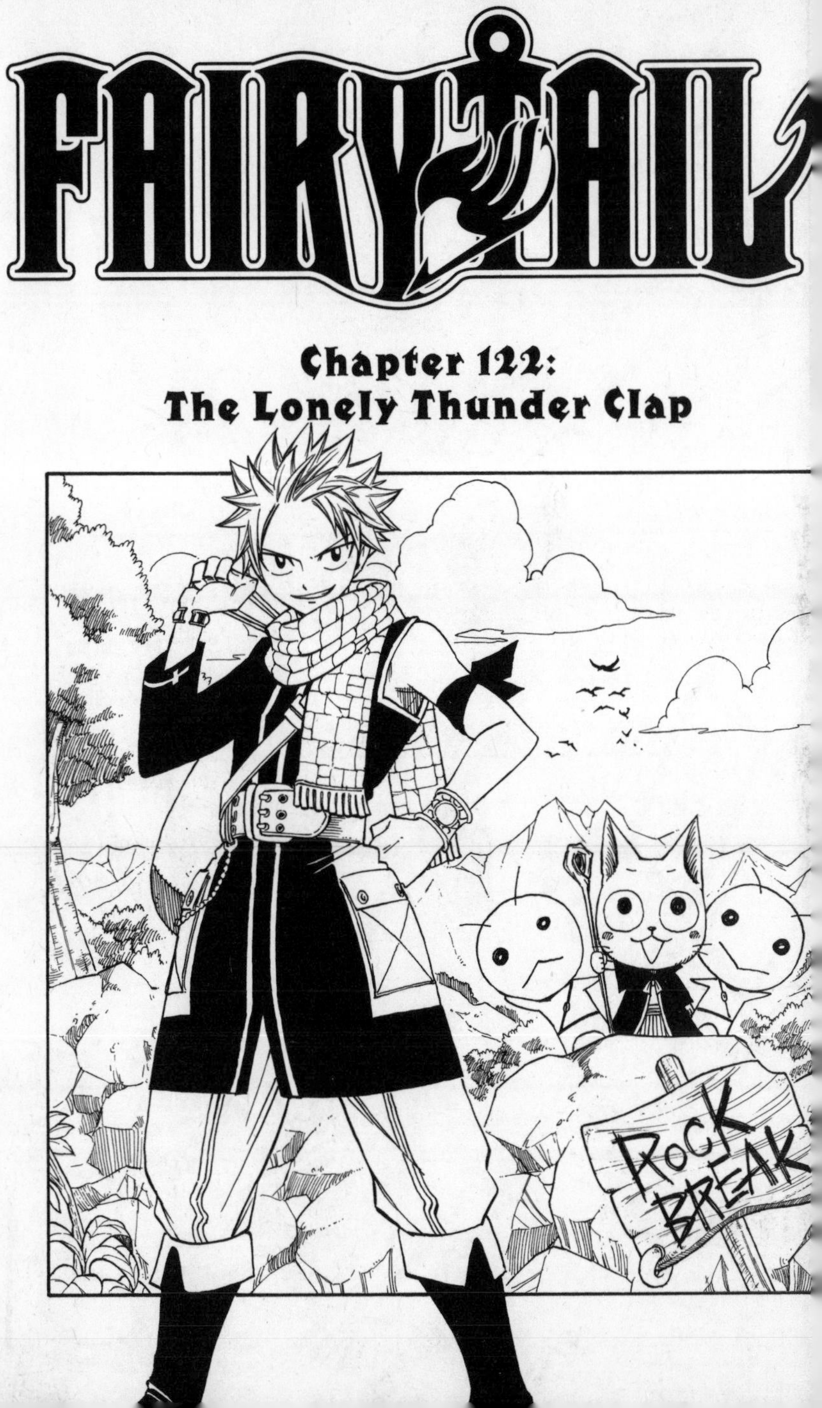
ROCK BREAK

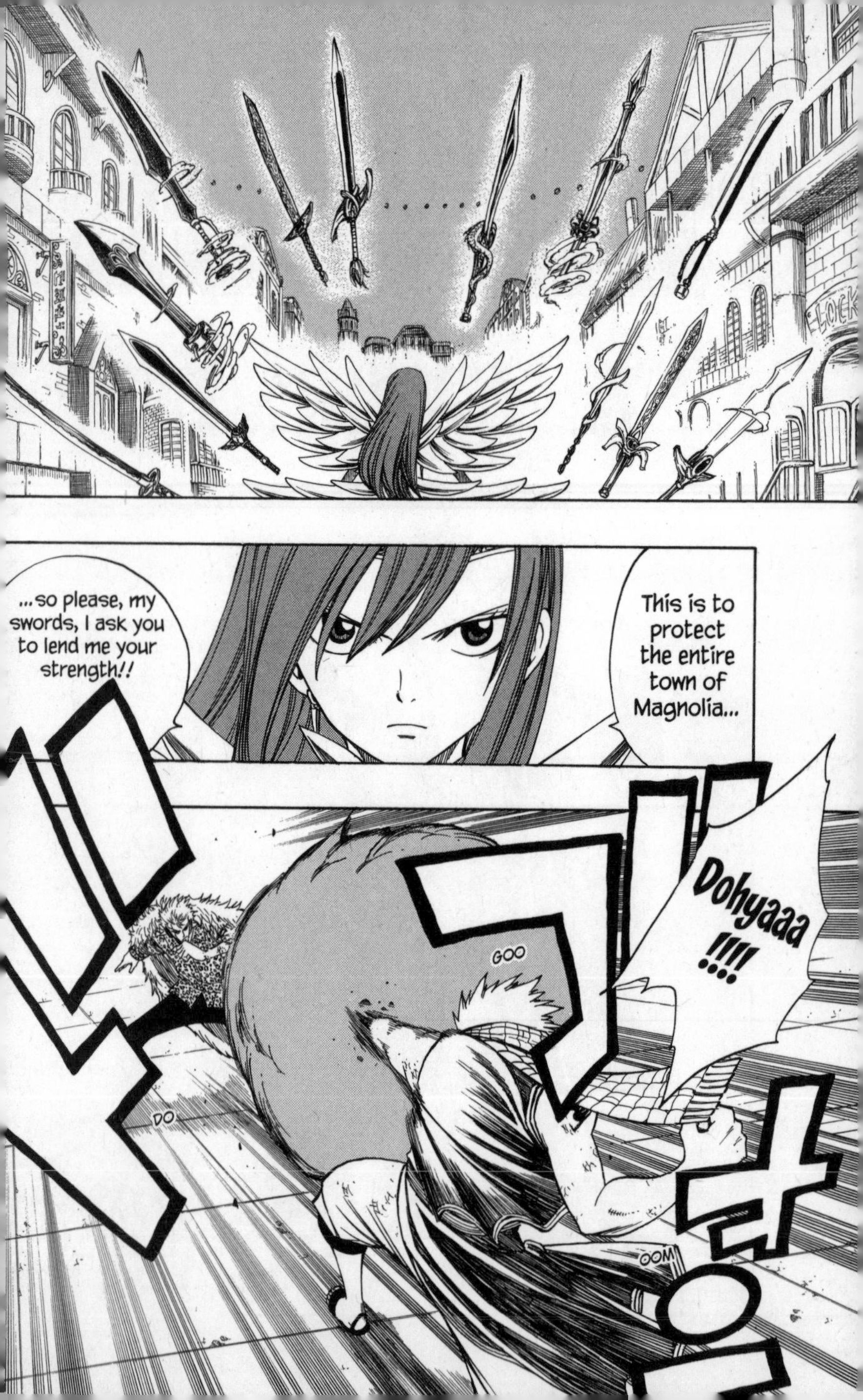

This is to protect the entire town of Magnolia...
...so please, my swords, I ask you to lend me your strength!!
Dohyaaa!!!!
GOO
OOM
DO

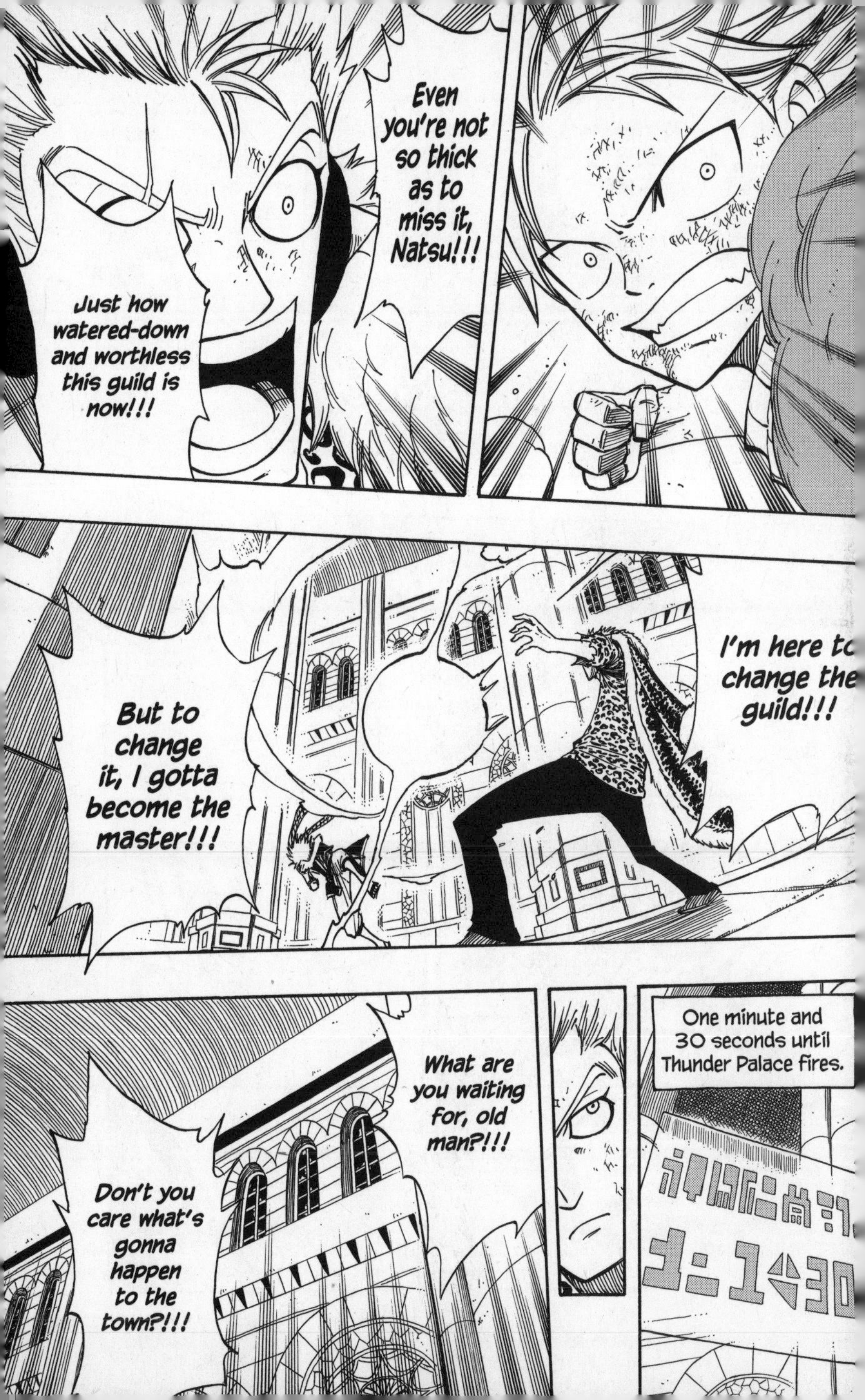
Even you're not so thick as to miss it, Natsu!!!
Just how watered-down and worthless this guild is now!!!
I'm here to change the guild!!!
But to change it, I gotta become the master!!!
One minute and 30 seconds until Thunder Palace fires.
What are you waiting for, old man?!!!
Don't you care what's gonna happen to the town?!!!

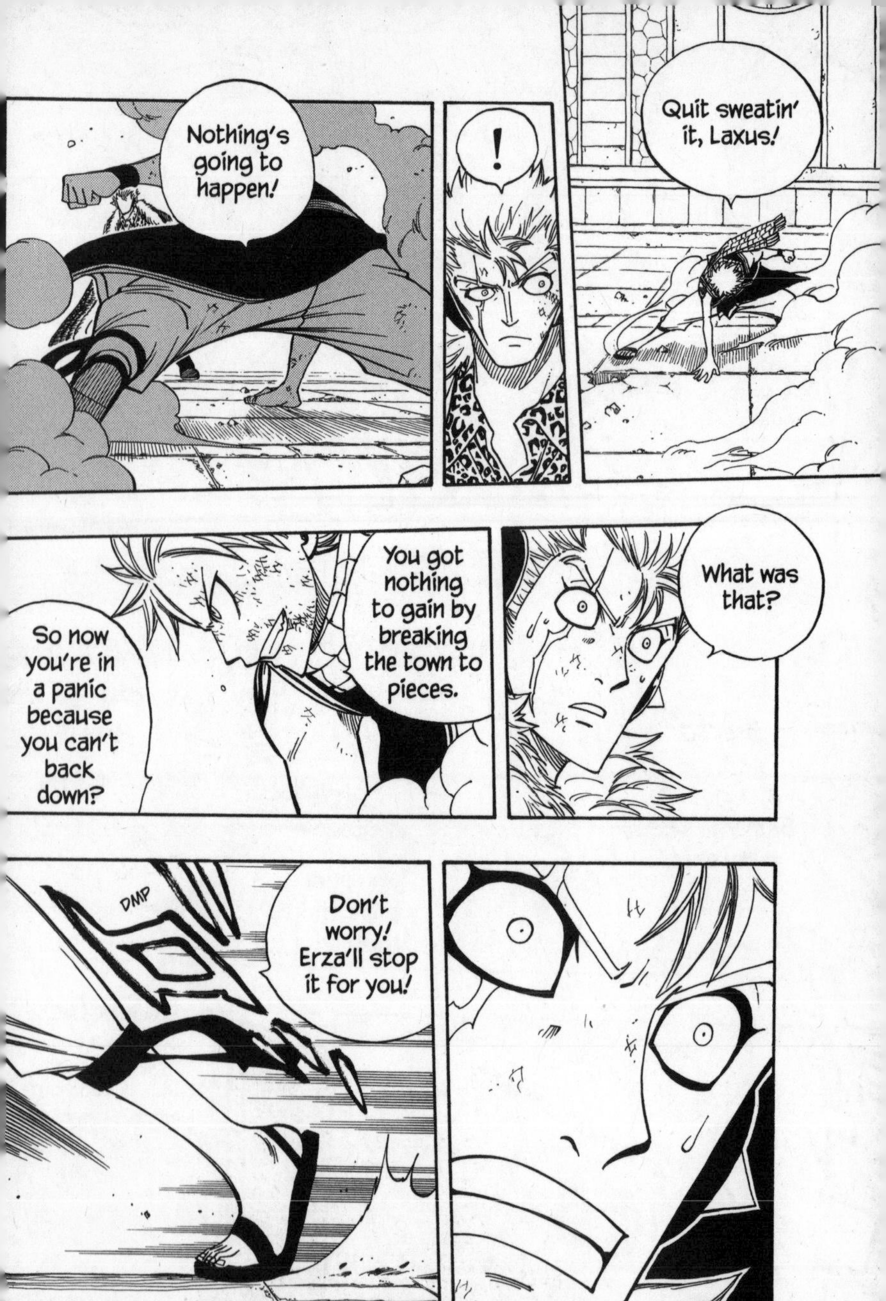
Quit sweatin' it, Laxus!
!
Nothing's going to happen!
What was that?
You got nothing to gain by breaking the town to pieces.
So now you're in a panic because you can't back down?
Don't worry! Erza'll stop it for you!
DMP

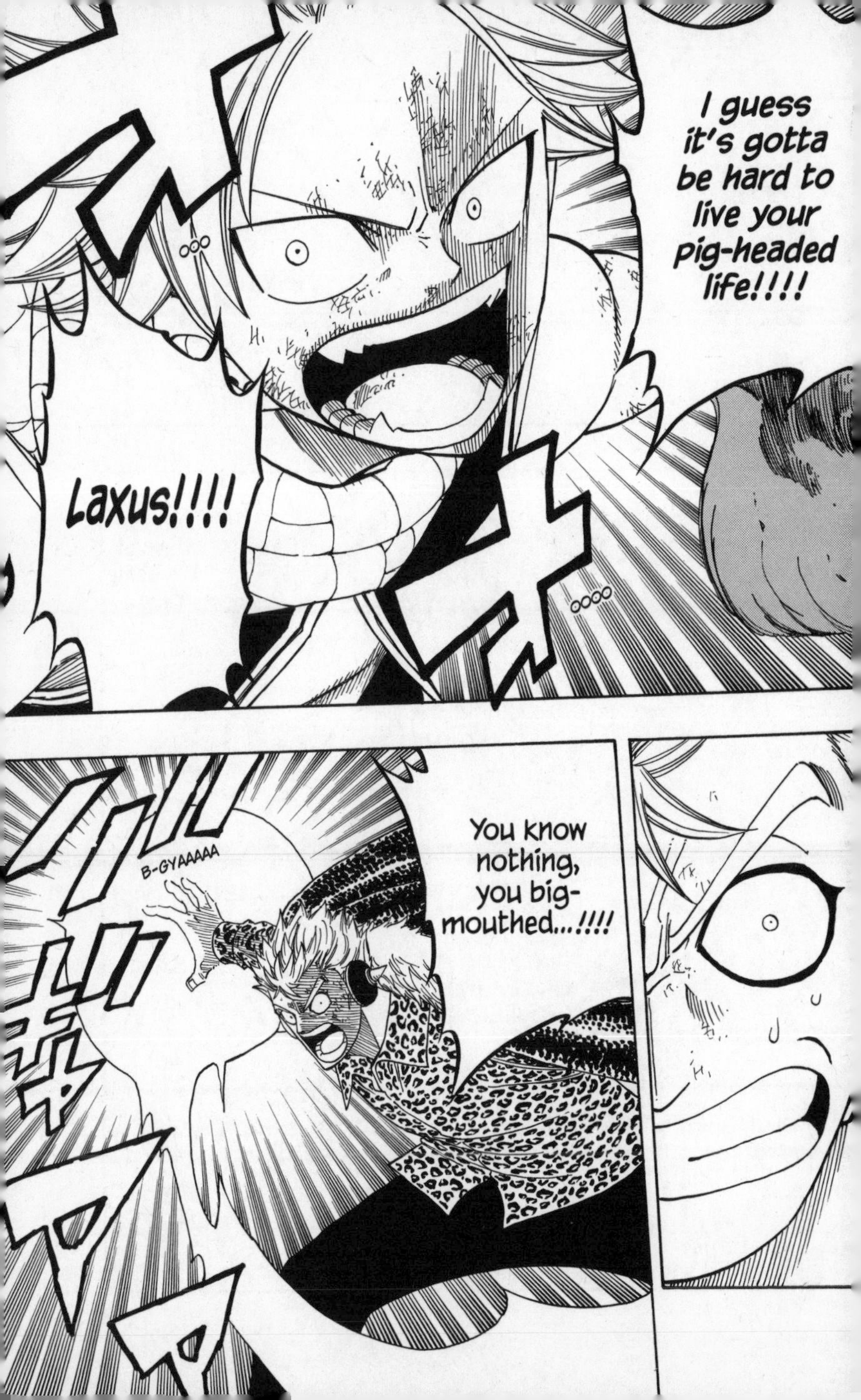
I guess it's gotta be hard to live your pig-headed life!!!!
Laxus!!!!
You know nothing, you big-mouthed...!!!!
B-GYAAAAA

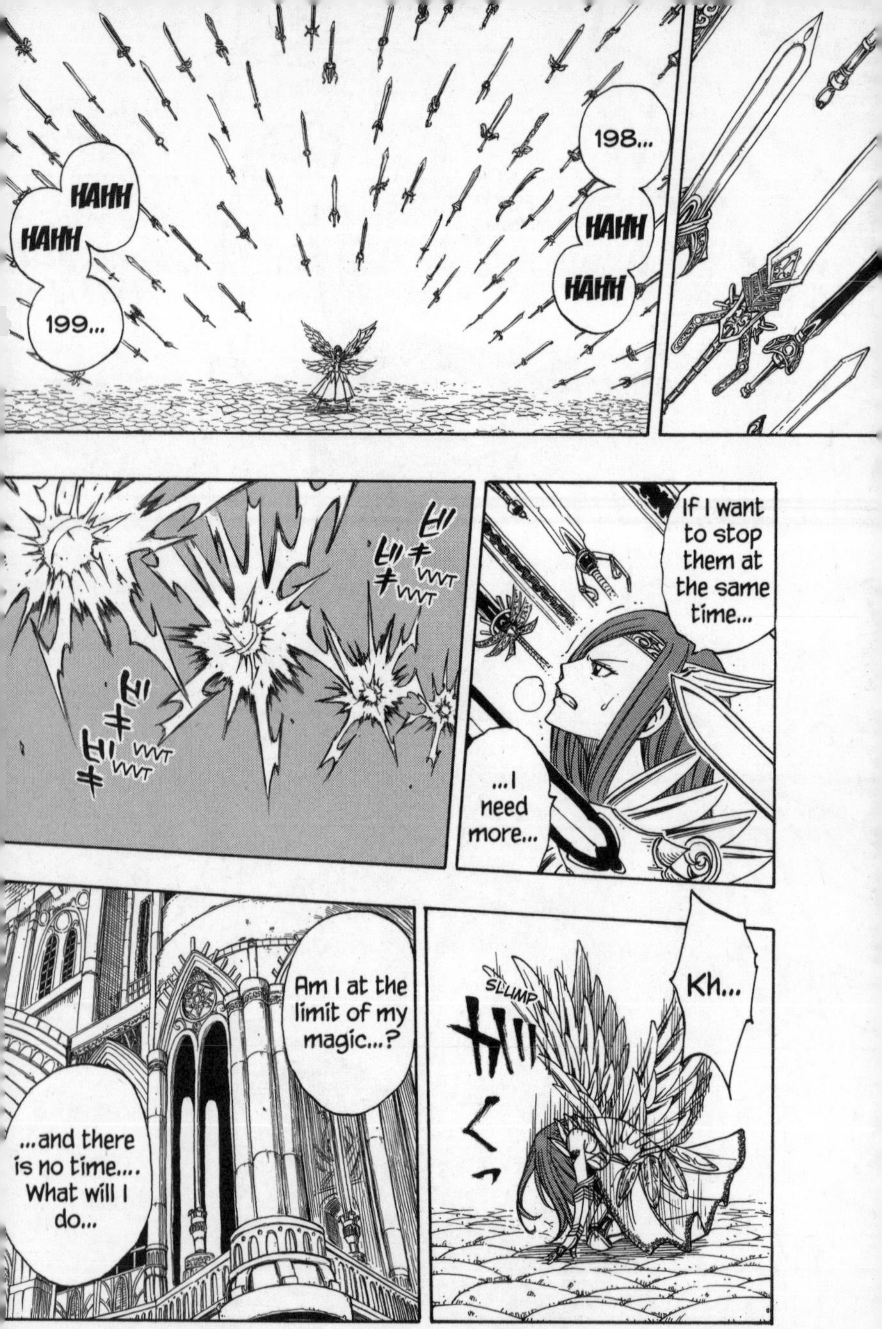
198...
HAHH HAHH
HAHH HAHH
199...
If I want to stop them at the same time...
...I need more...
VVVT VVVT
VVVT VVVT
Kh...
SLUMP
Am I at the limit of my magic...?
...and there is no time.... What will I do...

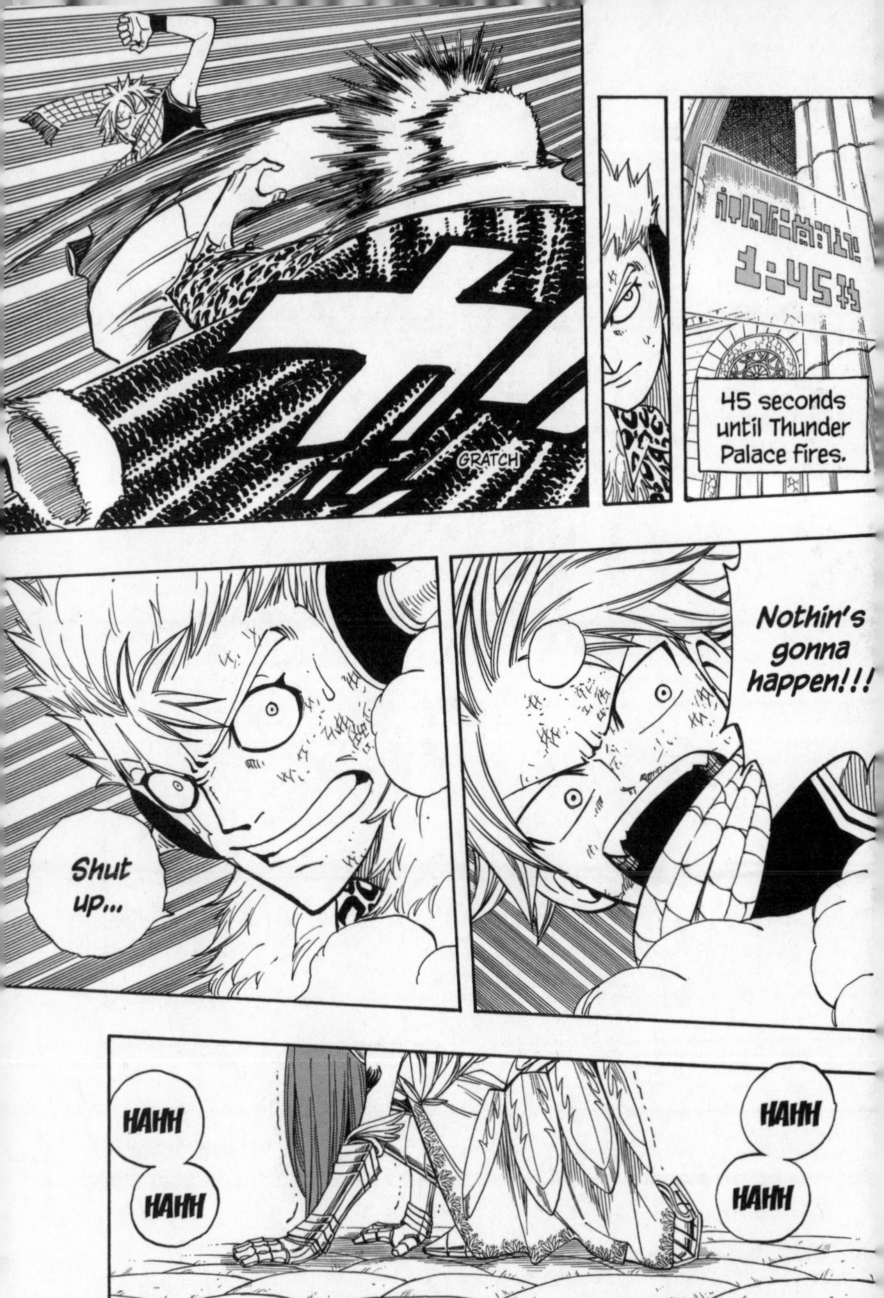
45 seconds until Thunder Palace fires.
GRATCH
Nothin's gonna happen!!!
Shut up...
HAHH
HAHH
HAHH
HAHH

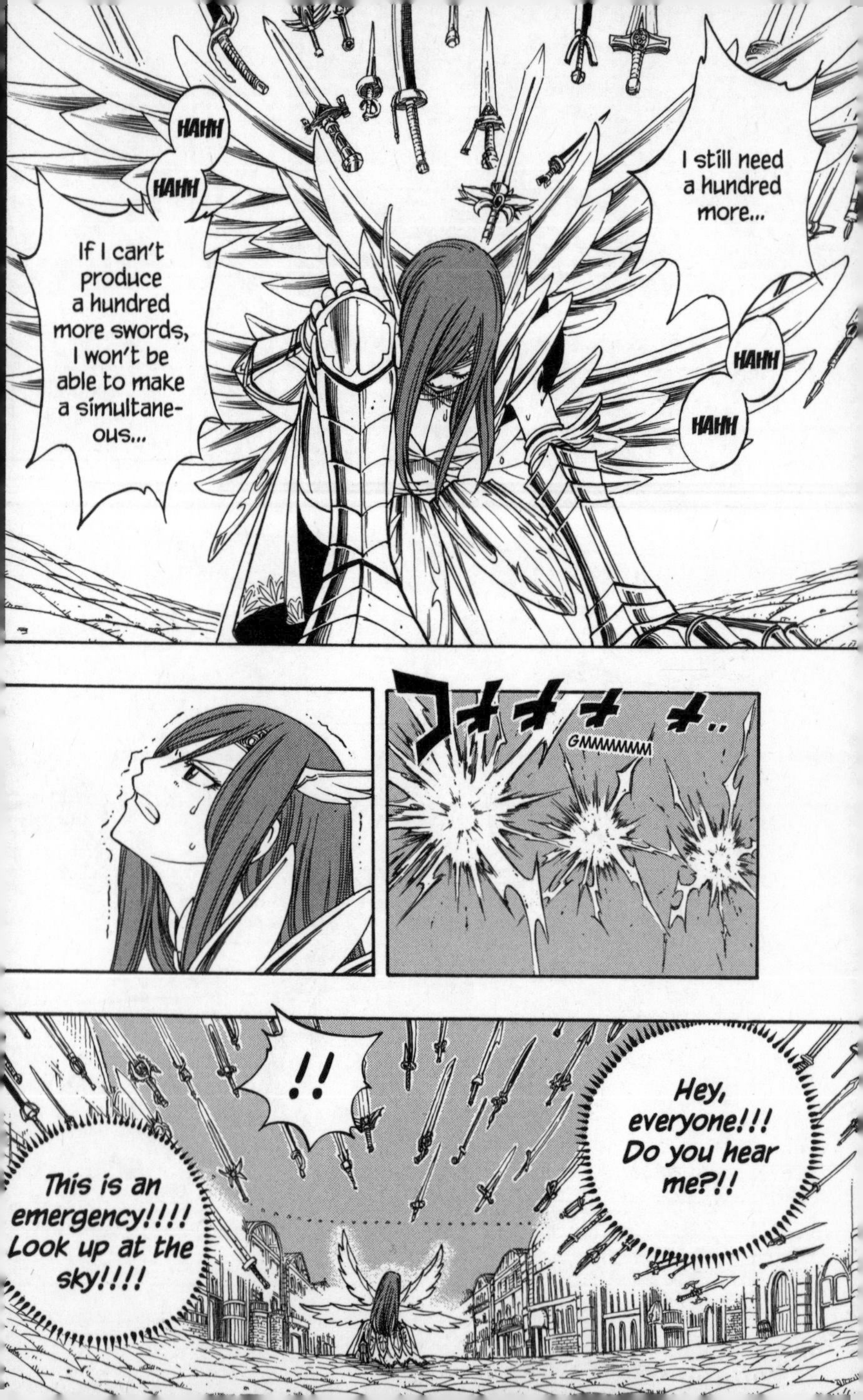
I still need a hundred more...
HAHH
HAHH
HAHH
HAHH
If I can't produce a hundred more swords, I won't be able to make a simultane-ous...
GMMMMMMM
Hey, everyone!!! Do you hear me?!!
!!
This is an emergency!!!! Look up at the sky!!!!

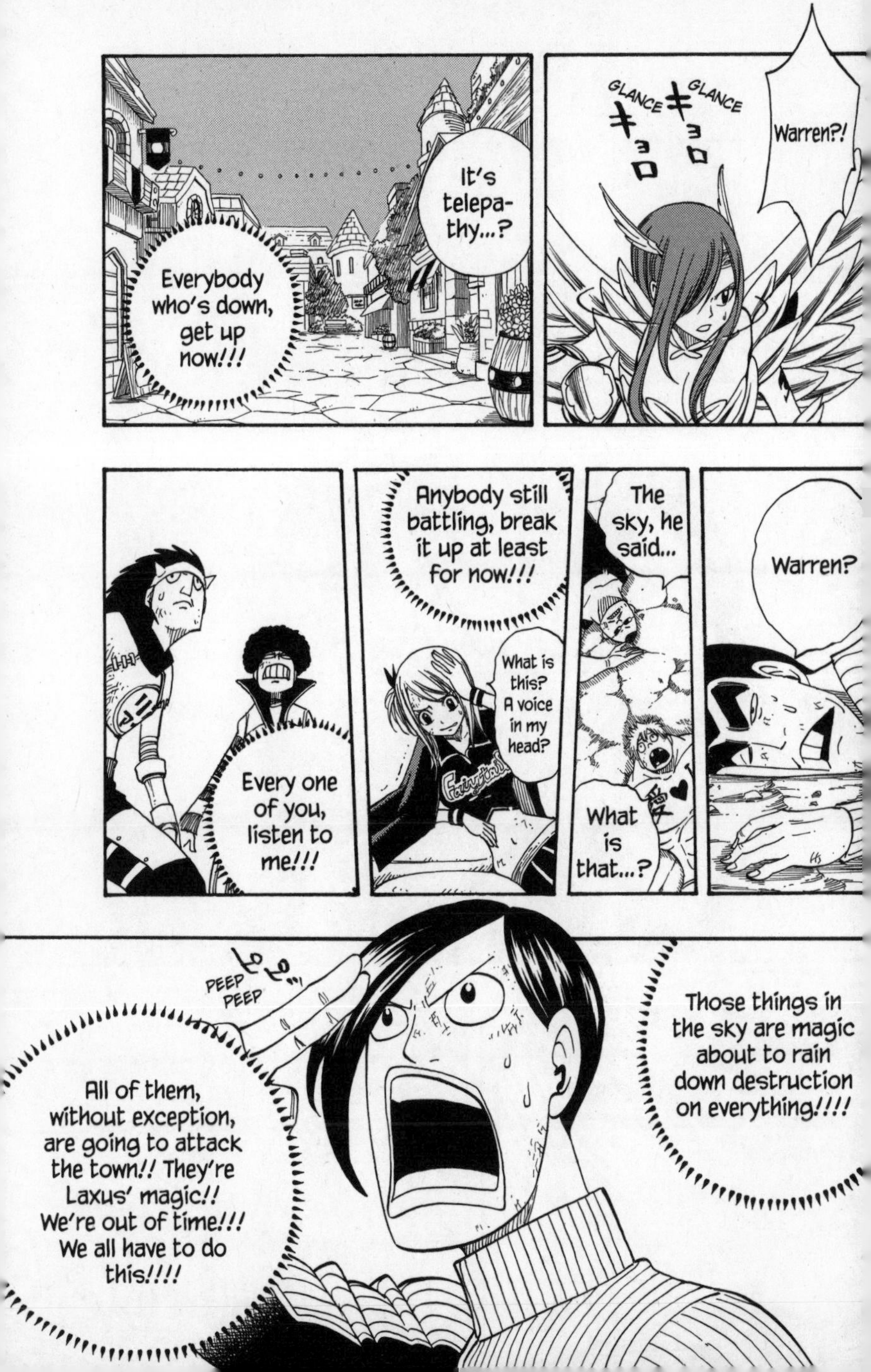

Warren?!
GLANCE GLANCE
キョロキョロ
It's telepa-thy...?
Everybody who's down, get up now!!!
Warren?
The sky, he said...
What is that...?
Anybody still battling, break it up at least for now!!!
What is this? A voice in my head?
Every one of you, listen to me!!!
Those things in the sky are magic about to rain down destruction on everything!!!!
PEEP PEEP
All of them, without exception, are going to attack the town!! They're Laxus' magic!! We're out of time!!! We all have to do this!!!!

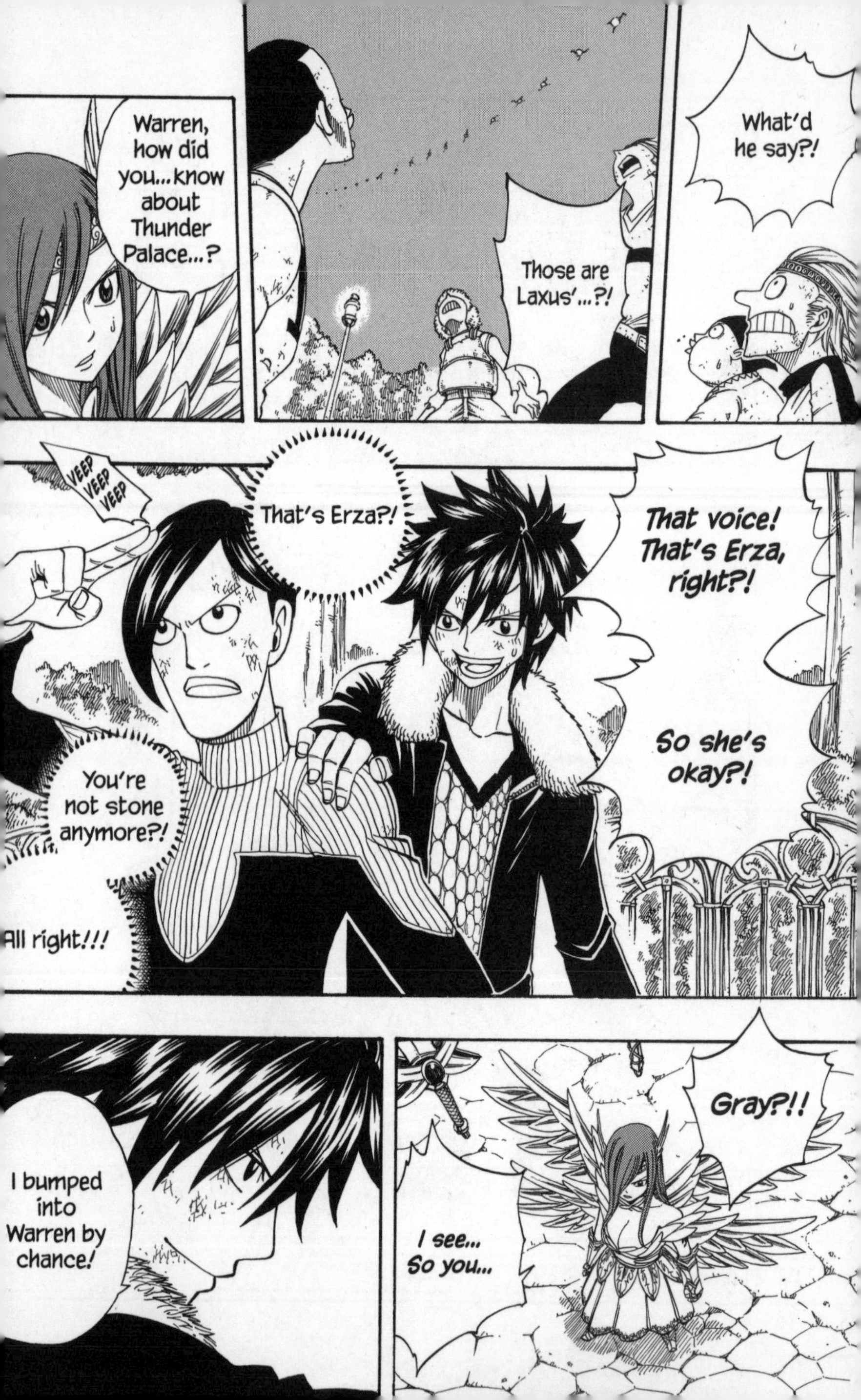

What'd he say?!
Those are Laxus'...?!
Warren, how did you...know about Thunder Palace...?
That voice! That's Erza, right?!
So she's okay?!
That's Erza?!
VEEP VEEP VEEP
You're not stone anymore?!
All right!!!
Gray?!!
I see... So you...
I bumped into Warren by chance!

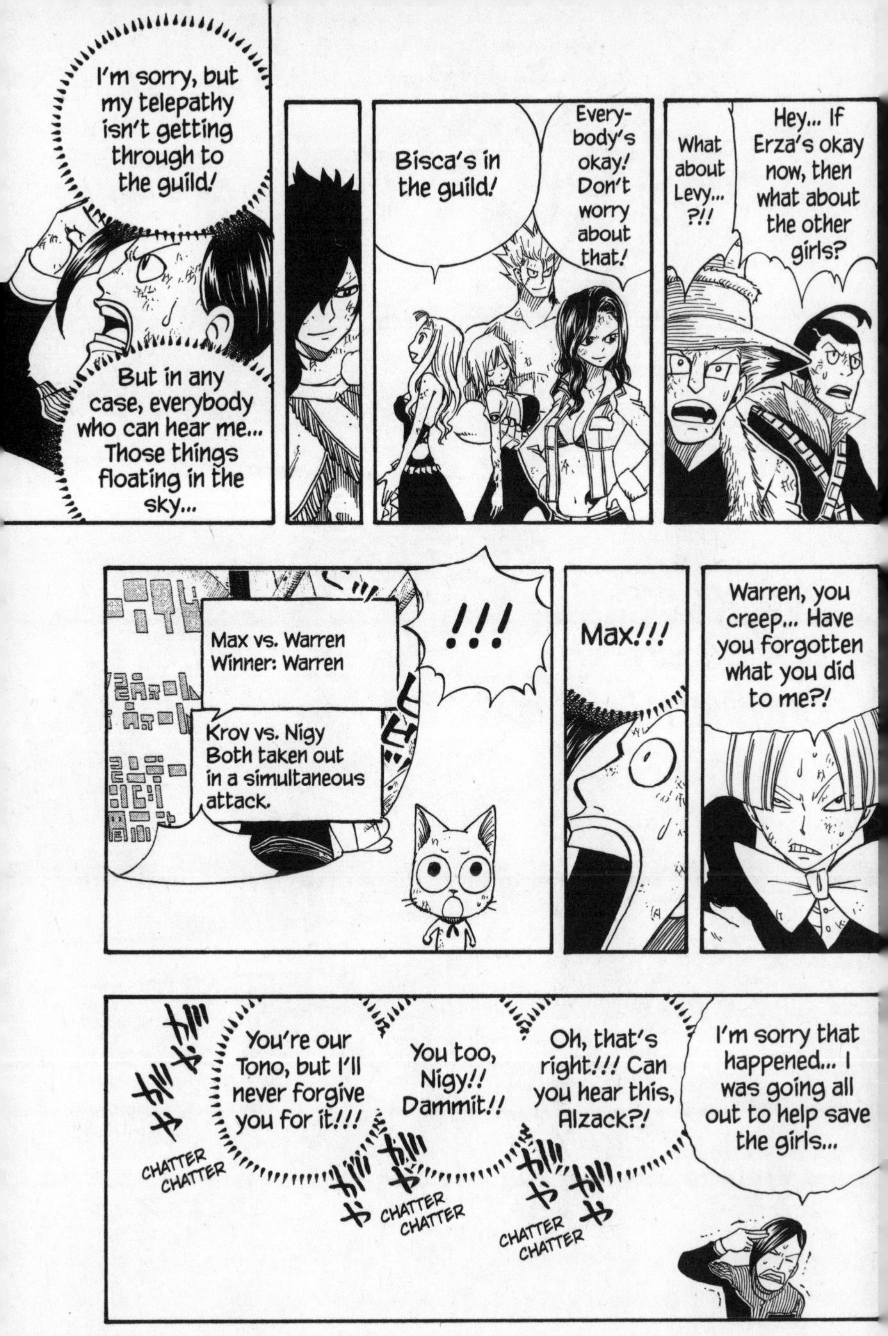
Hey... If Erza's okay now, then what about the other girls?
What about Levy...?!!
Everybody's okay! Don't worry about that!
Bisca's in the guild!
I'm sorry, but my telepathy isn't getting through to the guild!
But in any case, everybody who can hear me... Those things floating in the sky...
Warren, you creep... Have you forgotten what you did to me?!
Max!!!
!!!
Max vs. Warren
Winner: Warren
Krov vs. Nigy
Both taken out in a simultaneous attack.
I'm sorry that happened... I was going all out to help save the girls...
Oh, that's right!!! Can you hear this, Alzack?!
You too, Nigy!! Dammit!!
You're our Tono, but I'll never forgive you for it!!!
CHATTER CHATTER
CHATTER CHATTER
CHATTER CHATTER

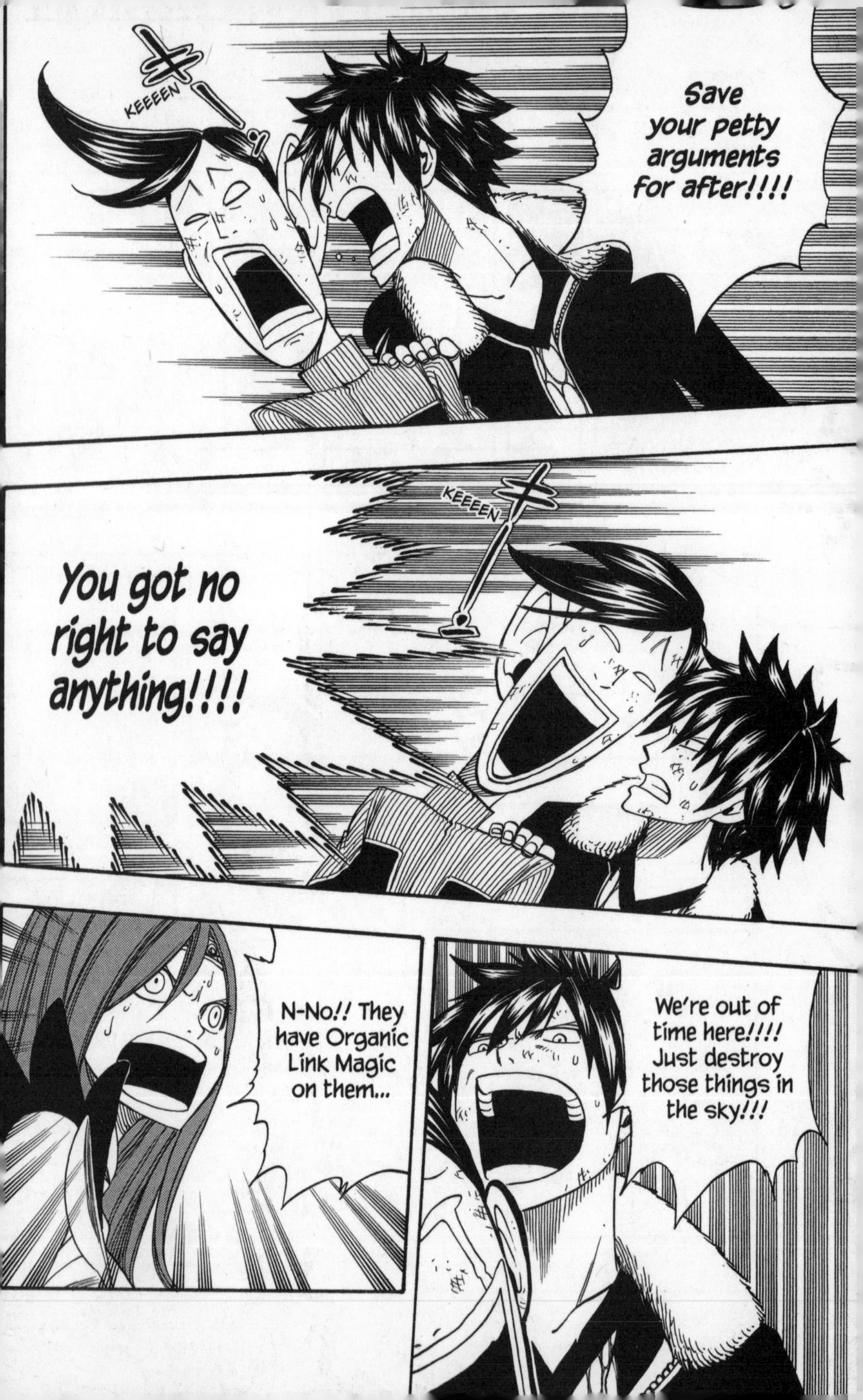
KEEEEN
Save your petty arguments for after!!!!
KEEEEN
You got no right to say anything!!!!
We're out of time here!!!! Just destroy those things in the sky!!!
N-No!! They have Organic Link Magic on them...

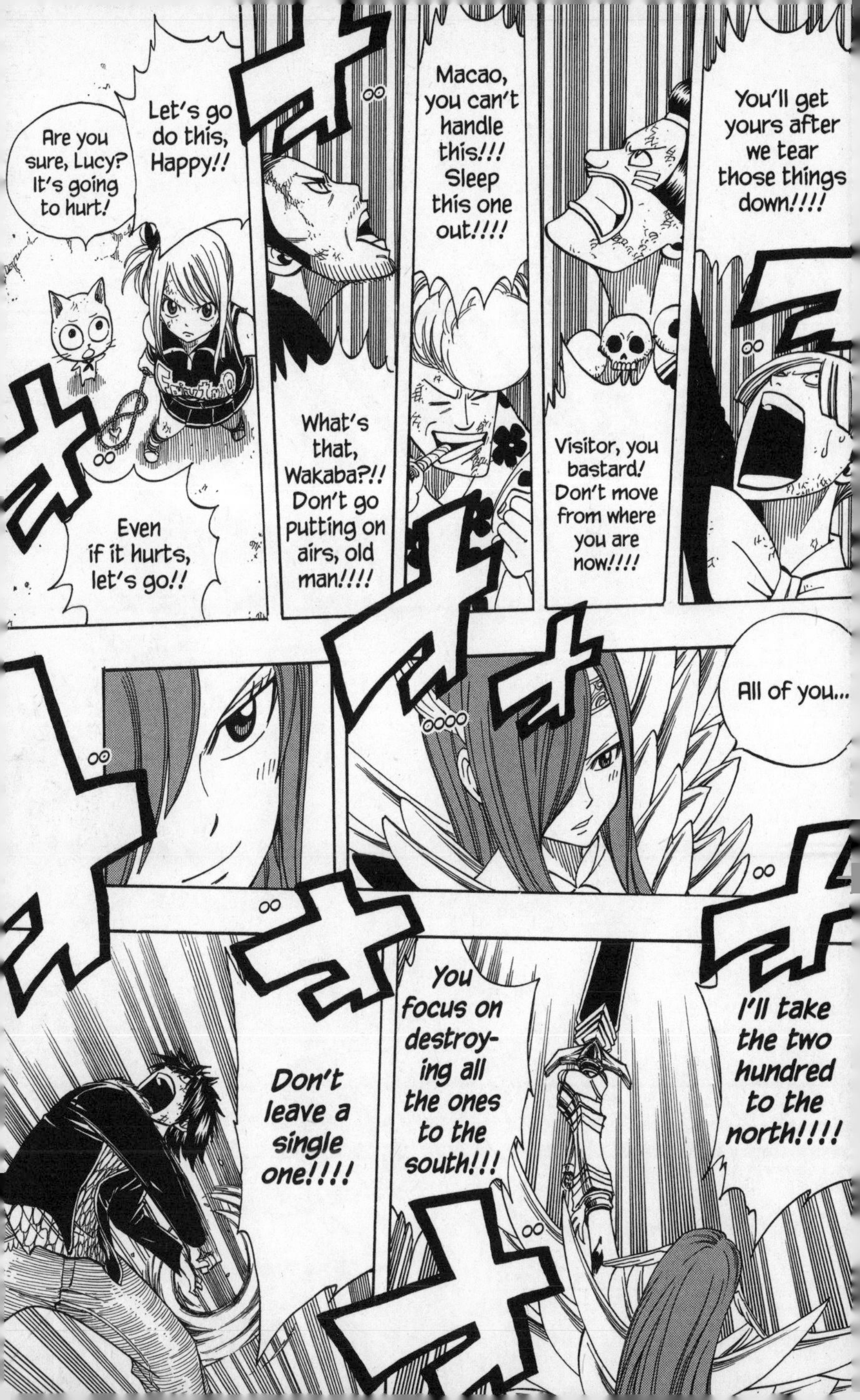
You'll get yours after we tear those things down!!!!
Visitor, you bastard! Don't move from where you are now!!!!
Macao, you can't handle this!!! Sleep this one out!!!!
What's that, Wakaba?!! Don't go putting on airs, old man!!!!
Let's go do this, Happy!!
Are you sure, Lucy? It's going to hurt!
Even if it hurts, let's go!!
All of you...
I'll take the two hundred to the north!!!!
You focus on destroying all the ones to the south!!!
Don't leave a single one!!!!

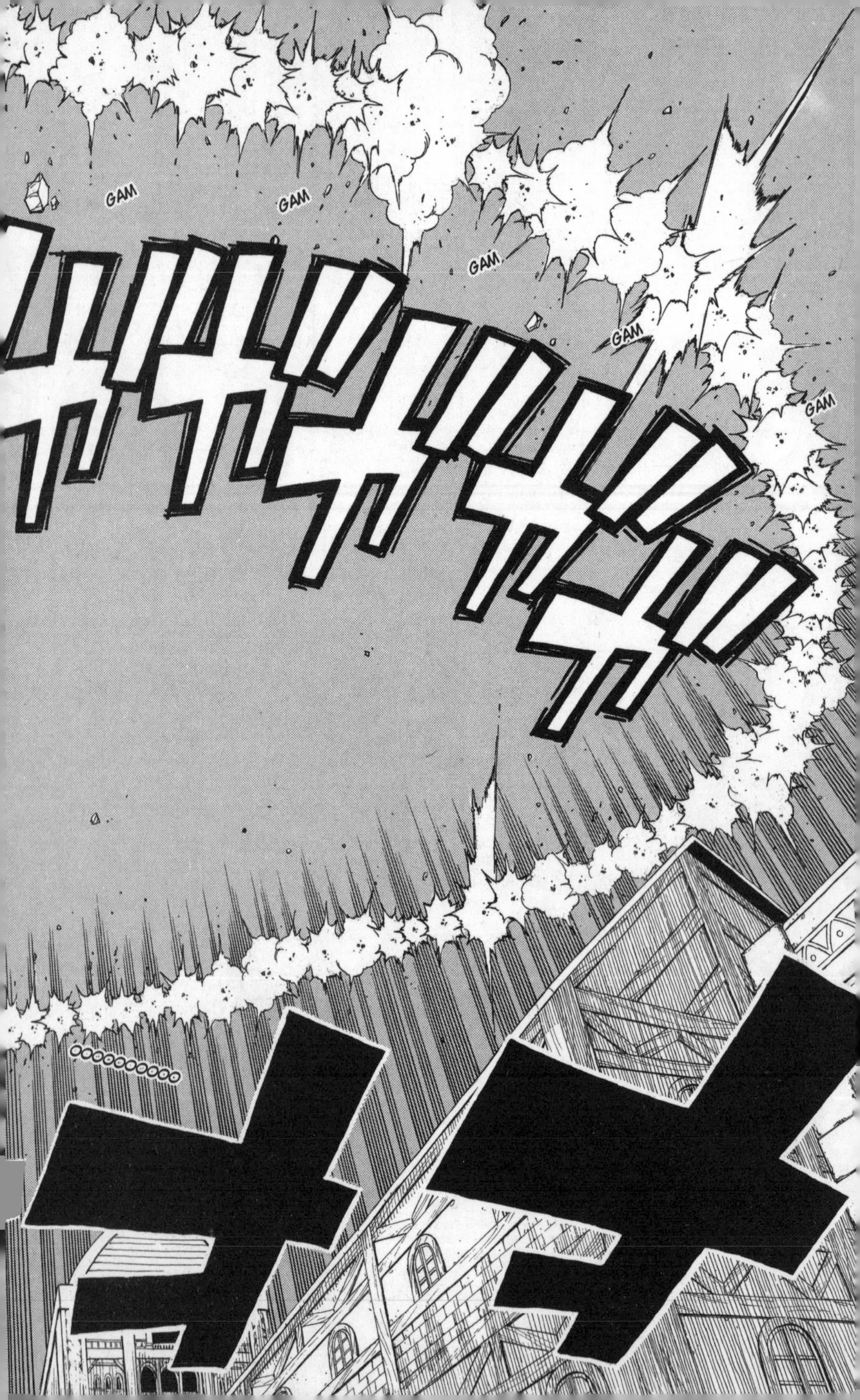
GAM
GAM
GAM
GAM
GAM
OOOOOOOOOO

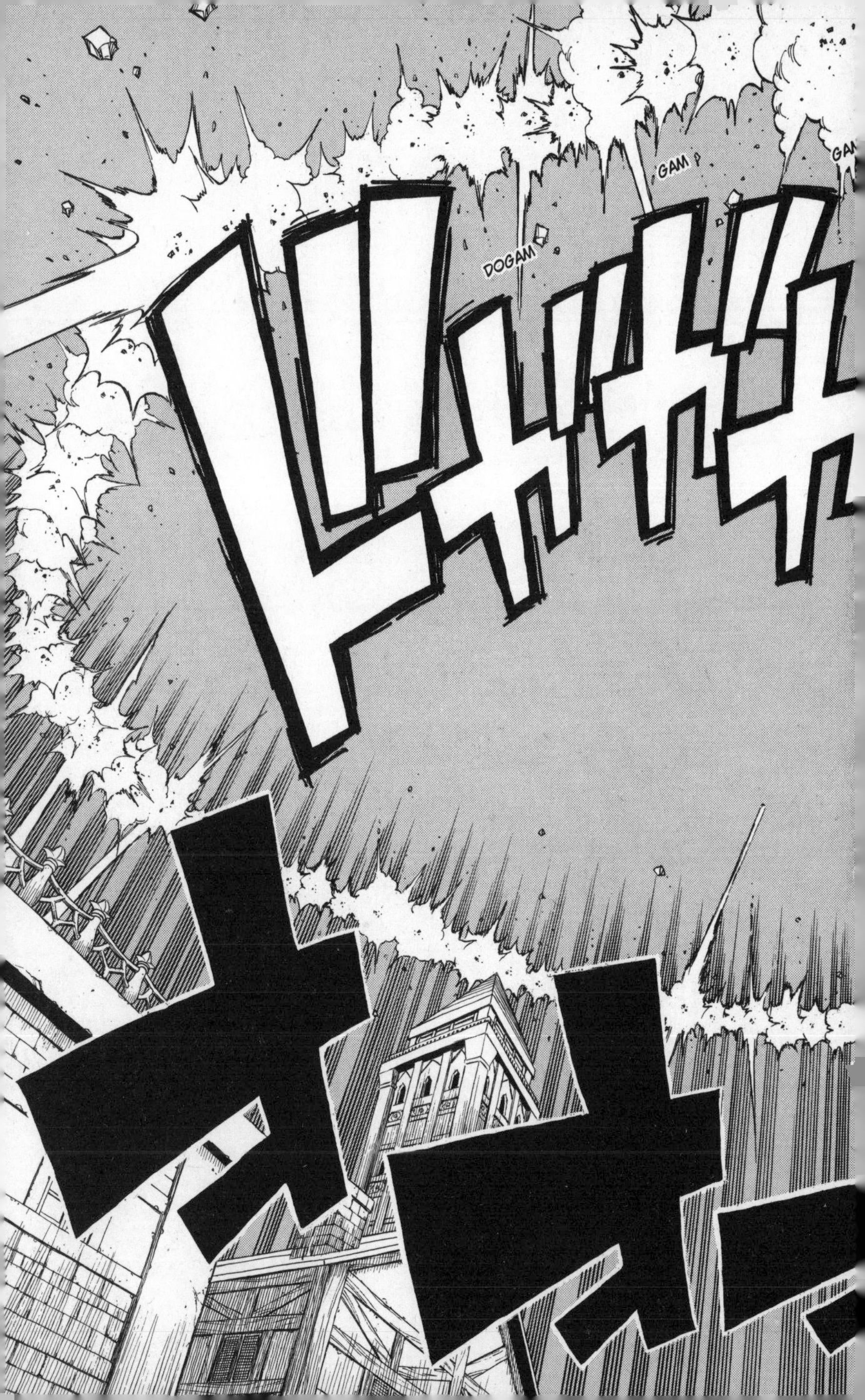
GAM
DOGAM

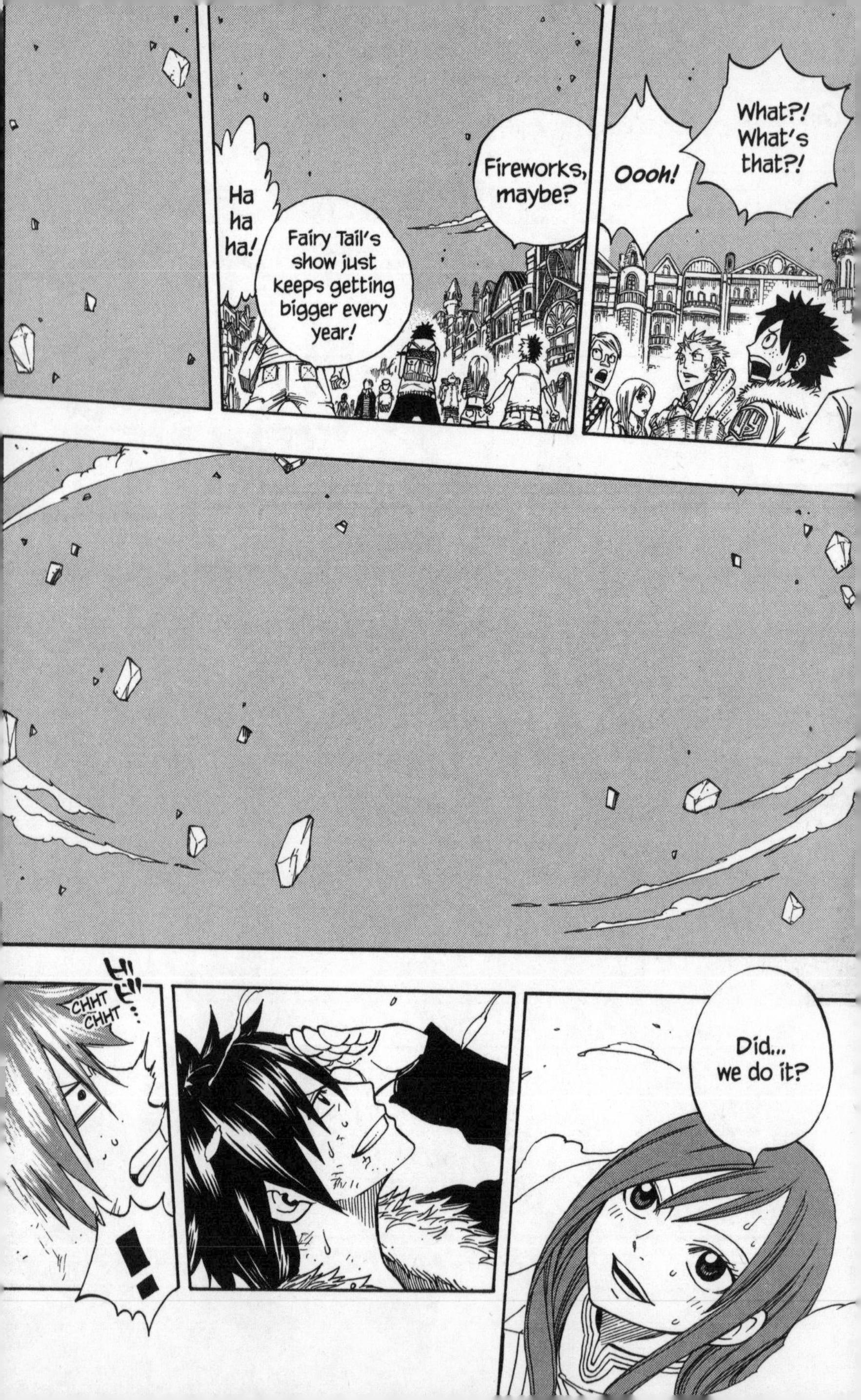
What?! What's that?!
Oooh!
Fireworks, maybe?
Fairy Tail's show just keeps getting bigger every year!
Ha ha ha!
Did... we do it?
CHHT CHHT
!!

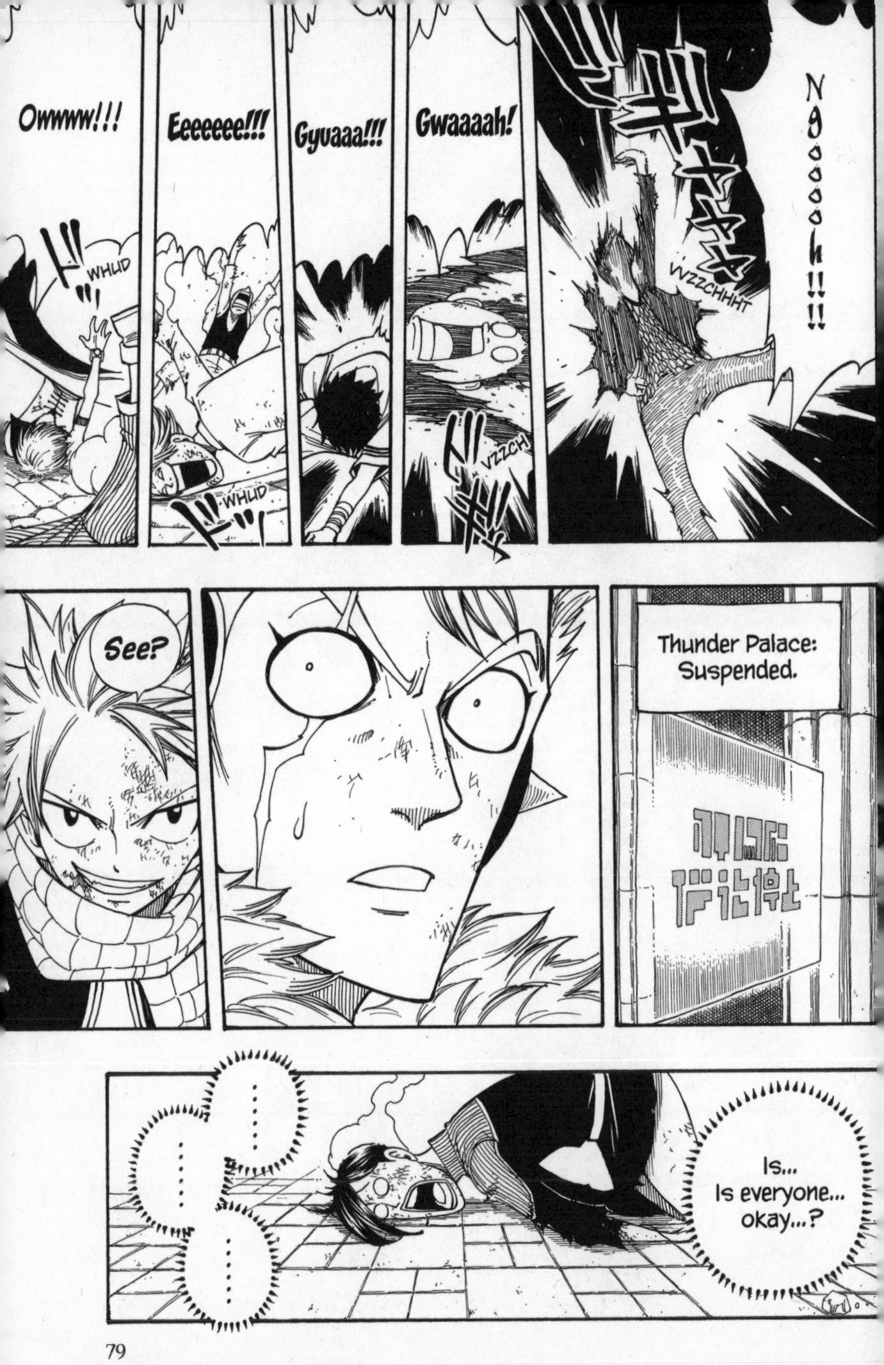

Ngooooh!!!!
VVZZCHHHT
Gwaaaah!
VZZCH
Gyuaaa!!!
Eeeeeee!!!
WHUD
Owwww!!!
WHUD
Thunder Palace: Suspended.
See?
Is... Is everyone... okay...?
......

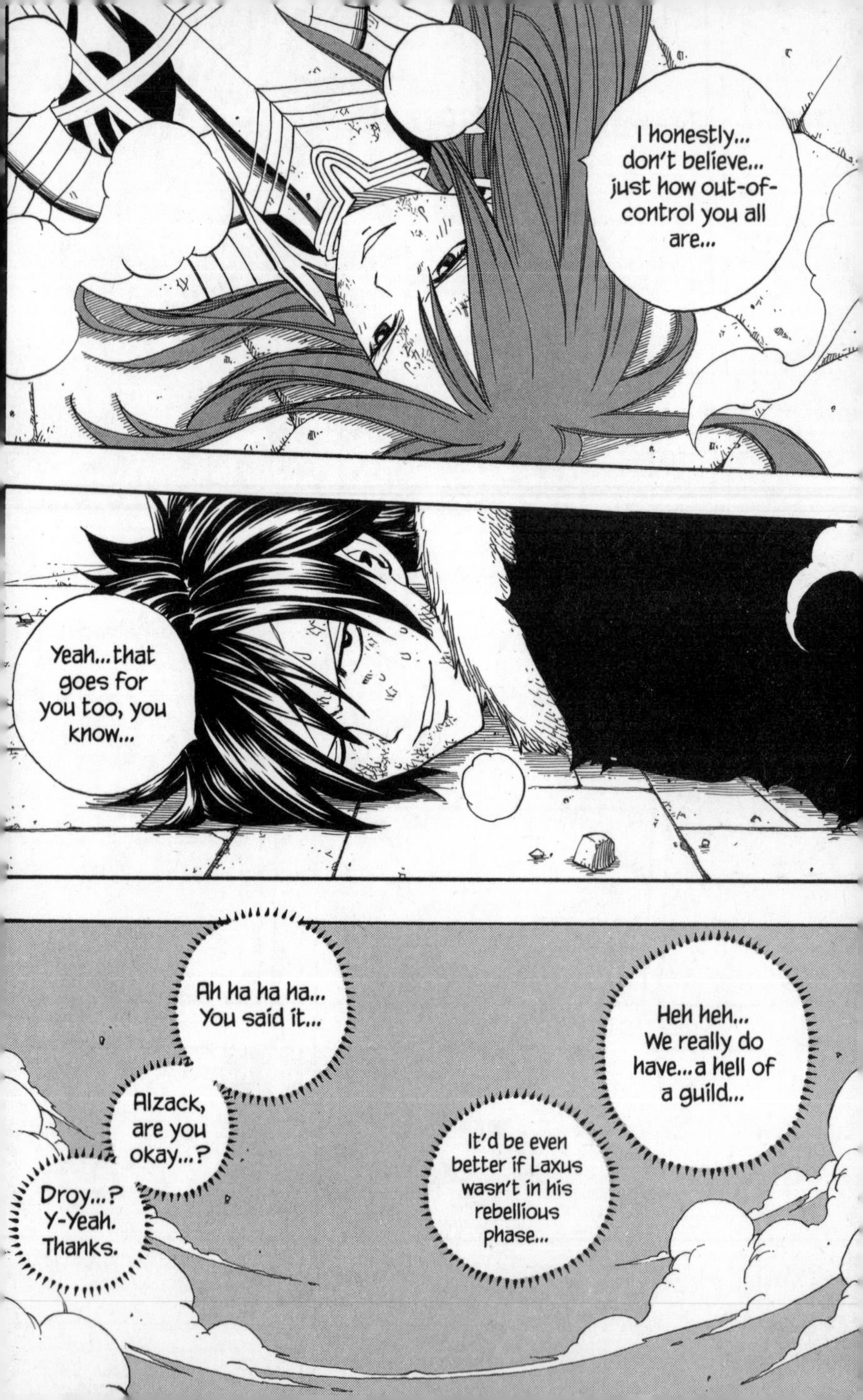
I honestly... don't believe... just how out-of-control you all are...
Yeah...that goes for you too, you know...
Heh heh... We really do have...a hell of a guild...
It'd be even better if Laxus wasn't in his rebellious phase...
Ah ha ha ha... You said it...
Alzack, are you okay...?
Droy...? Y-Yeah. Thanks.

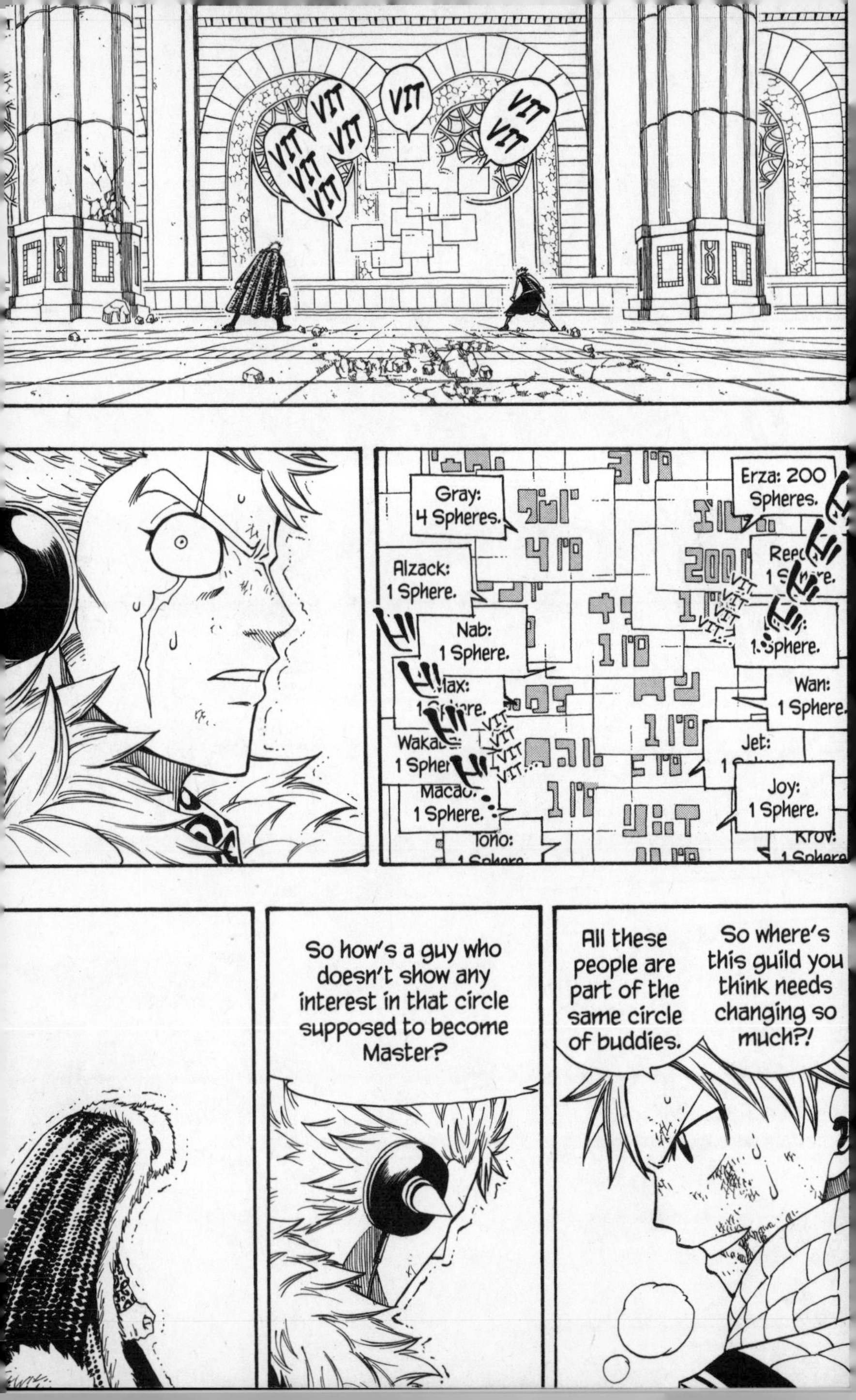
VIT VIT
VIT
VIT VIT
VIT VIT VIT
Erza: 200 Spheres.
Gray: 4 Spheres.
Alzack: 1 Sphere.
Nab: 1 Sphere.
Wan: 1 Sphere.
Joy: 1 Sphere.
Macao: 1 Sphere.
VIT VIT VIT VIT...
So where's this guild you think needs changing so much?!
All these people are part of the same circle of buddies.
So how's a guy who doesn't show any interest in that circle supposed to become Master?

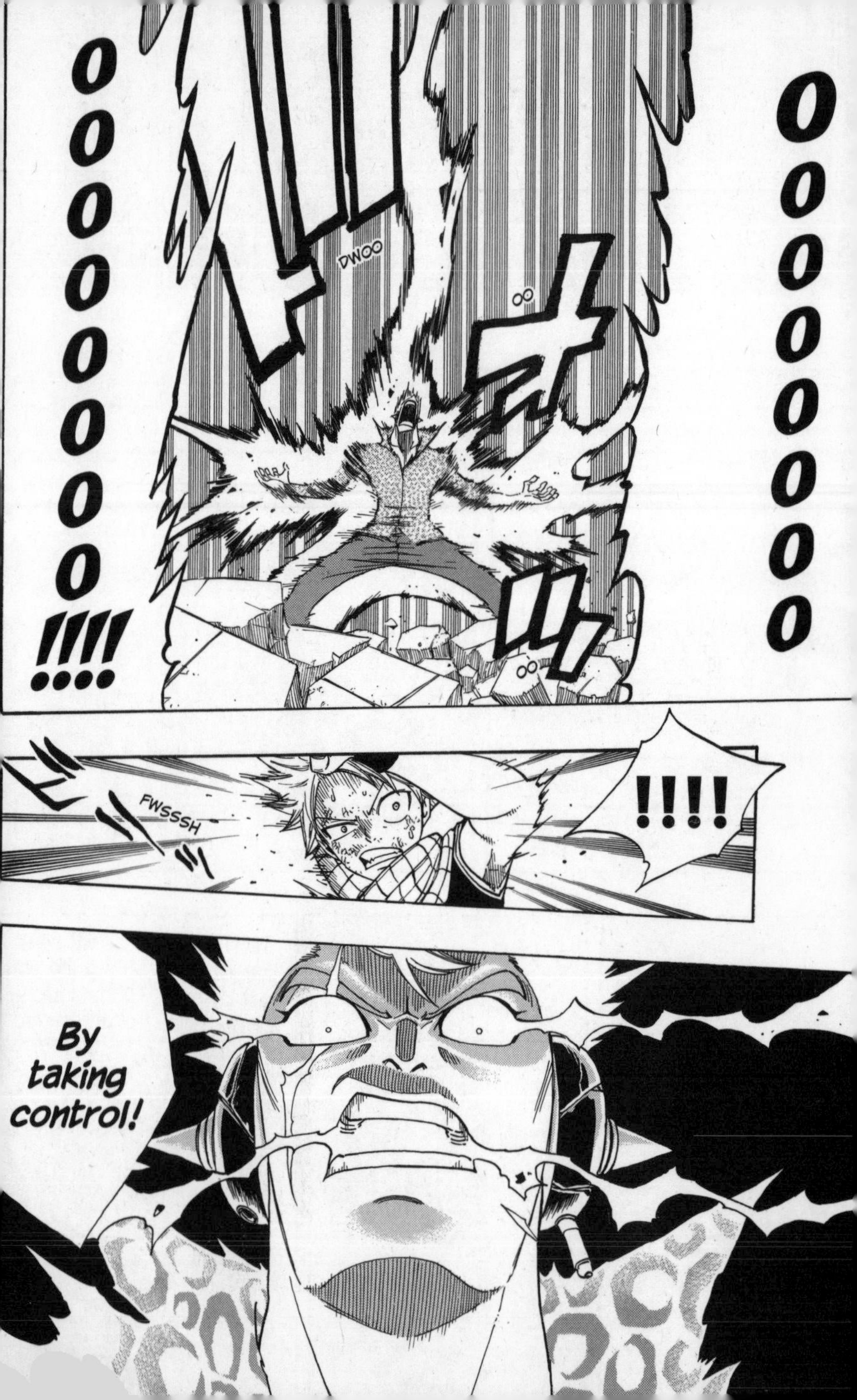
OOOOOOOO
DWOO
OOOOOOOO!!!!
FWSSSH
!!!!
By taking control!

FAIRY TAIL

Chapter 123: Double Dragon

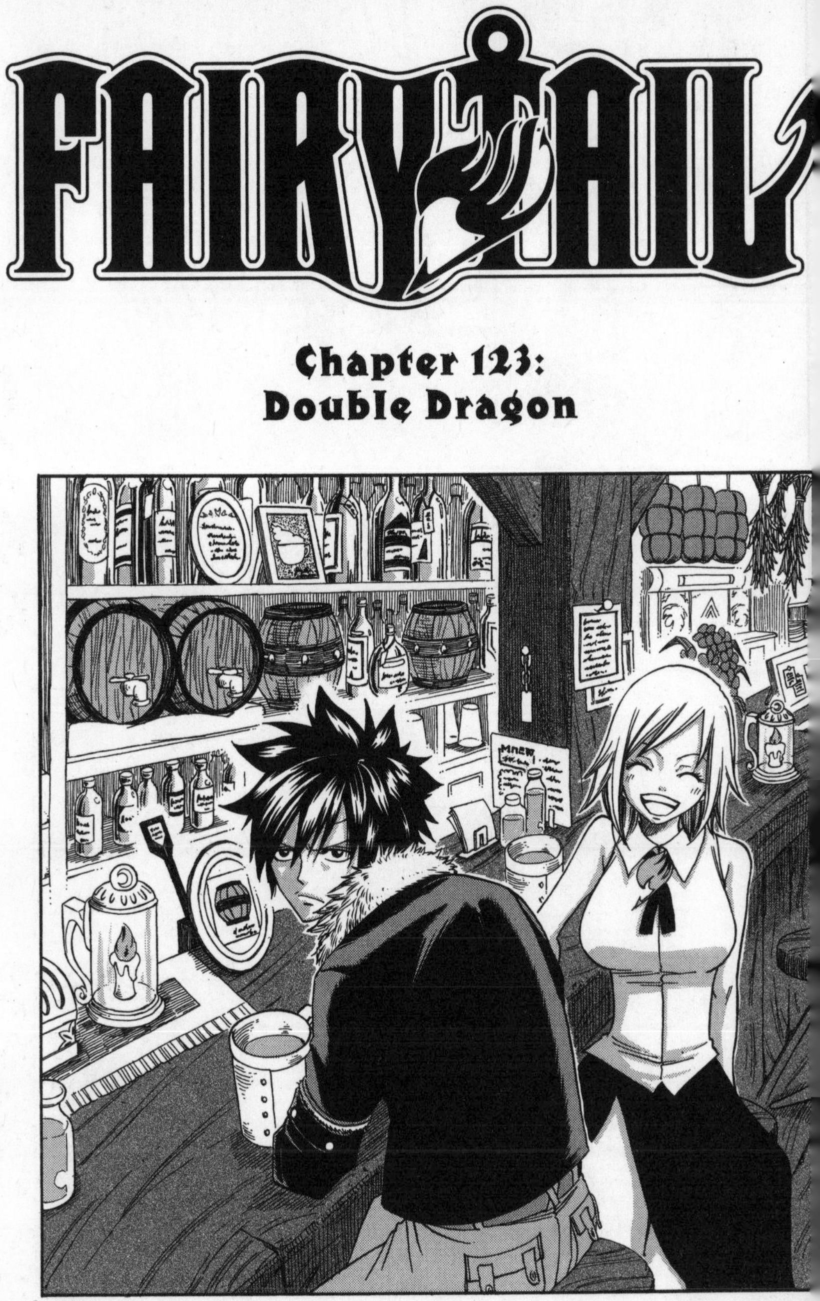

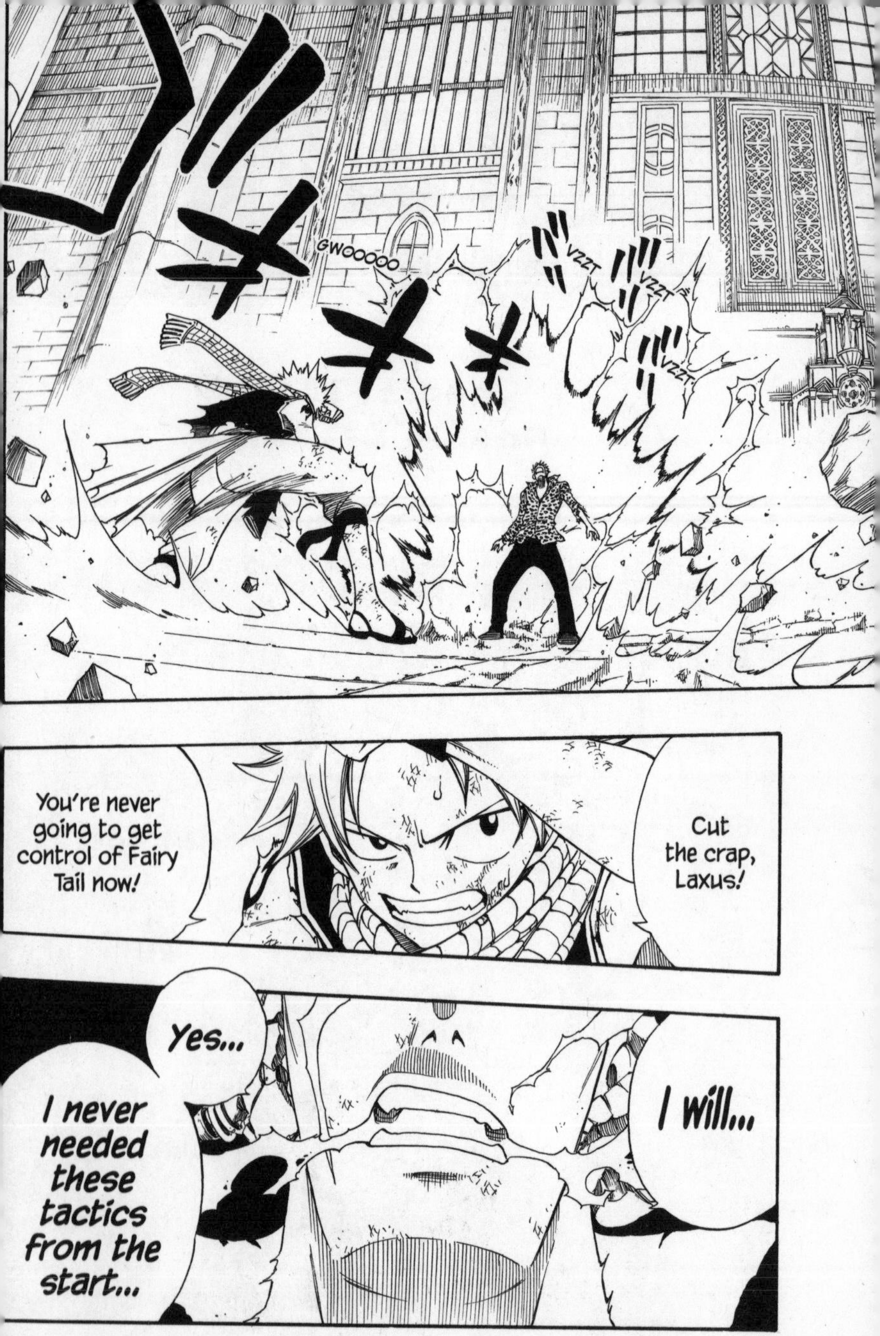
VZZT
VZZT
VZZT
GWOOOOO
Cut the crap, Laxus!
You're never going to get control of Fairy Tail now!
I will...
Yes...
I never needed these tactics from the start...

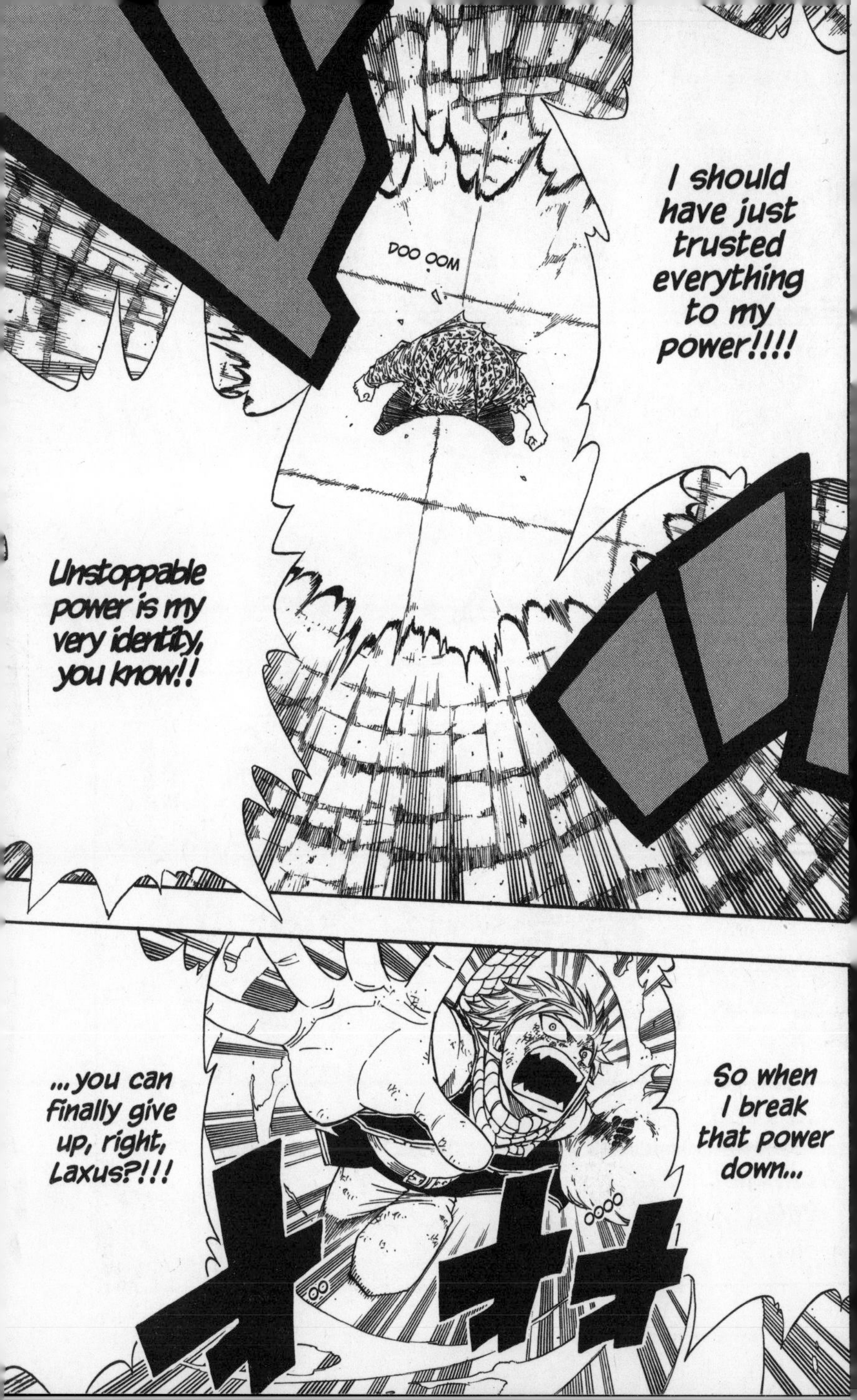
I should have just trusted everything to my power!!!!
DOO OOM
Unstoppable power is my very identity, you know!!
So when I break that power down...
...you can finally give up, right, Laxus?!!!

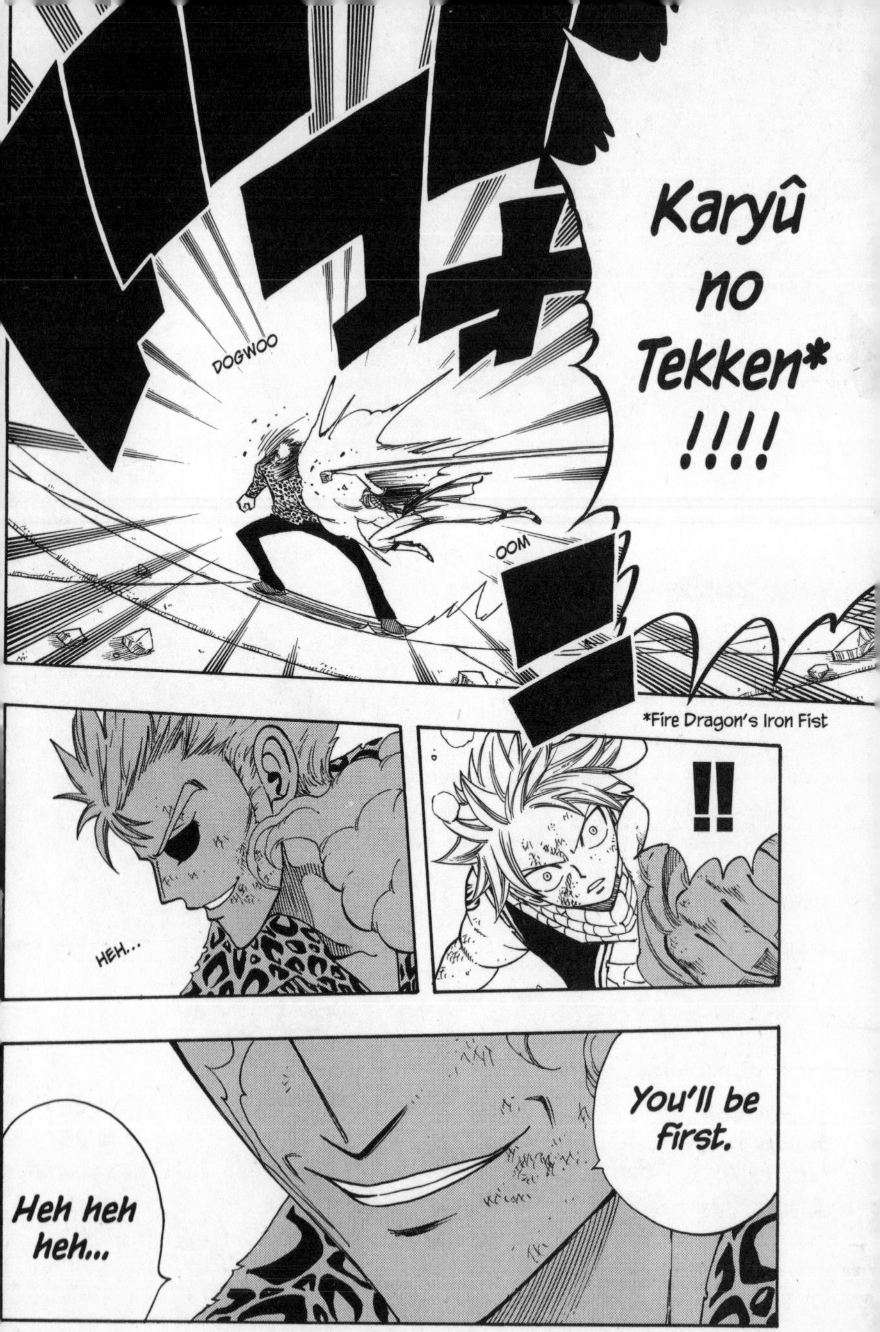
Karyû no Tekken* !!!!
DOGWOO
OOM
!!
HEH...
You'll be first.
Heh heh heh...

*Fire Dragon's Iron Fist

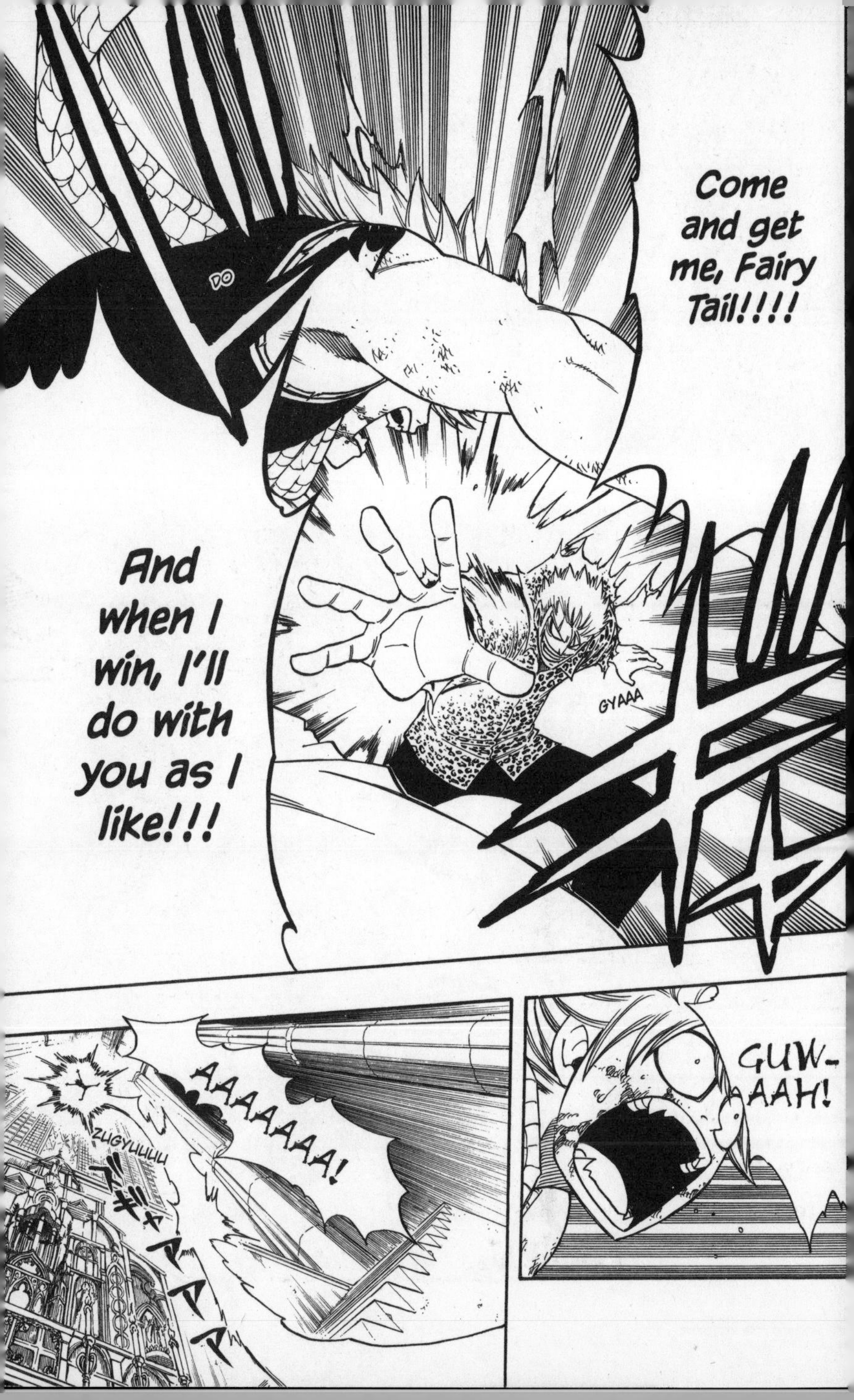
Come and get me, Fairy Tail!!!!
DO
And when I win, I'll do with you as I like!!!
GYAAA
GUW-AAH!
AAAAAAAA!
ZUGYUUUU

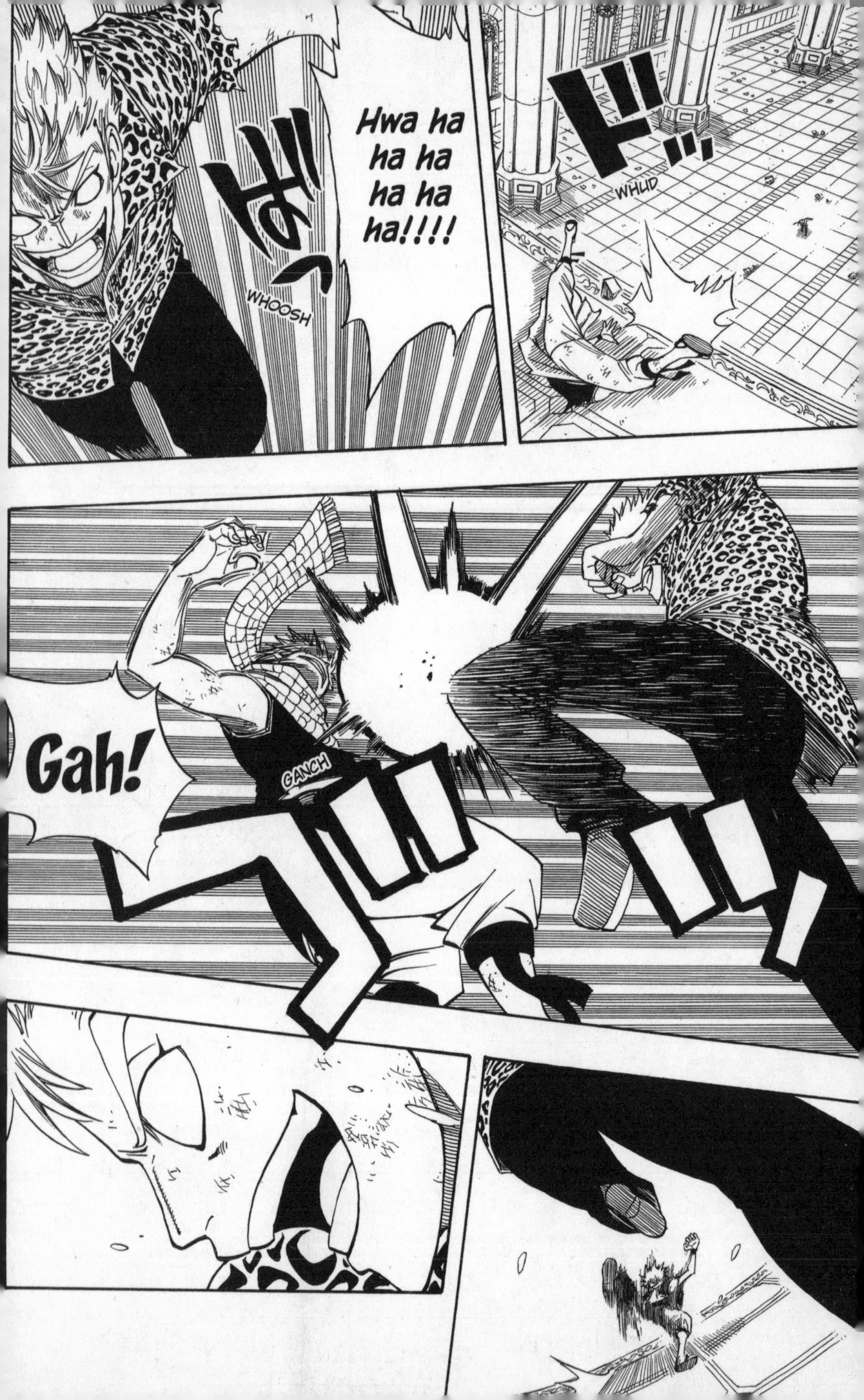
WHUD
Hwa ha ha ha ha ha ha!!!!
WHOOSH
GANCH
Gah!

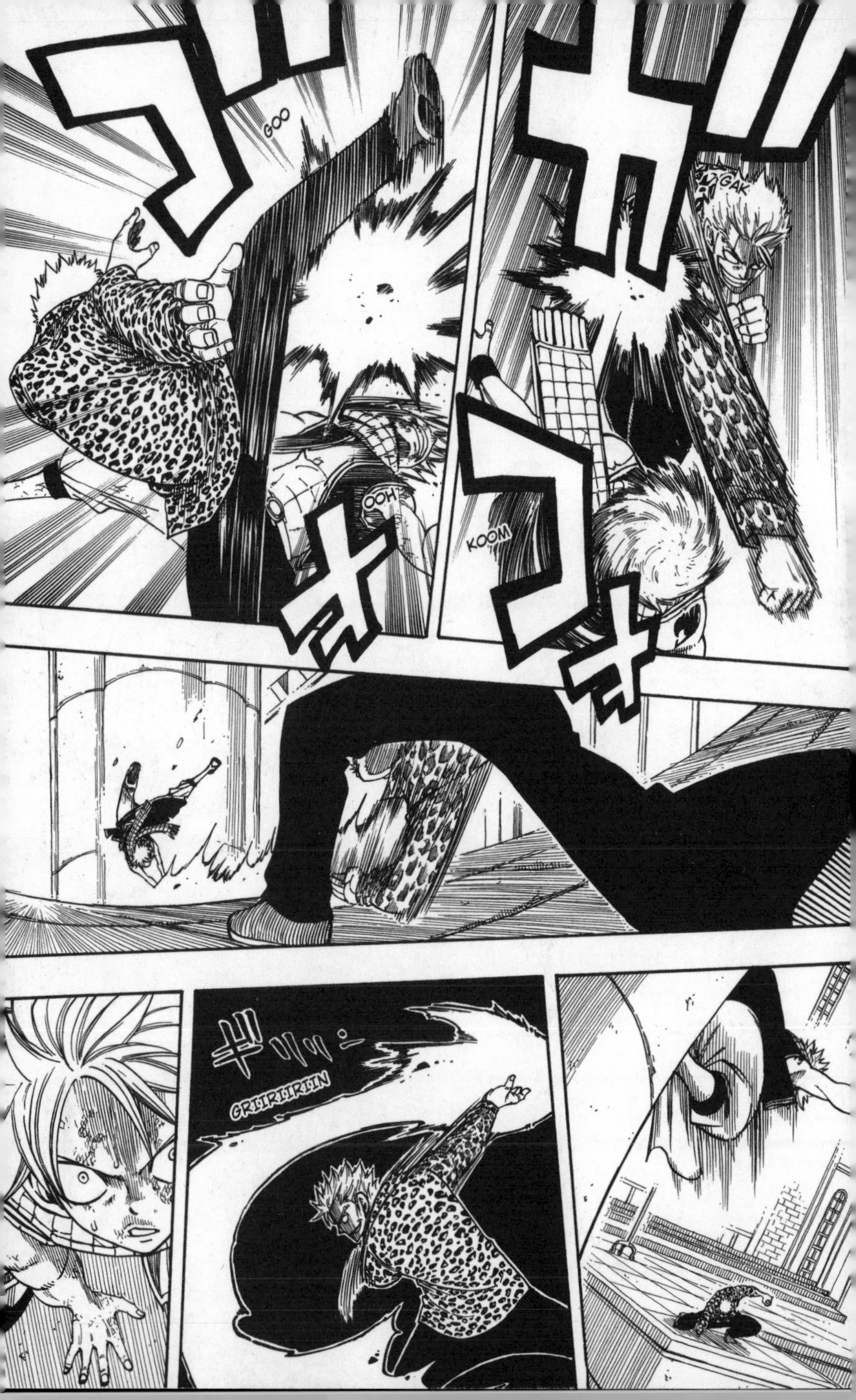
GAK
KOOM
GOO
OOH
GRIIIRIIIN

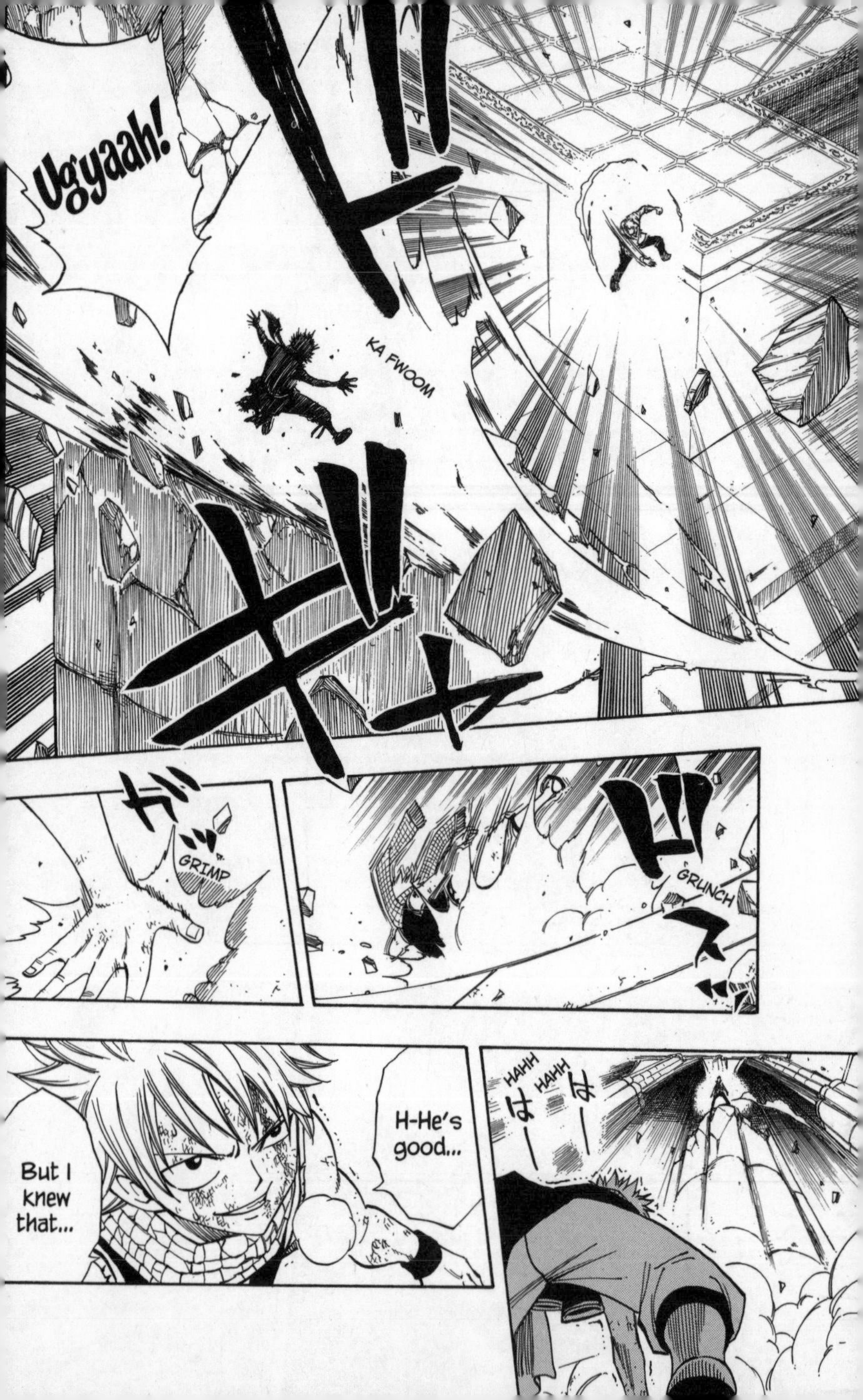
Ugyaah!
KA FWOOM
GRUNCH
GRIMP
HAHH HAHH
H-He's good...
But I knew that...

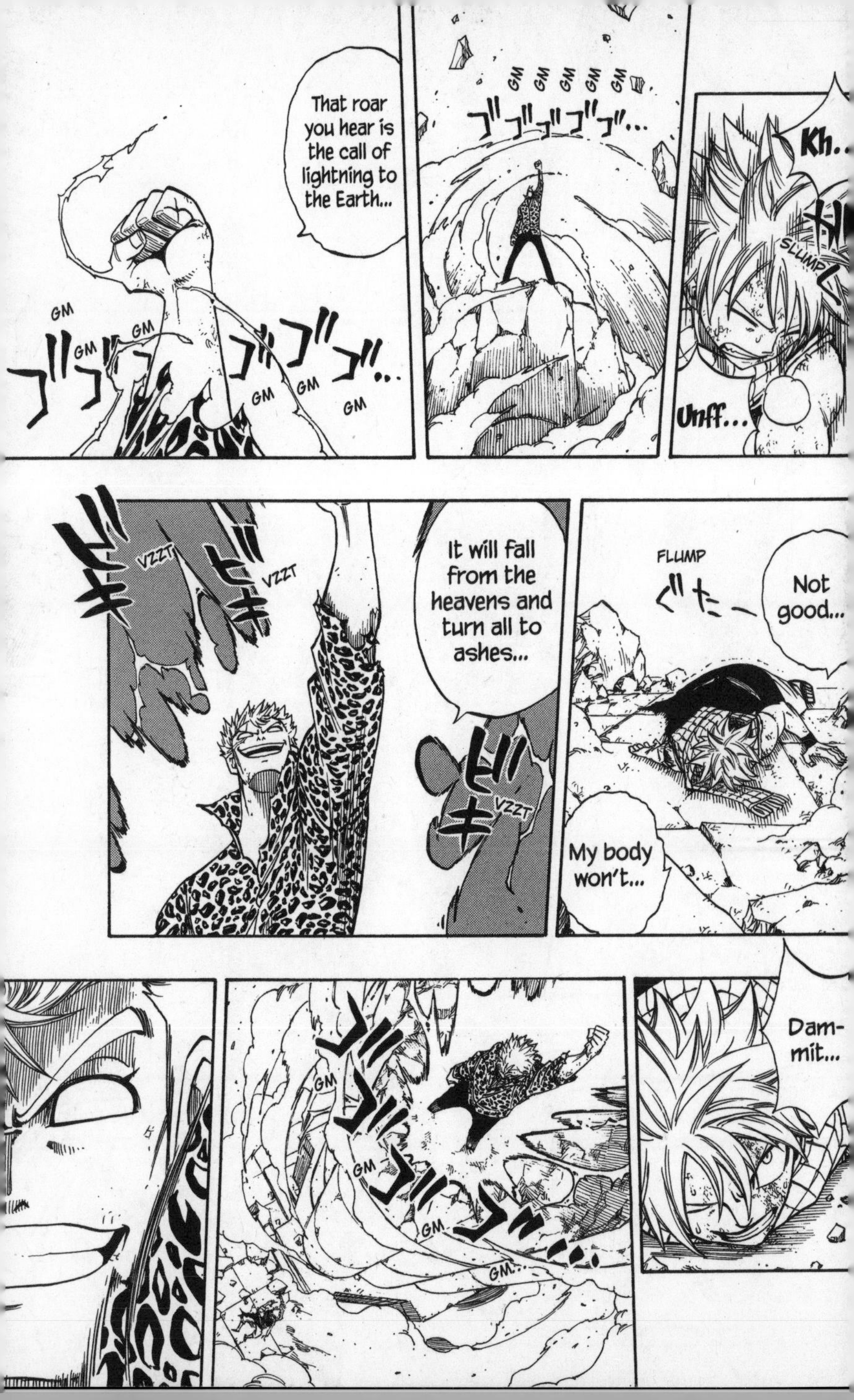
Kh..
SLUMP
Unff...
GM GM GM GM GM
That roar you hear is the call of lightning to the Earth...
GM GM GM GM GM GM
FLUMP
Not good...
My body won't...
It will fall from the heavens and turn all to ashes...
VZZT
VZZT
VZZT
Dam-mit...
GM
GM
GM
GM...

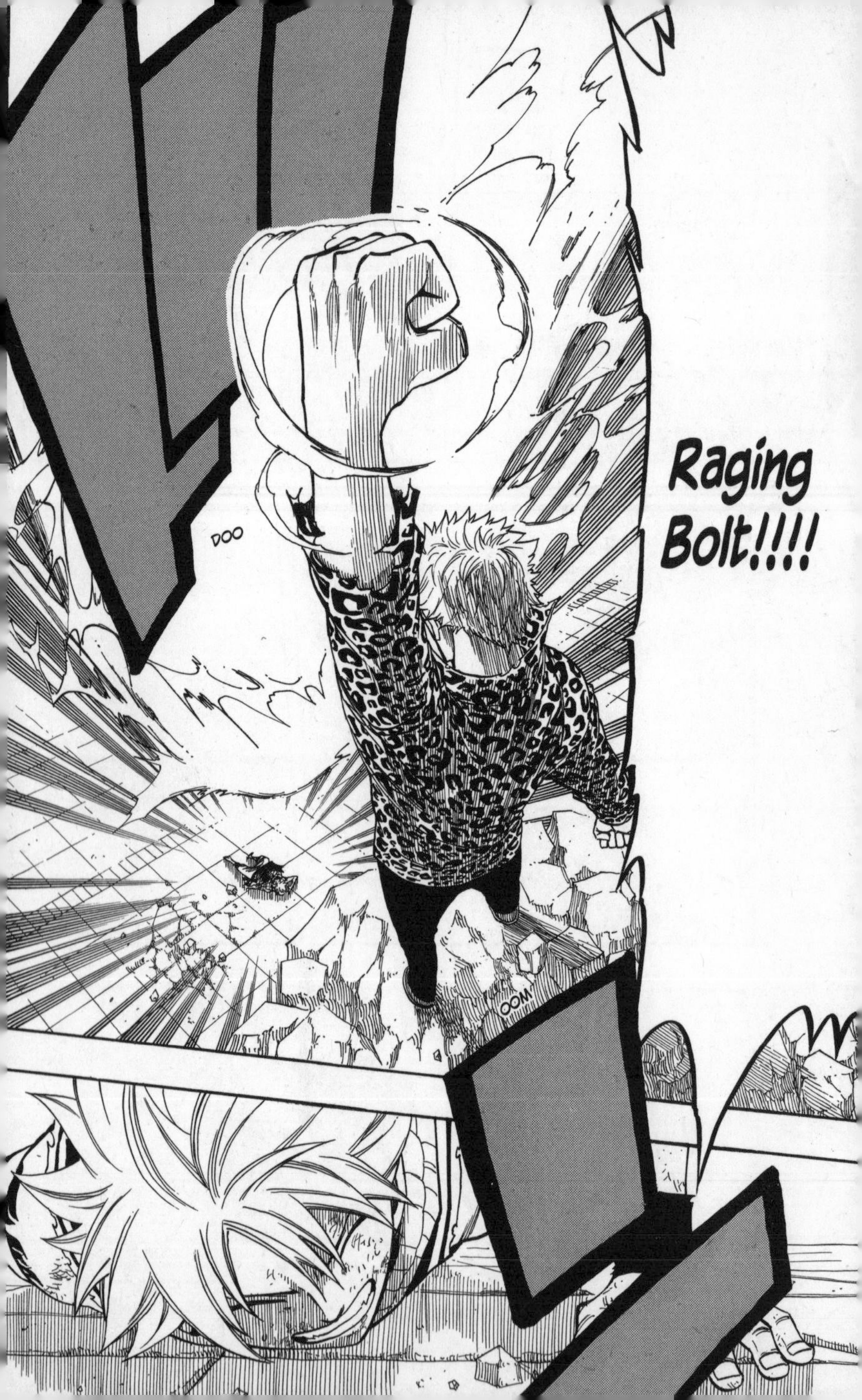
Raging Bolt!!!!
DOO
OOM

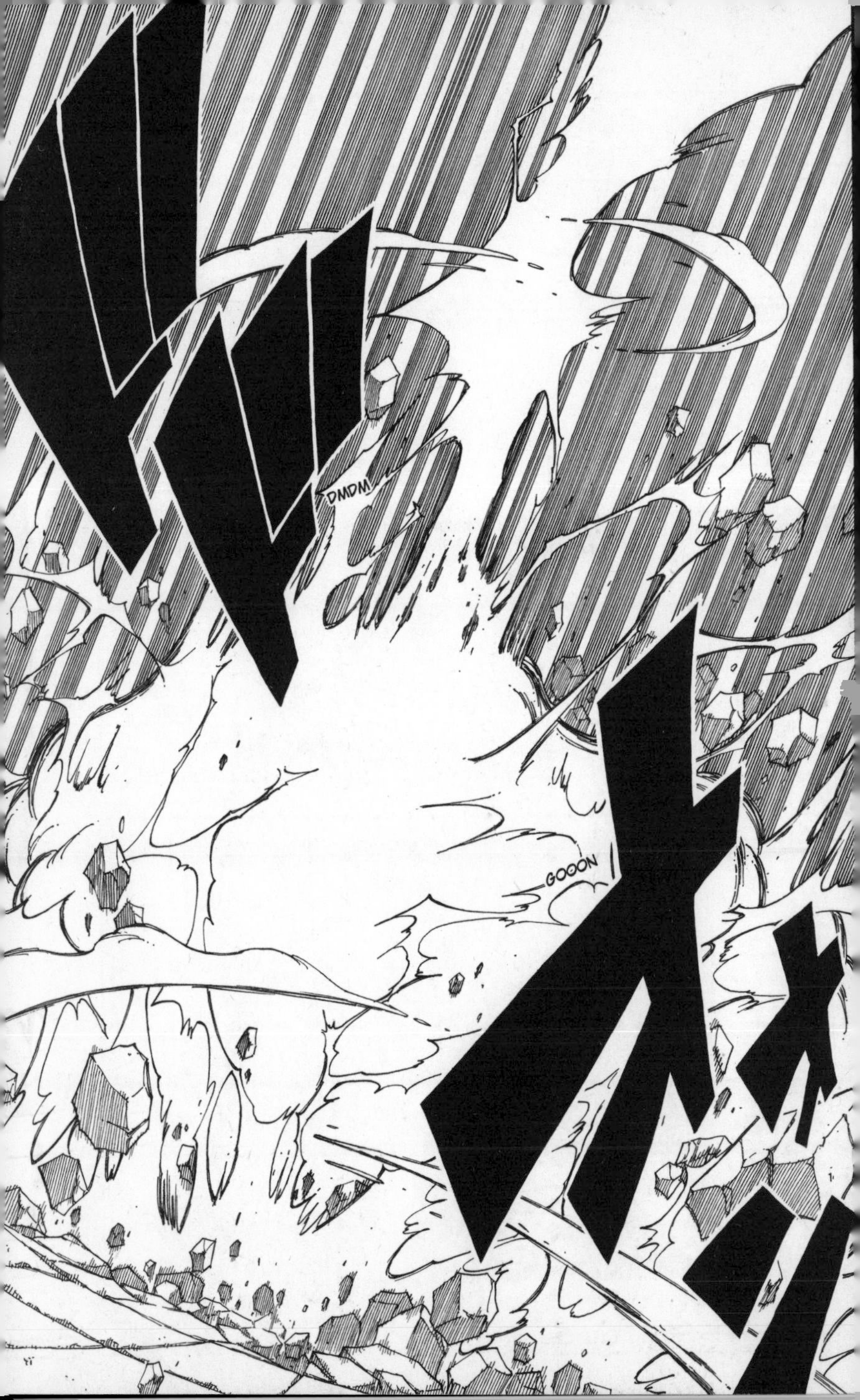
DMDM
GOOON

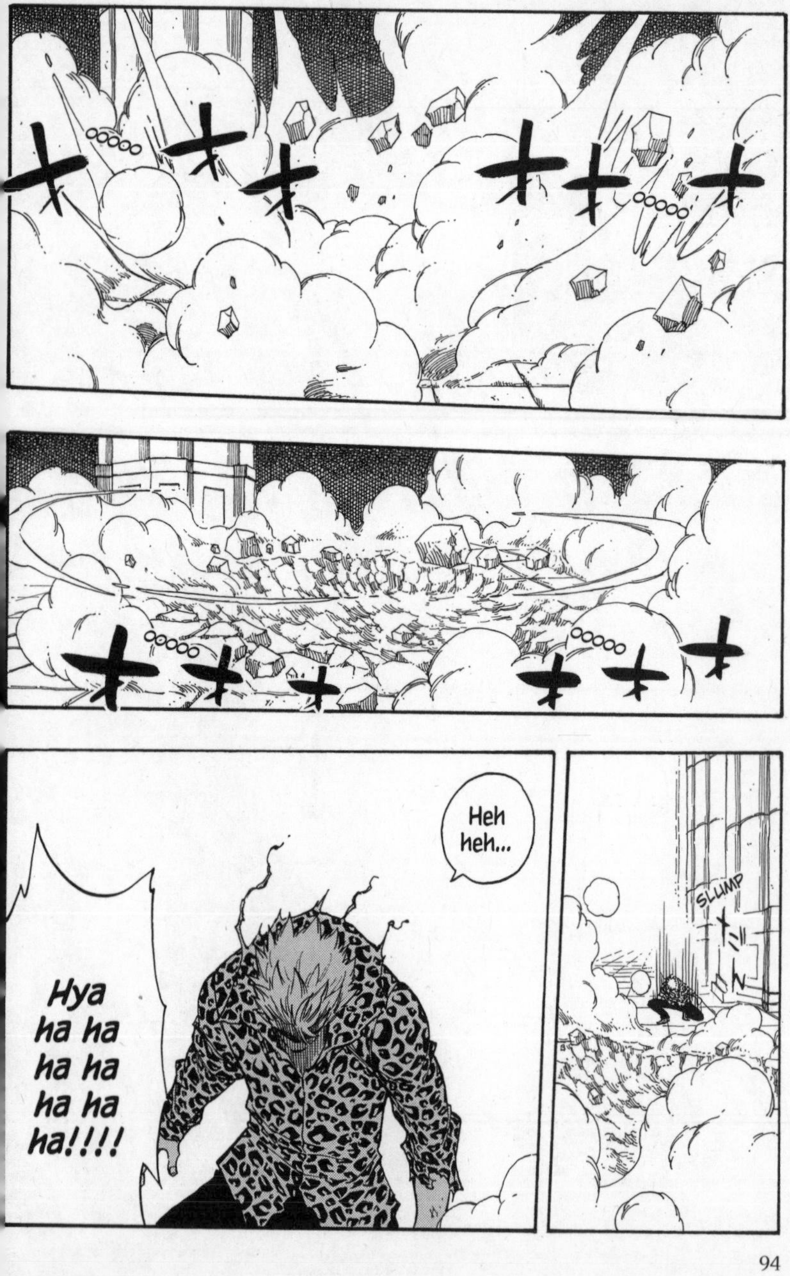
SLUMP
Heh heh...
Hya ha ha ha ha ha ha ha!!!!

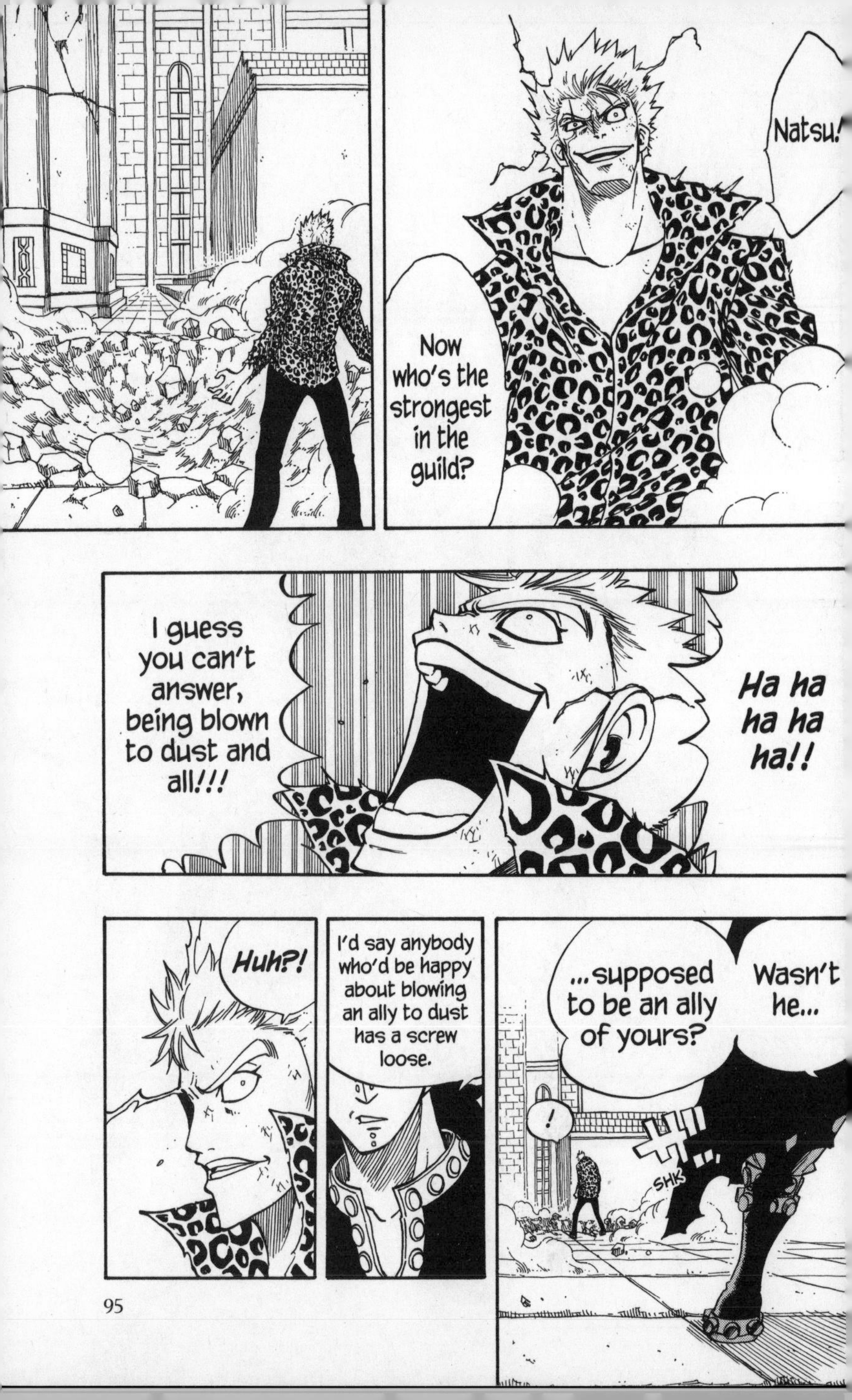

Natsu!
Now who's the strongest in the guild?
Ha ha ha ha ha!!
I guess you can't answer, being blown to dust and all!!!
Wasn't he...
...supposed to be an ally of yours?
!
SHK
I'd say anybody who'd be happy about blowing an ally to dust has a screw loose.
Huh?!

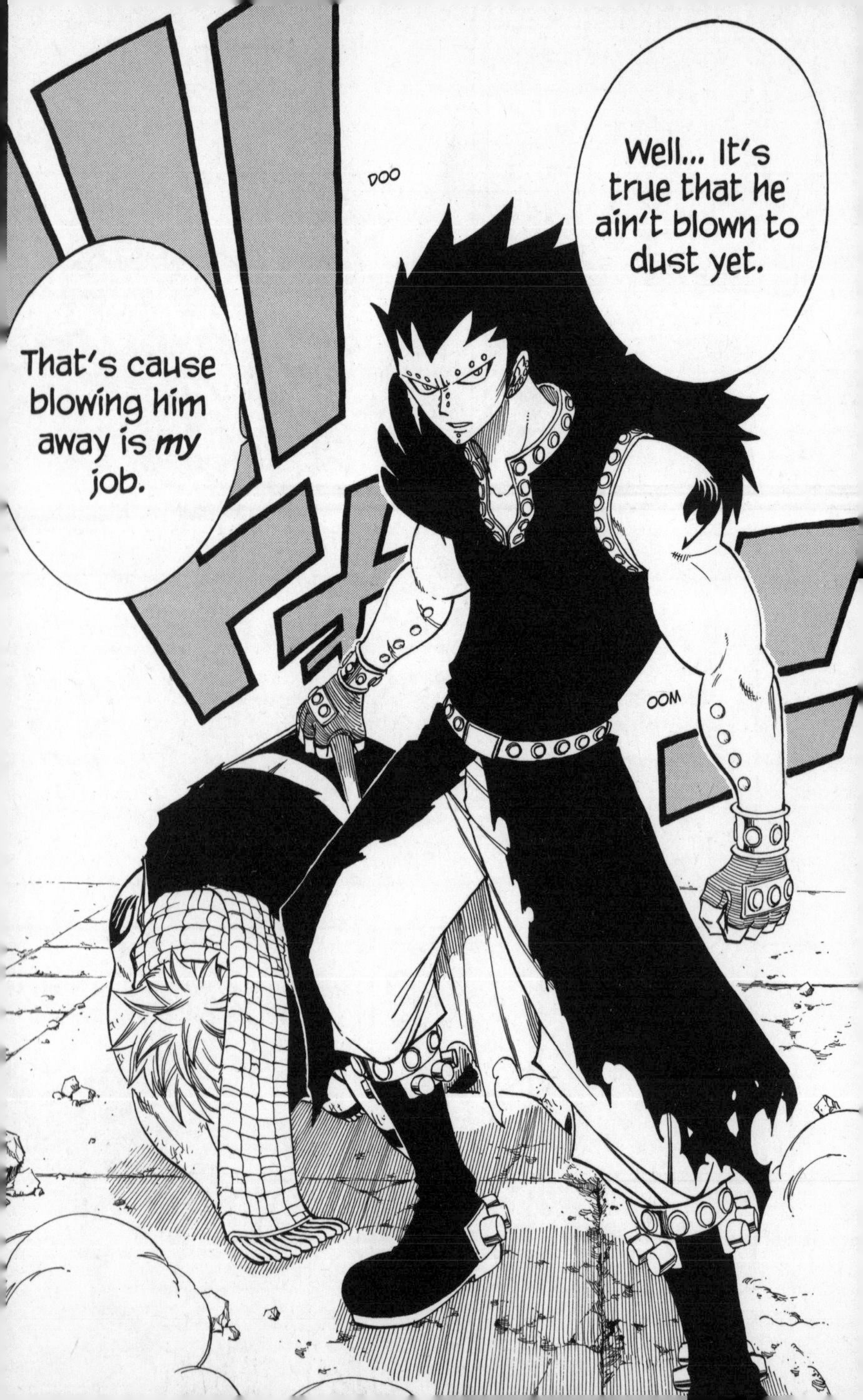
Well... It's true that he ain't blown to dust yet.
DOO
That's cause blowing him away is *my* job.
OOM

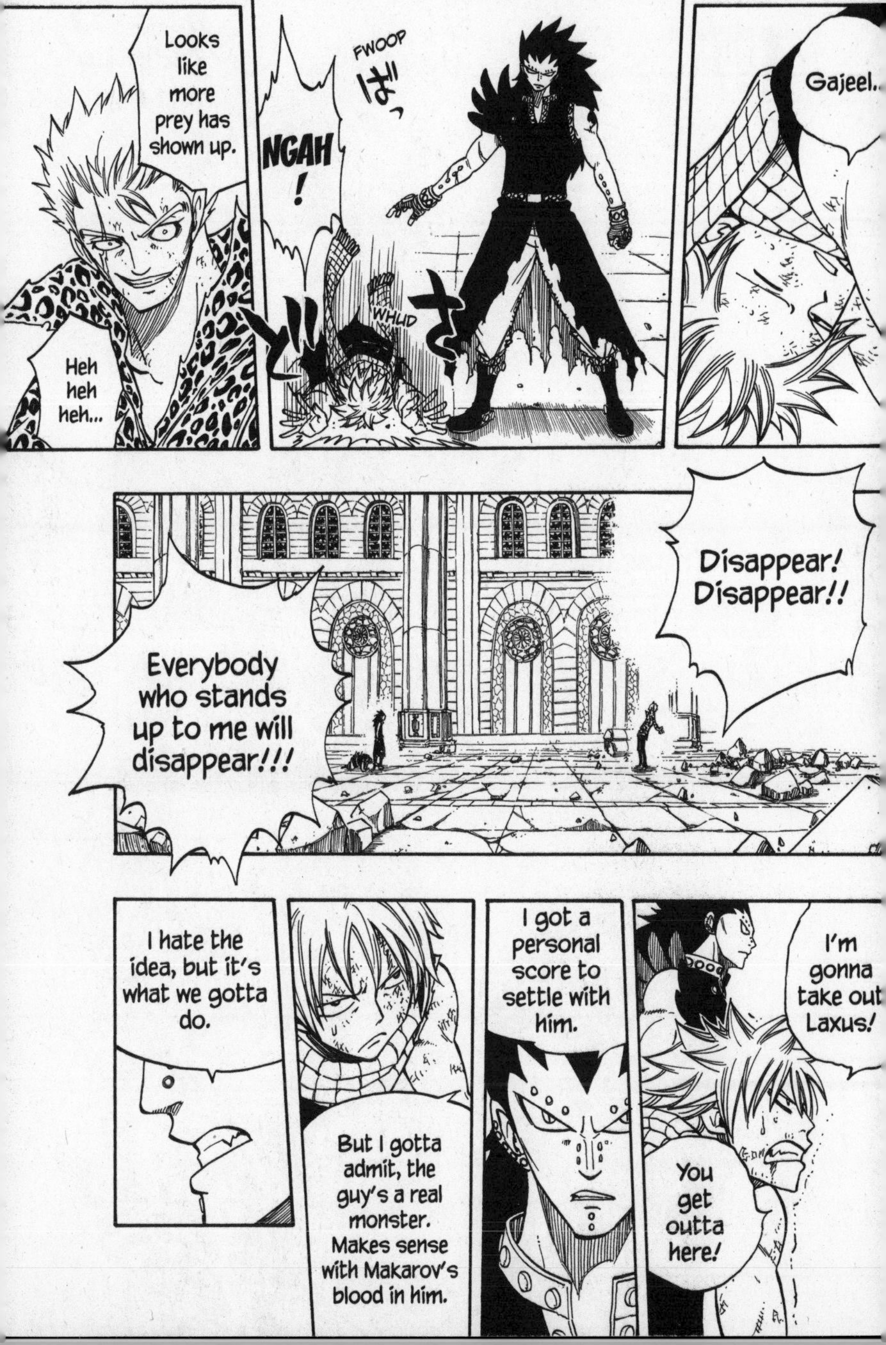
Gajeel..
FWOOP
ばっ
NGAH!
WHUD
Looks like more prey has shown up.
Heh heh heh...
Disappear! Disappear!!
Everybody who stands up to me will disappear!!!
I'm gonna take out Laxus!
You get outta here!
I got a personal score to settle with him.
But I gotta admit, the guy's a real monster. Makes sense with Makarov's blood in him.
I hate the idea, but it's what we gotta do.

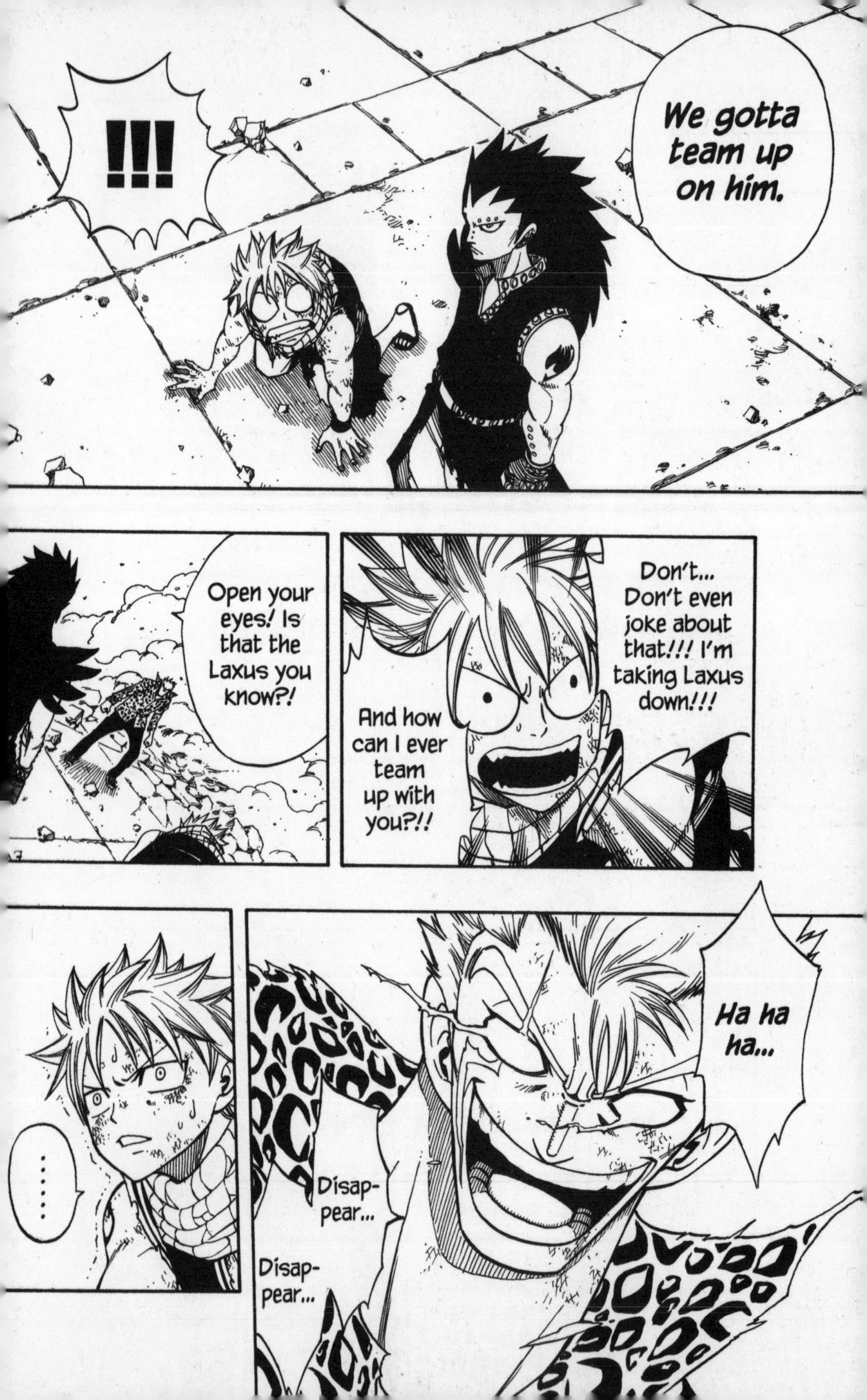
We gotta team up on him.
!!!
Don't... Don't even joke about that!!! I'm taking Laxus down!!!
And how can I ever team up with you?!!
Open your eyes! Is that the Laxus you know?!
Ha ha ha...
Disap- pear...
Disap- pear...
......

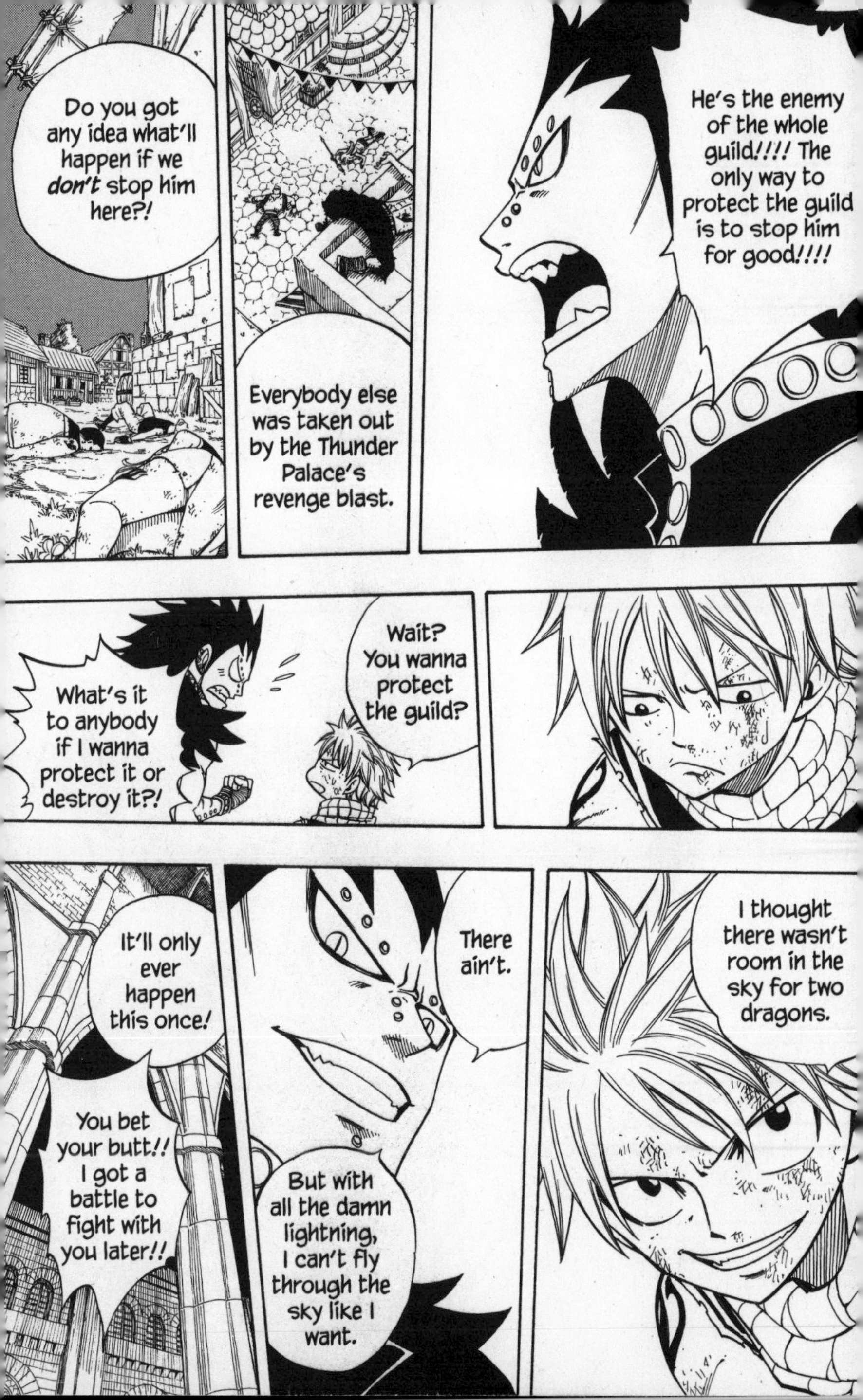
He's the enemy of the whole guild!!!! The only way to protect the guild is to stop him for good!!!!
Everybody else was taken out by the Thunder Palace's revenge blast.
Do you got any idea what'll happen if we *don't* stop him here?!
Wait? You wanna protect the guild?
What's it to anybody if I wanna protect it or destroy it?!
I thought there wasn't room in the sky for two dragons.
There ain't.
But with all the damn lightning, I can't fly through the sky like I want.
It'll only ever happen this once!
You bet your butt!! I got a battle to fight with you later!!

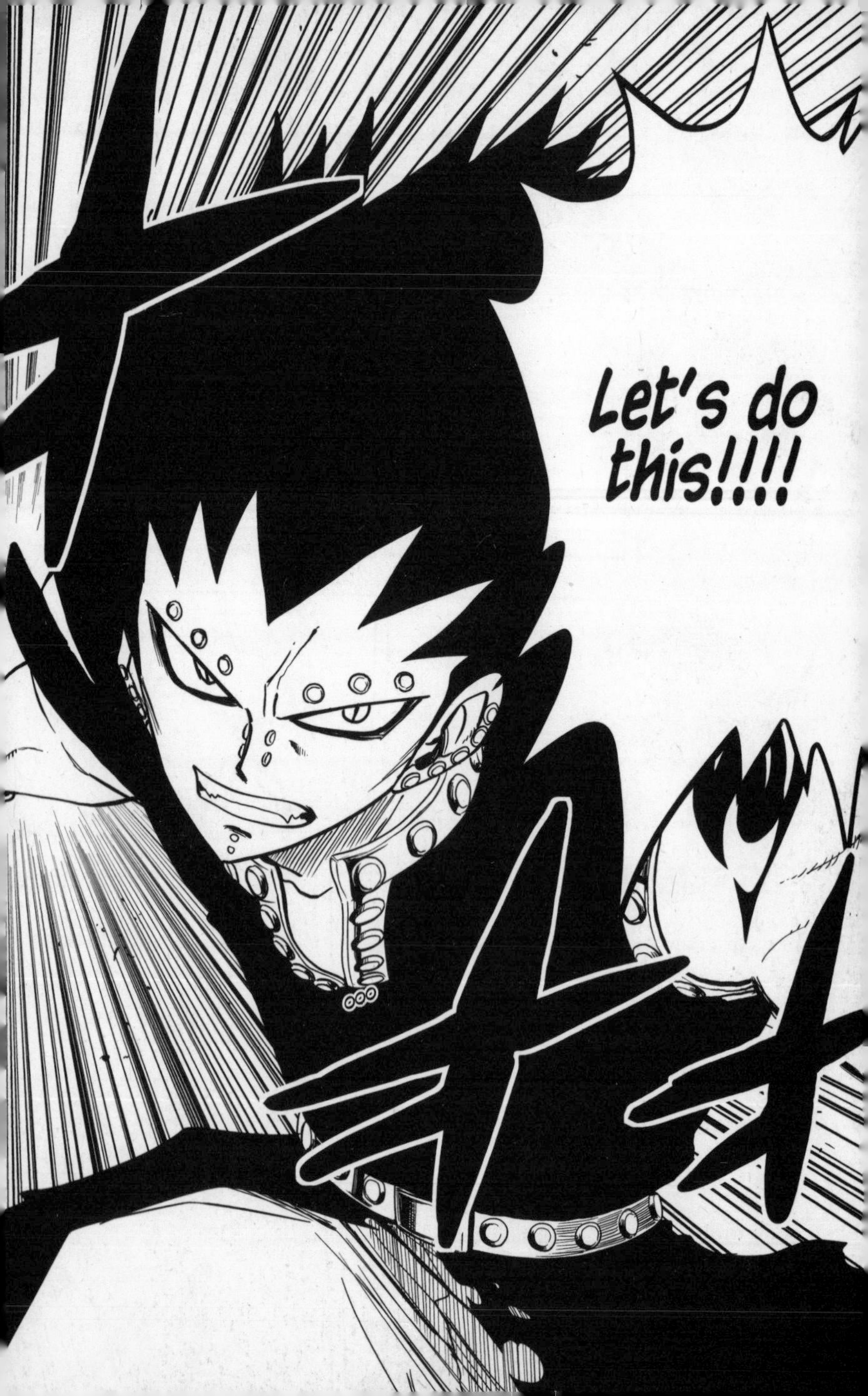
Let's do this!!!!

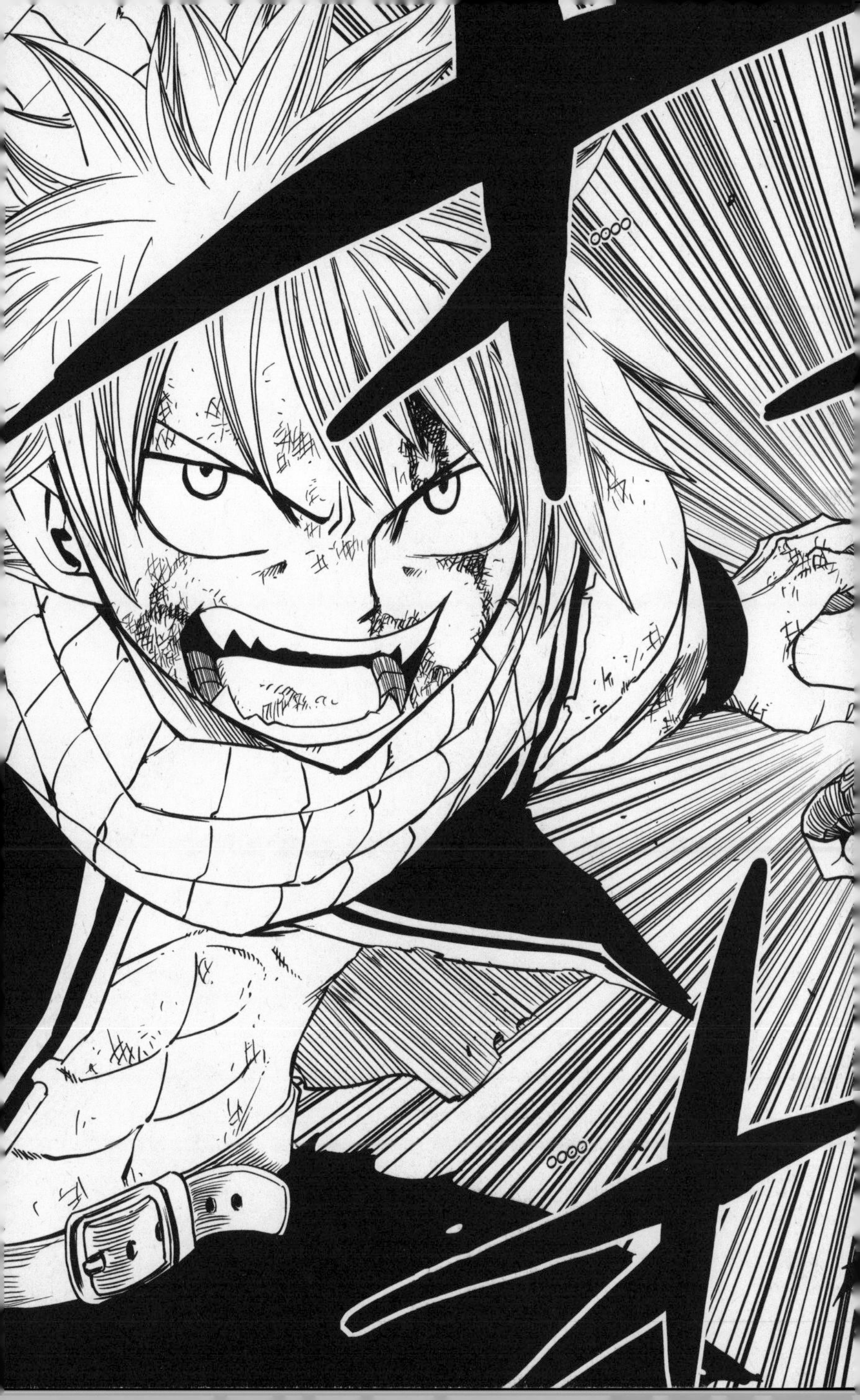

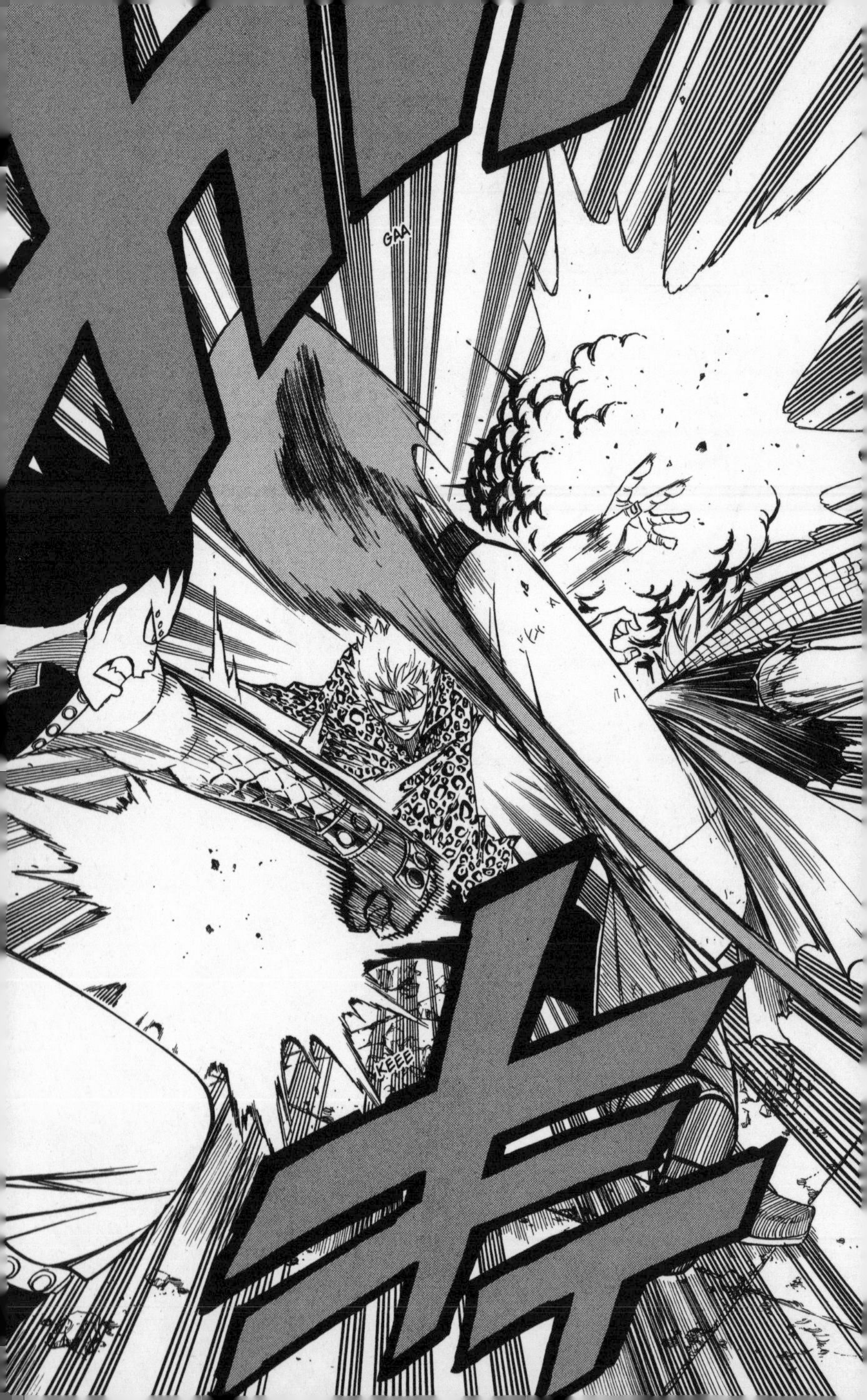
GAA
KEEE

FAIRY TAIL

Chapter 124: Triple Dragon

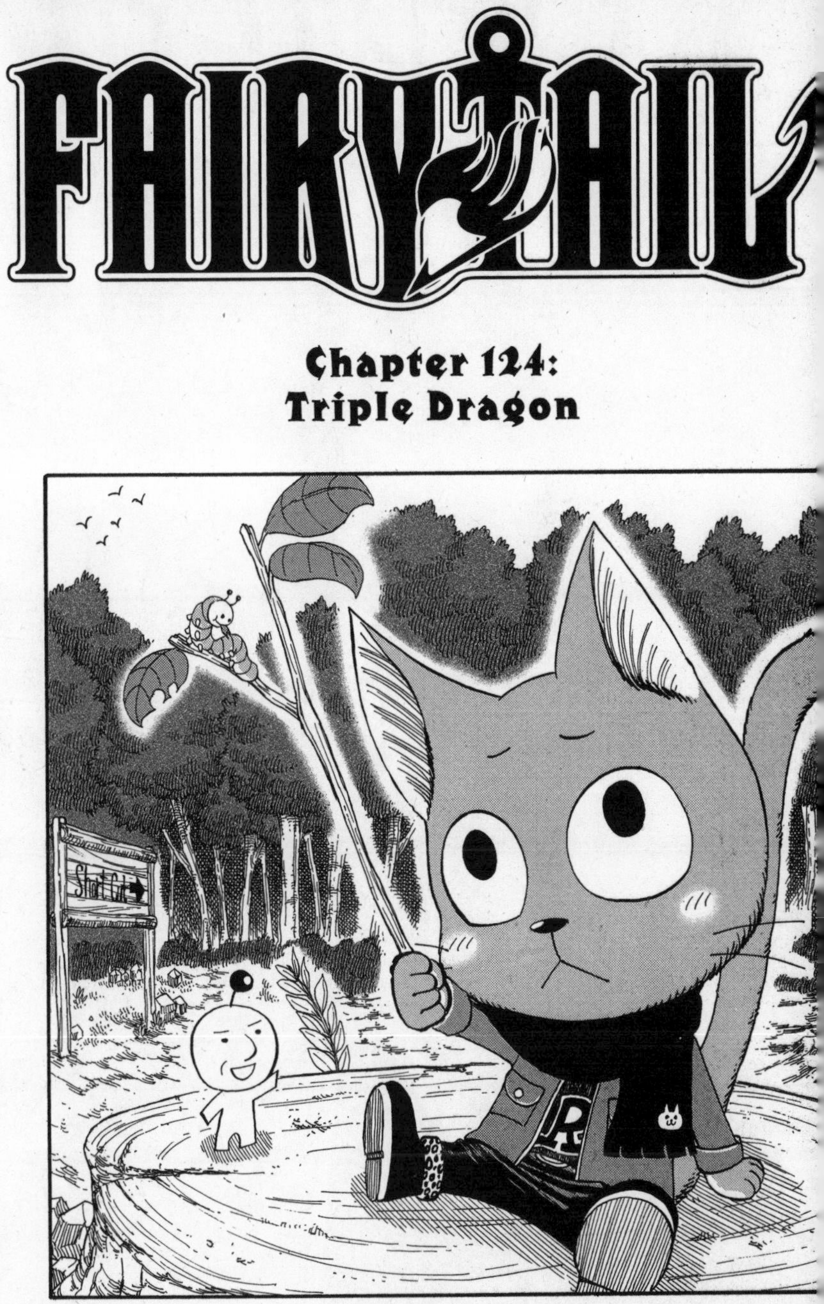
Short Cut

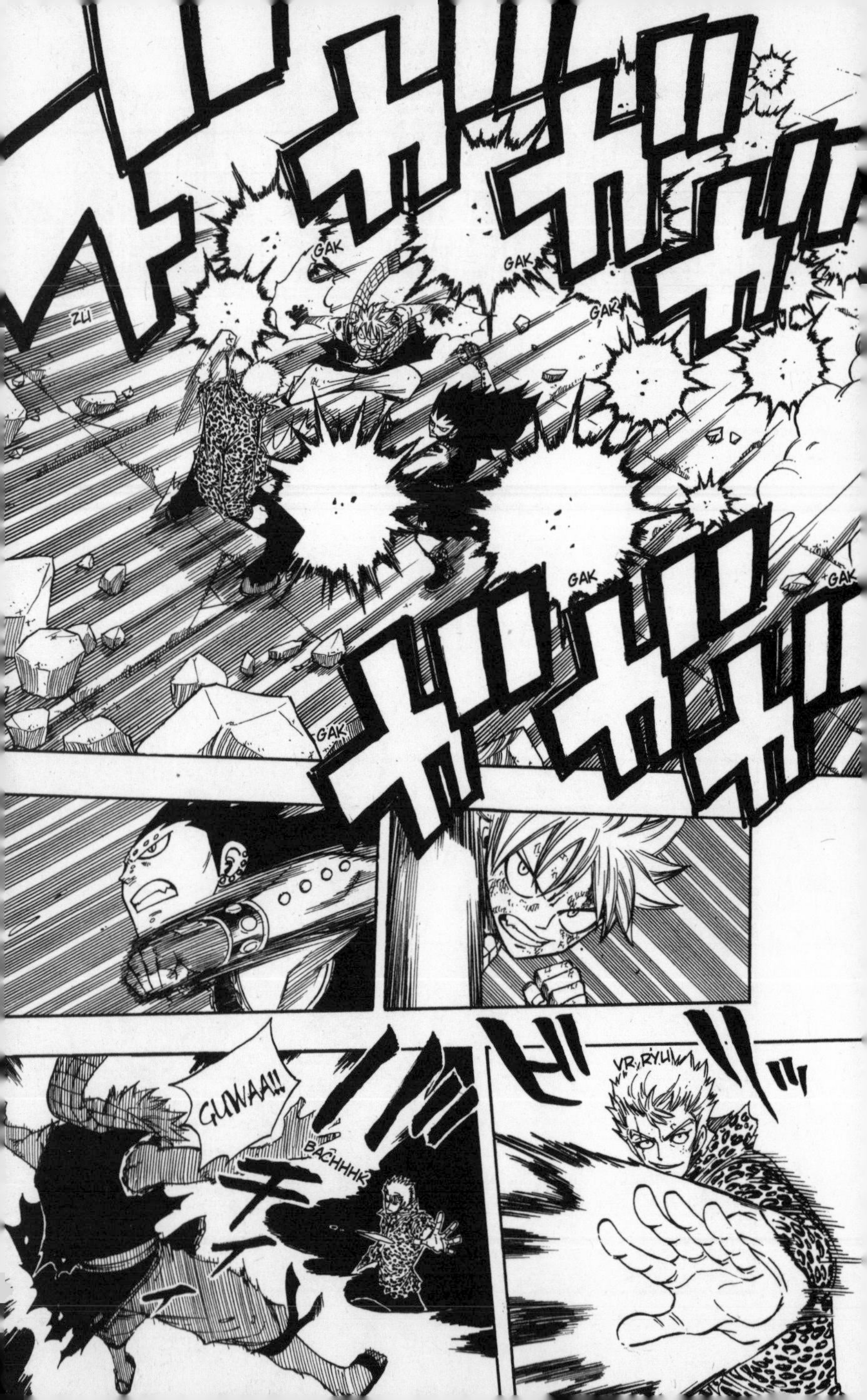
GAK
GAK
GAK
ZU
GAK
GAK
GAK
VR RYU
GUWAA!!
BACHHHK

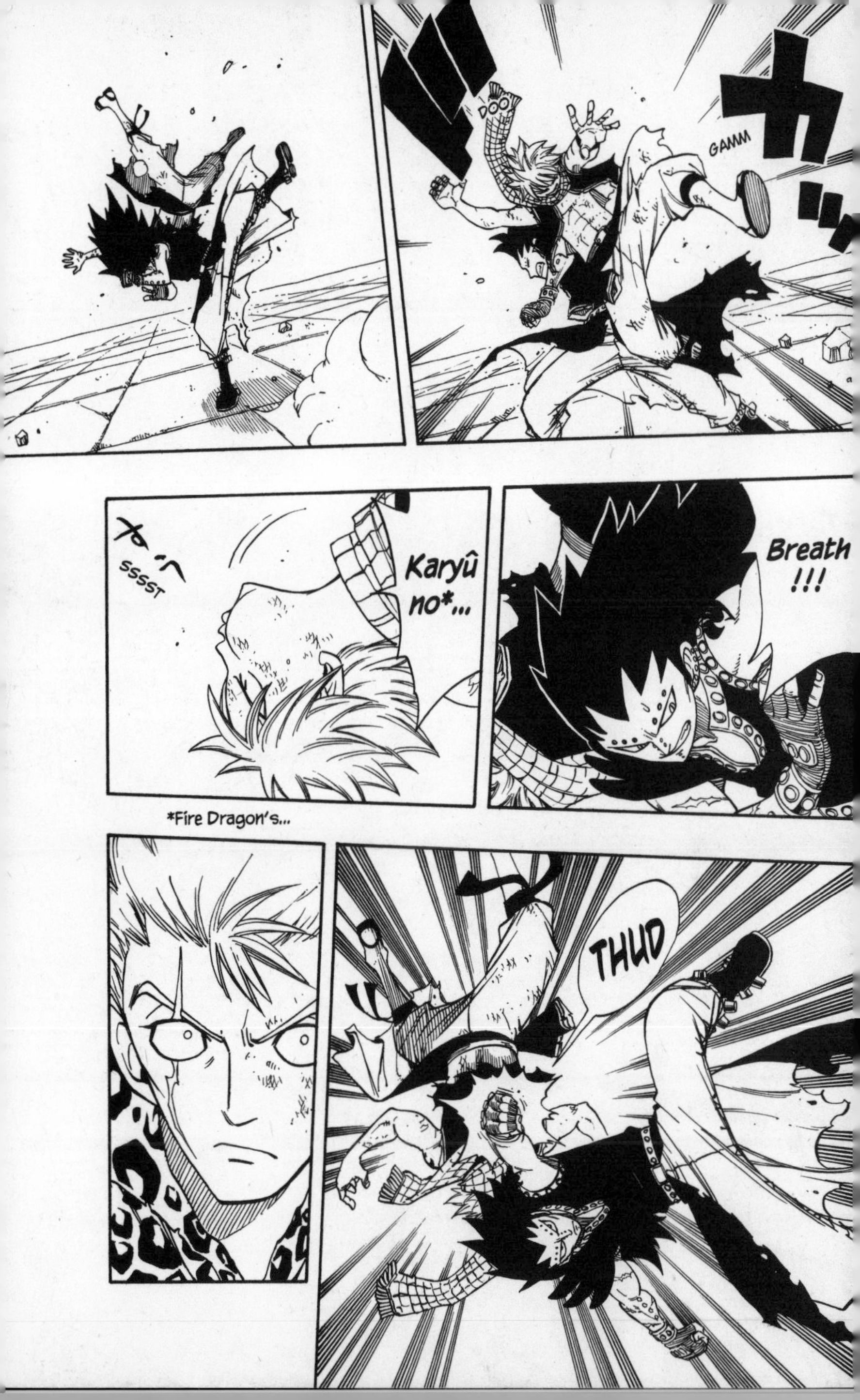
GAMM
DOO
Breath !!!
Karyû no*...
SSSST
THUD
*Fire Dragon's...

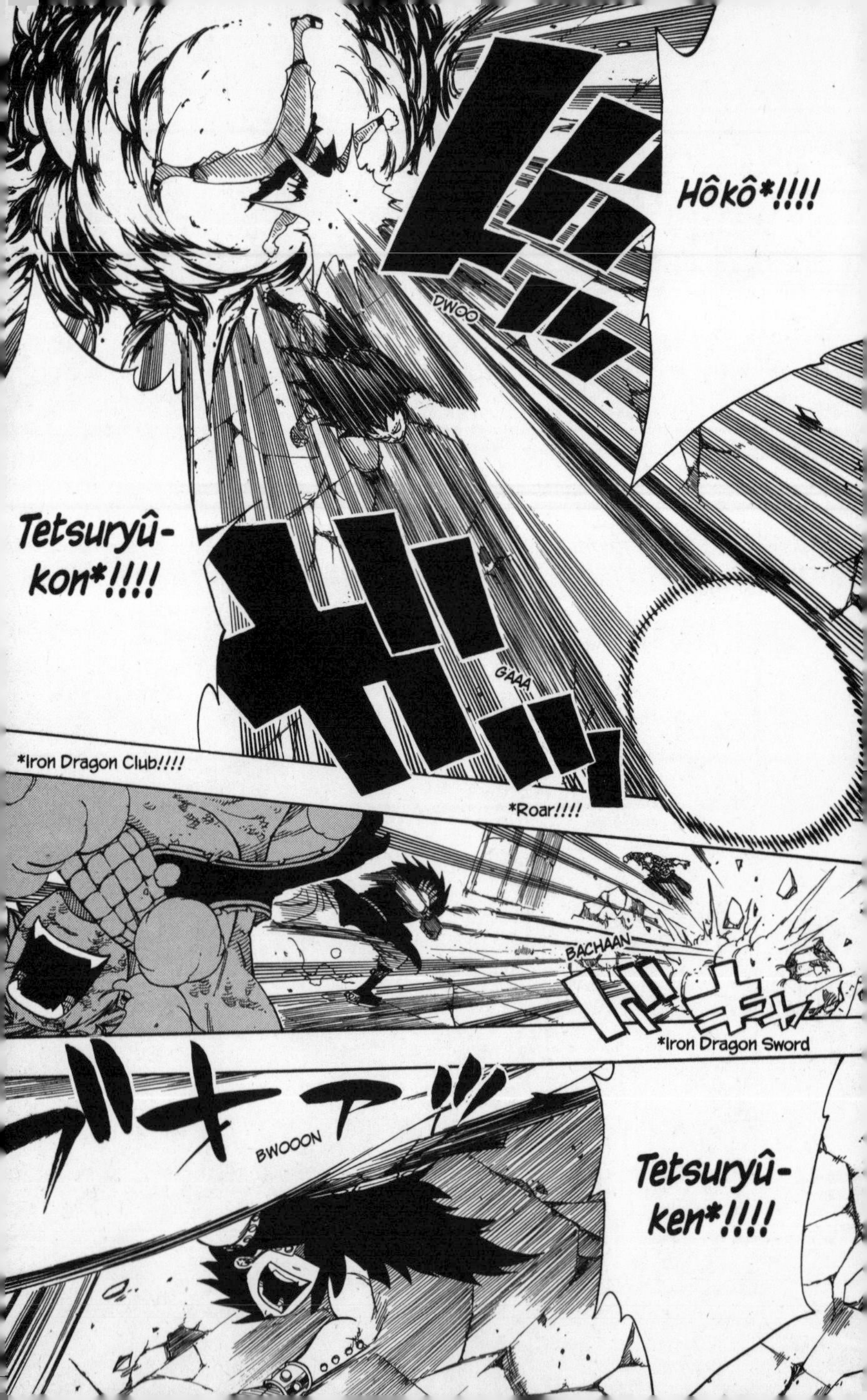
Hôkô*!!!!
DWOO
Tetsuryû-kon*!!!!
GAAA
*Roar!!!!
*Iron Dragon Club!!!!
BACHAAN
*Iron Dragon Sword
Tetsuryû-ken*!!!!
BWOOON

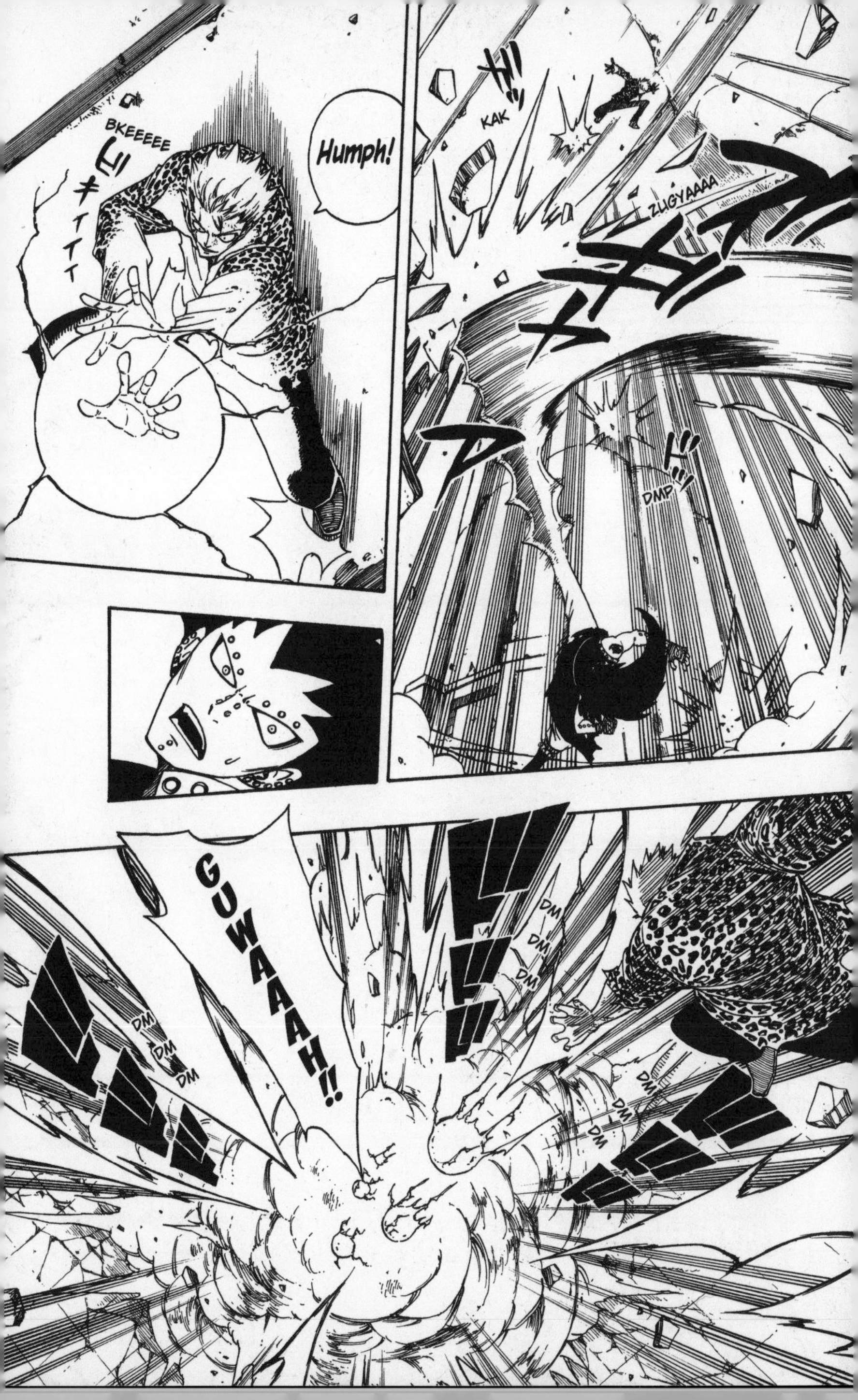
KAK
ZUGYAAAA
DMP
Humph!
BKEEEEE
GUWAAAAH!!
DM DM DM
DM DM DM
DM DM DM

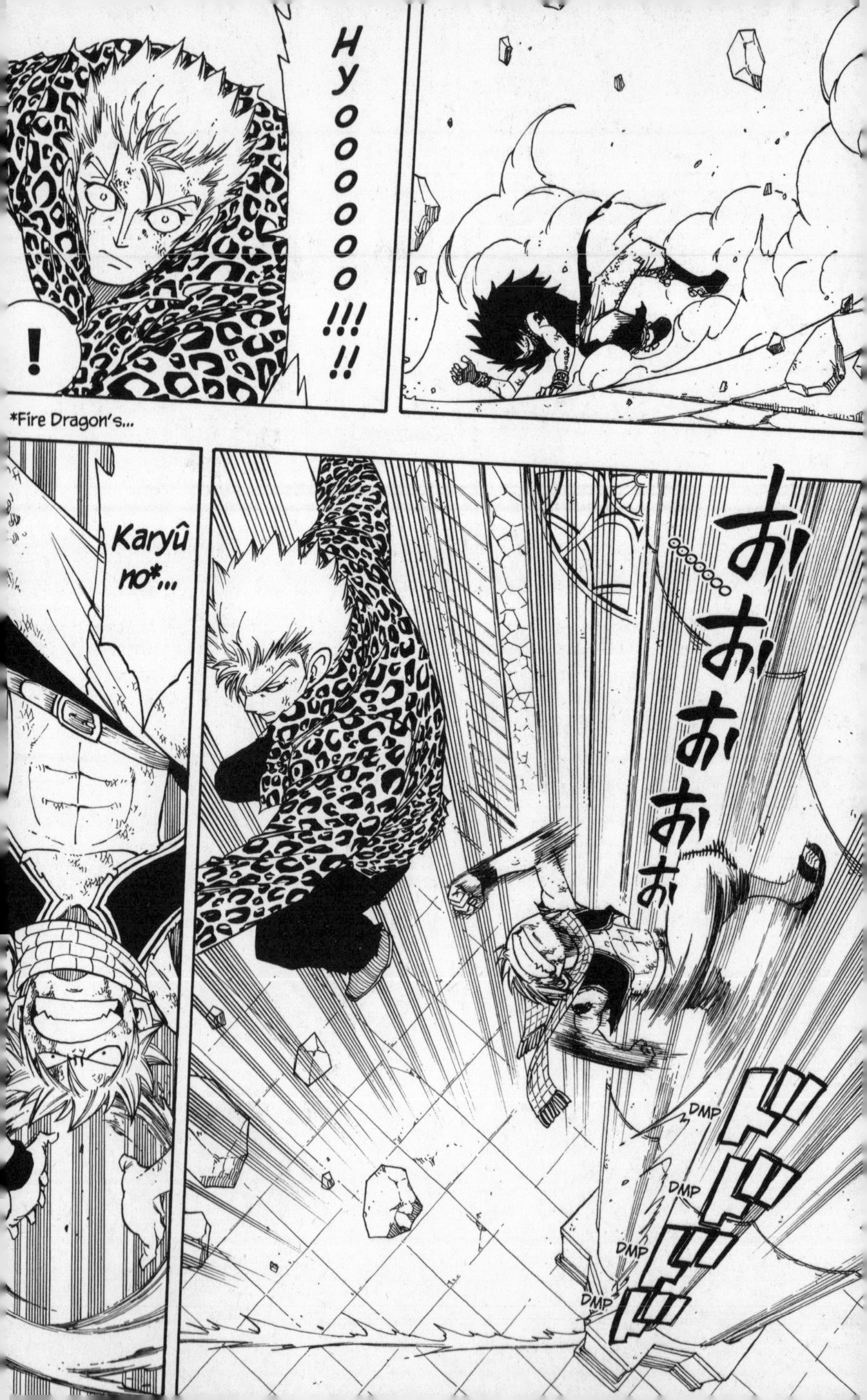
Hyoooooo!!!!!
!
*Fire Dragon's...
おおおおお
DMP
DMP
DMP
DMP
ドドドド
Karyû no*...

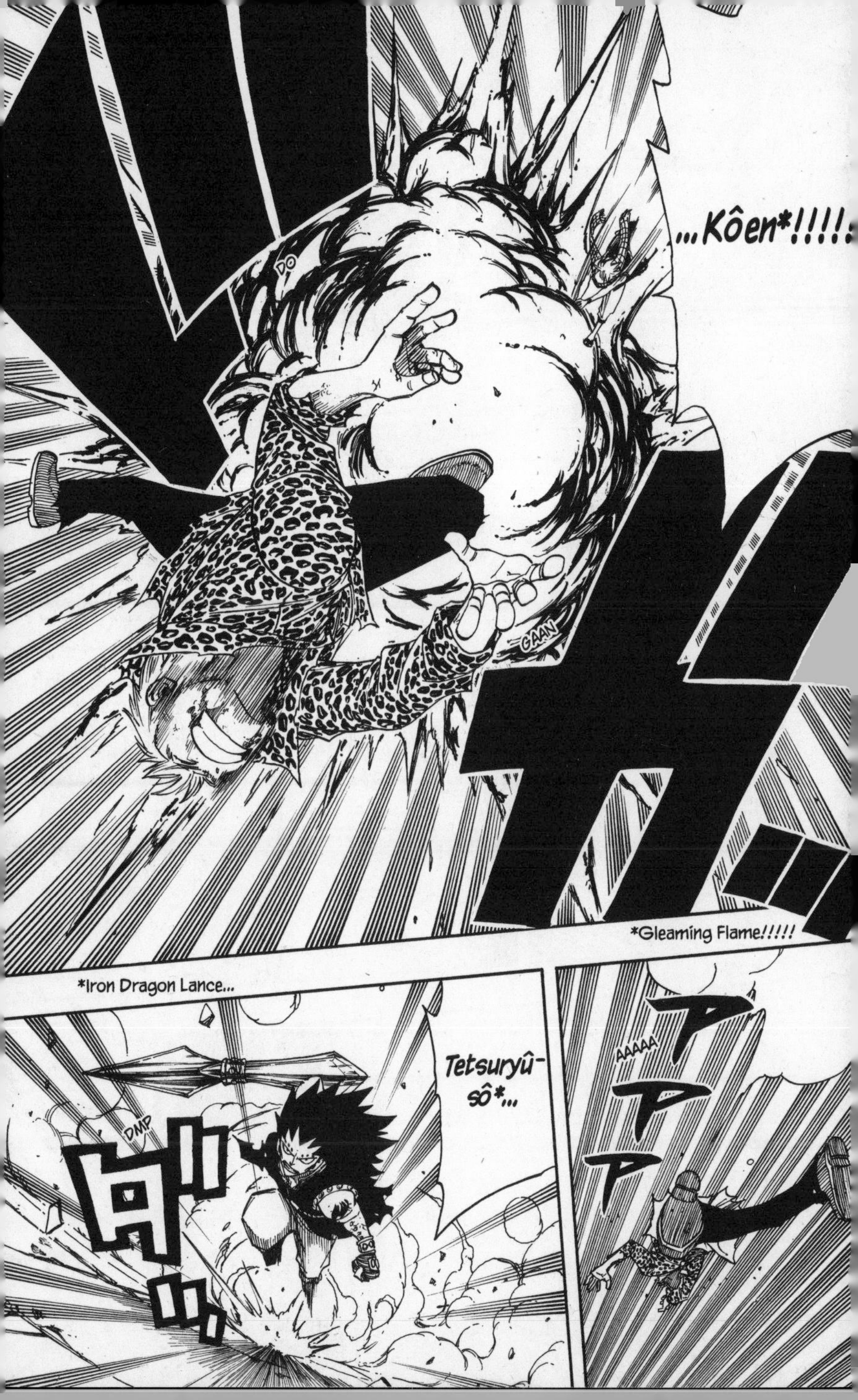
...Kôen*!!!!!
DO
GAAN
*Gleaming Flame!!!!!
AAAAA
Tetsuryû-sô*...
DMP
*Iron Dragon Lance...

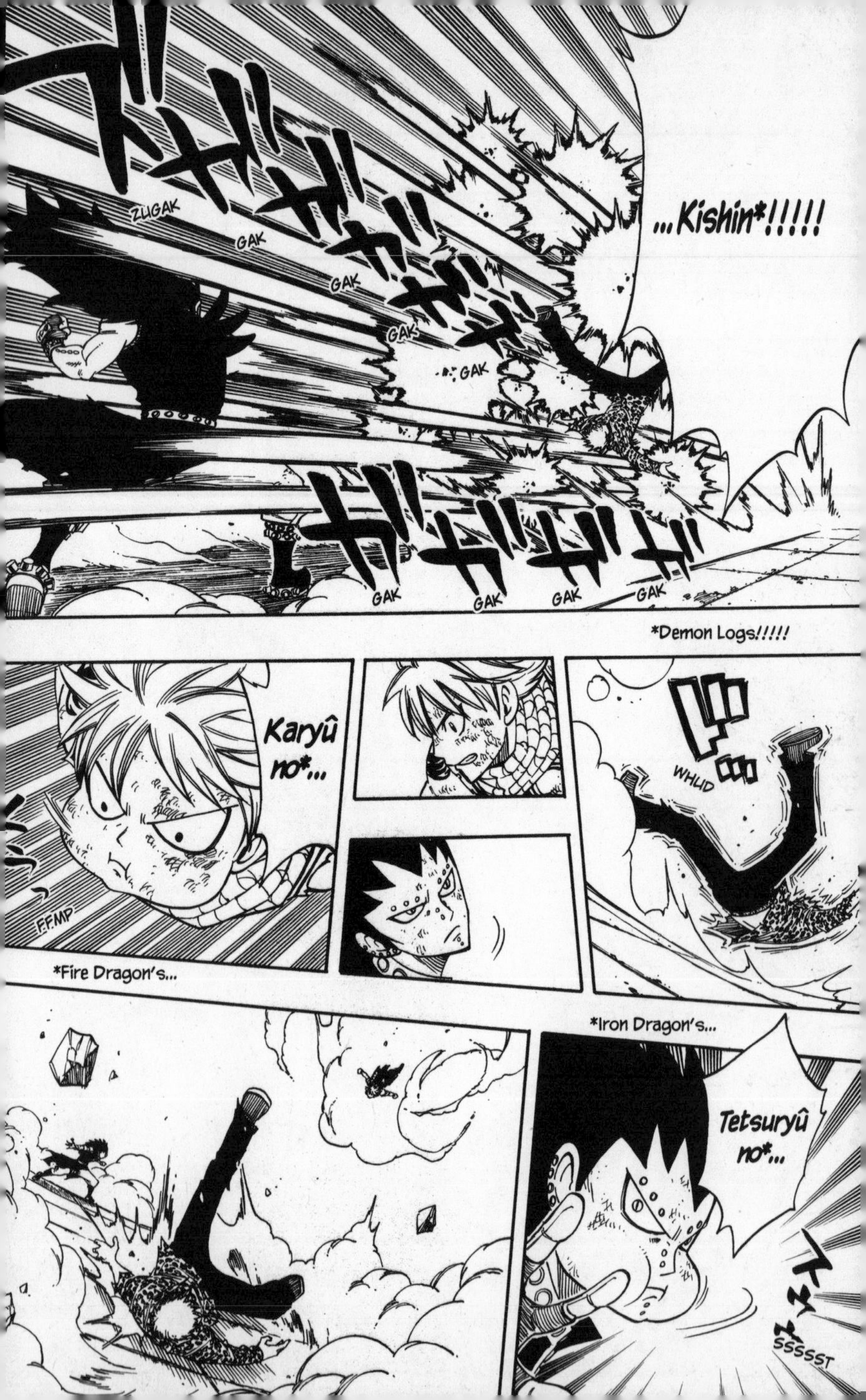
...Kishin*!!!!!
ZUGAK
GAK
GAK
GAK
GAK
GAK
GAK
GAK
GAK
*Demon Logs!!!!!
WHUD
Karyû no*...
F.F.MP
*Fire Dragon's...
*Iron Dragon's...
Tetsuryû no*...
SSSSST

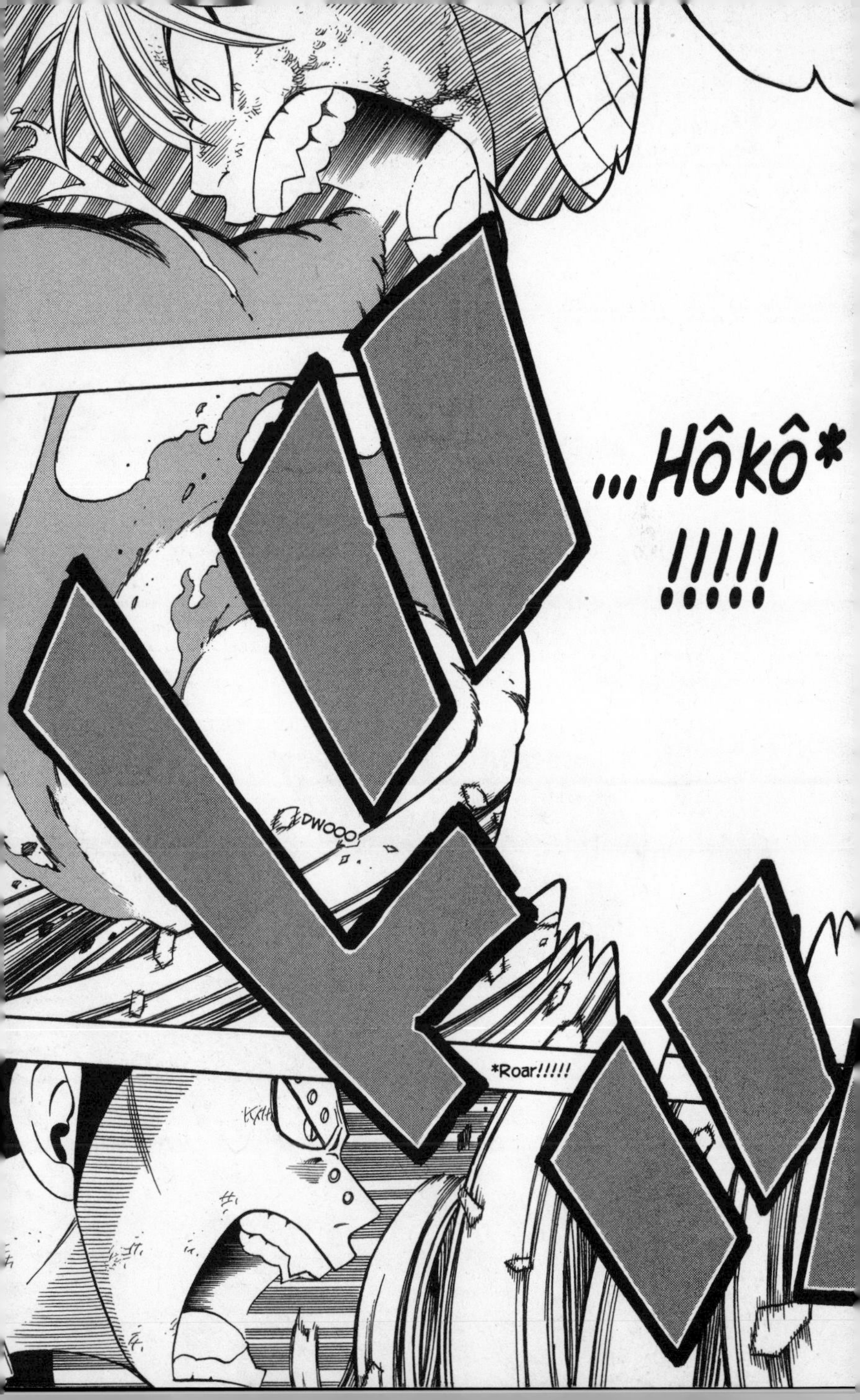
...Hôkô*
!!!!!
DWOOO
*Roar!!!!!

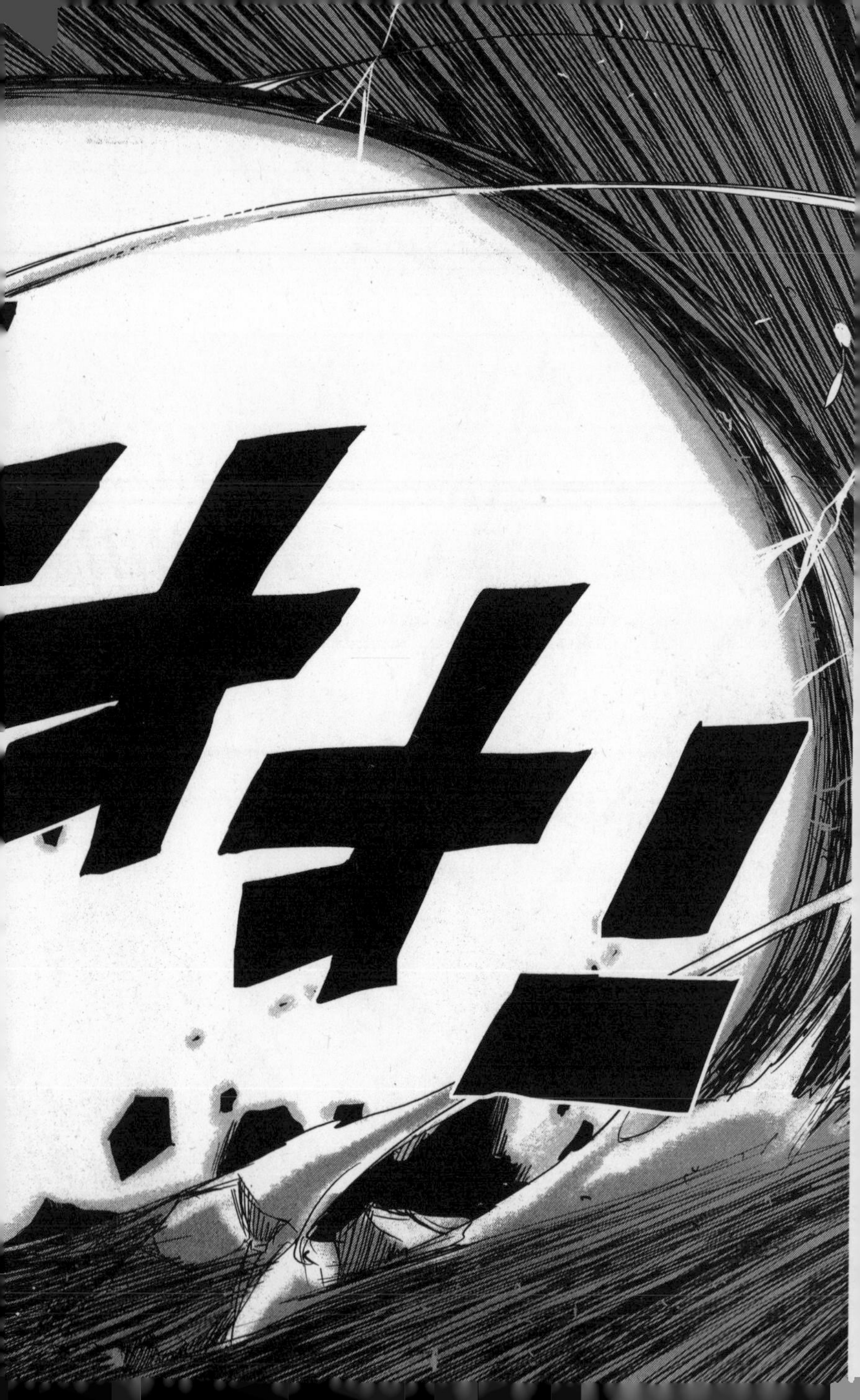
オオ！

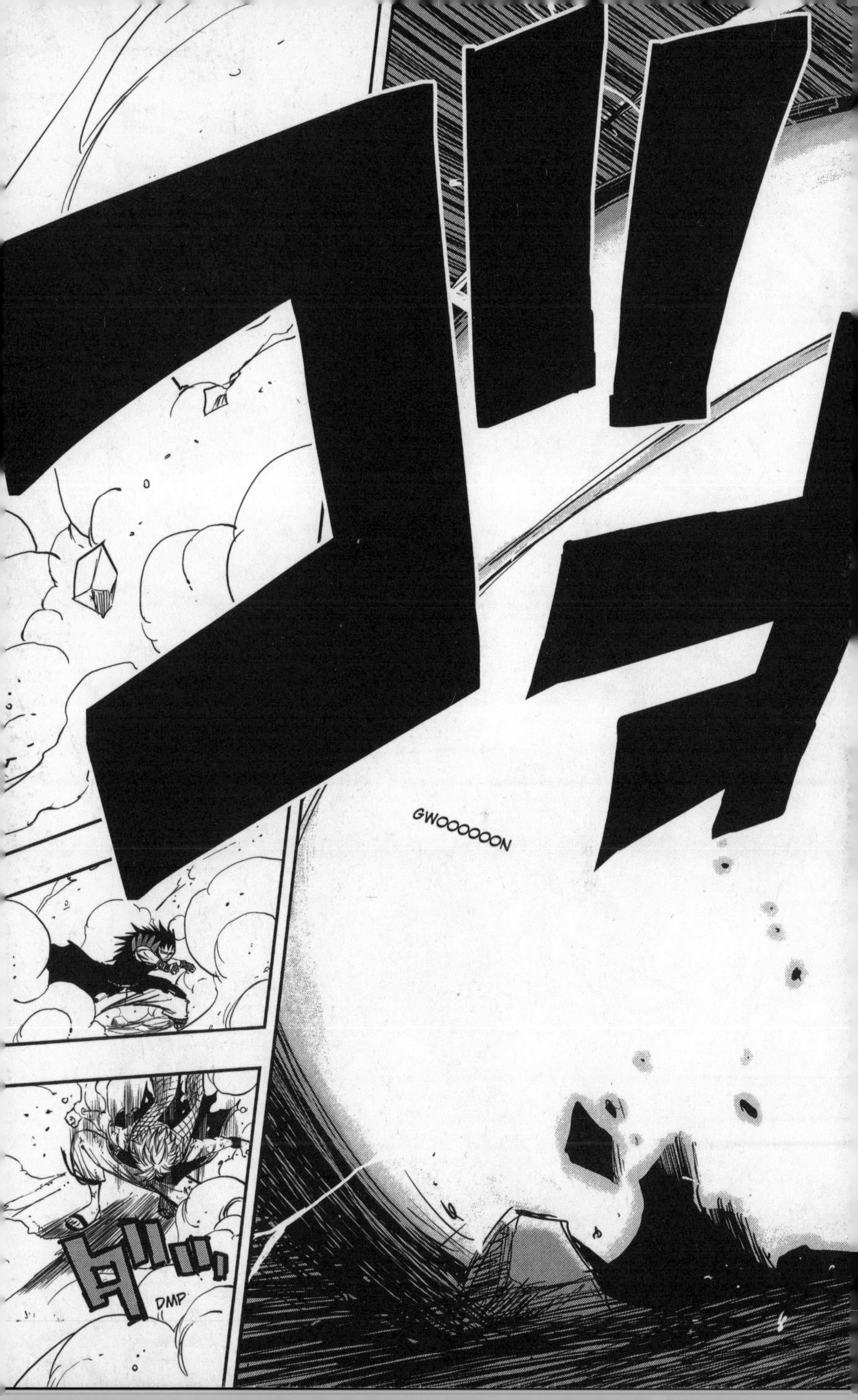
GWOOOOOON
DMP

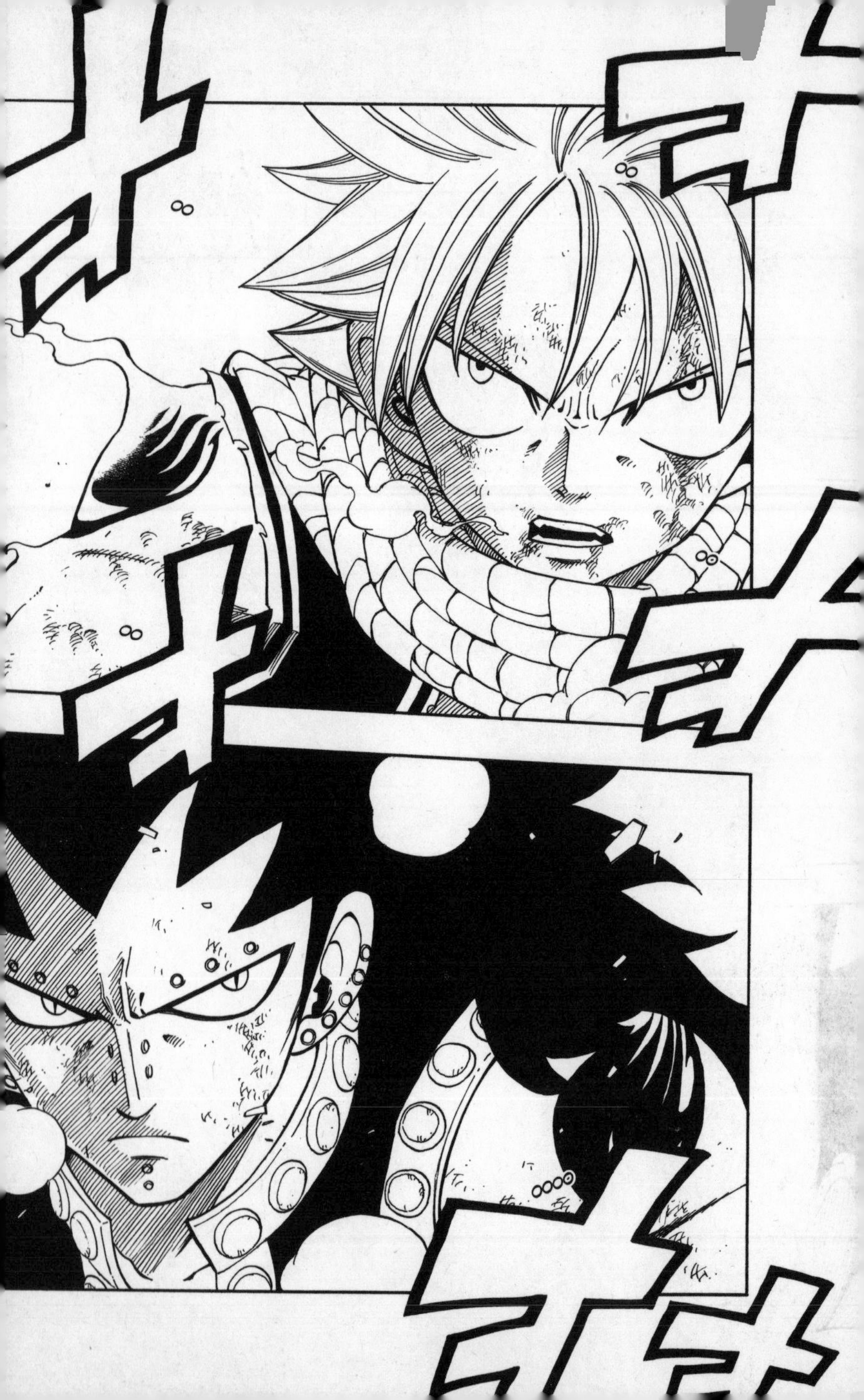

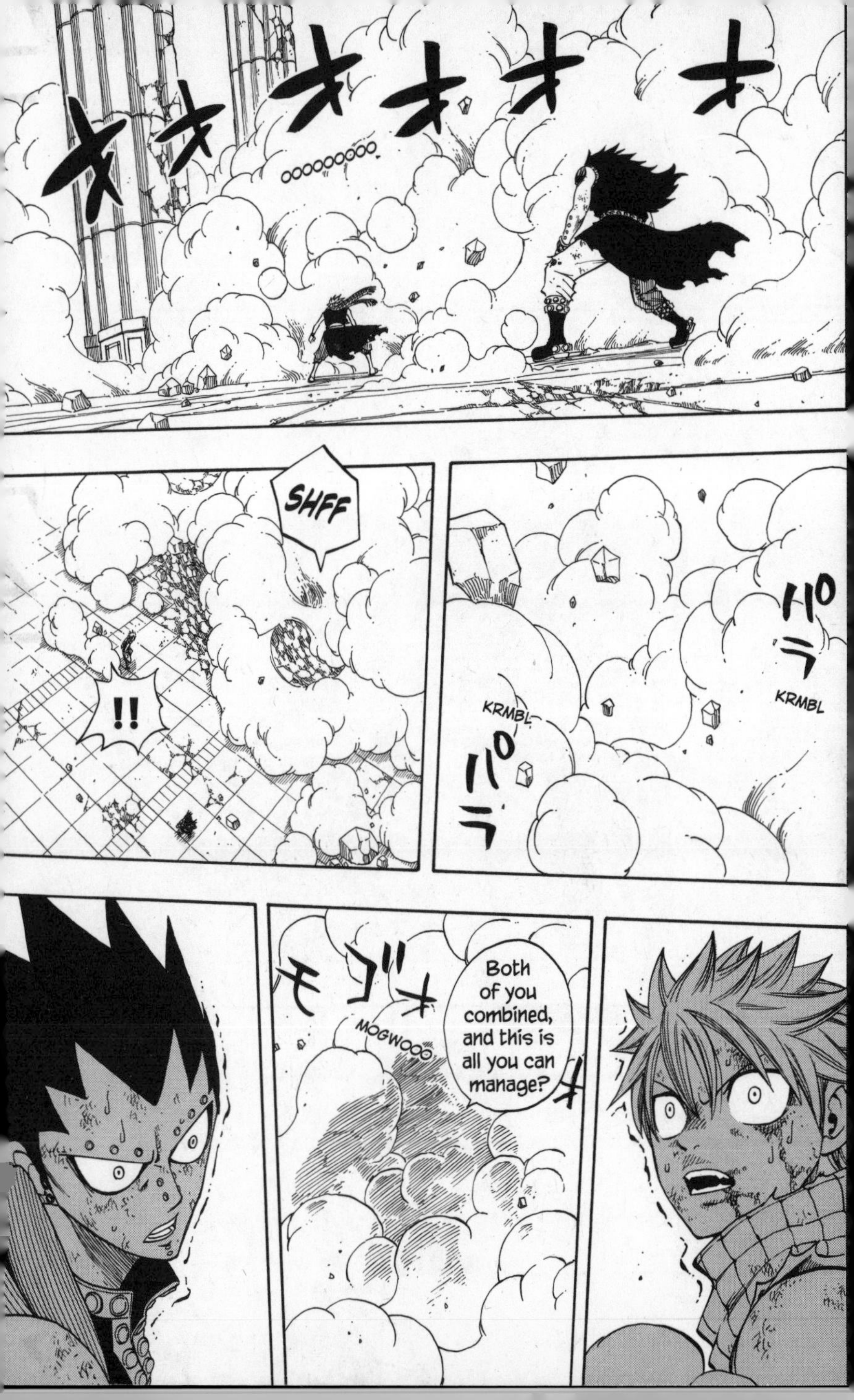
OOOOOOOOO
KRMBL
KRMBL
SHFF
!!
MOGWOOO
Both of you combined, and this is all you can manage?

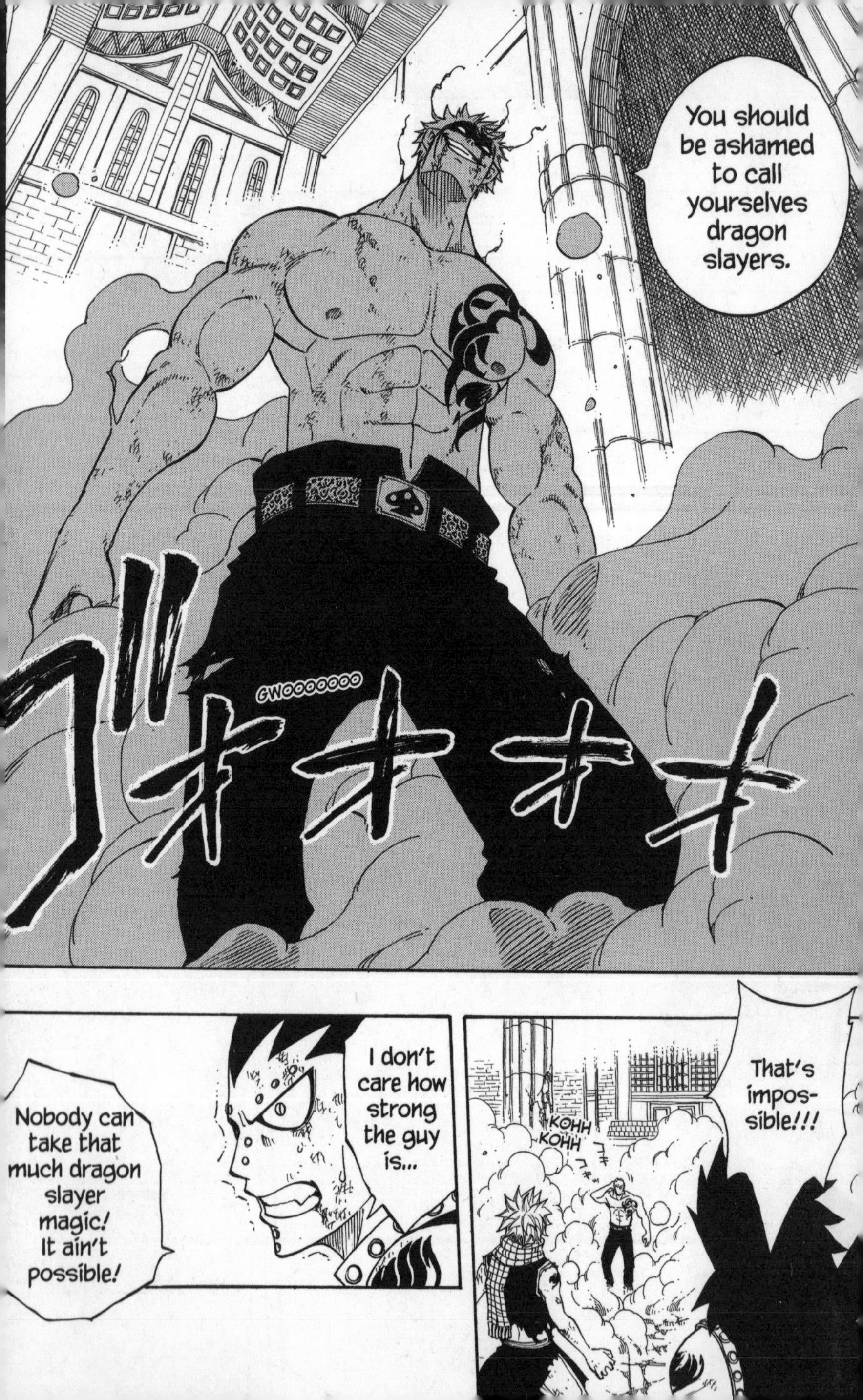
You should be ashamed to call yourselves dragon slayers.
ゴオオオオ
GWOOOOOOO
That's impos-sible!!!
KOHH KOHH
I don't care how strong the guy is...
Nobody can take that much dragon slayer magic! It ain't possible!

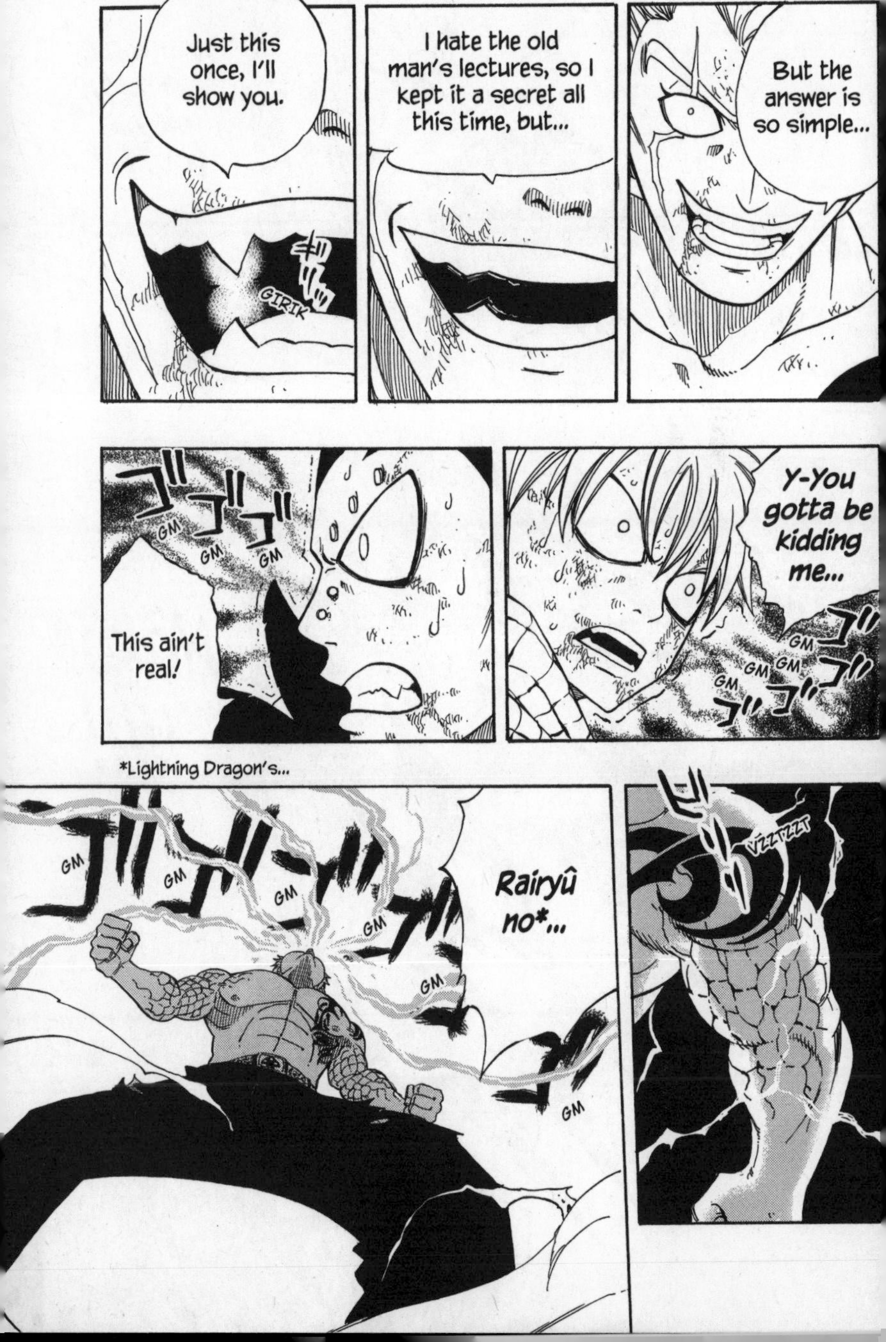
But the answer is so simple...
I hate the old man's lectures, so I kept it a secret all this time, but...
Just this once, I'll show you.
GIRIK
Y-You gotta be kidding me...
GM GM GM GM
GM GM GM
This ain't real!
VZZTZZT
GM GM GM GM GM GM
Rairyû no*...
*Lightning Dragon's...

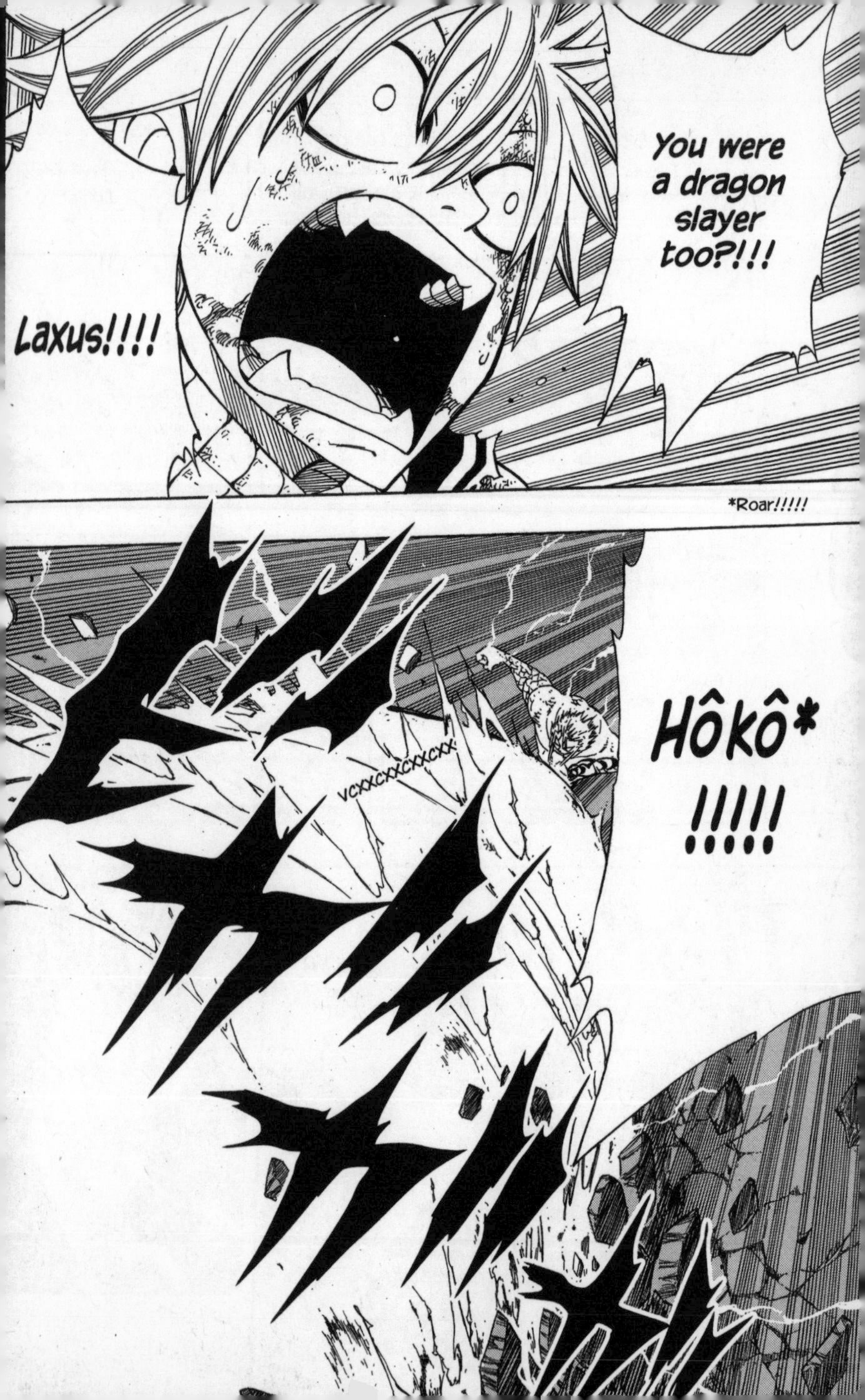
You were a dragon slayer too?!!!
Laxus!!!!
*Roar!!!!!
Hôkô* !!!!!
VCXXCXXCXXCXX

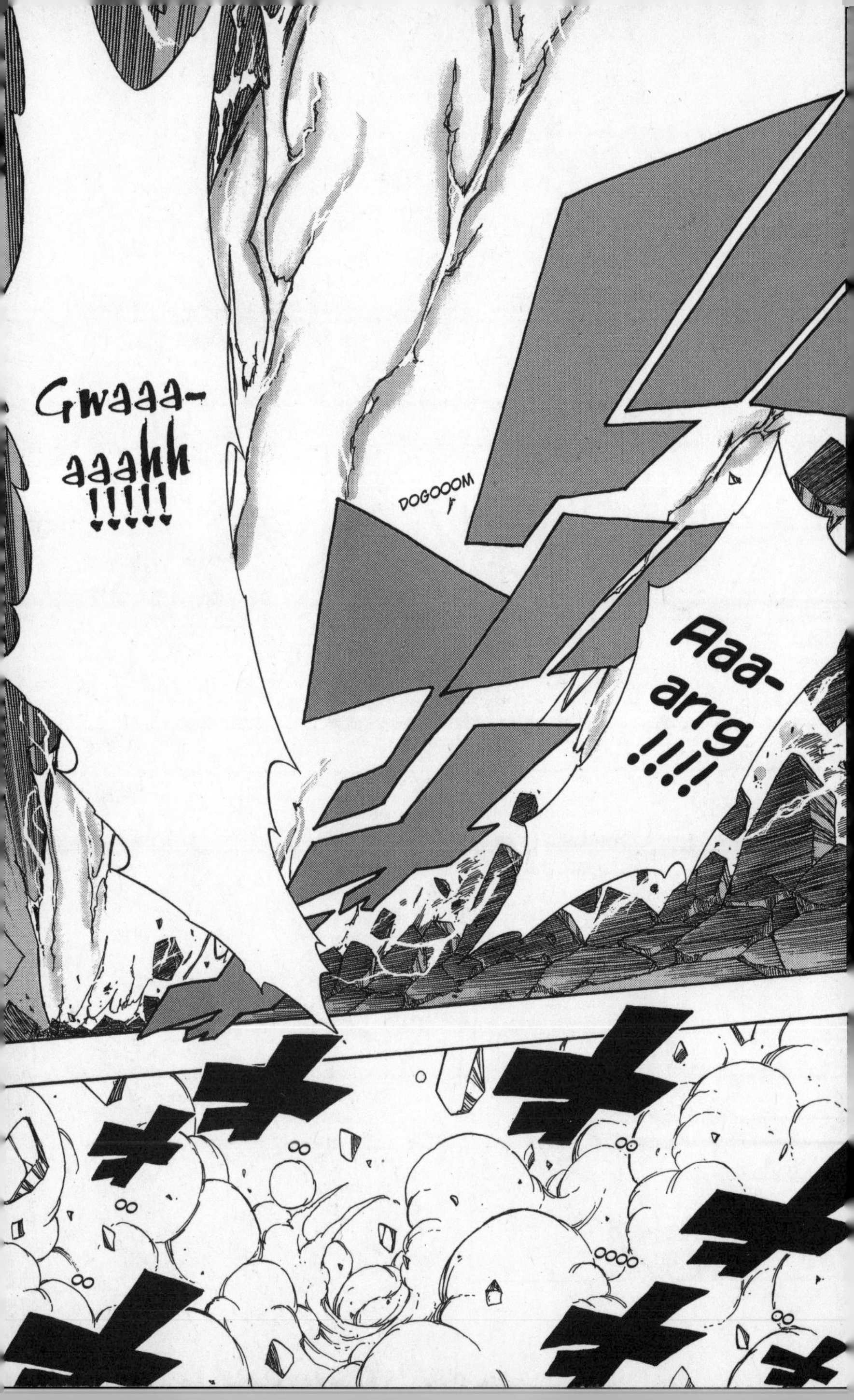
Aaa-
arrg
!!!!
DOGOOOM
Gwaaa-
aaahh
!!!!!

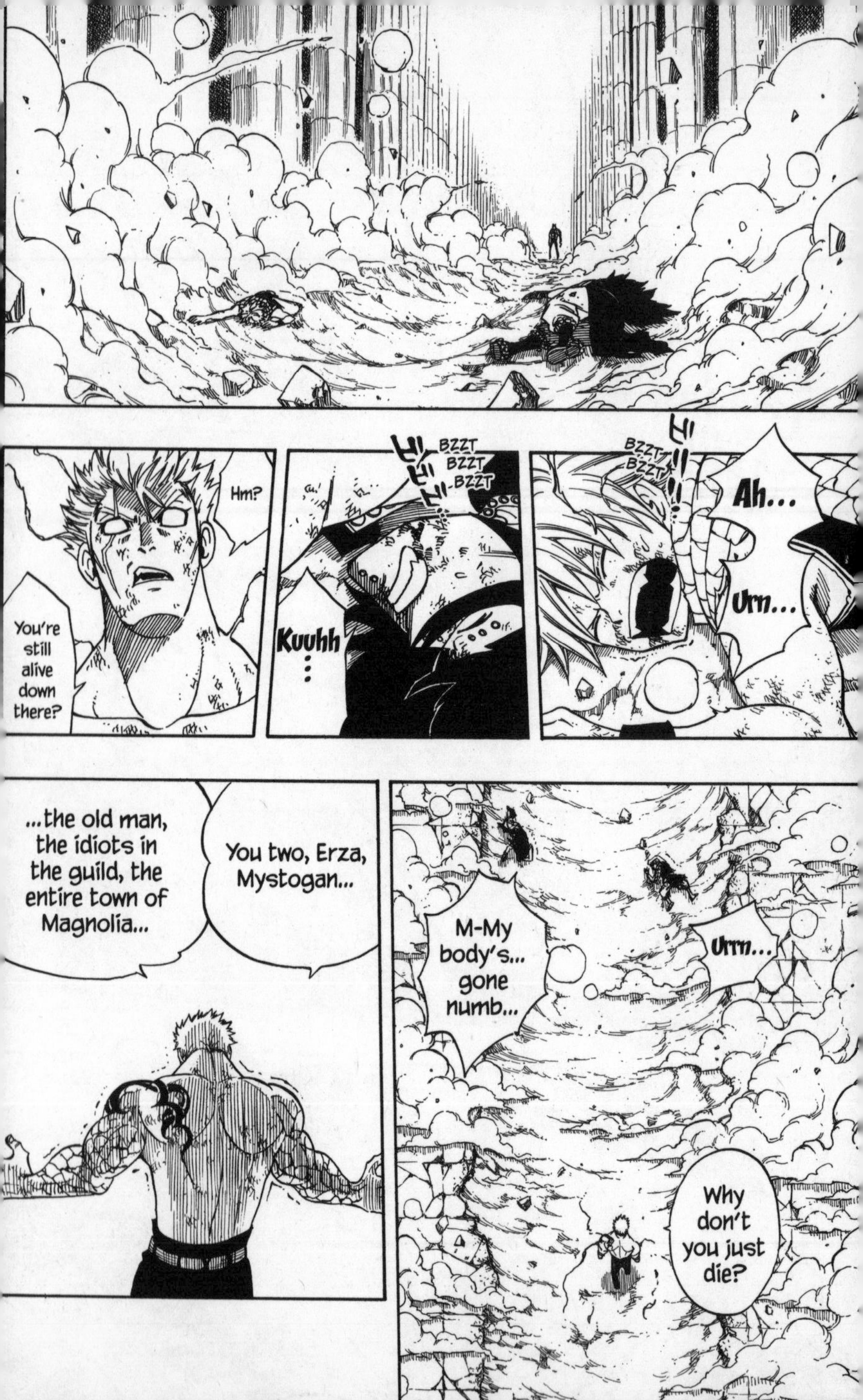
BZZT
BZZT
Ah...
Urn...
BZZT
BZZT
BZZT
Kuuhh...
Hm?
You're still alive down there?
Urn...
M-My body's... gone numb...
Why don't you just die?
You two, Erza, Mystogan...
...the old man, the idiots in the guild, the entire town of Magnolia...

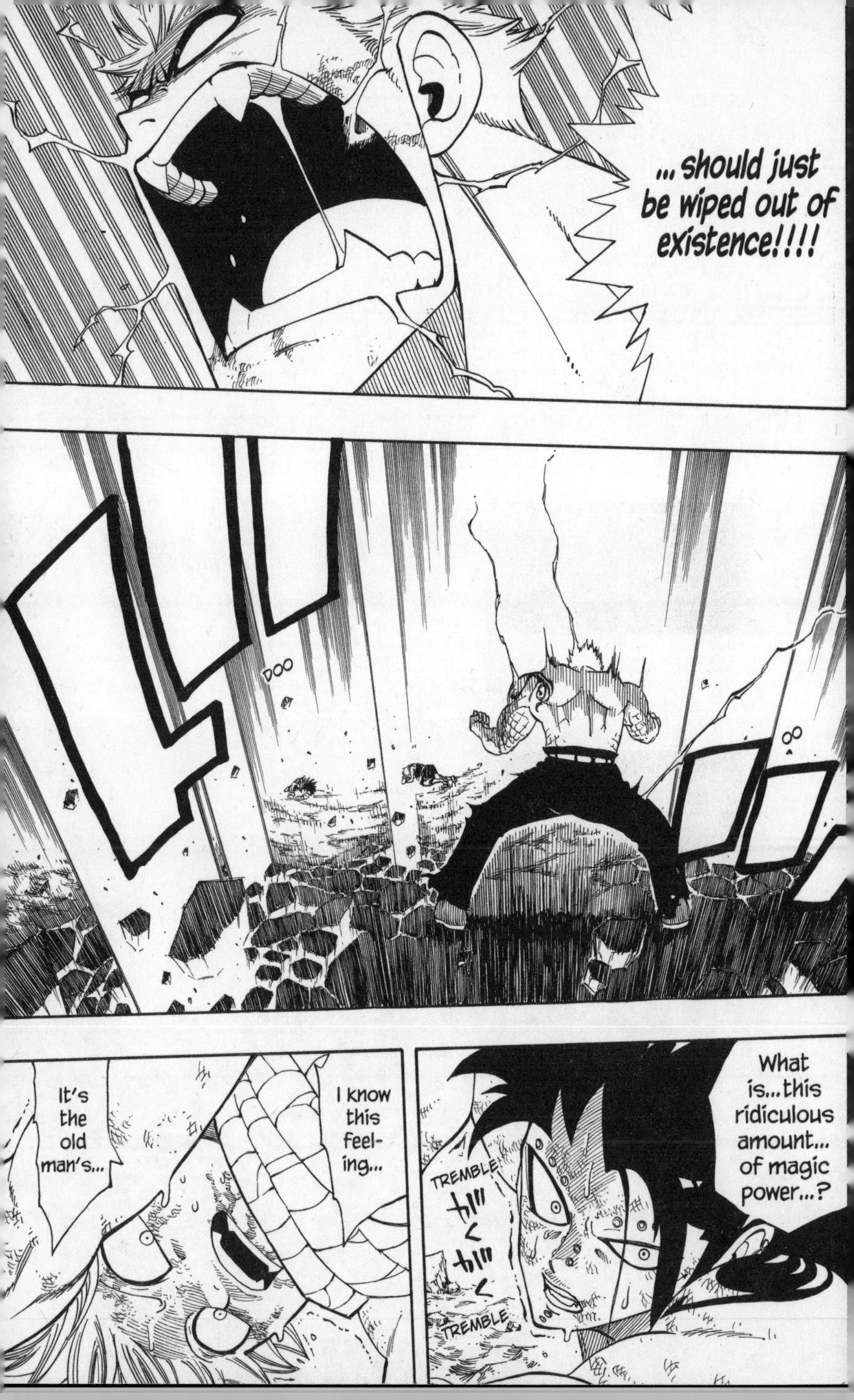
...should just be wiped out of existence!!!!
DOO
OO
What is...this ridiculous amount... of magic power...?
TREMBLE
TREMBLE
I know this feel-ing...
It's the old man's...

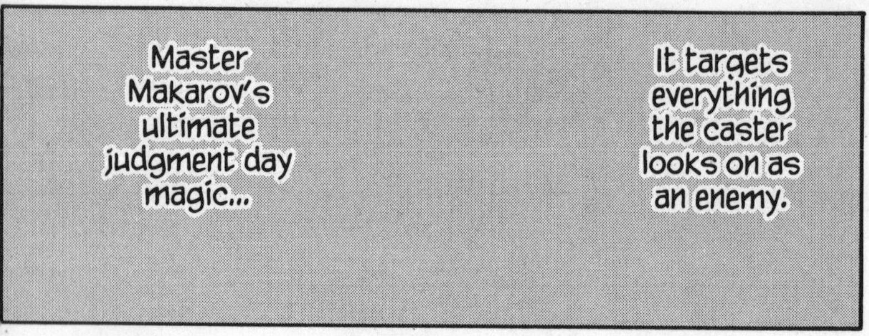
It targets everything the caster looks on as an enemy.
Master Makarov's ultimate judgment day magic...
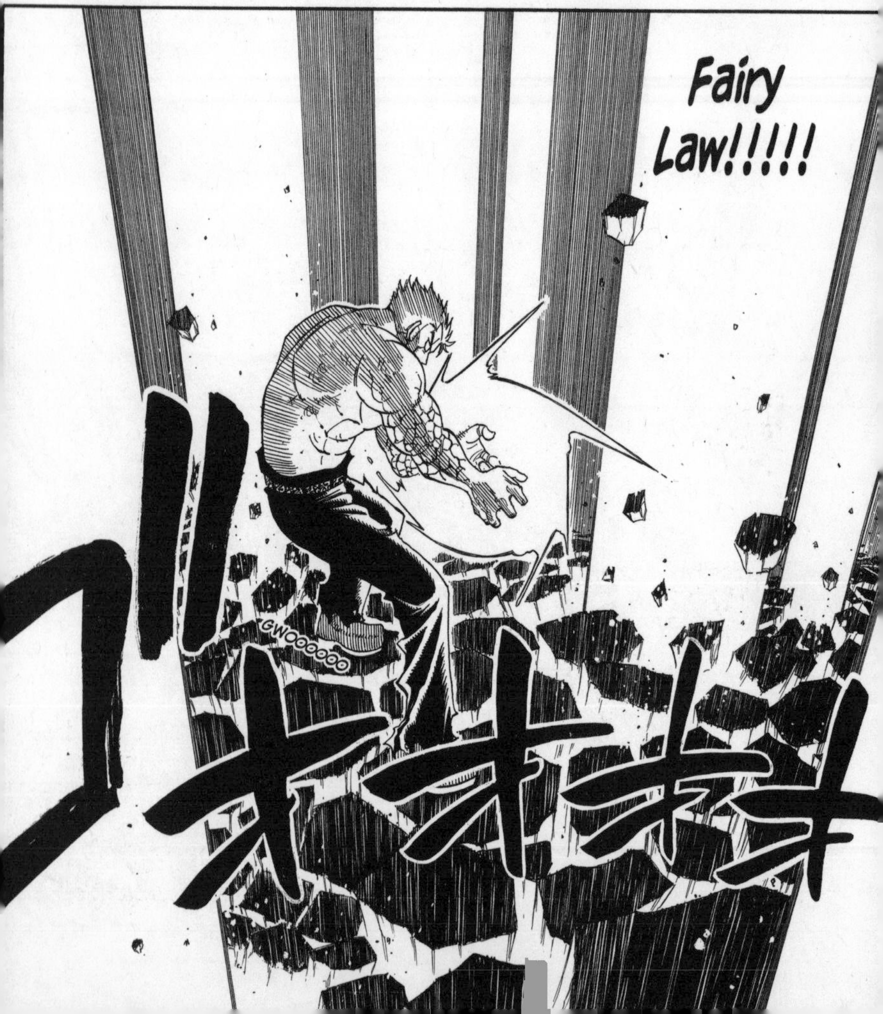
Fairy Law!!!!!
ゴオオオオ
GWOOOOOO

FAIRY TAIL

Chapter 125: Face of a Devil, Heart of an Angel

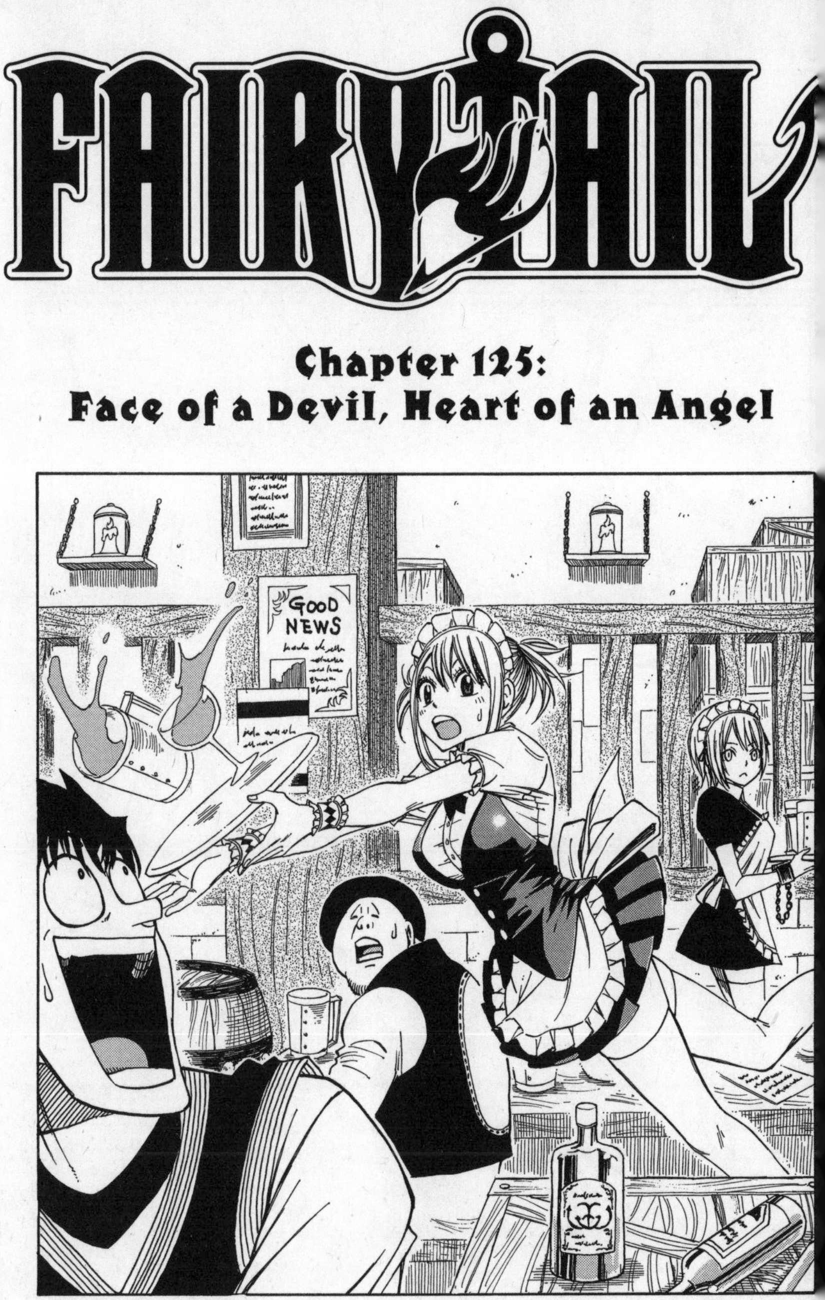
GOOD NEWS

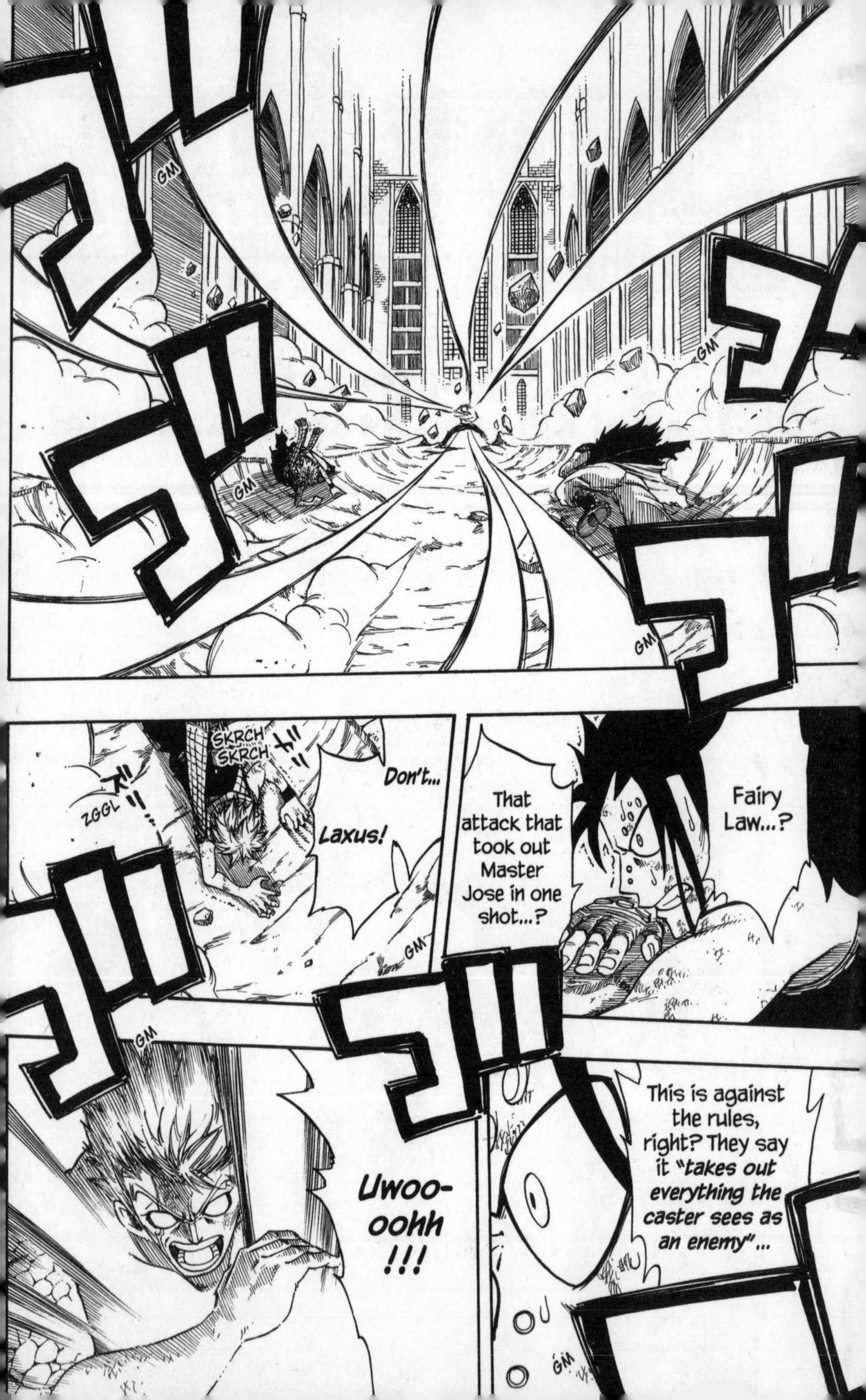
GM
GM
GM
GM
GM
Fairy Law...?
That attack that took out Master Jose in one shot...?
SKRCH SKRCH
ZGGL
Don't...
Laxus!
GM
This is against the rules, right? They say it "*takes out everything the caster sees as an enemy*"...
GM
GM
Uwoo-oohh!!!

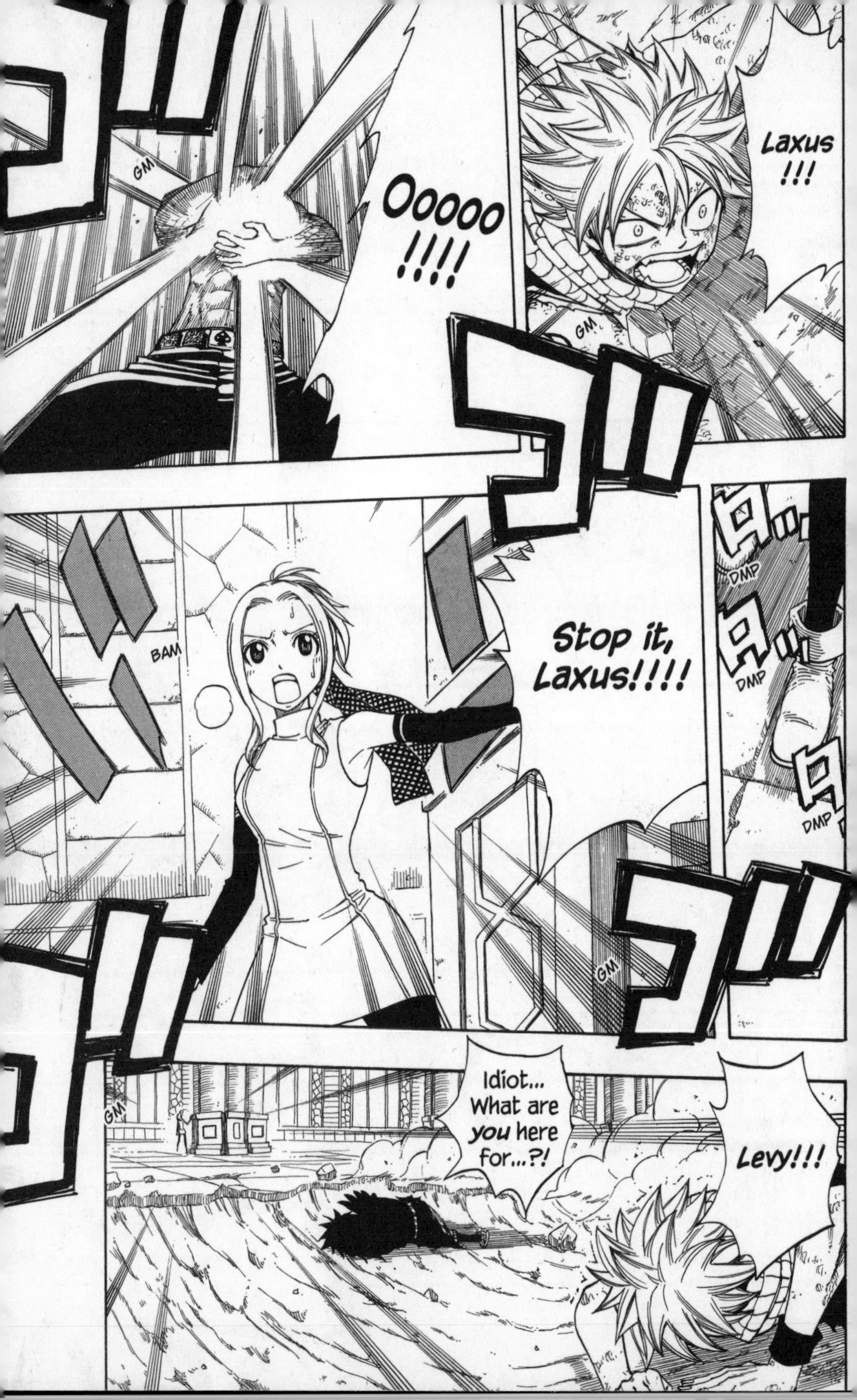
Laxus!!!
GM
Ooooo!!!!
GM
DMP
DMP
DMP
Stop it, Laxus!!!!
BAM
GM
Levy!!!
Idiot... What are you here for...?!
GM

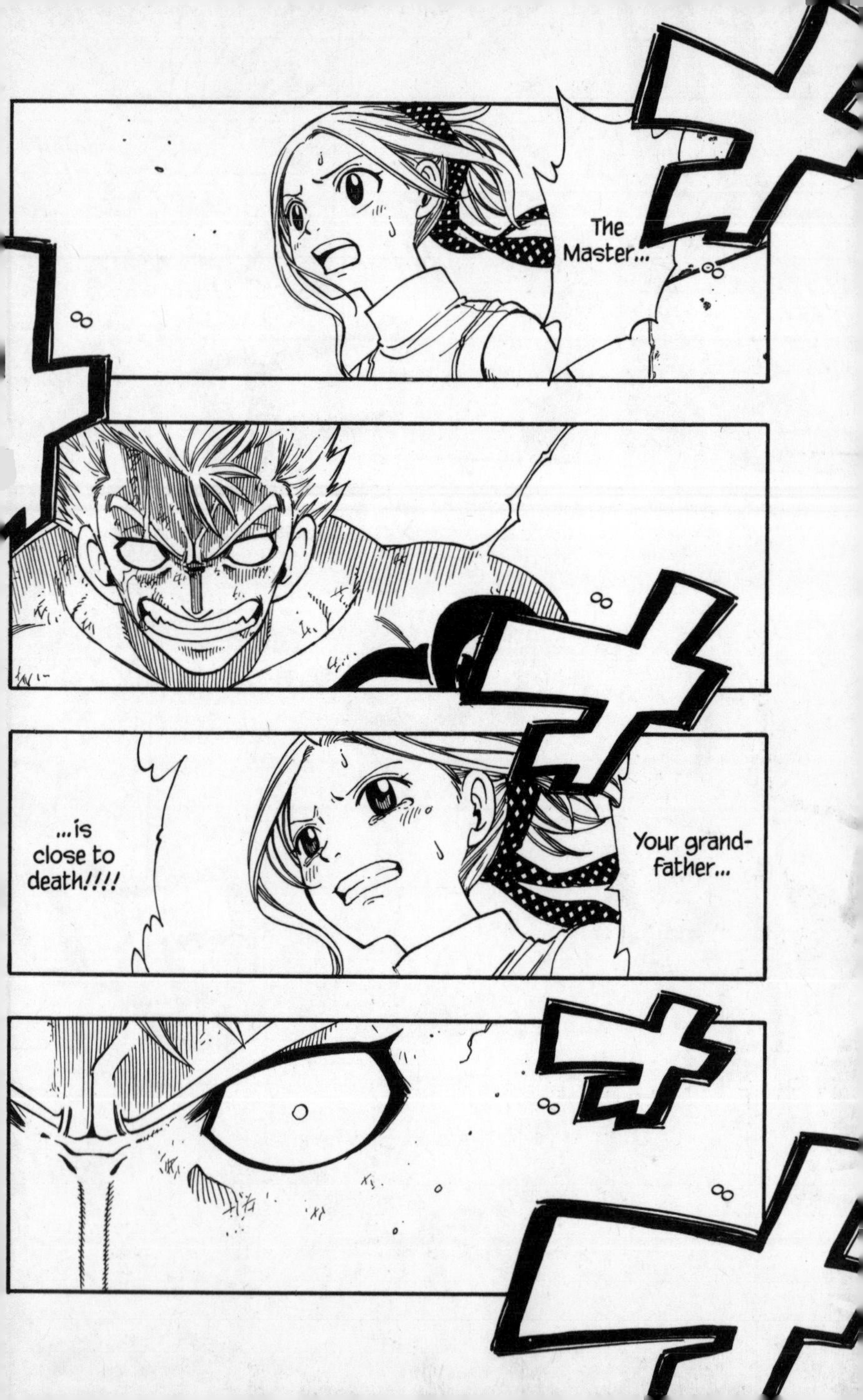
The Master...
Your grand-father...
...is close to death!!!!

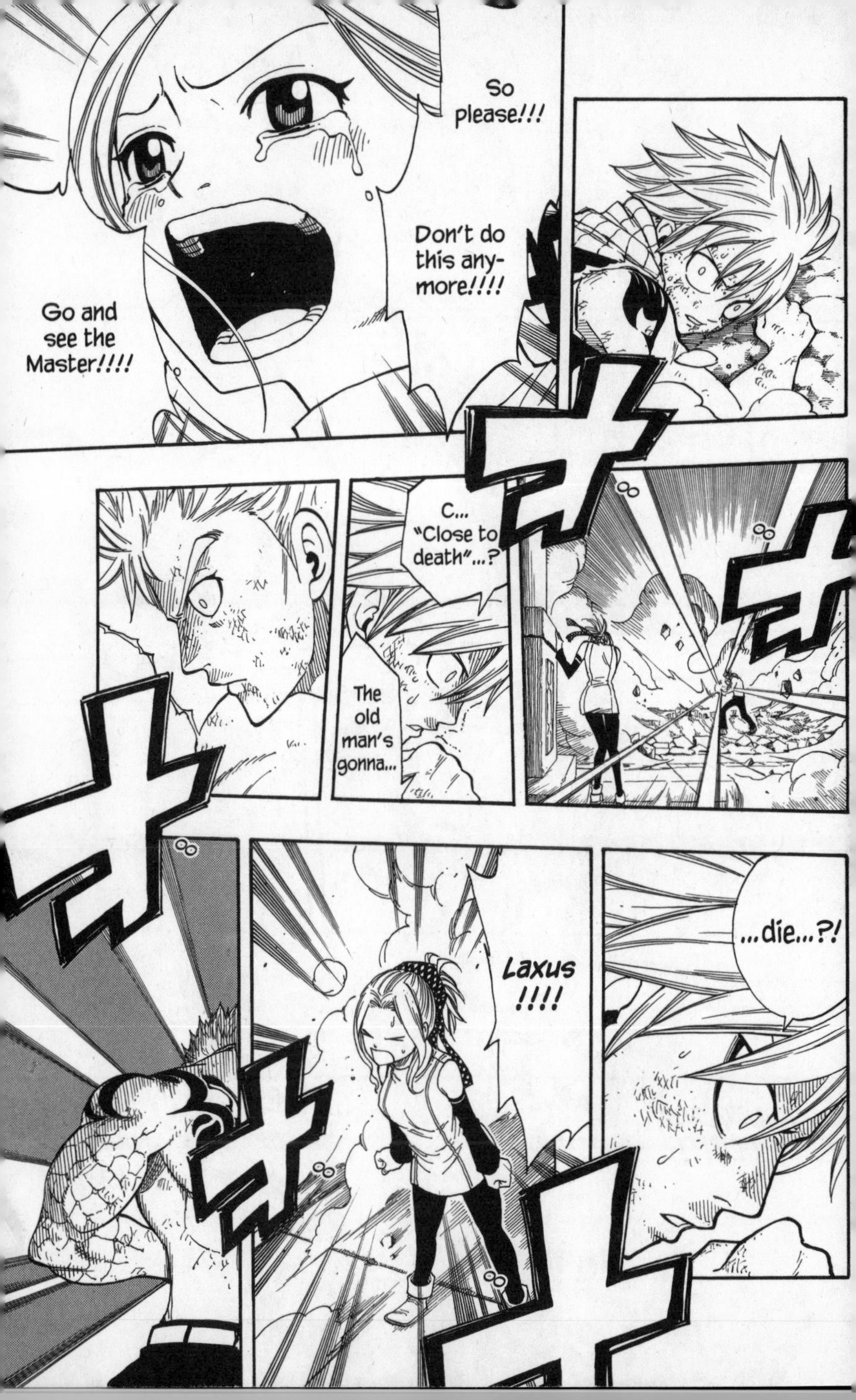
So please!!!
Don't do this anymore!!!!
Go and see the Master!!!!
C... "Close to death"...?
The old man's gonna...
...die...?!
Laxus !!!!

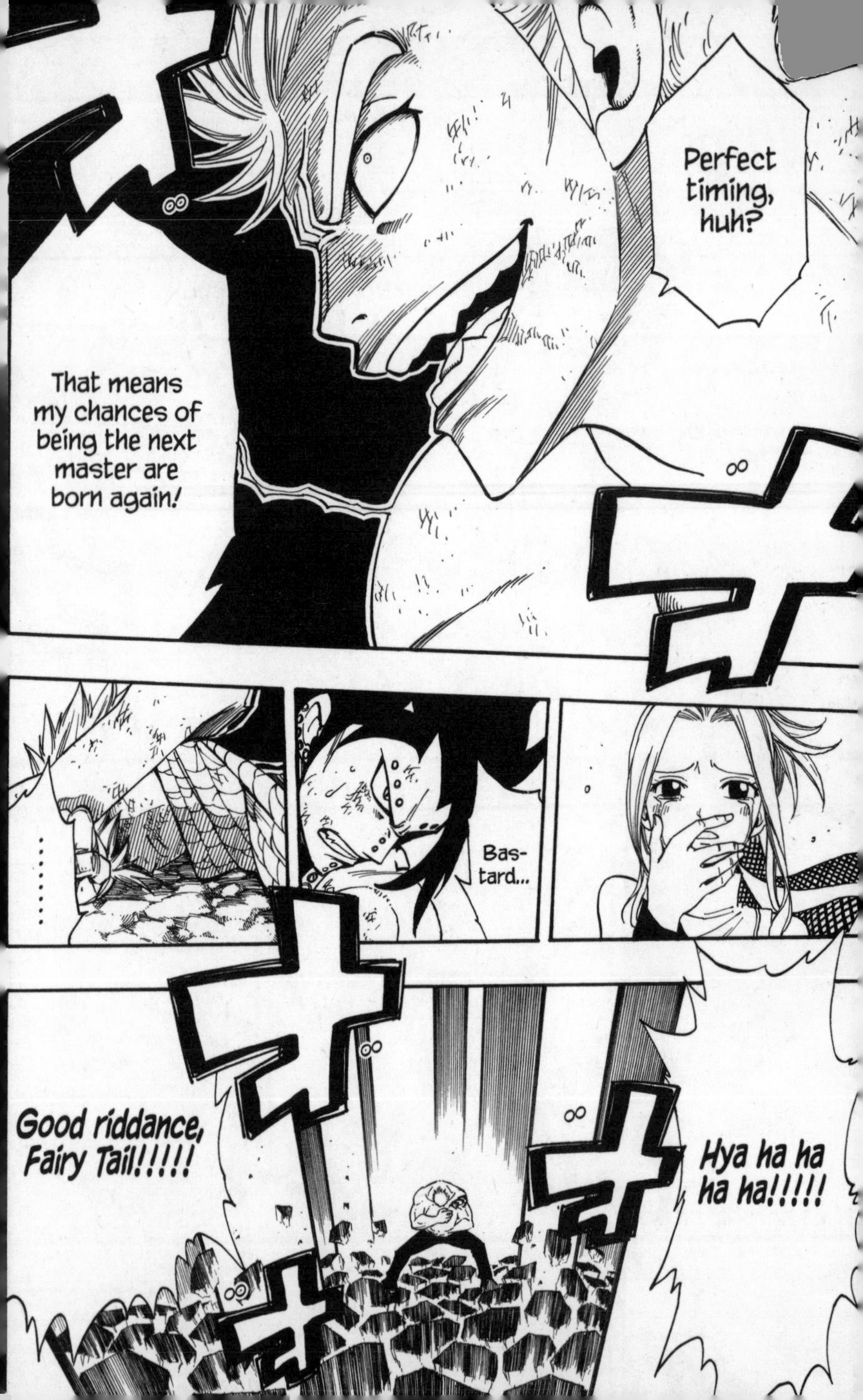
Perfect timing, huh?
That means my chances of being the next master are born again!
Bas-tard...
......
Hya ha ha ha ha!!!!!
Good riddance, Fairy Tail!!!!!

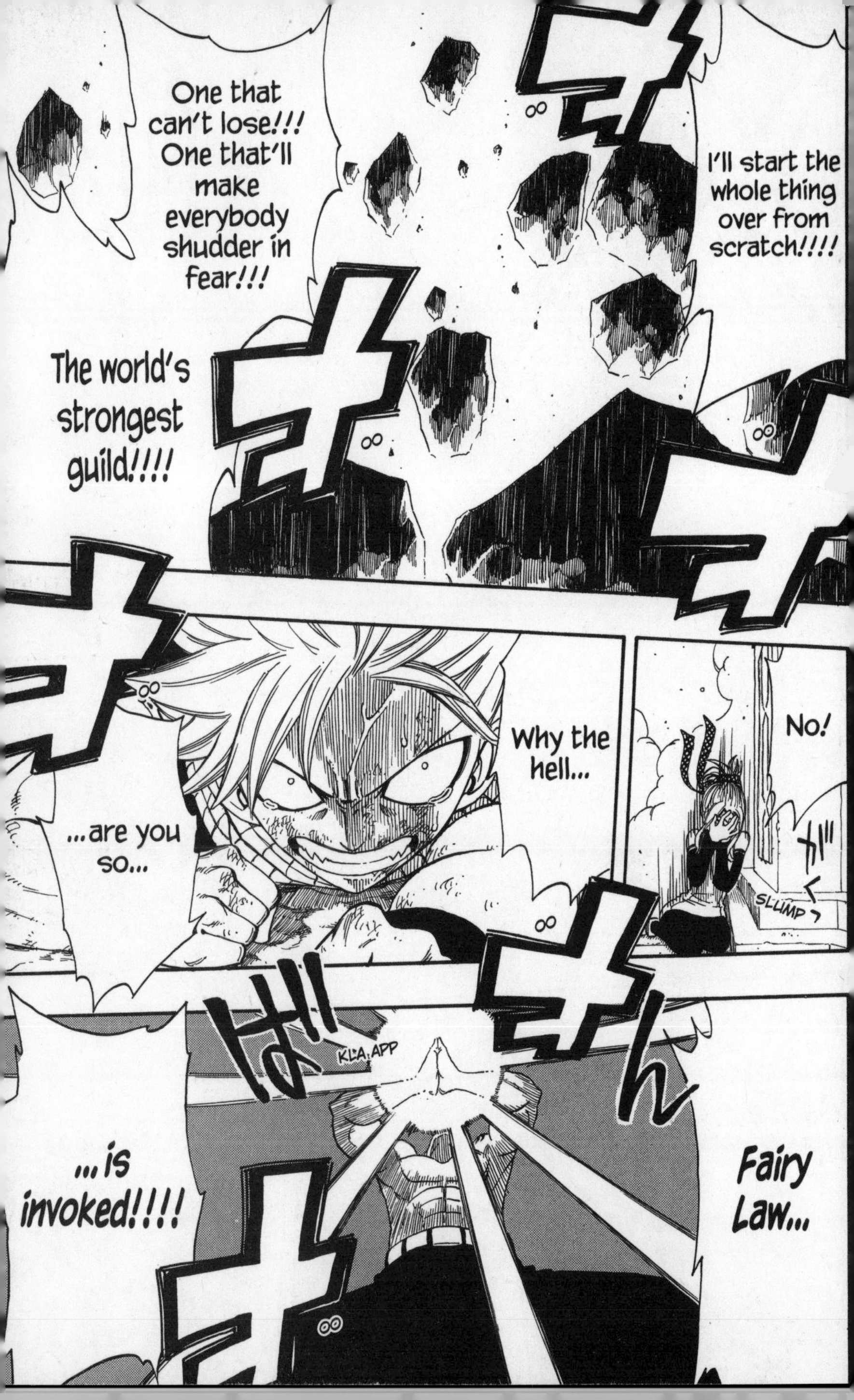
I'll start the whole thing over from scratch!!!!
One that can't lose!!! One that'll make everybody shudder in fear!!!
The world's strongest guild!!!!
No!
SLUMP
Why the hell...
...are you so...
Fairy Law...
KLAAPP
...is invoked!!!!

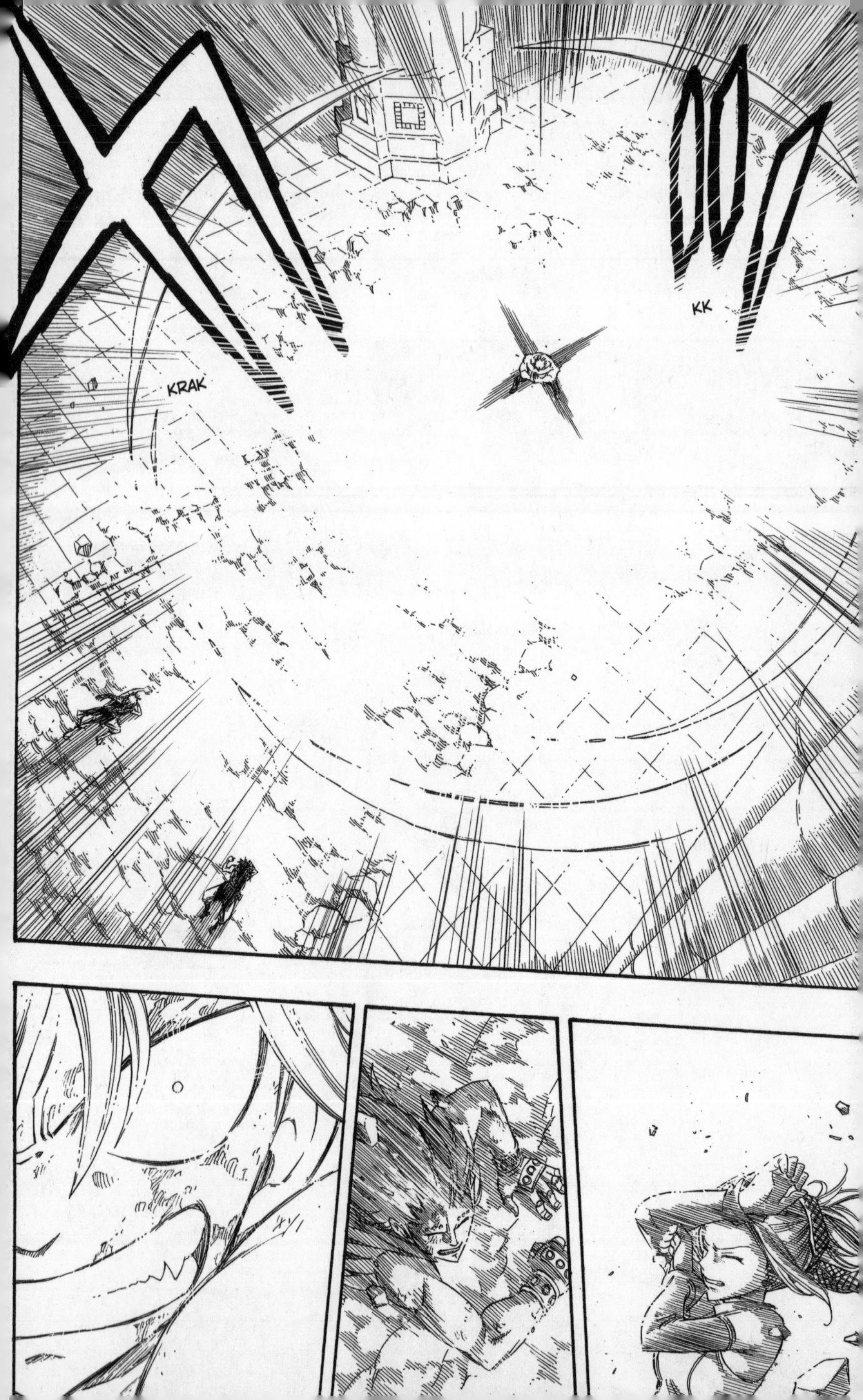
KK
KRAK

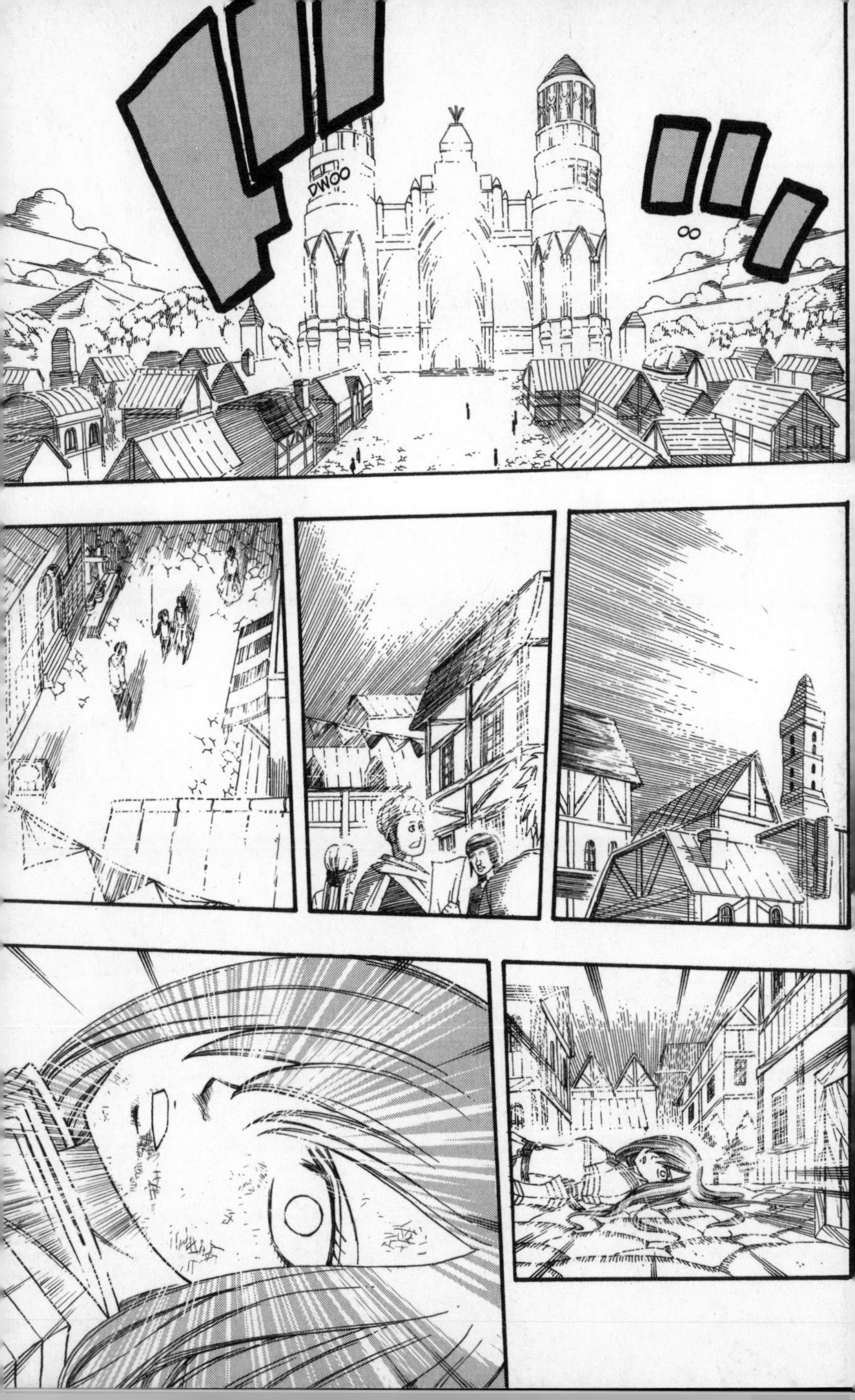
DWOO

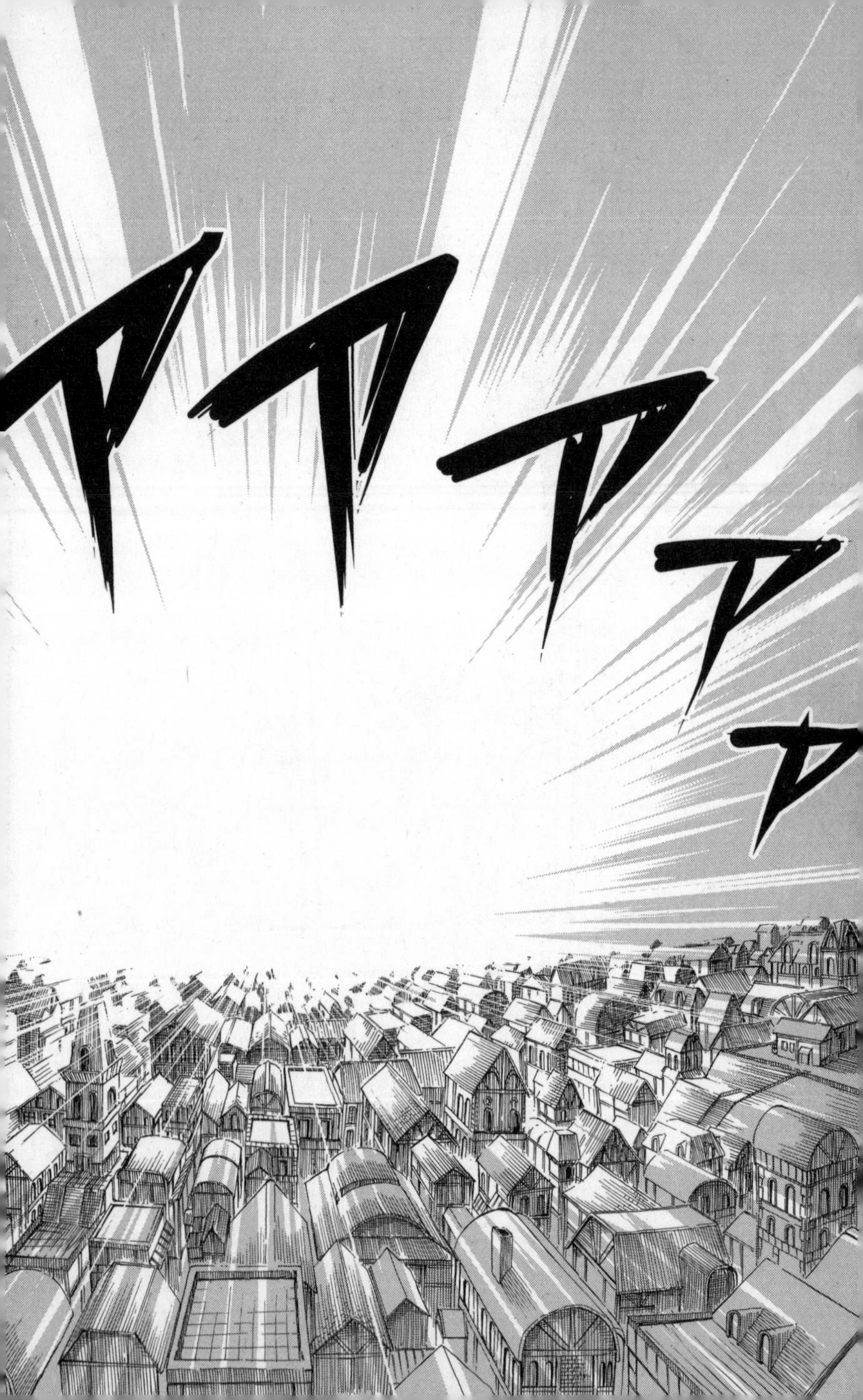
アアアアァ

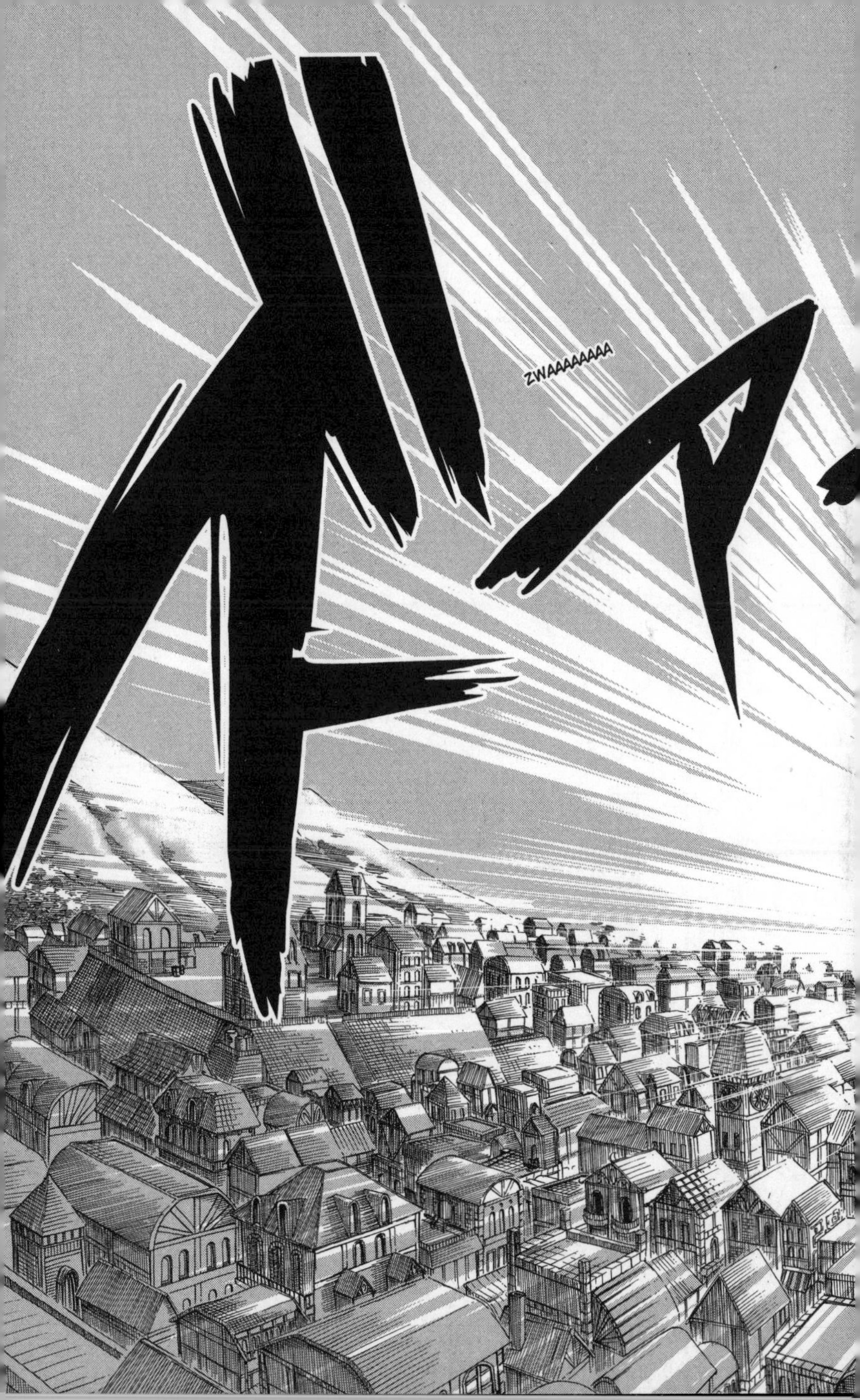
ZWAAAAAAAA

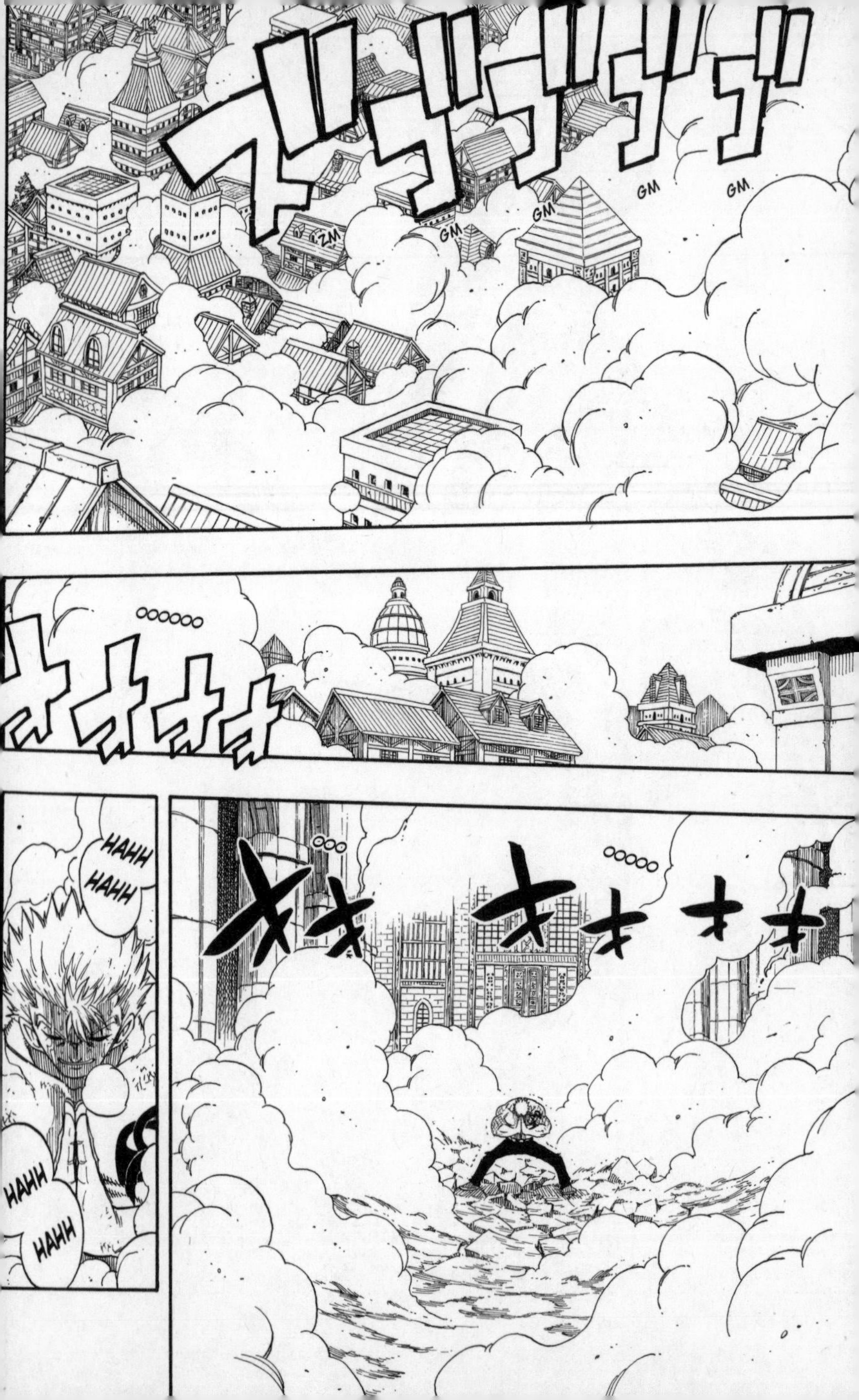

GM
GM
GM
GM
ZM
OOOOOO
OOOOO
OOO
HAHH HAHH
HAHH HAHH

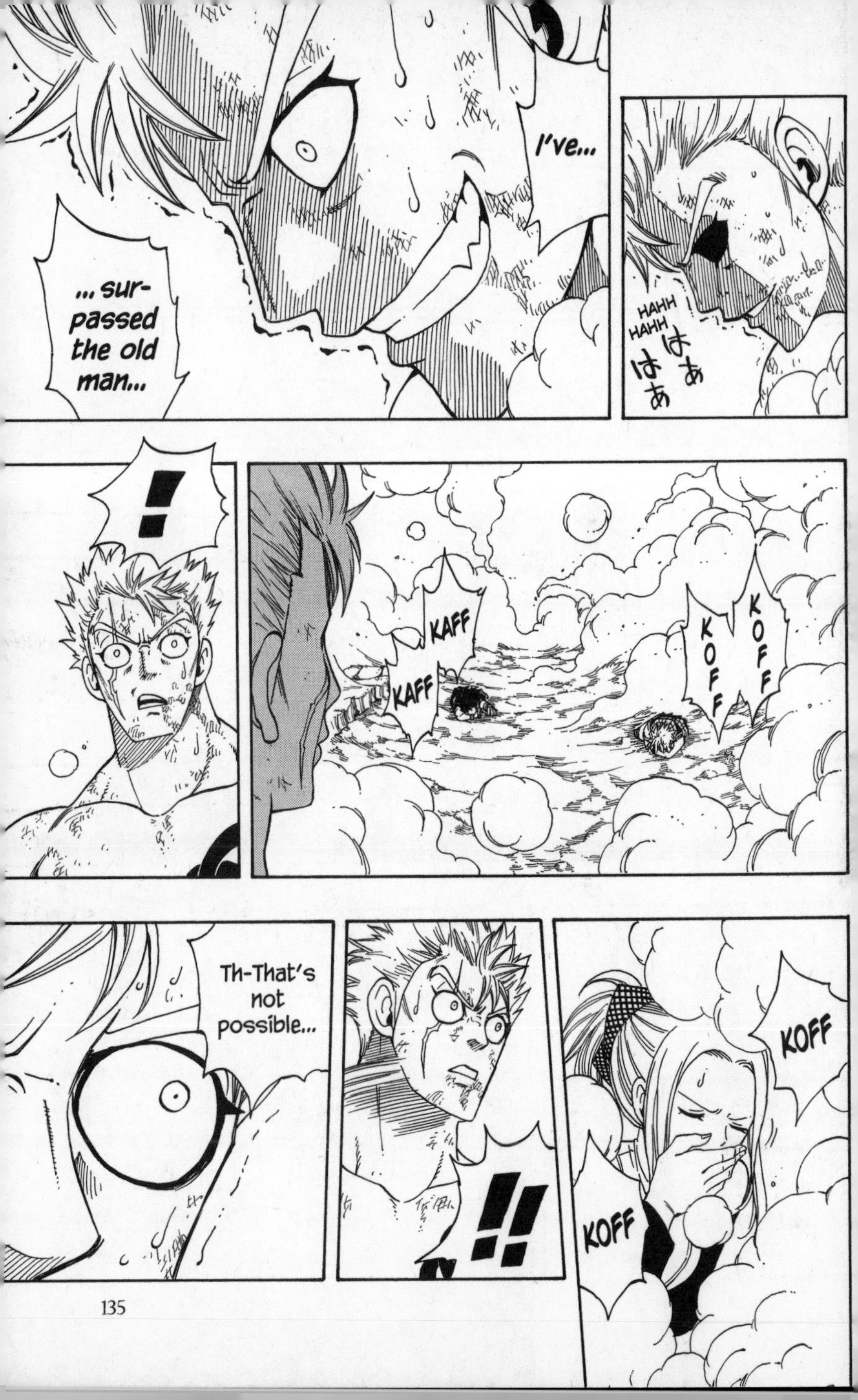
HAHH HAHH
はぁはぁ
I've...
... sur-passed the old man...
KOFF KOFF
KOFF KOFF
KAFF
KAFF
!
KOFF
KOFF
!!
Th-That's not possible...

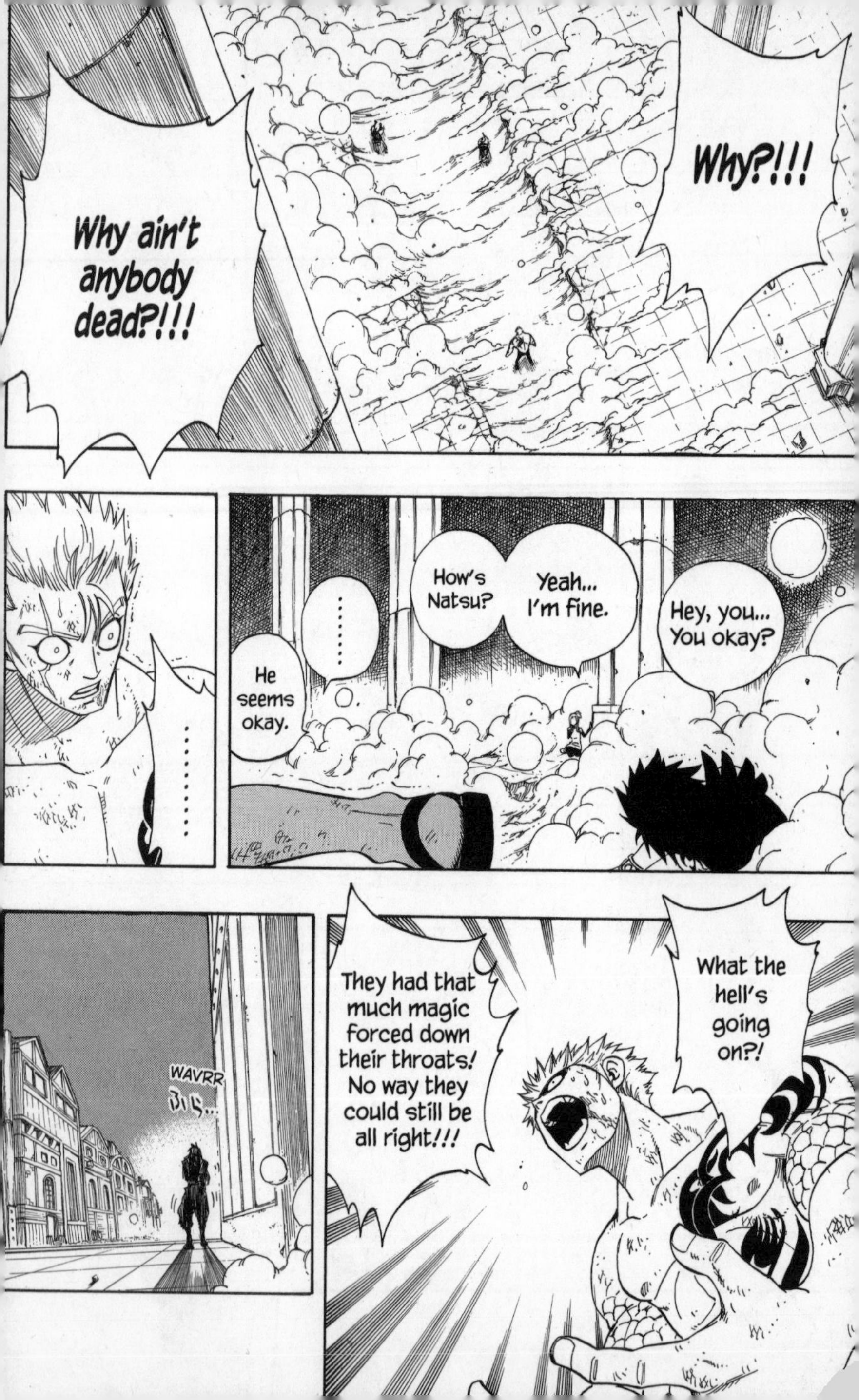
Why?!!!
Why ain't anybody dead?!!!
Hey, you... You okay?
Yeah... I'm fine.
How's Natsu?
......
He seems okay.
......
What the hell's going on?!
They had that much magic forced down their throats! No way they could still be all right!!!
WAVRR
ふら…

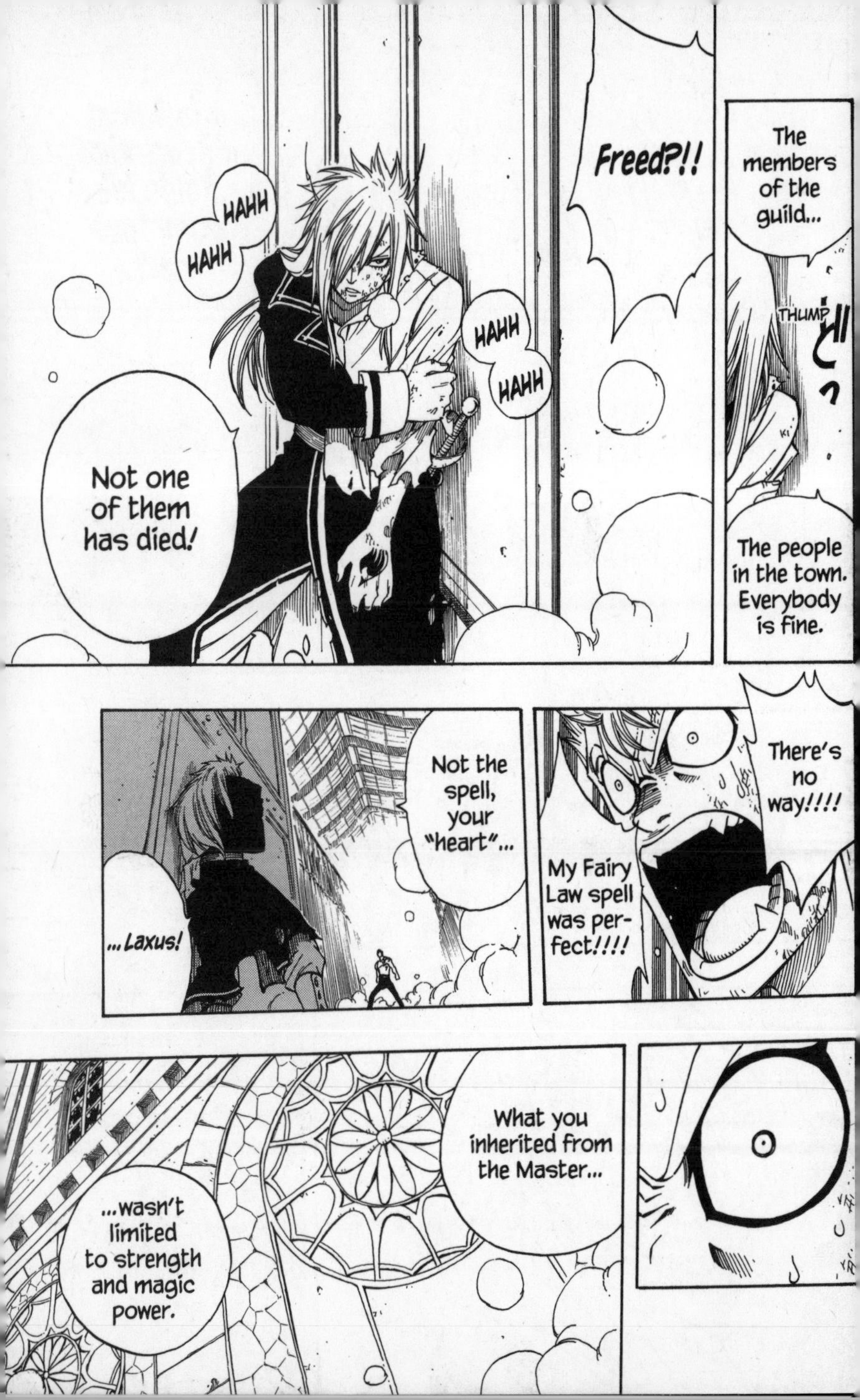
The members of the guild...
THUMP
The people in the town. Everybody is fine.
Freed?!!
HAHH
HAHH
HAHH
HAHH
Not one of them has died!
There's no way!!!!
My Fairy Law spell was perfect!!!!
Not the spell, your "heart"...
...Laxus!
What you inherited from the Master...
...wasn't limited to strength and magic power.

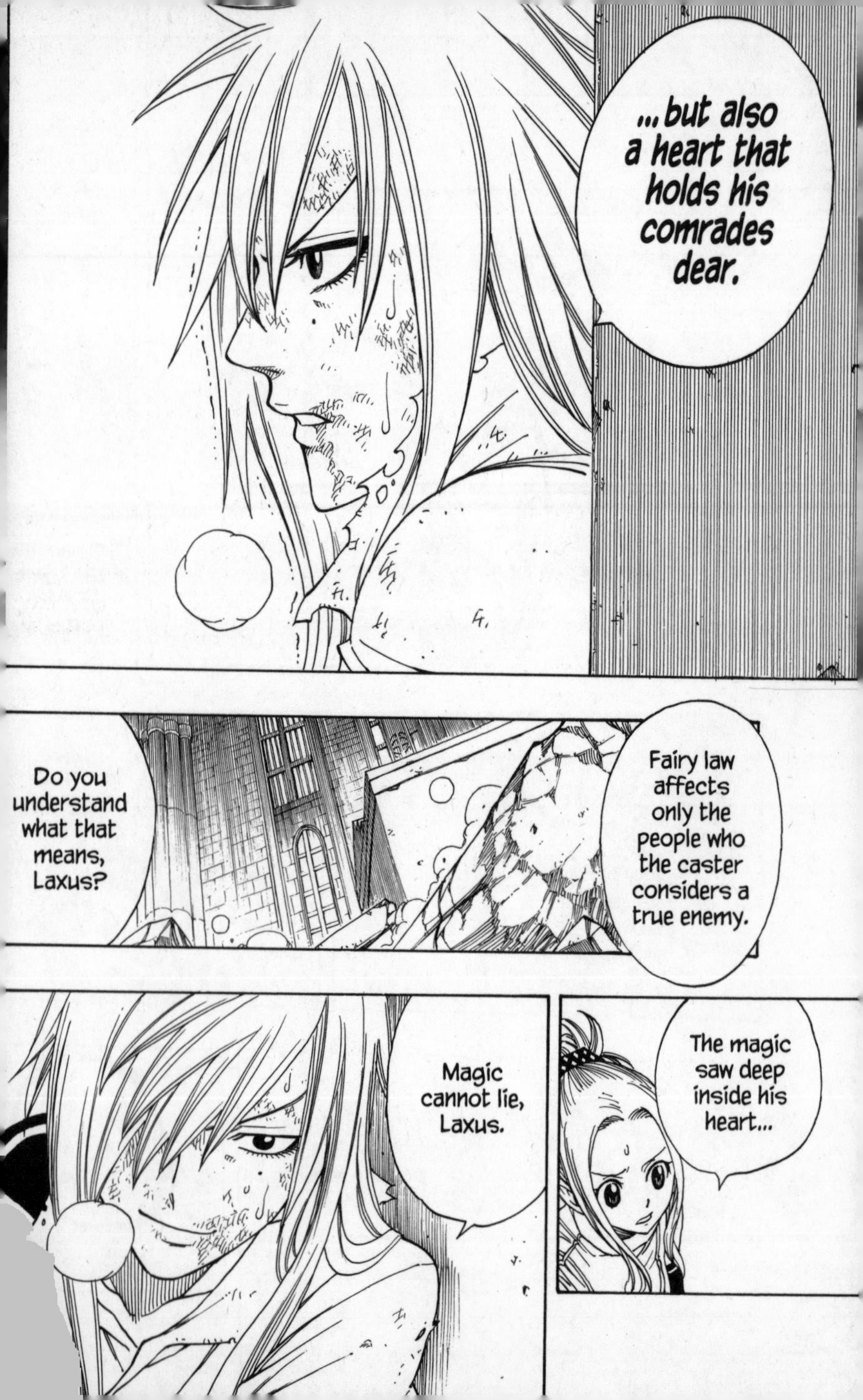
...but also a heart that holds his comrades dear.
Fairy law affects only the people who the caster considers a true enemy.
Do you understand what that means, Laxus?
The magic saw deep inside his heart...
Magic cannot lie, Laxus.

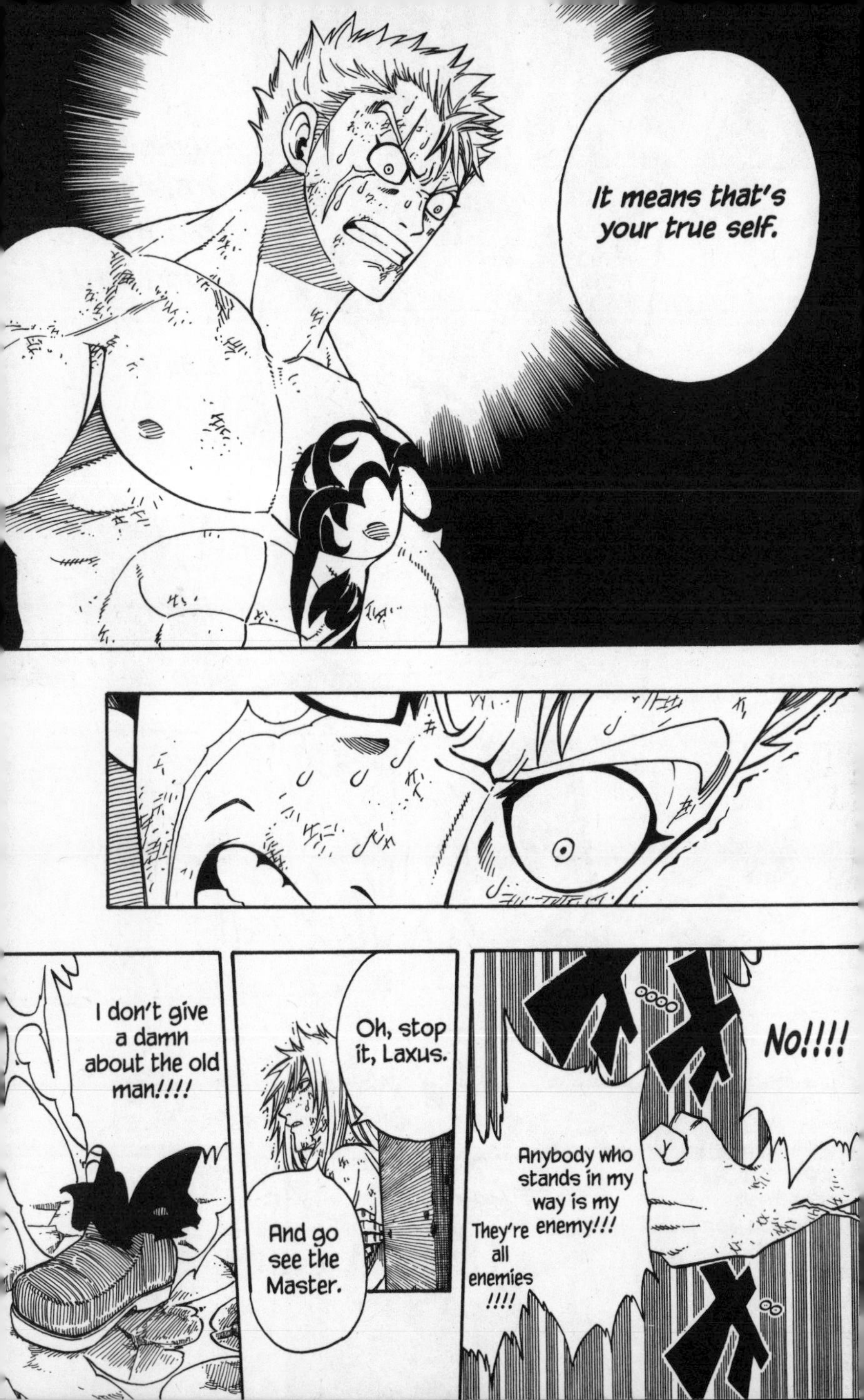

It means that's your true self.
No!!!!
Anybody who stands in my way is my enemy!!!
They're all enemies!!!!
Oh, stop it, Laxus.
And go see the Master.
I don't give a damn about the old man!!!!

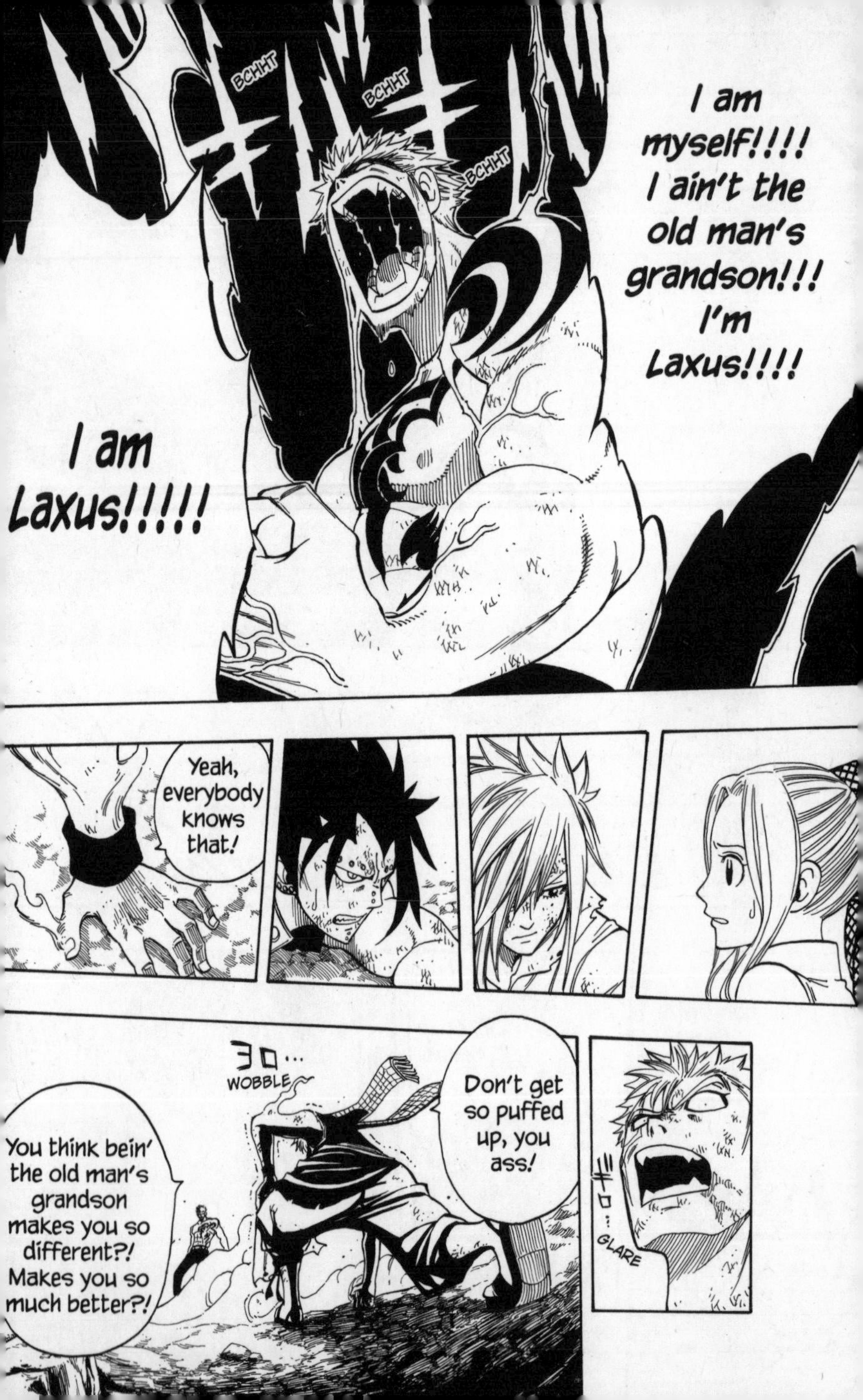
BCHHT
BCHHT
BCHHT
I am myself!!!! I ain't the old man's grandson!!! I'm Laxus!!!!
I am Laxus!!!!!
Yeah, everybody knows that!
ギロ… GLARE
ヨロ… WOBBLE
Don't get so puffed up, you ass!
You think bein' the old man's grandson makes you so different?! Makes you so much better?!

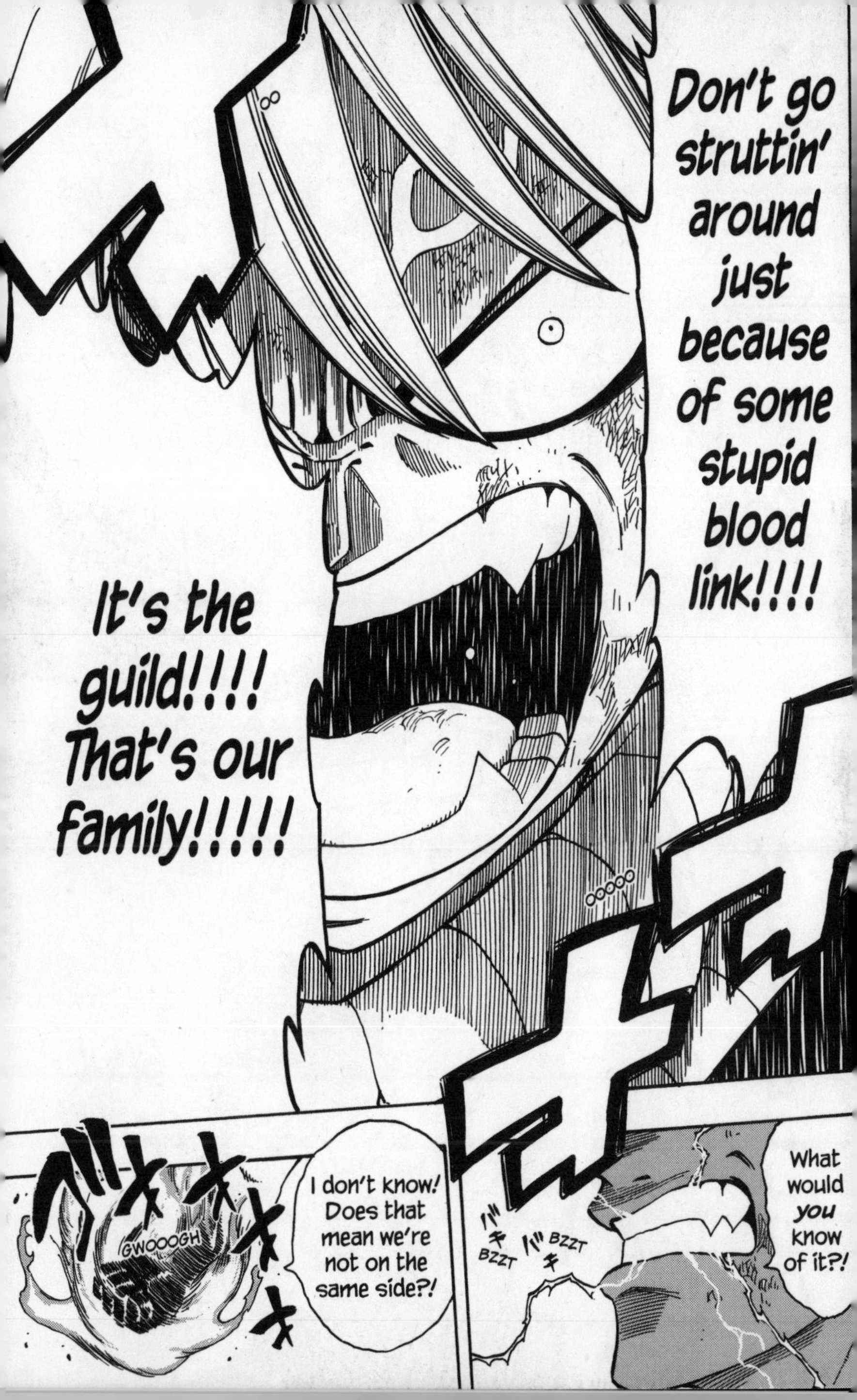
Don't go struttin' around just because of some stupid blood link!!!!
It's the guild!!!! That's our family!!!!!
What would *you* know of it?!
BZZT
BZZT
I don't know! Does that mean we're not on the same side?!
GWOOOGH

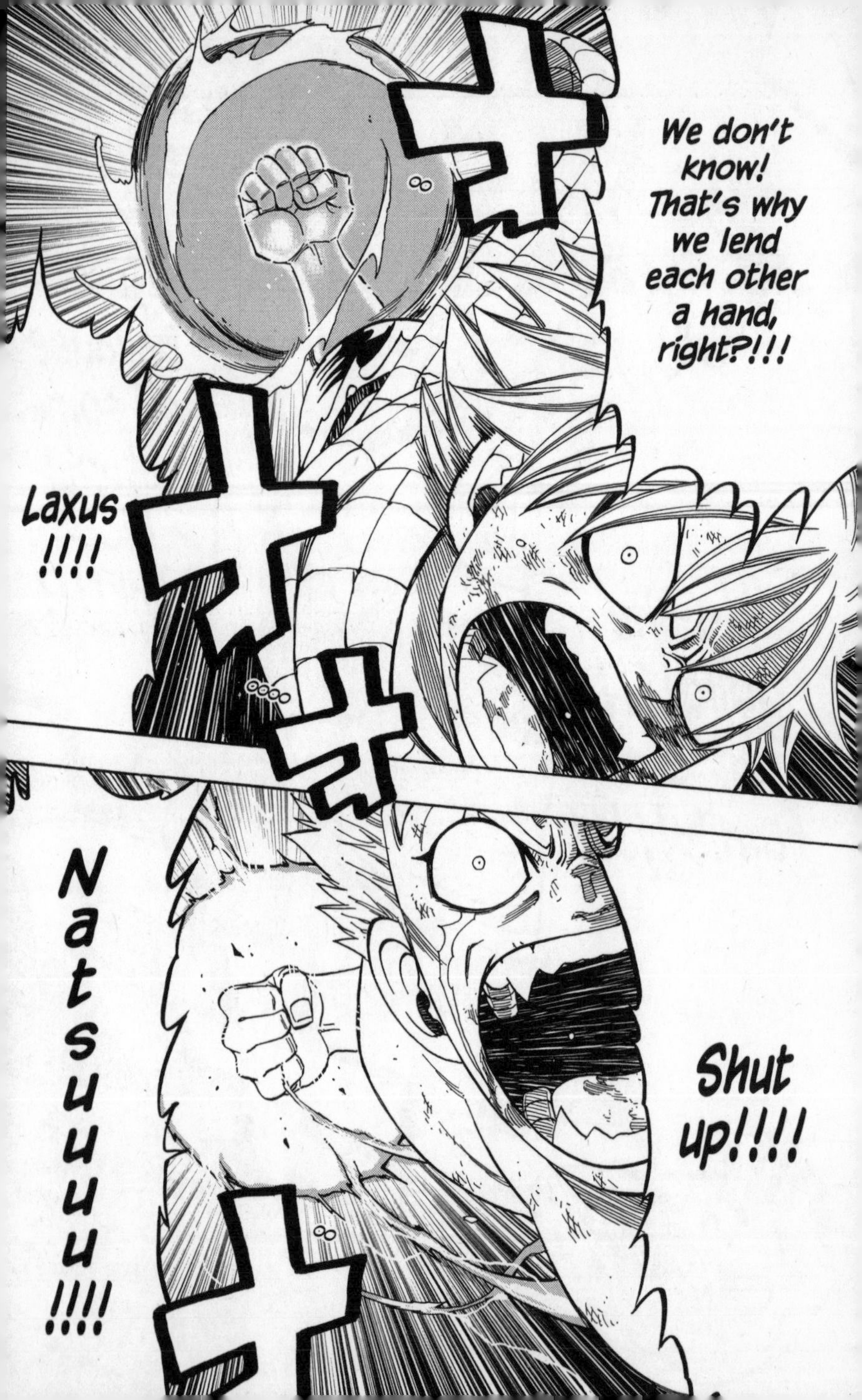
We don't know! That's why we lend each other a hand, right?!!!
Laxus !!!!
Shut up!!!!
Natsuuuu !!!!

FAIRY TAIL

Chapter 126: Stand Up!!!!

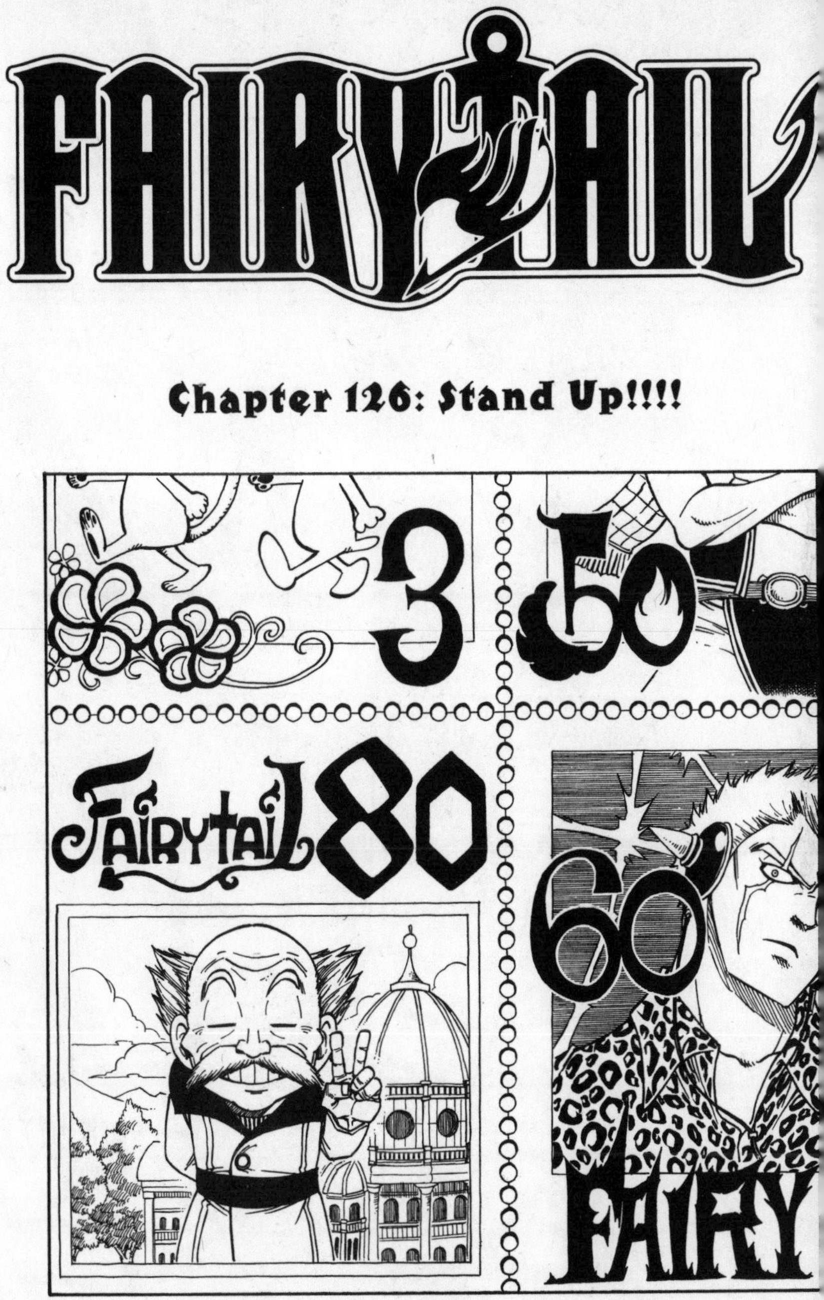
50
3
60
FAIRY
FAIRY TAIL
80

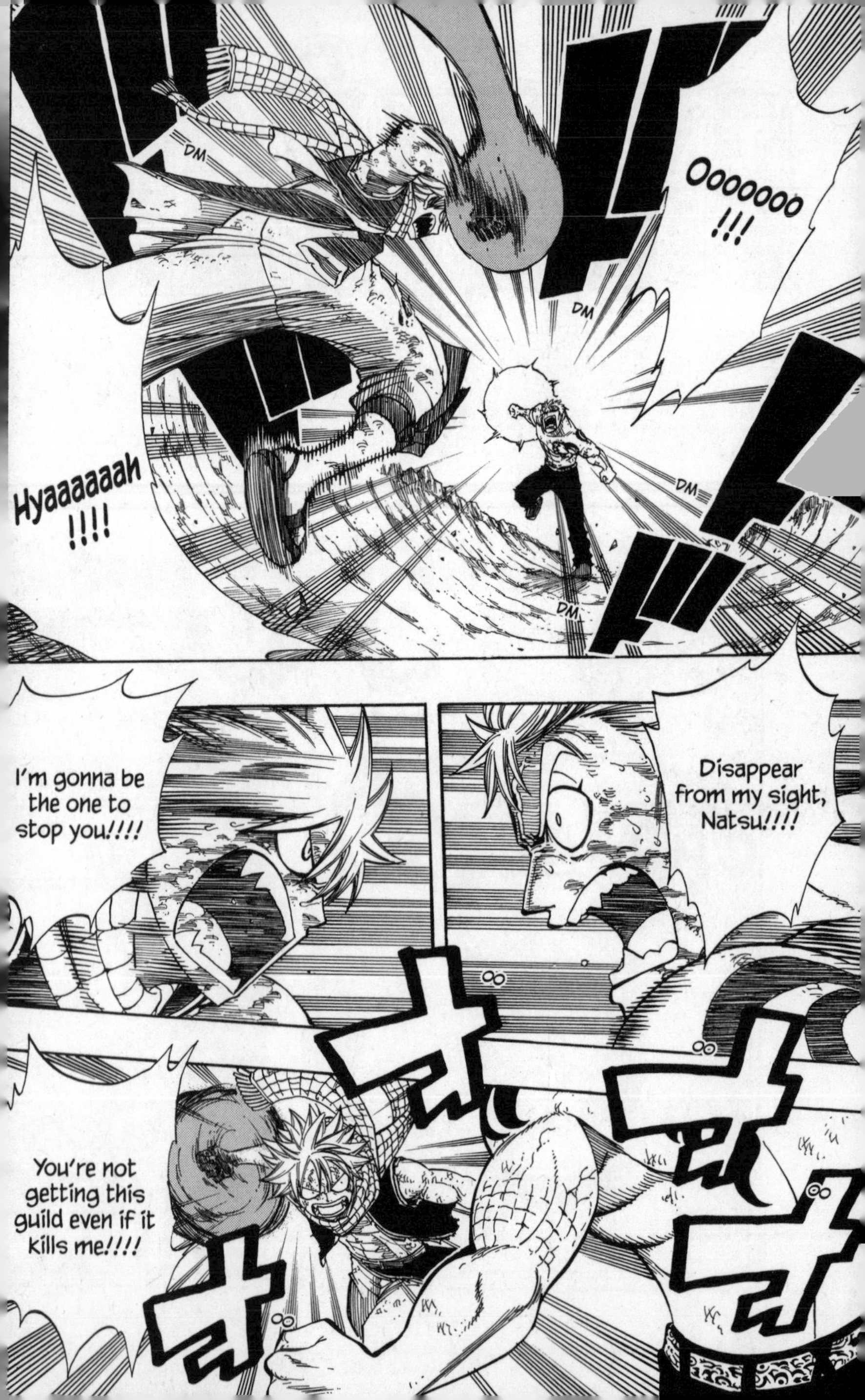
Oooooo !!!
DM
DM
DM
DM
Hyaaaaaah !!!!
Disappear from my sight, Natsu!!!!
I'm gonna be the one to stop you!!!!
You're not getting this guild even if it kills me!!!!

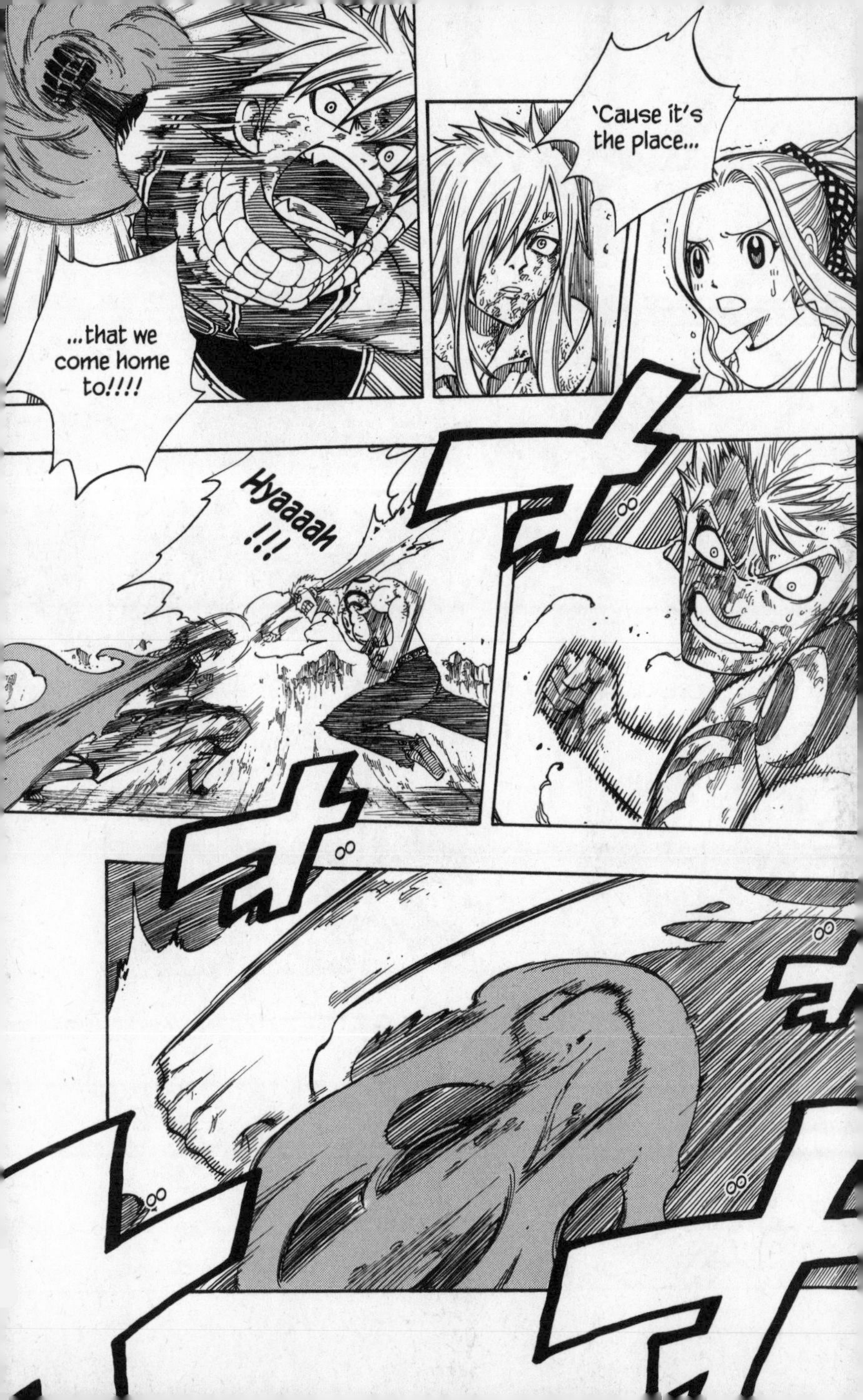
'Cause it's the place...
...that we come home to!!!!
Hyaaaaah!!!

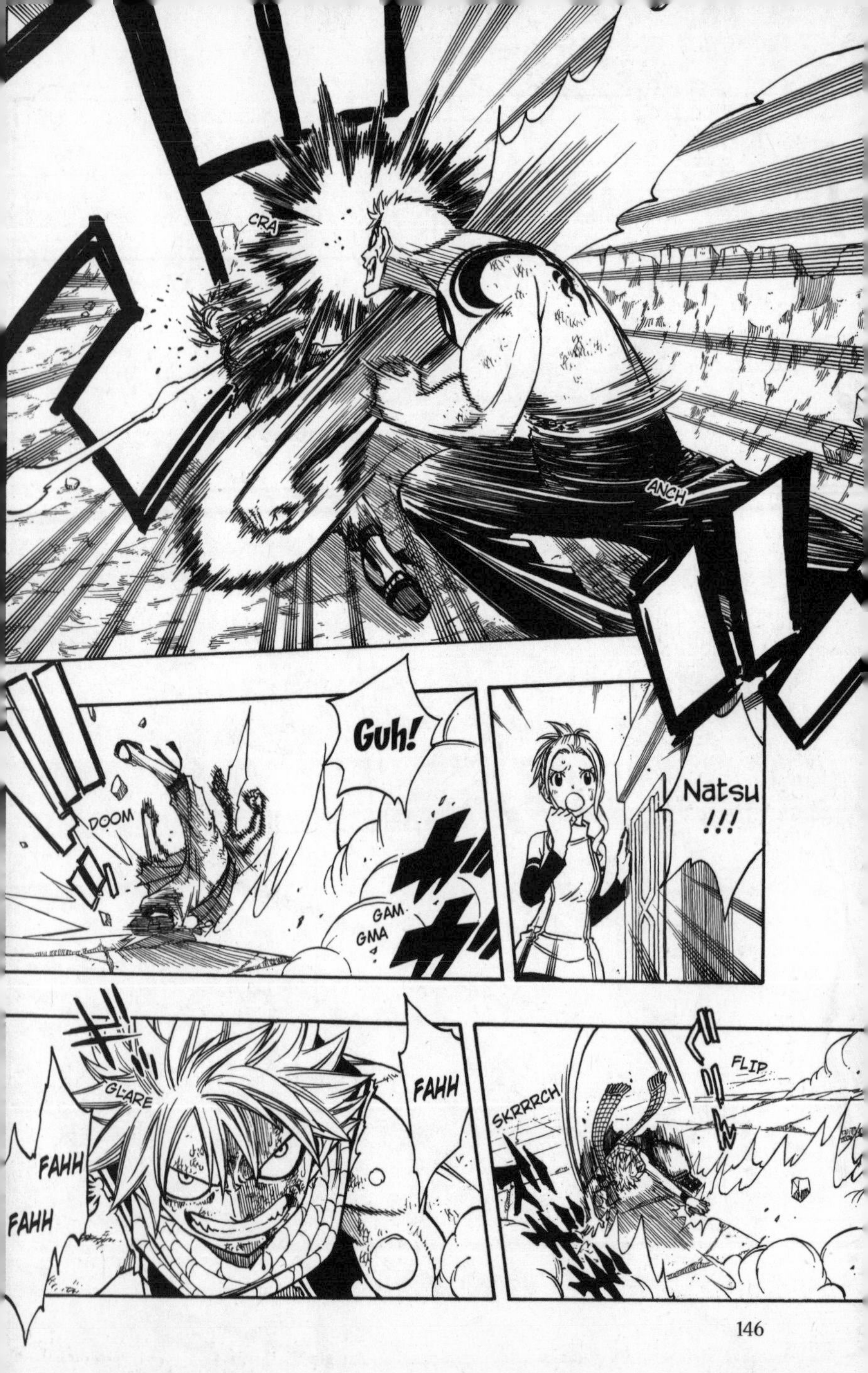
CRA
ANCH
Natsu !!!
Guh!
DOOM
GAM
GMA
FLIP
SKRRRCH
FAHH
GLARE
FAHH
FAHH

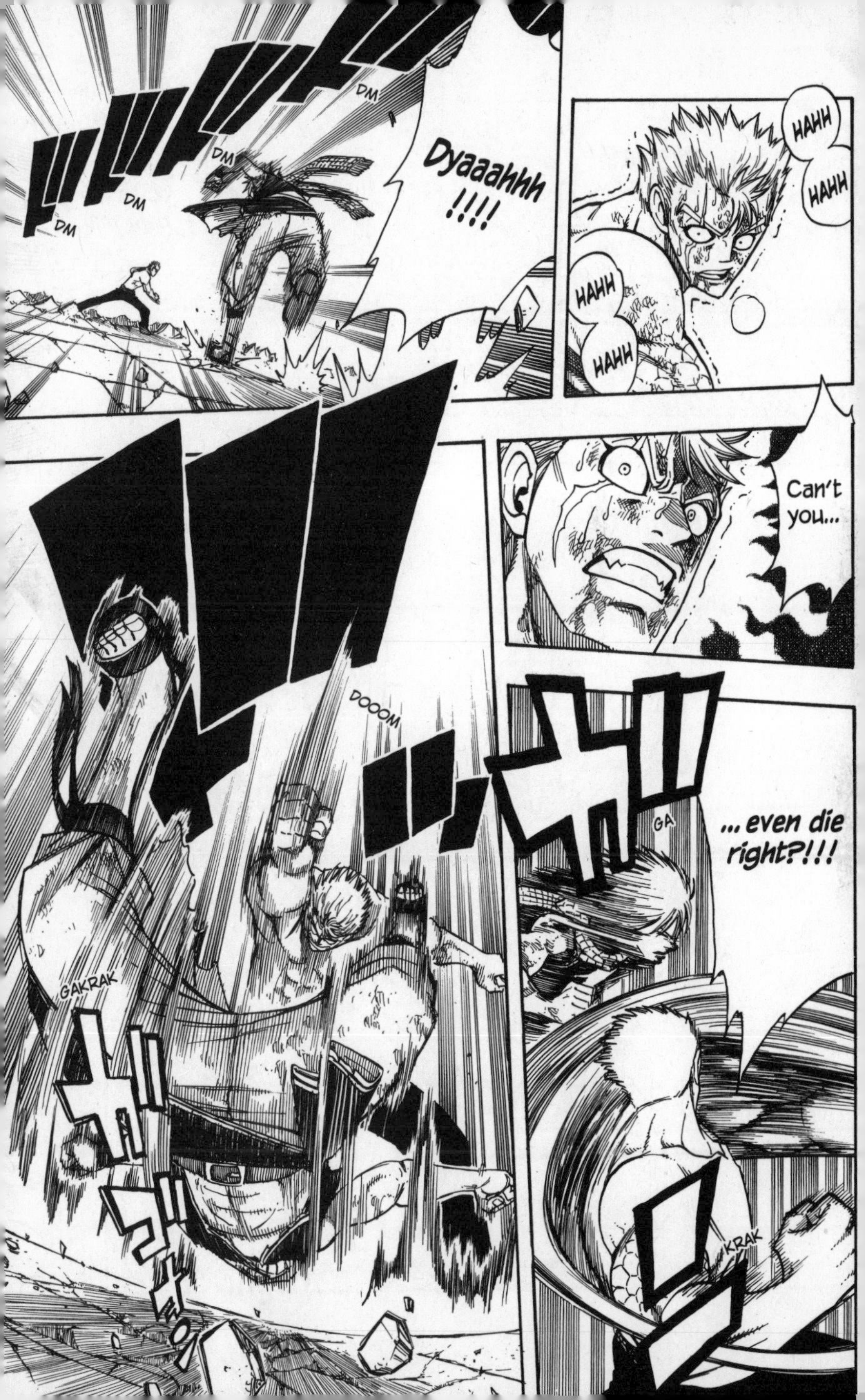
HAHH
HAHH
HAHH
HAHH
Dyaaahhh !!!!
DM
DM
DM
DM
Can't you...
GA
...even die right?!!!
KRAK
DOOOM
GAKRAK

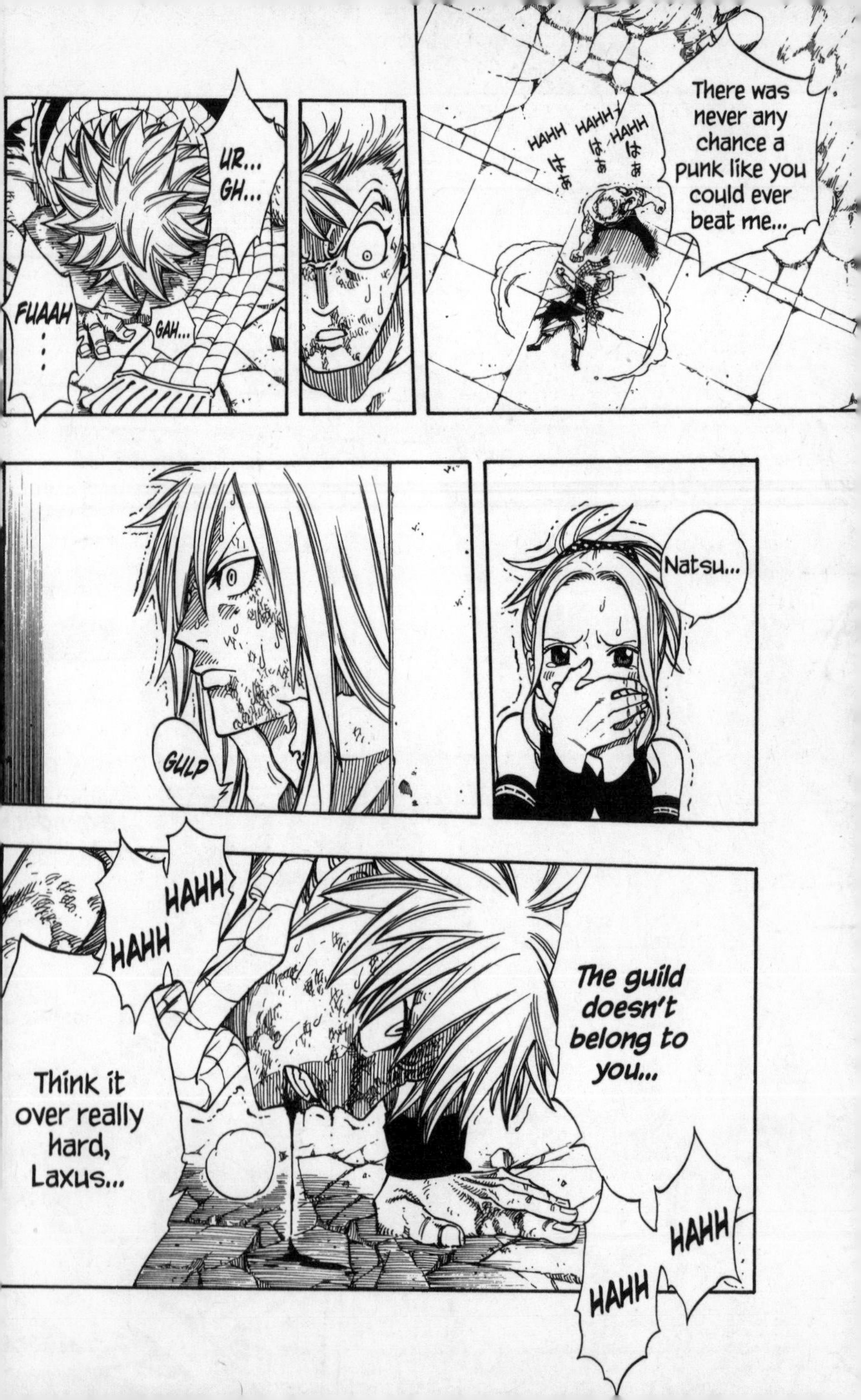
There was never any chance a punk like you could ever beat me...
HAHH HAHH HAHH
はぁ はぁ はぁ
UR... GH...
GAH...
FUAAH...
Natsu...
GULP
HAHH HAHH
The guild doesn't belong to you...
Think it over really hard, Laxus...
HAHH HAHH

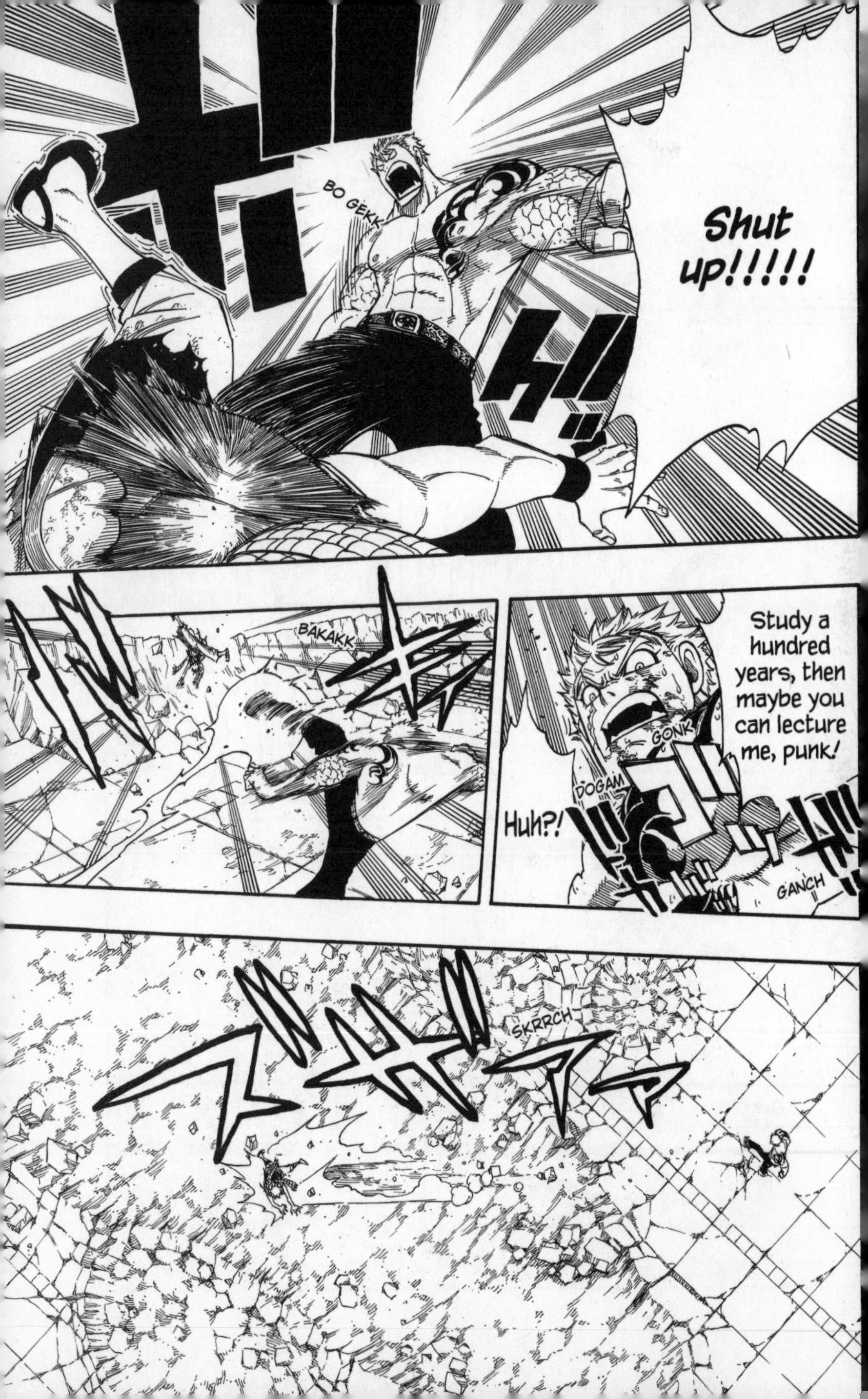
Shut up!!!!!
BO GEKK
Study a hundred years, then maybe you can lecture me, punk!
GONK
DOGAM
Huh?!
GANCH
BAKAKK
SKRRCH

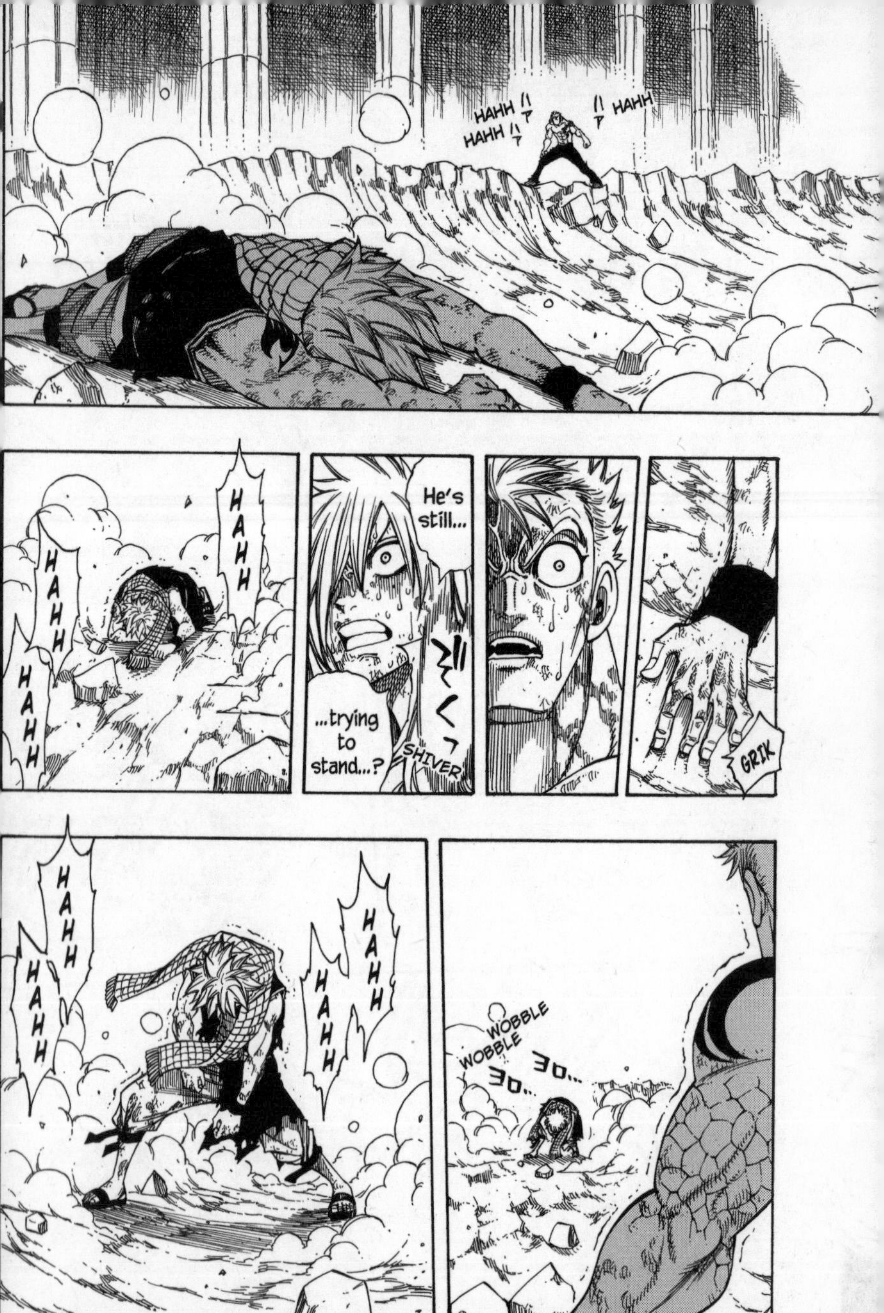
HAHH
HAHH
HAHH
GRIK
He's still...
...trying to stand...?
SHIVER
HAHH
HAHH
HAHH
WOBBLE
WOBBLE
HAHH
HAHH
HAHH
HAHH

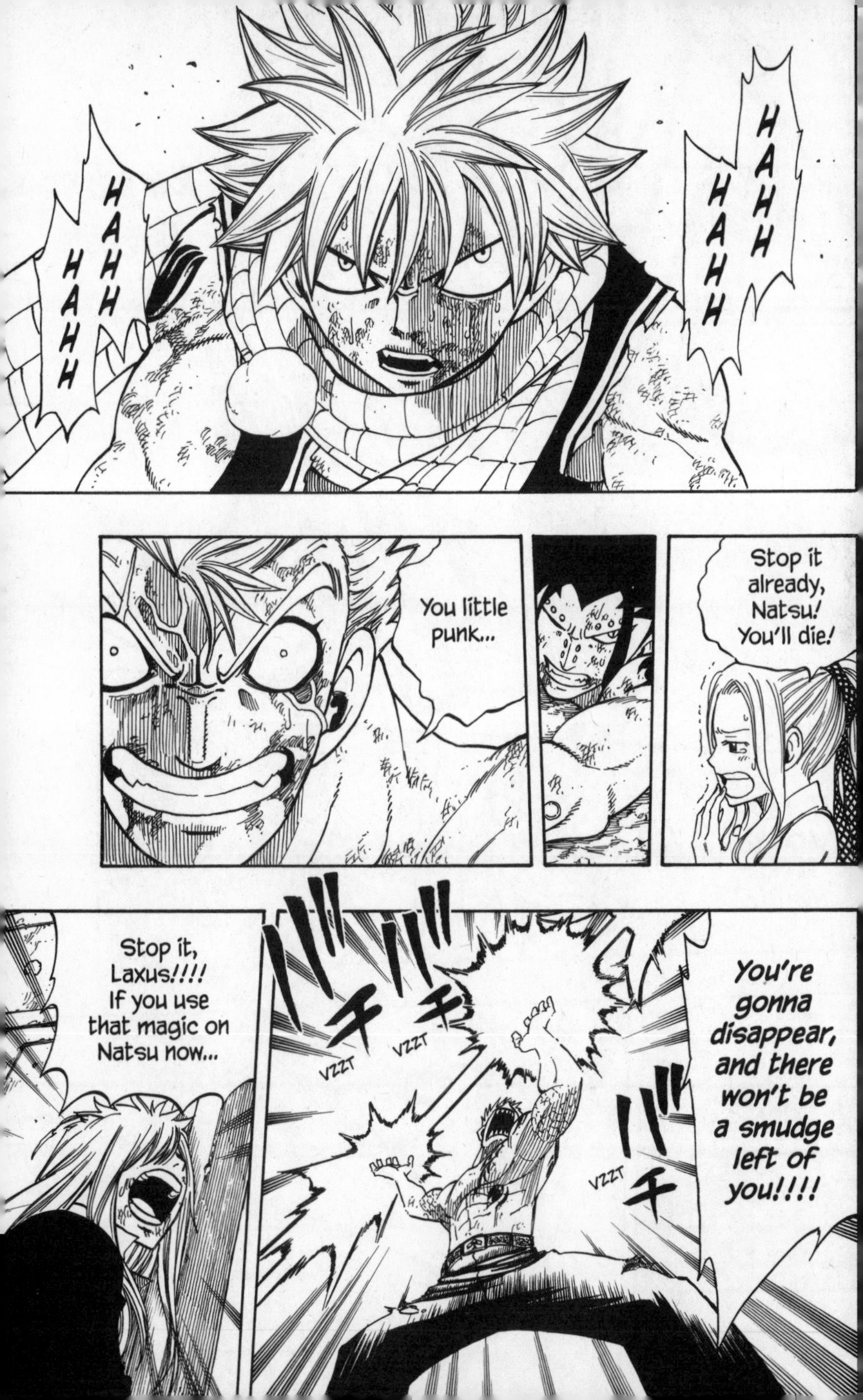
HAHH HAHH
HAHH HAHH
Stop it already, Natsu! You'll die!
You little punk...
You're gonna disappear, and there won't be a smudge left of you!!!!
VZZT
VZZT
VZZT
Stop it, Laxus!!!! If you use that magic on Natsu now...

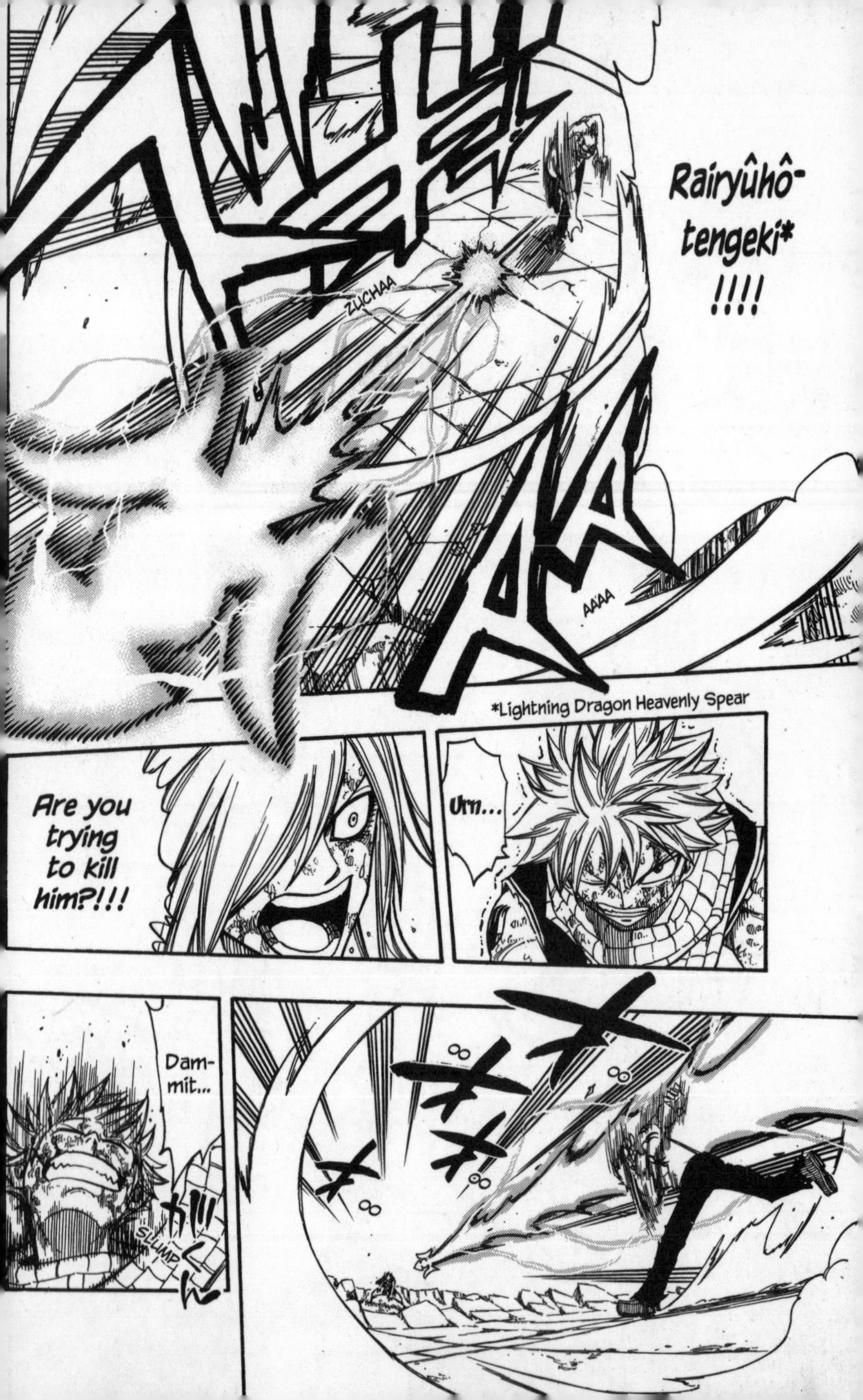
Rairyûhô-tengeki*!!!!
ZUCHAA
AAAA
*Lightning Dragon Heavenly Spear
Urn...
Are you trying to kill him?!!!
Dam-mit...
SLUMP

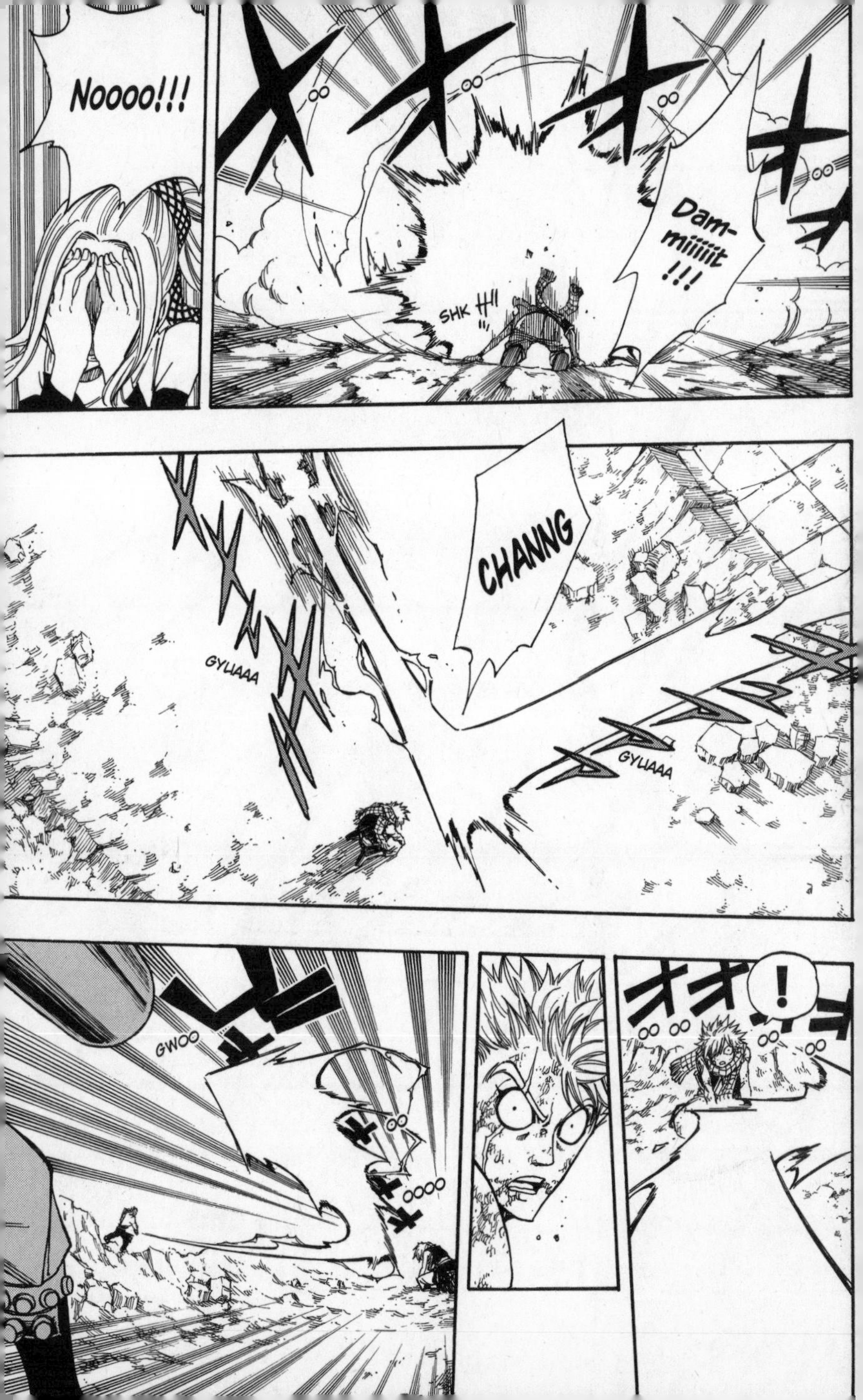
Dam-miiiiit!!!
SHK
Noooo!!!
CHANNG
GYUAAA
GYUAAA
!
GWOO
OOOO

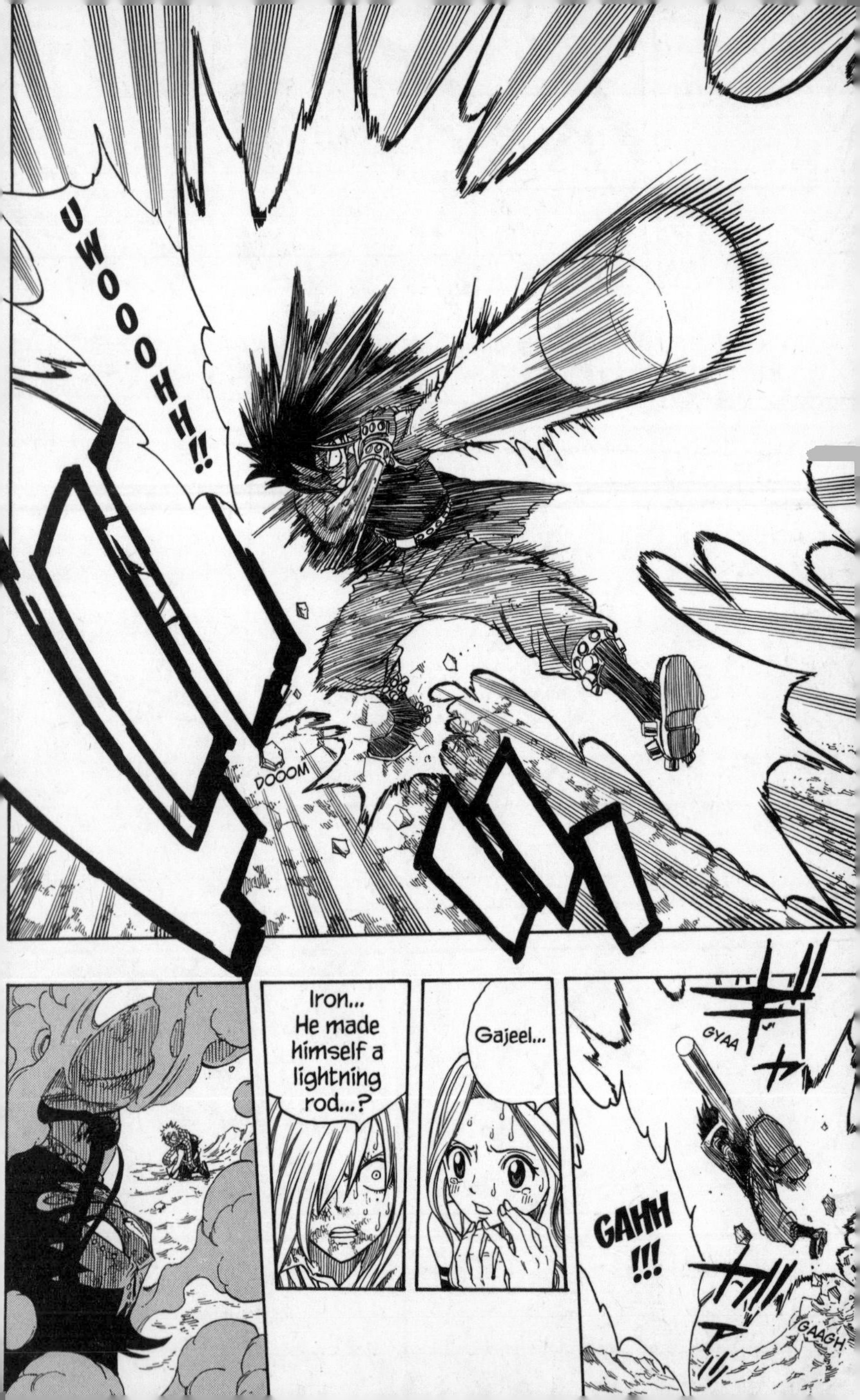
UWOOOOHH!!
DOOOM
GYAA
GAHH!!!
GAAGH
Gajeel...
Iron... He made himself a lightning rod...?

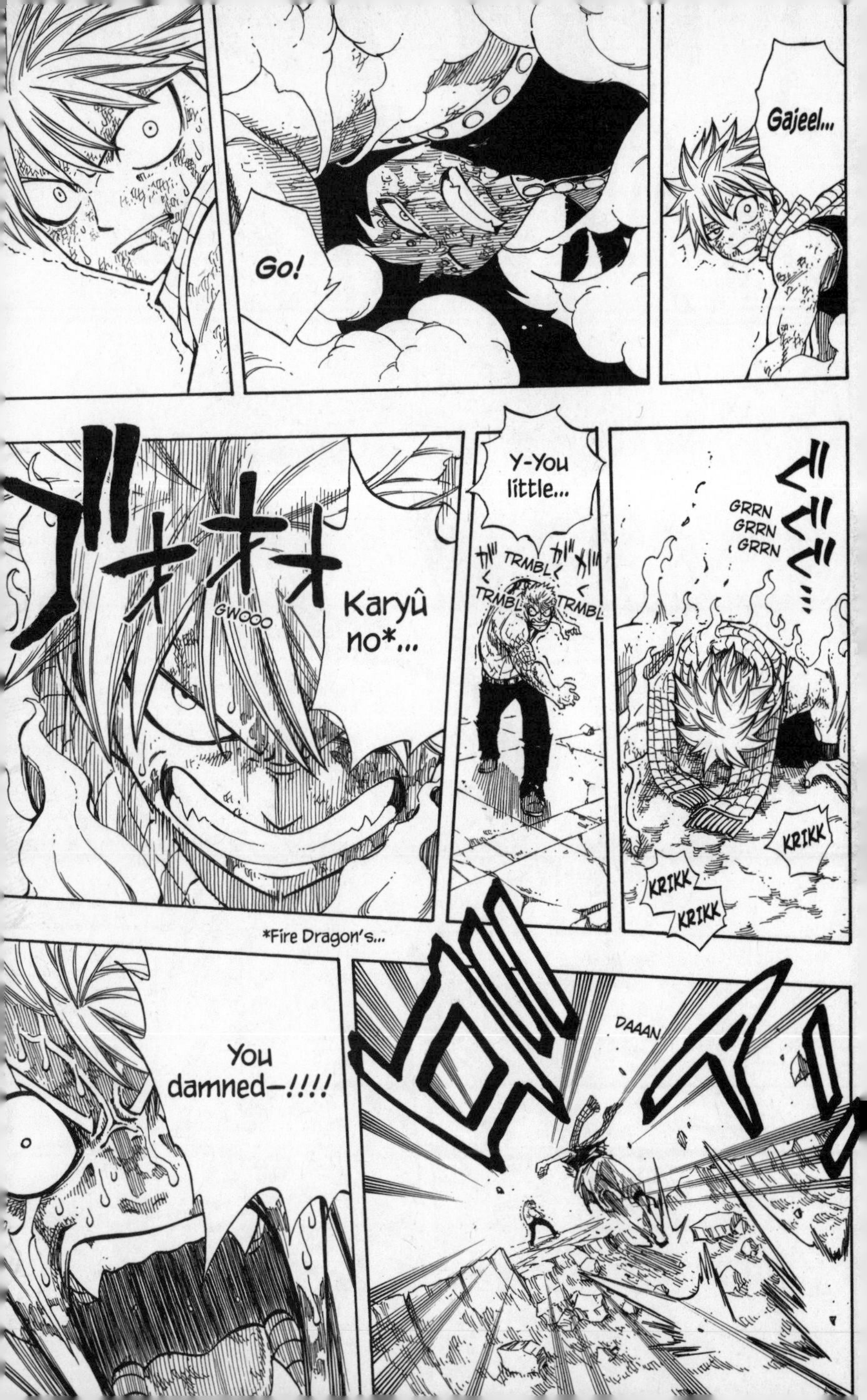
Gajeel...
Go!
GRRN
GRRN
GRRN
KRIKK
KRIKK
KRIKK
Y-You little...
TRMBL
TRMBL
TRMBL
GWOOO
Karyû no*...
DAAAN
You damned—!!!!
*Fire Dragon's...

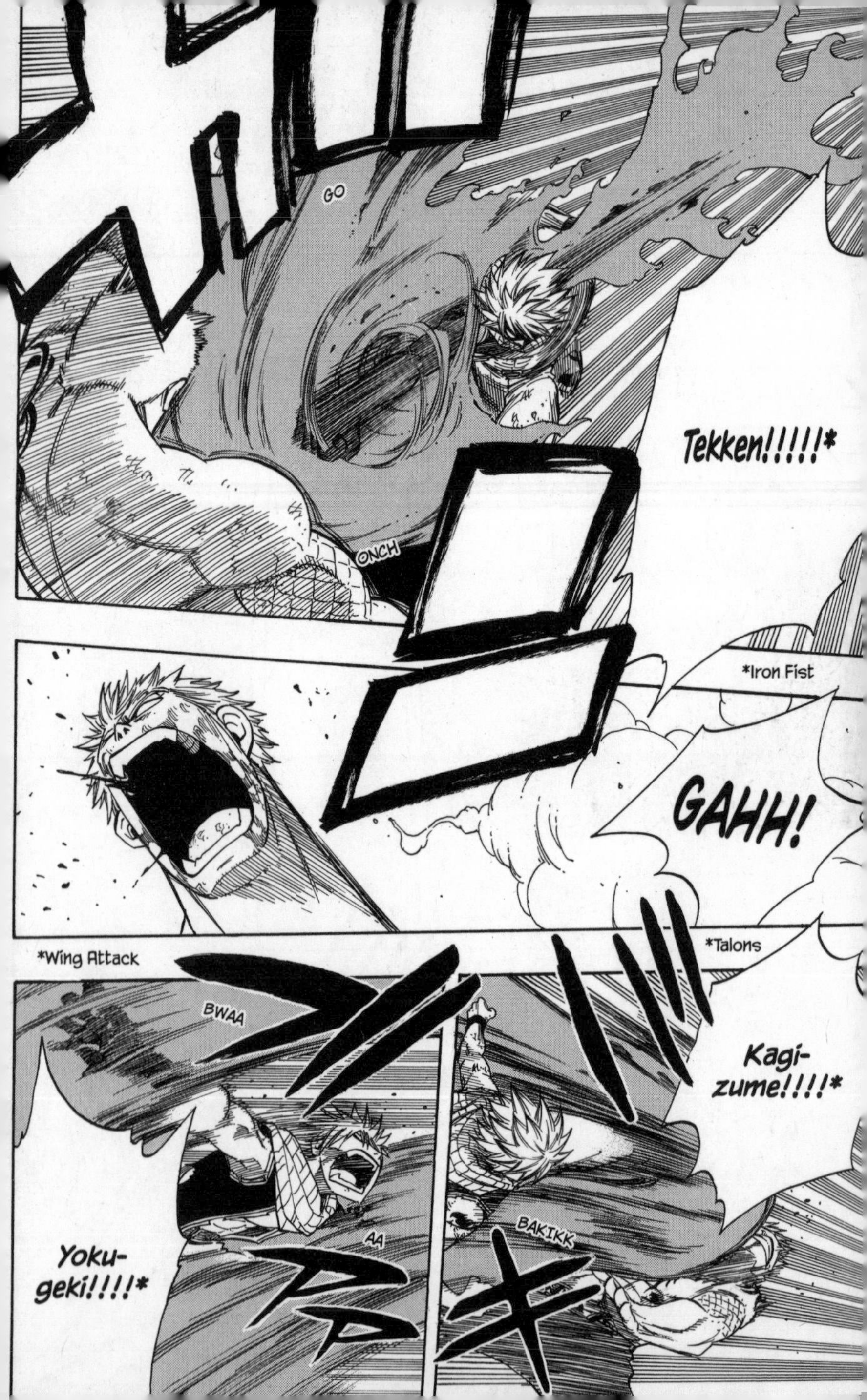
GO
Tekken!!!!!*
ONCH
*Iron Fist
GAHH!
*Talons
Kagi-
zume!!!!*
BAKIKK
*Wing Attack
BWAA
AA
Yoku-
geki!!!!*

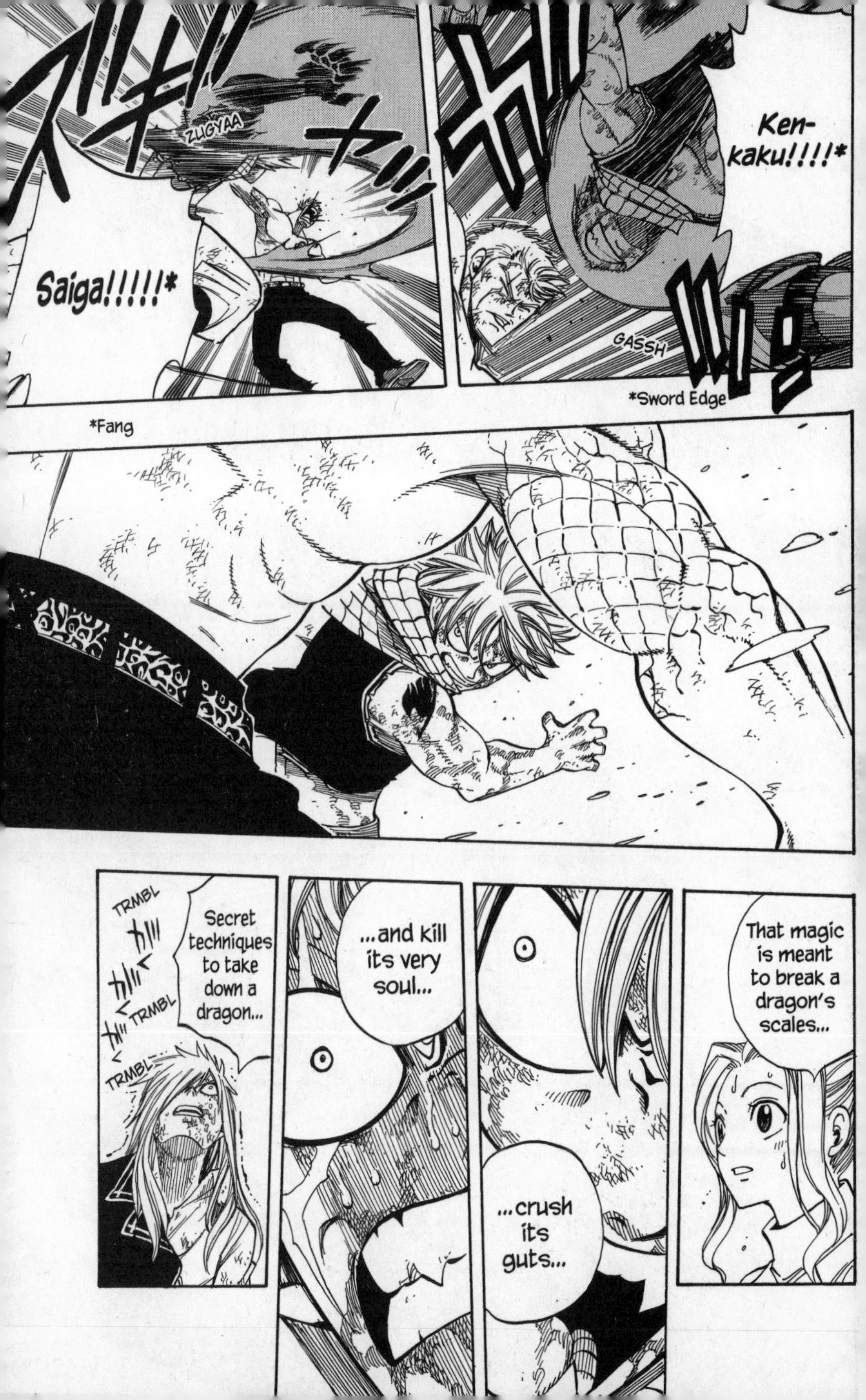
Ken-kaku!!!!*
GASSH
*Sword Edge
ZUGYAA
Saiga!!!!!*
*Fang
That magic is meant to break a dragon's scales...
...crush its guts...
...and kill its very soul...
TRMBL
TRMBL
TRMBL
Secret techniques to take down a dragon...

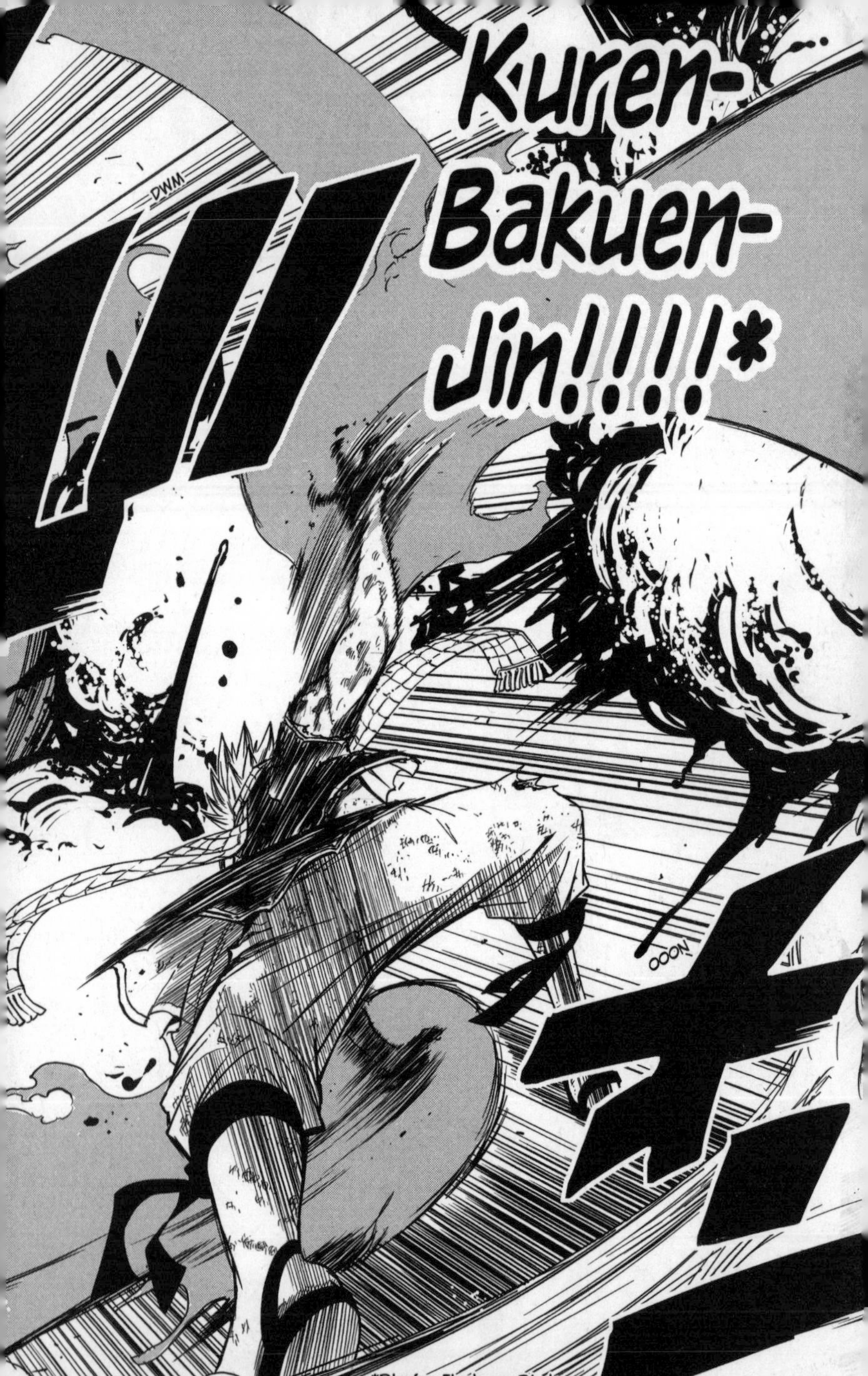
Kuren-Bakuen-Jin!!!!*
DWM
OOON

*Blazing Flashover Blade

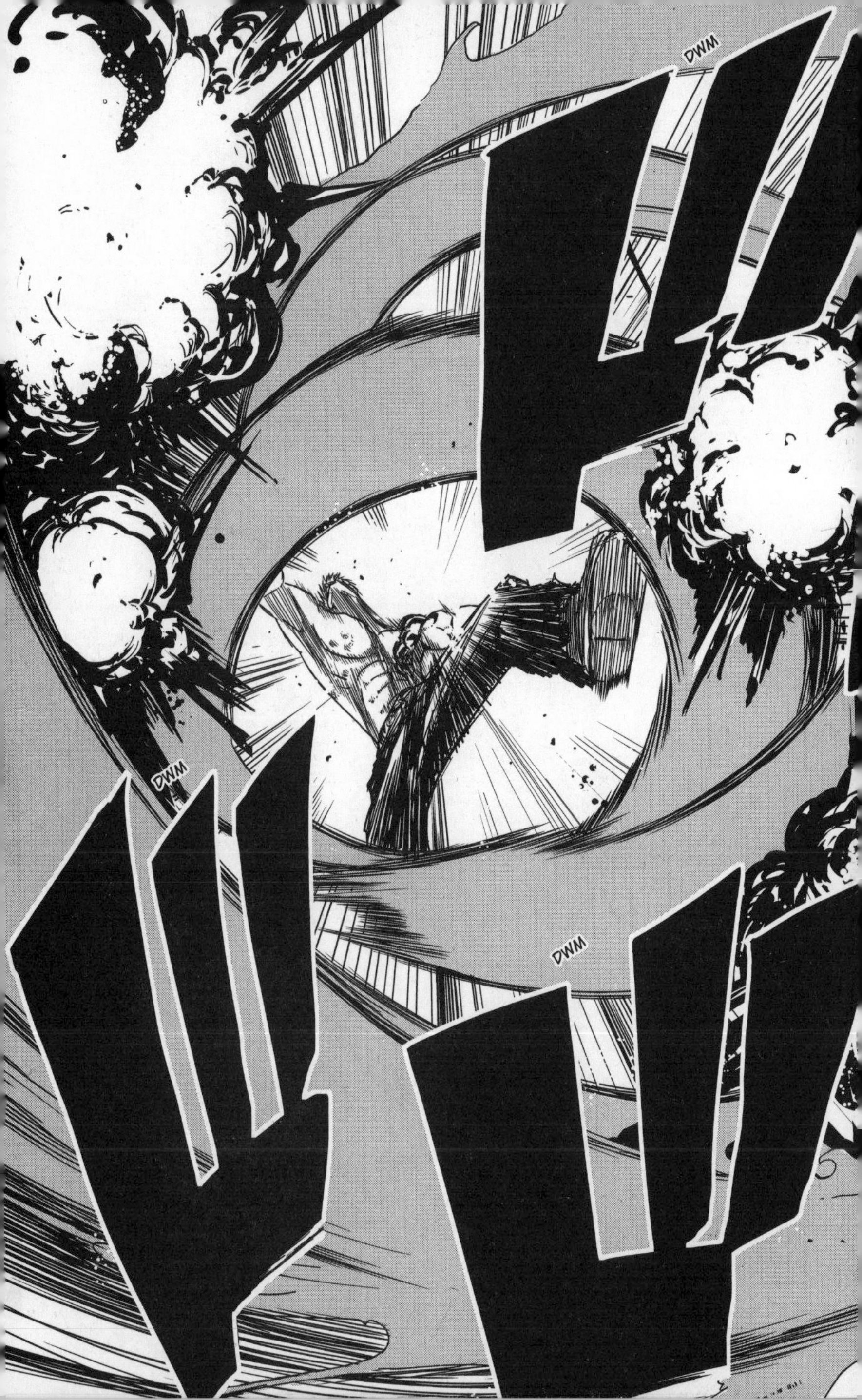
DWM
DWM
DWM

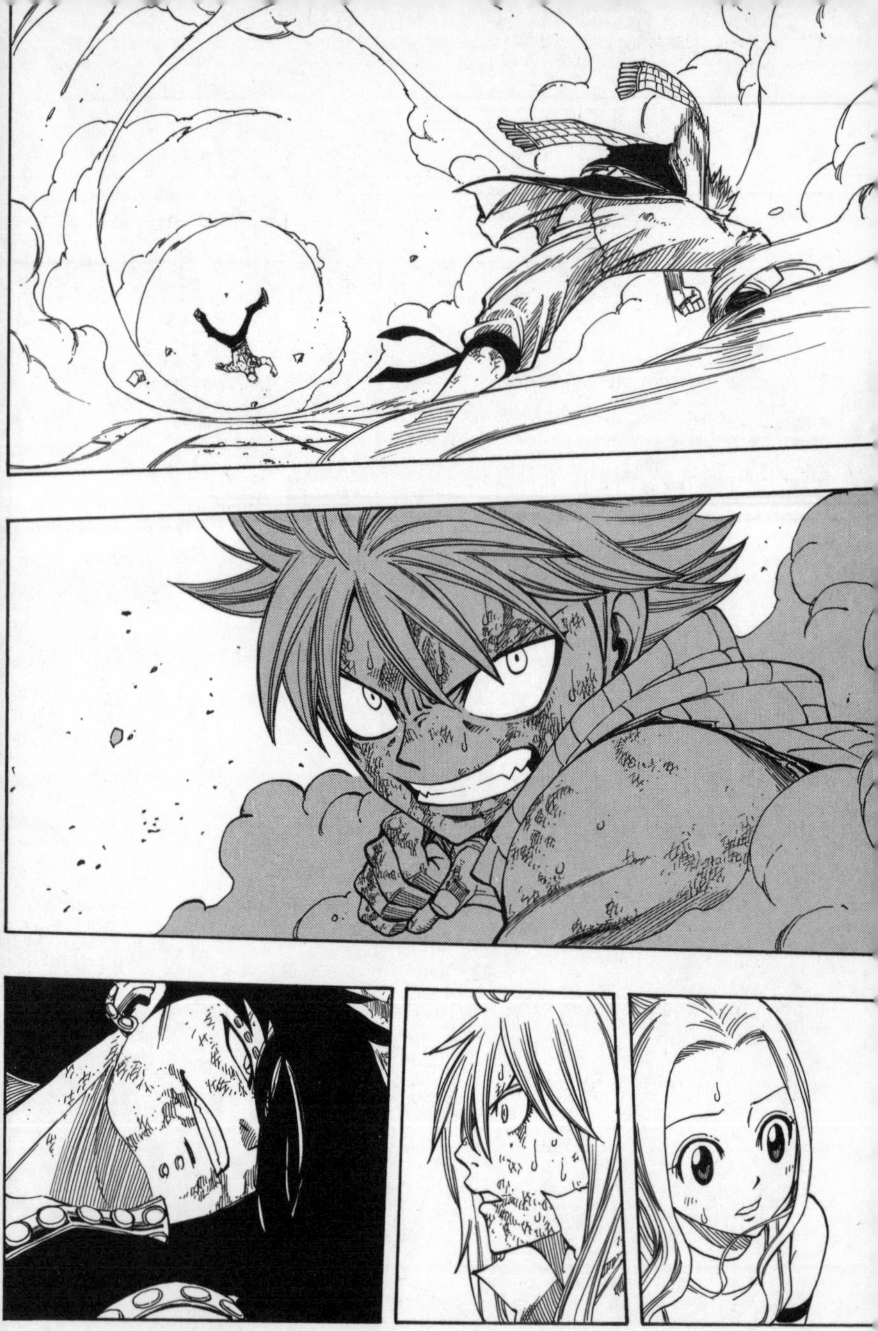

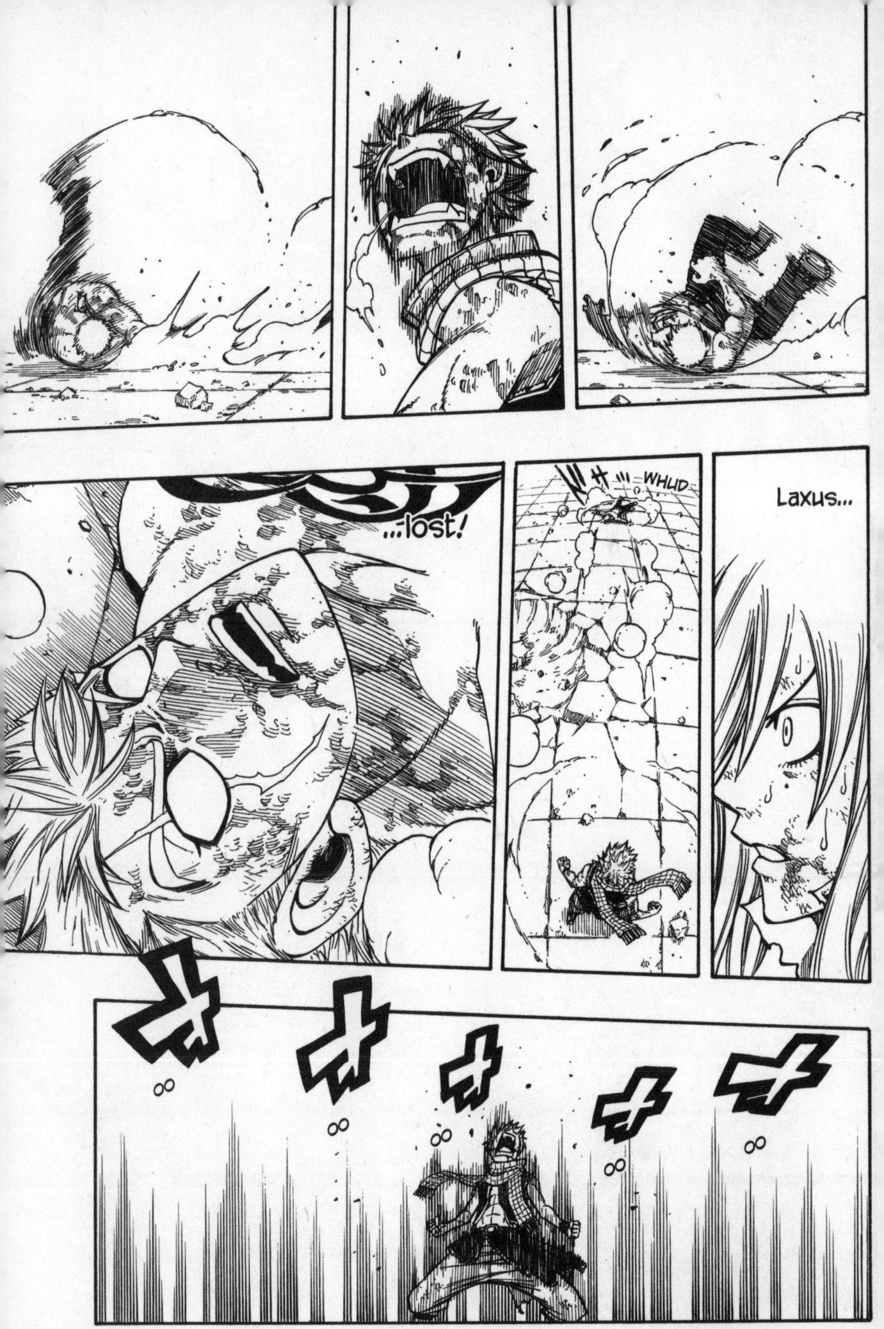
Laxus...
WHUD
...lost!

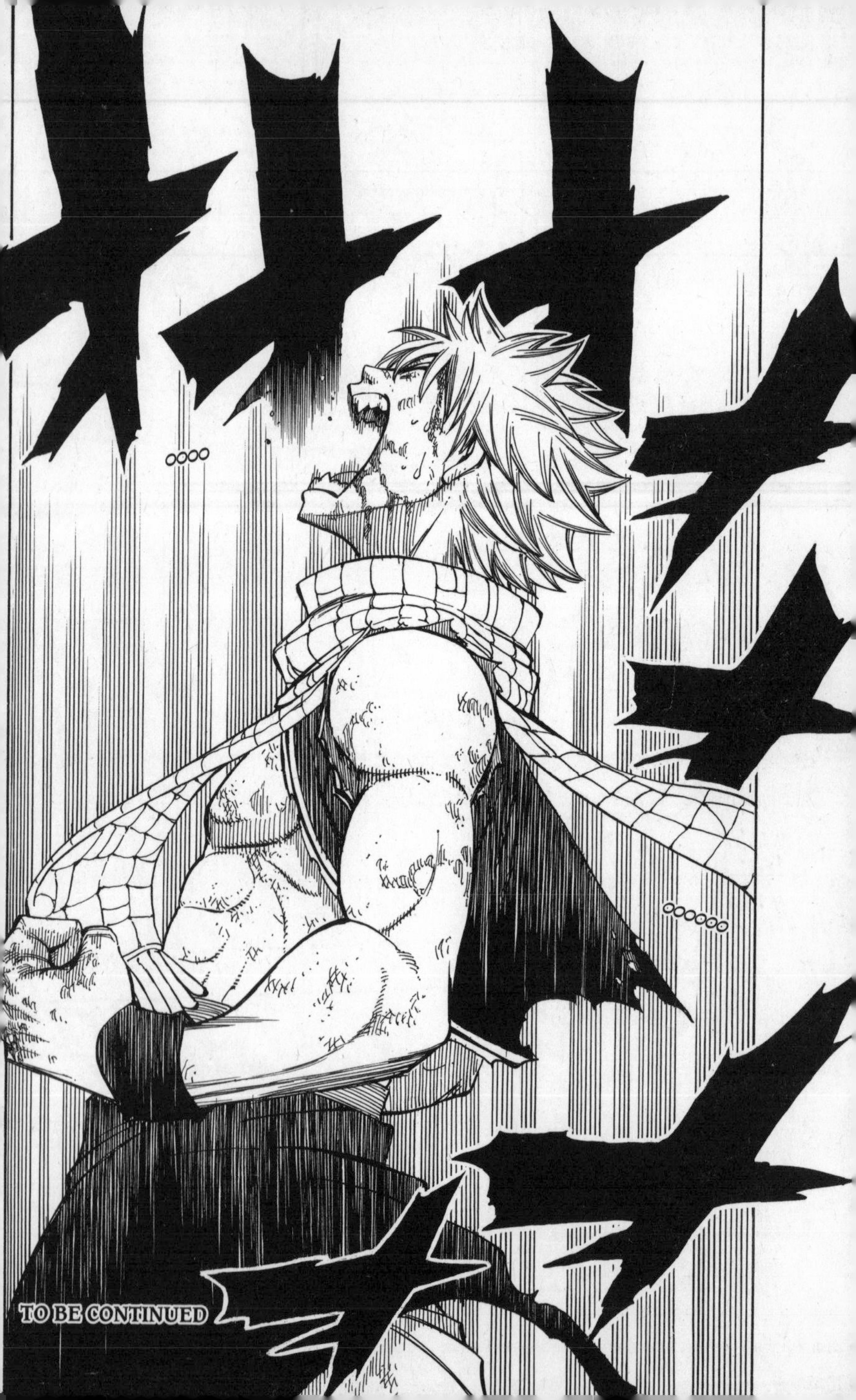
OOOO
OOOOOO
TO BE CONTINUED

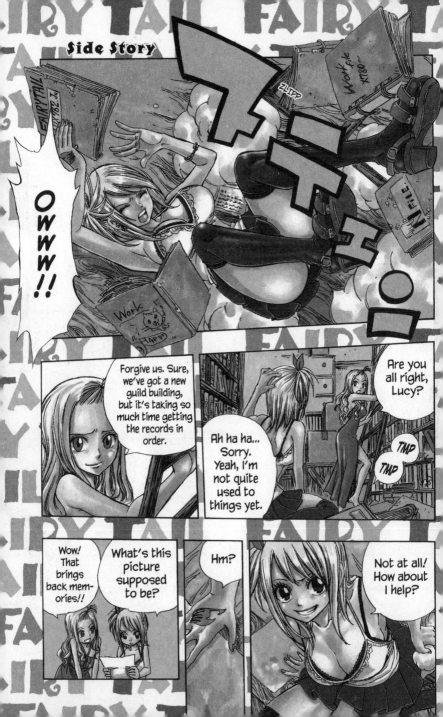

Side Story

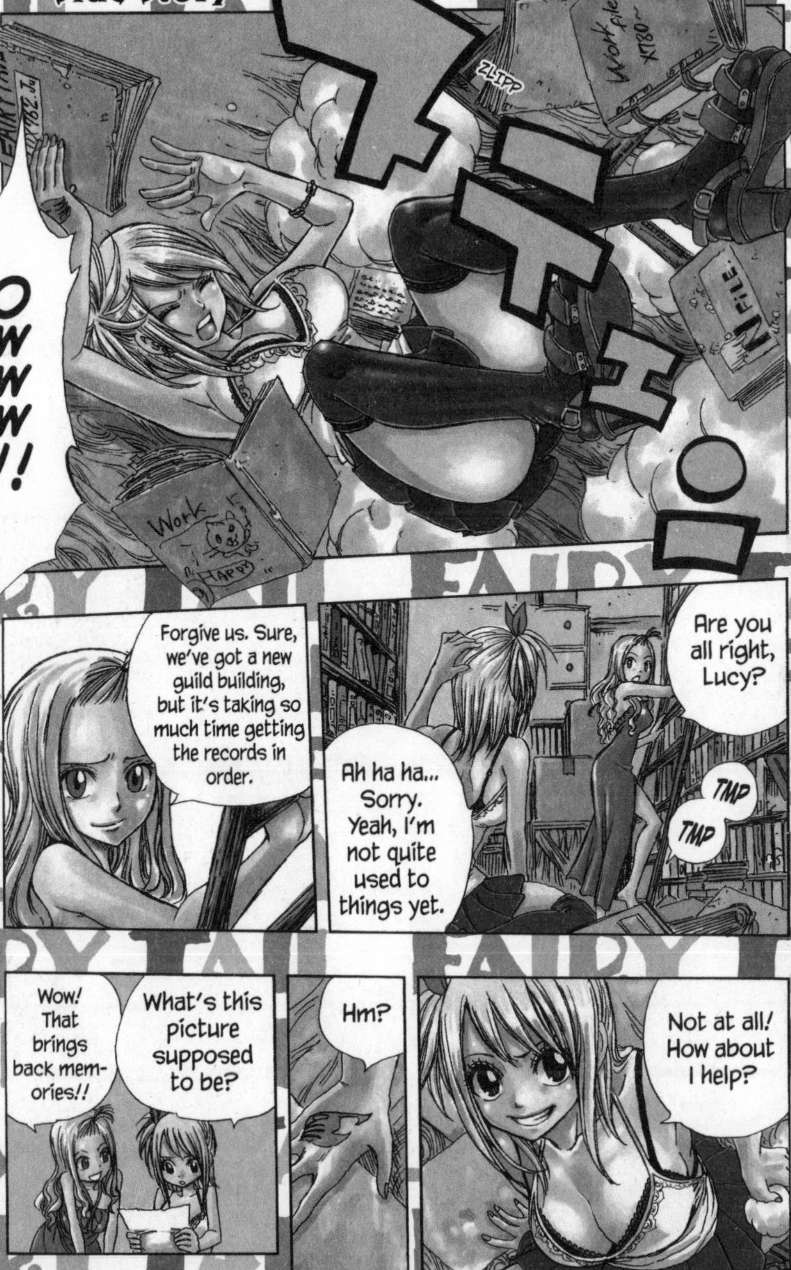
ZLIPP
FAIRYTAIL
Work file
FILE
Work
OWWW!!
Are you all right, Lucy?
TMP
TMP
Ah ha ha... Sorry. Yeah, I'm not quite used to things yet.
Forgive us. Sure, we've got a new guild building, but it's taking so much time getting the records in order.
Not at all! How about I help?
Hm?
What's this picture supposed to be?
Wow! That brings back memories!!

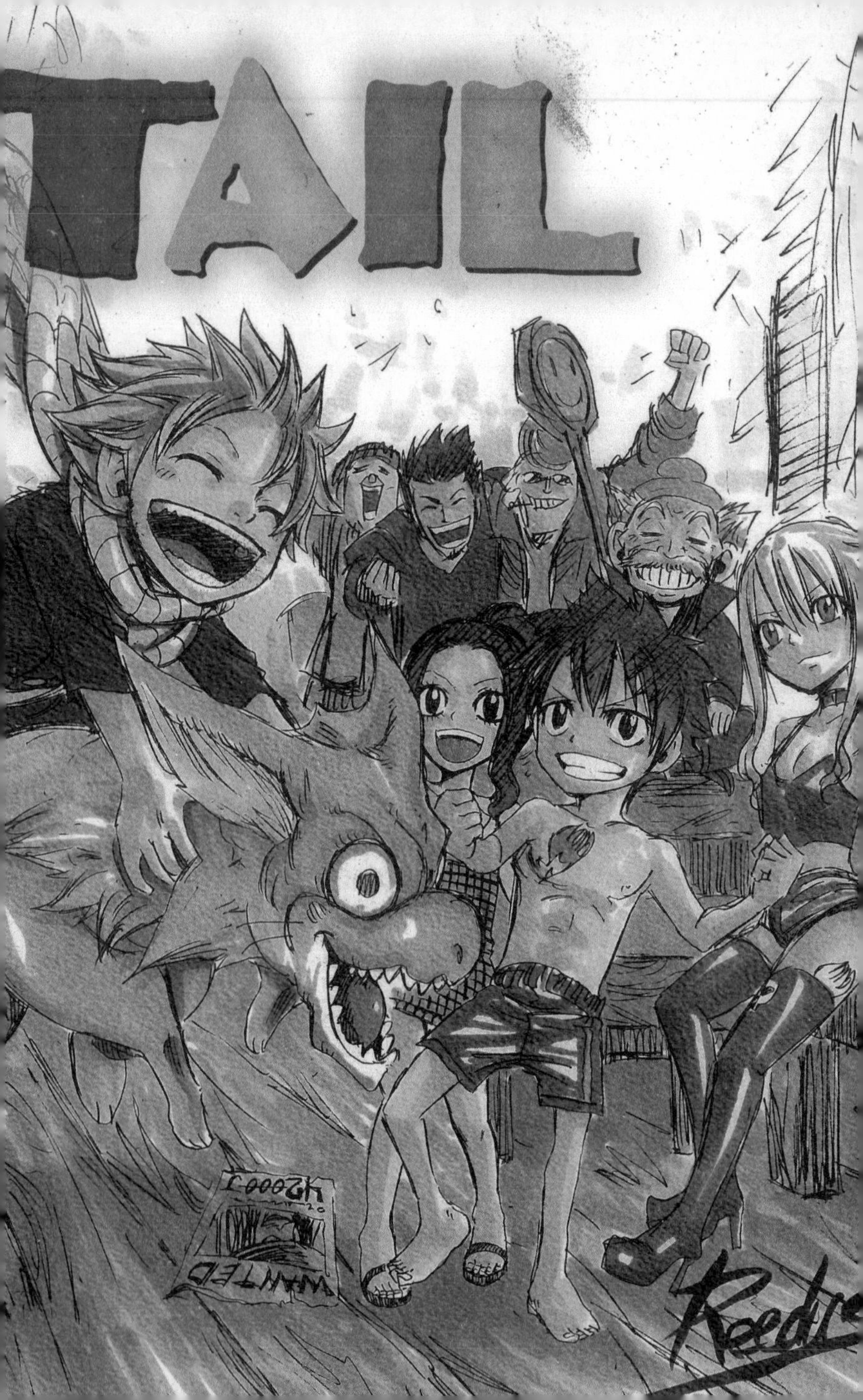
TAIL
WANTED

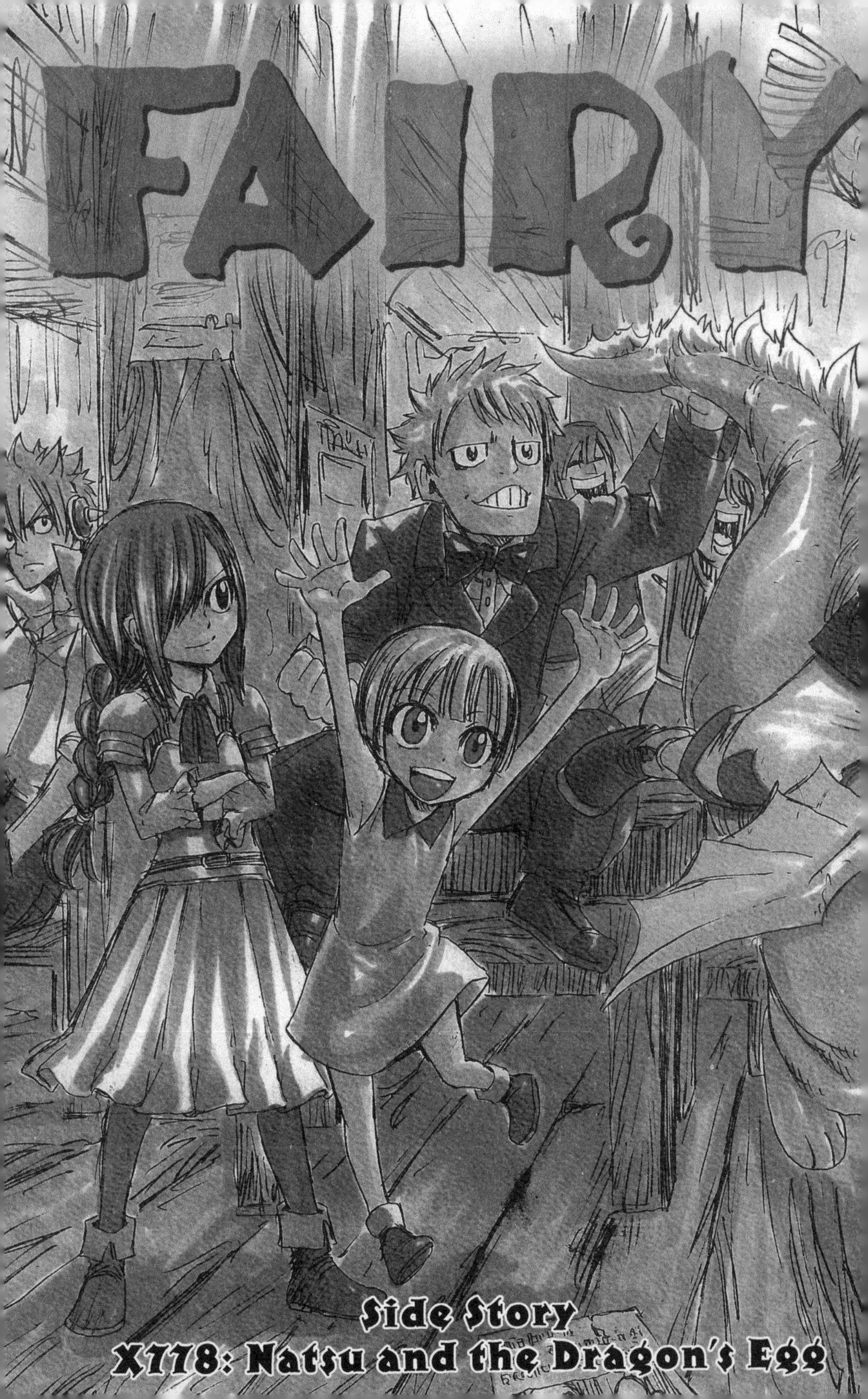
FAIRY
Side Story
X778: Natsu and the Dragon's Egg

FAIRY TAIL

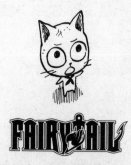

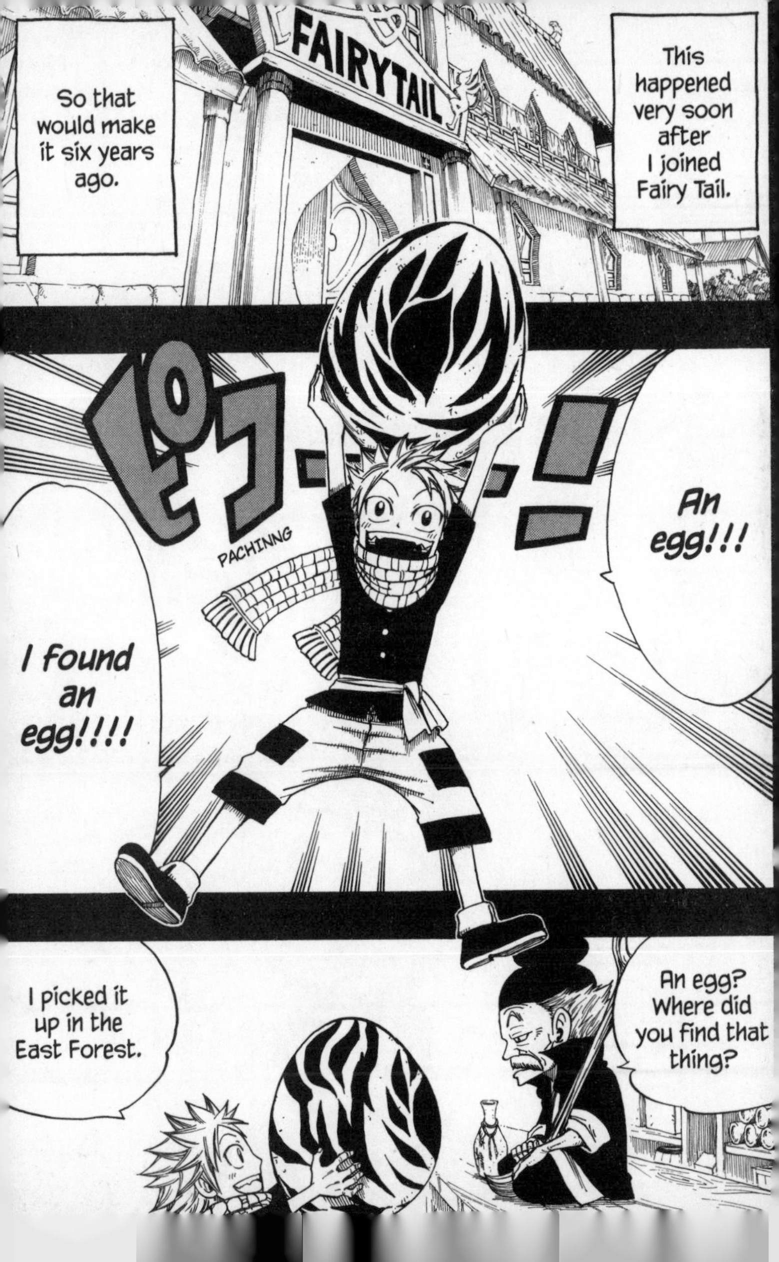
This happened very soon after I joined Fairy Tail.
FAIRY TAIL
So that would make it six years ago.
An egg!!!
PACHINNG
I found an egg!!!!
An egg? Where did you find that thing?
I picked it up in the East Forest.

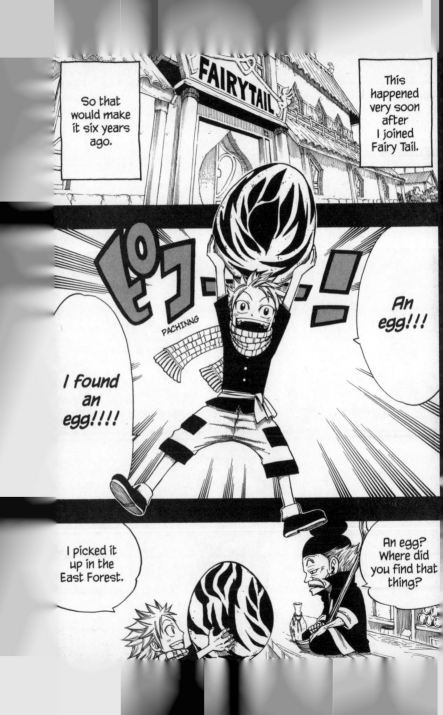

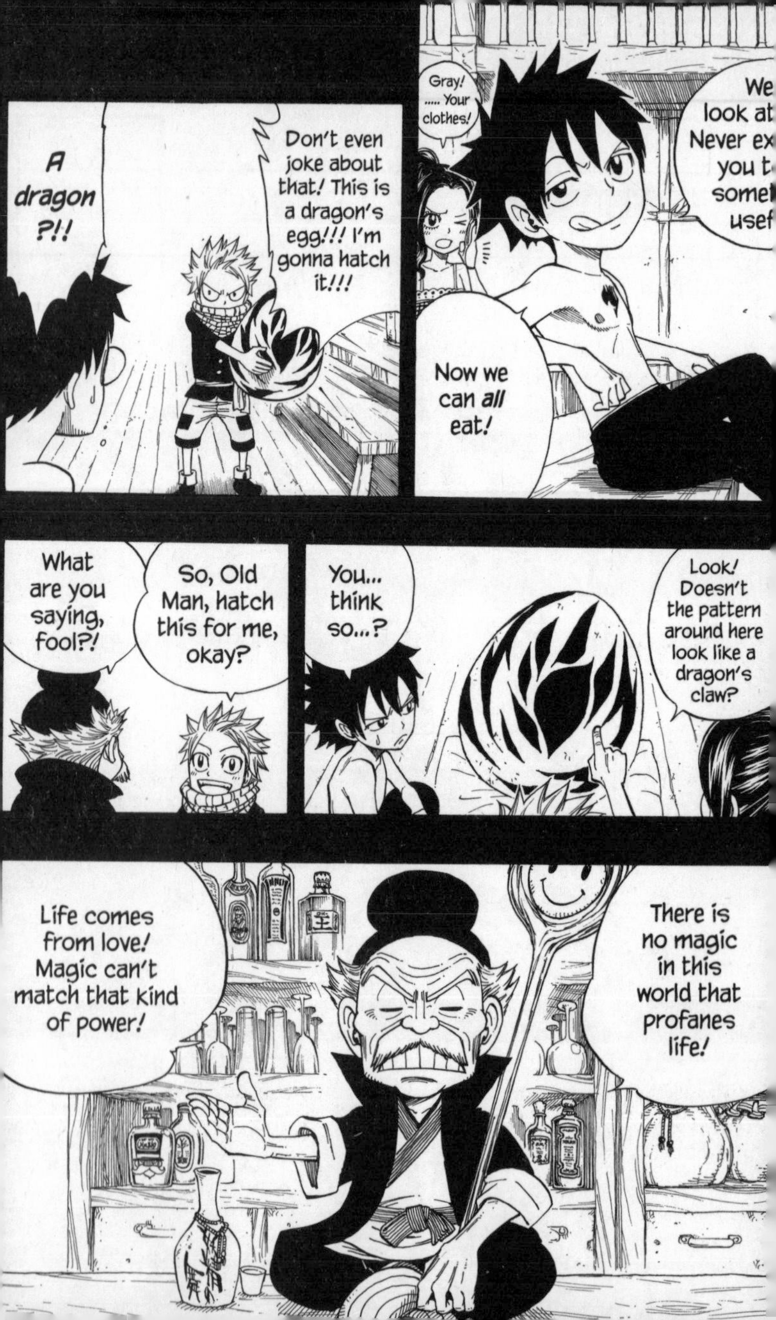
We look at Never ex you t somet usef
Gray! ..... Your clothes!
Now we can *all* eat!
Don't even joke about that! This is a dragon's egg!!! I'm gonna hatch it!!!
A dragon ?!!
Look! Doesn't the pattern around here look like a dragon's claw?
You... think so...?
So, Old Man, hatch this for me, okay?
What are you saying, fool?!
There is no magic in this world that profanes life!
Life comes from love! Magic can't match that kind of power!

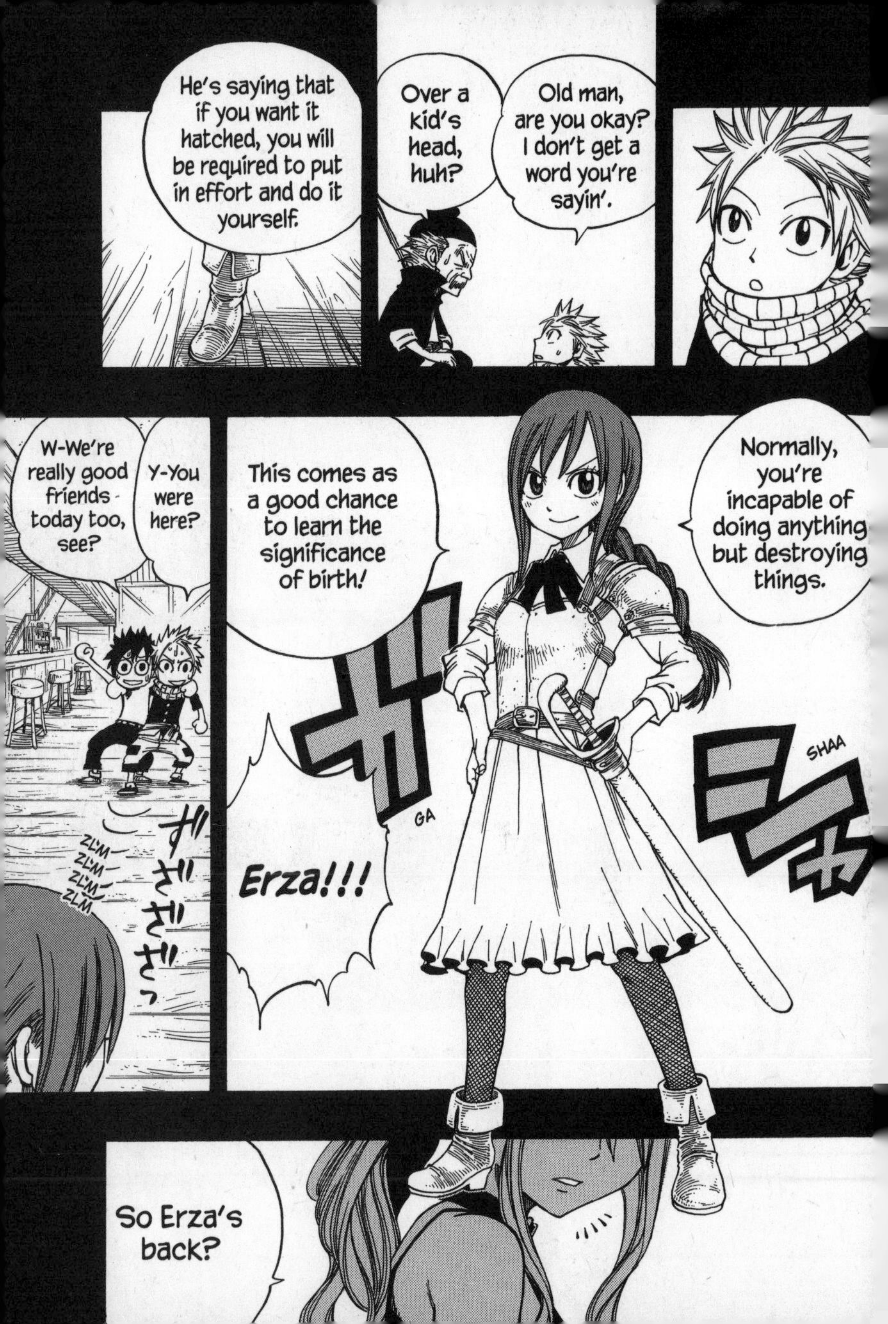

Old man, are you okay? I don't get a word you're sayin'.
Over a kid's head, huh?
He's saying that if you want it hatched, you will be required to put in effort and do it yourself.
Normally, you're incapable of doing anything but destroying things.
SHAA
GA
This comes as a good chance to learn the significance of birth!
Erza!!!
Y-You were here?
W-We're really good friends today too, see?
ZLM ZLM ZLM ZLM
ずざざざっ
So Erza's back?

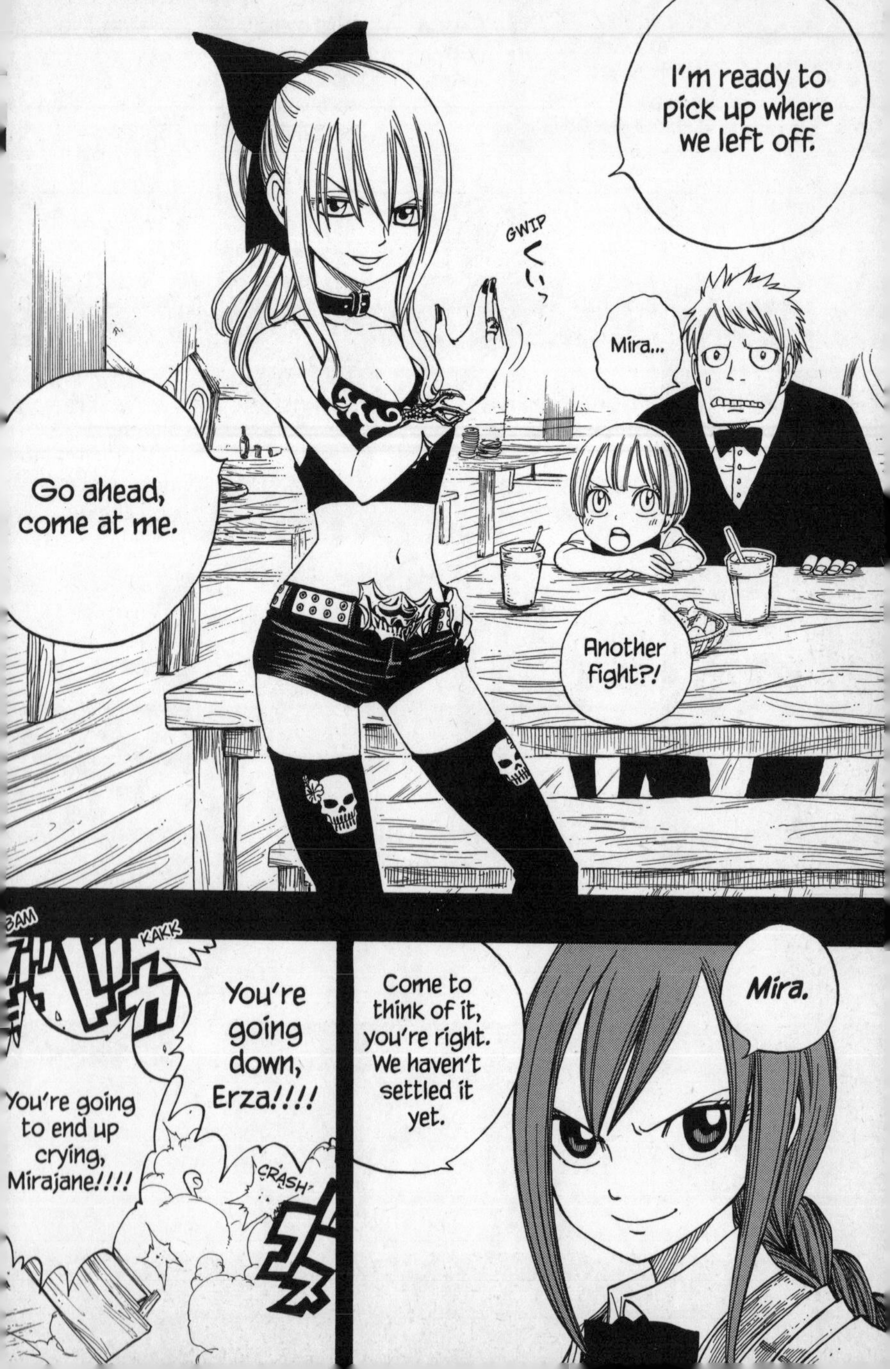
I'm ready to pick up where we left off.
GWIP
Mira...
Another fight?!
Go ahead, come at me.
Mira.
Come to think of it, you're right. We haven't settled it yet.
KAKK
BAM
You're going down, Erza!!!!
You're going to end up crying, Mirajane!!!!
CRASH

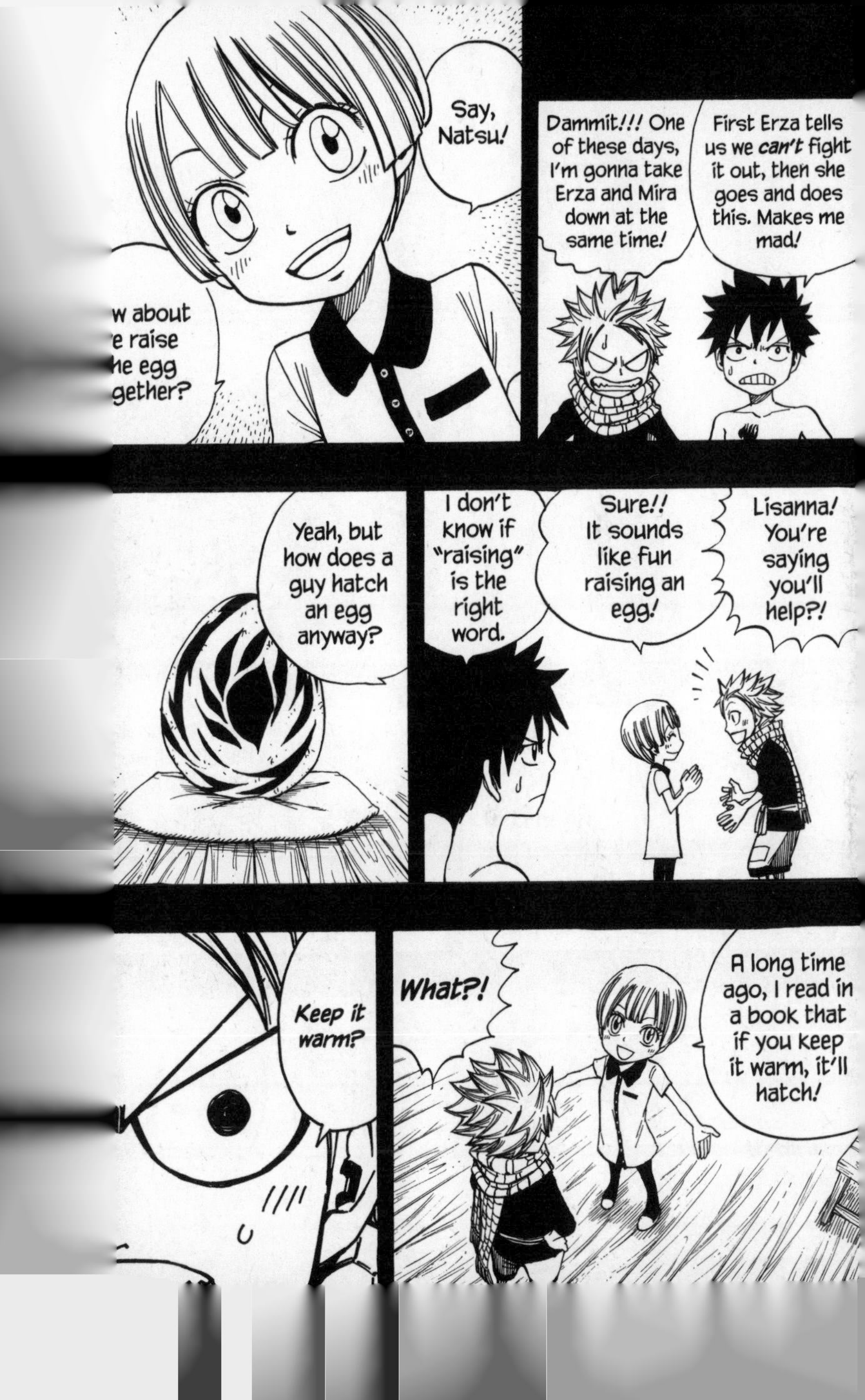
First Erza tells us we *can't* fight it out, then she goes and does this. Makes me mad!
Dammit!!! One of these days, I'm gonna take Erza and Mira down at the same time!
Say, Natsu!
w about e raise he egg gether?
Lisanna! You're saying you'll help?!
Sure!! It sounds like fun raising an egg!
I don't know if "raising" is the right word.
Yeah, but how does a guy hatch an egg anyway?
A long time ago, I read in a book that if you keep it warm, it'll hatch!
What?!
Keep it warm?

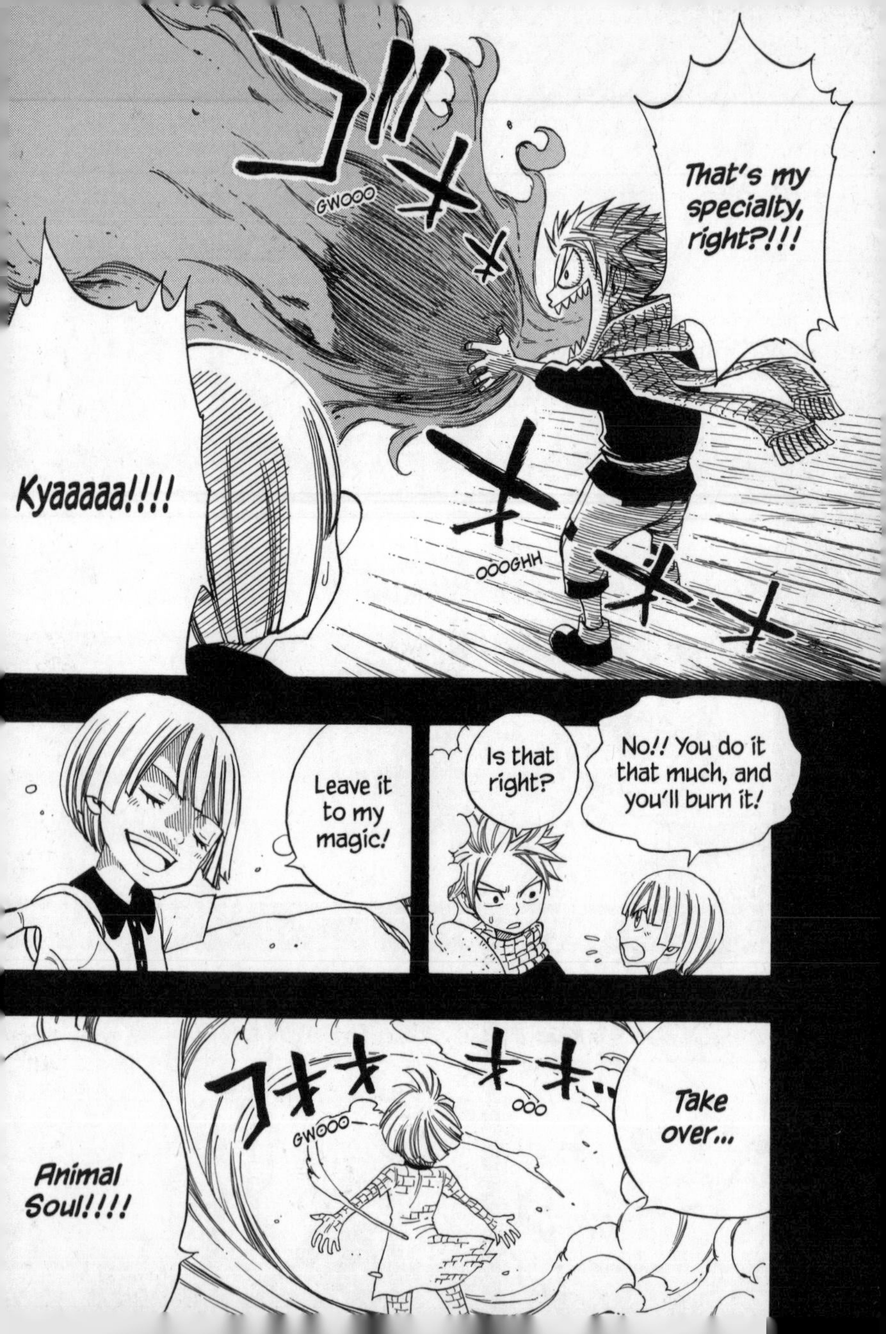
That's my specialty, right?!!!
GWOOO
OOOGHH
Kyaaaaa!!!!
No!! You do it that much, and you'll burn it!
Is that right?
Leave it to my magic!
Take over...
OOO
GWOOO
Animal Soul!!!!

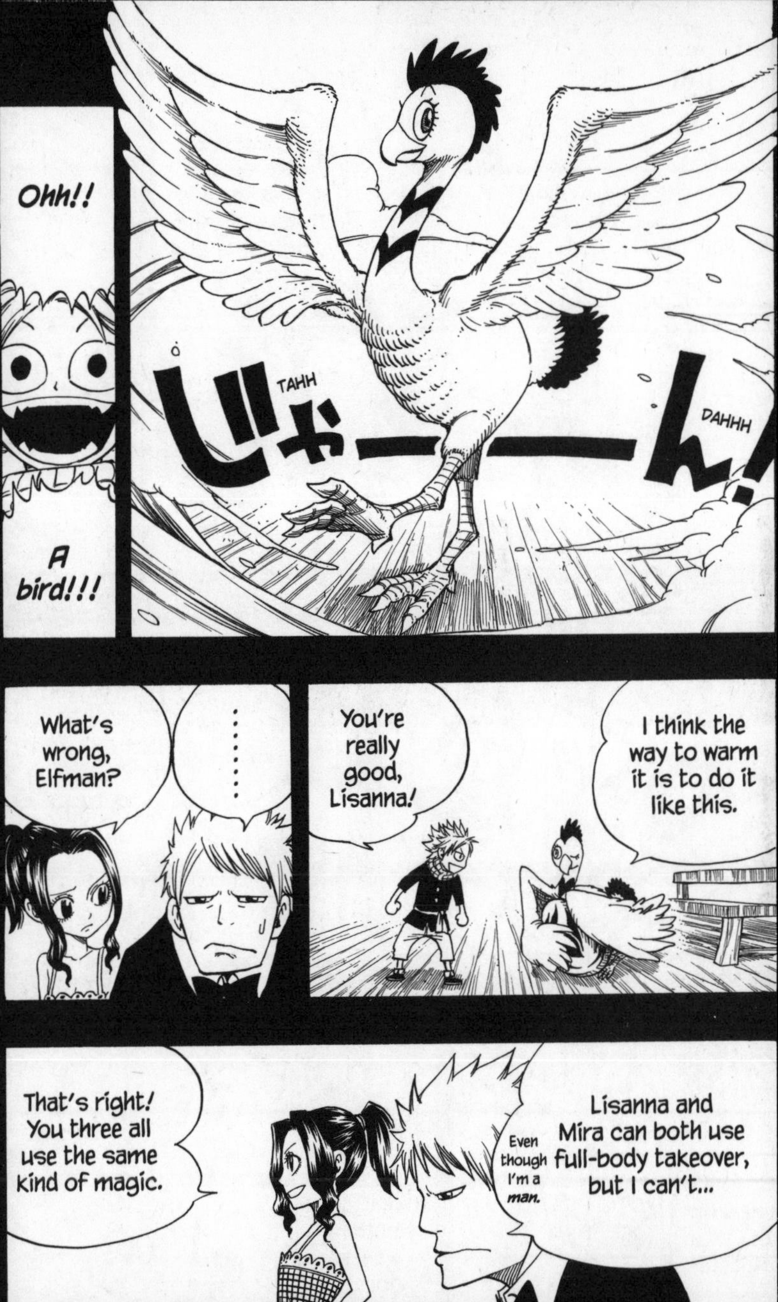

じゃーーーん!
TAHH
DAHHH
Ohh!!
A bird!!!
I think the way to warm it is to do it like this.
You're really good, Lisanna!
......
What's wrong, Elfman?
Lisanna and Mira can both use full-body takeover, but I can't...
Even though I'm a *man.*
That's right! You three all use the same kind of magic.

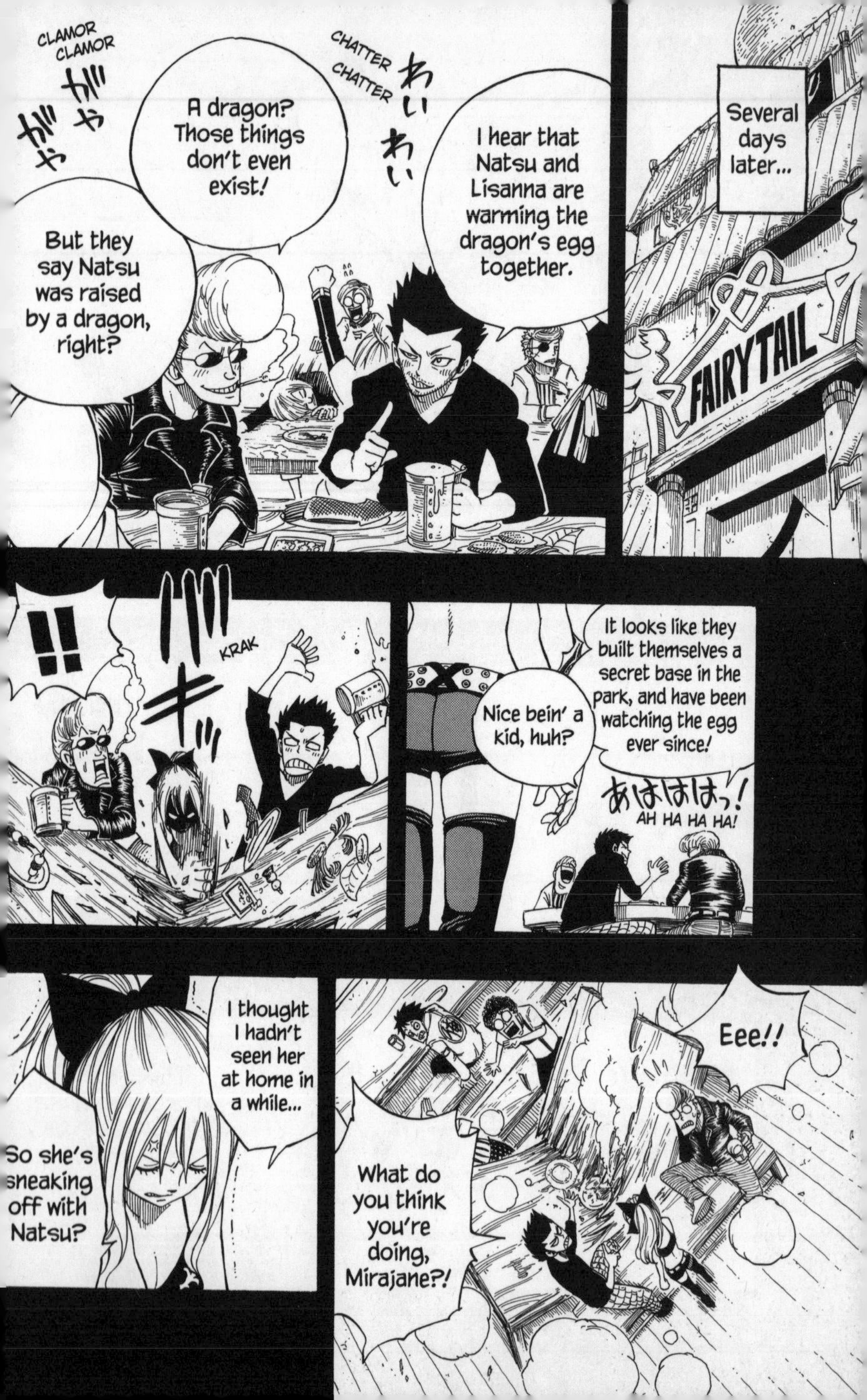
Several days later...
CHATTER CHATTER
わいわい
I hear that Natsu and Lisanna are warming the dragon's egg together.
A dragon? Those things don't even exist!
CLAMOR CLAMOR
ガやガや
But they say Natsu was raised by a dragon, right?
It looks like they built themselves a secret base in the park, and have been watching the egg ever since!
Nice bein' a kid, huh?
あははははっ!
AH HA HA HA!
KRAK
!!
Eee!!
What do you think you're doing, Mirajane?!
I thought I hadn't seen her at home in a while...
So she's sneaking off with Natsu?

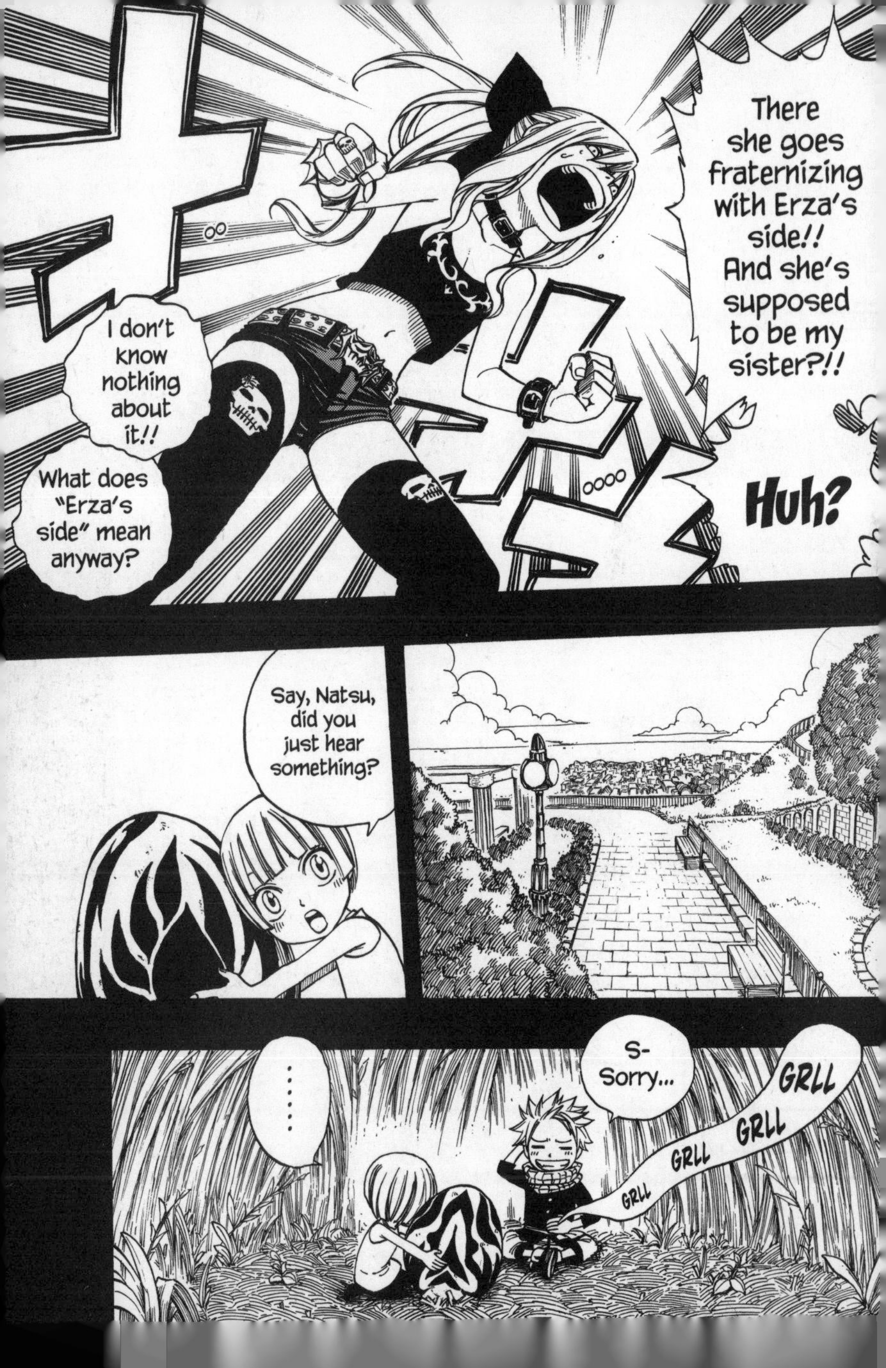
There she goes fraternizing with Erza's side!! And she's supposed to be my sister?!!
Huh?
I don't know nothing about it!!
What does "Erza's side" mean anyway?
Say, Natsu, did you just hear something?
S- Sorry...
GRLL GRLL GRLL GRLL
......

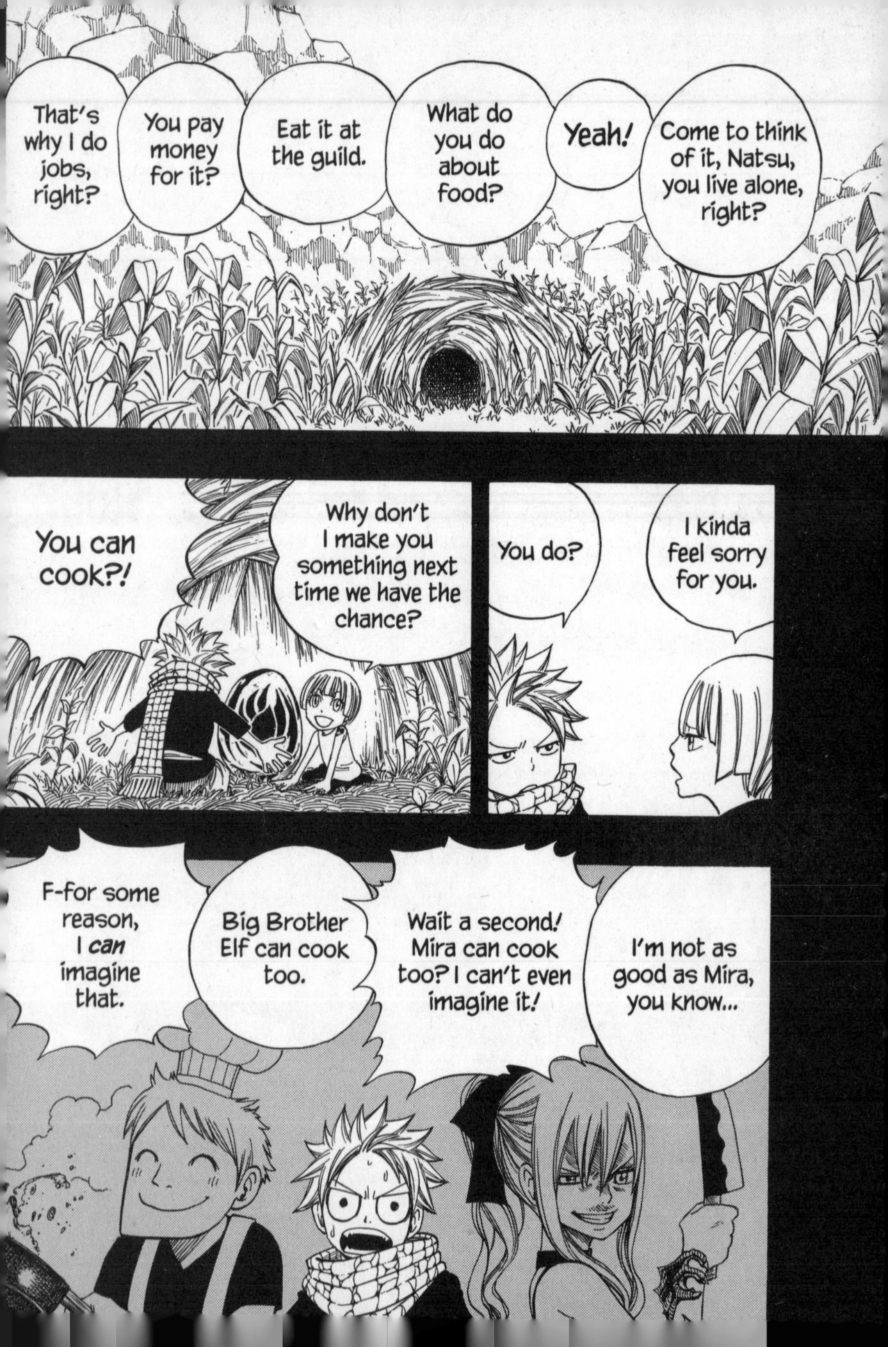
Come to think of it, Natsu, you live alone, right?
Yeah!
What do you do about food?
Eat it at the guild.
You pay money for it?
That's why I do jobs, right?
I kinda feel sorry for you.
You do?
Why don't I make you something next time we have the chance?
You can cook?!
I'm not as good as Mira, you know...
Wait a second! Mira can cook too? I can't even imagine it!
Big Brother Elf can cook too.
F-for some reason, I *can* imagine that.

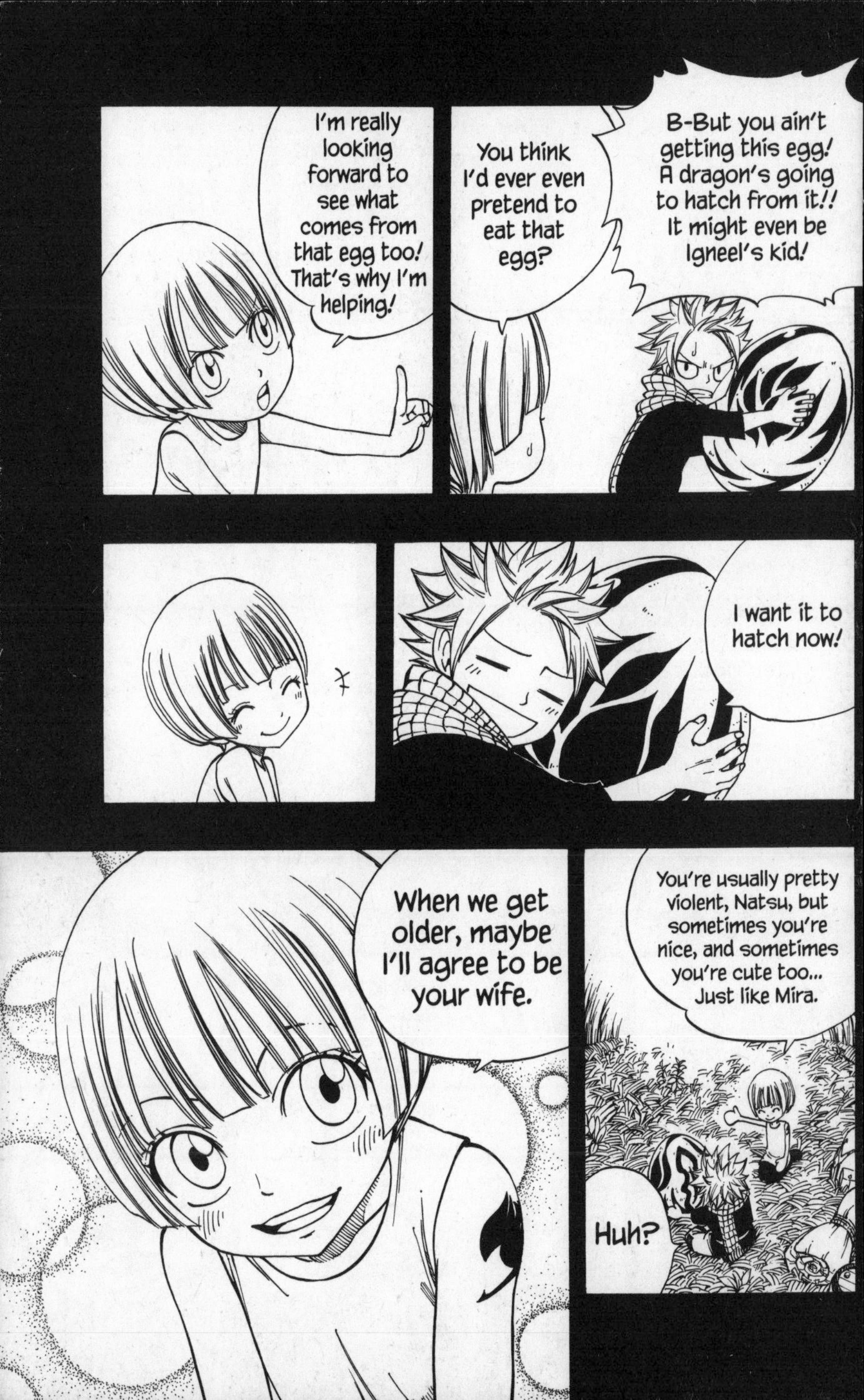
B-But you ain't getting this egg! A dragon's going to hatch from it!! It might even be Igneel's kid!
You think I'd ever even pretend to eat that egg?
I'm really looking forward to see what comes from that egg too! That's why I'm helping!
I want it to hatch now!
You're usually pretty violent, Natsu, but sometimes you're nice, and sometimes you're cute too... Just like Mira.
Huh?
When we get older, maybe I'll agree to be your wife.

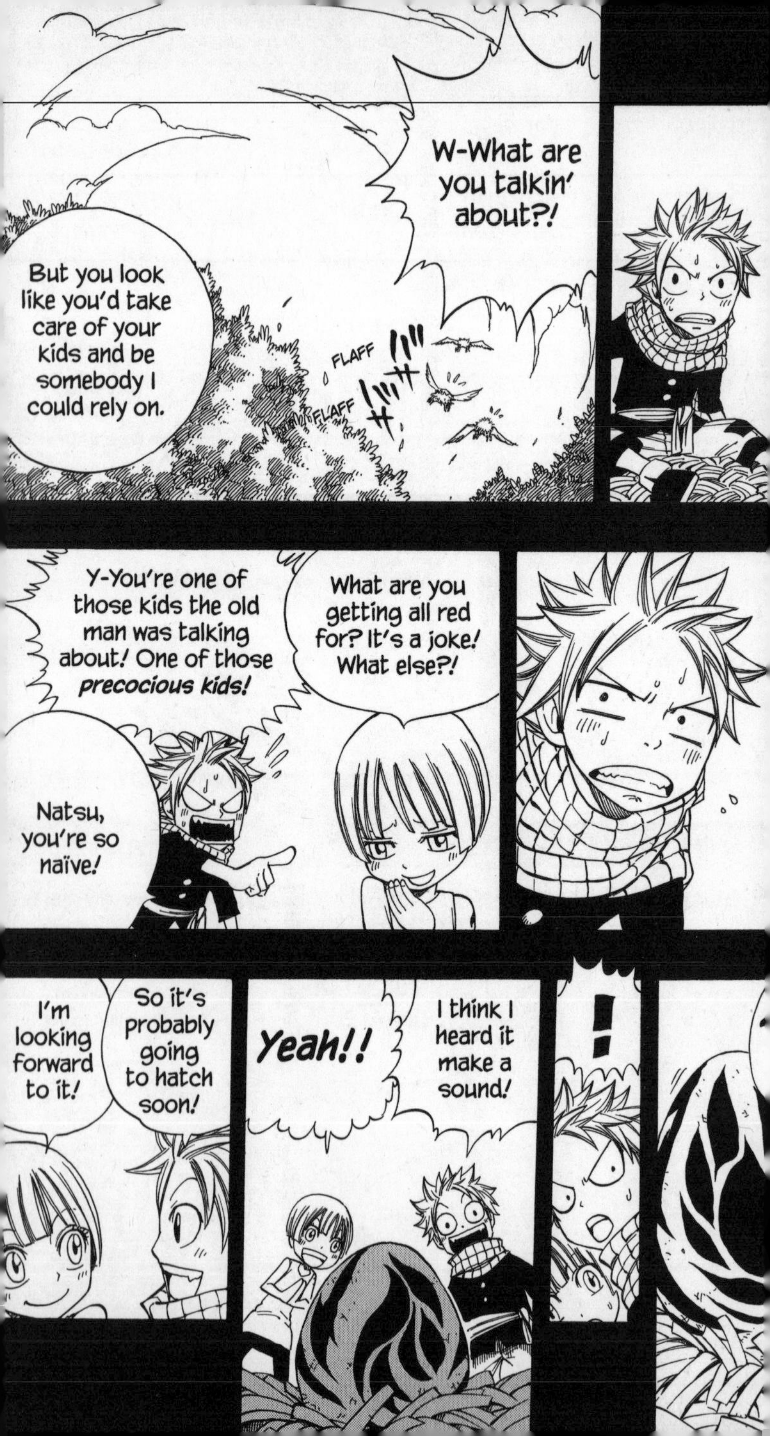

W-What are you talkin' about?!
FLAFF
FLAFF
But you look like you'd take care of your kids and be somebody I could rely on.
What are you getting all red for? It's a joke! What else?!
Y-You're one of those kids the old man was talking about! One of those *precocious kids!*
Natsu, you're so naïve!
!
I think I heard it make a sound!
Yeah!!
So it's probably going to hatch soon!
I'm looking forward to it!

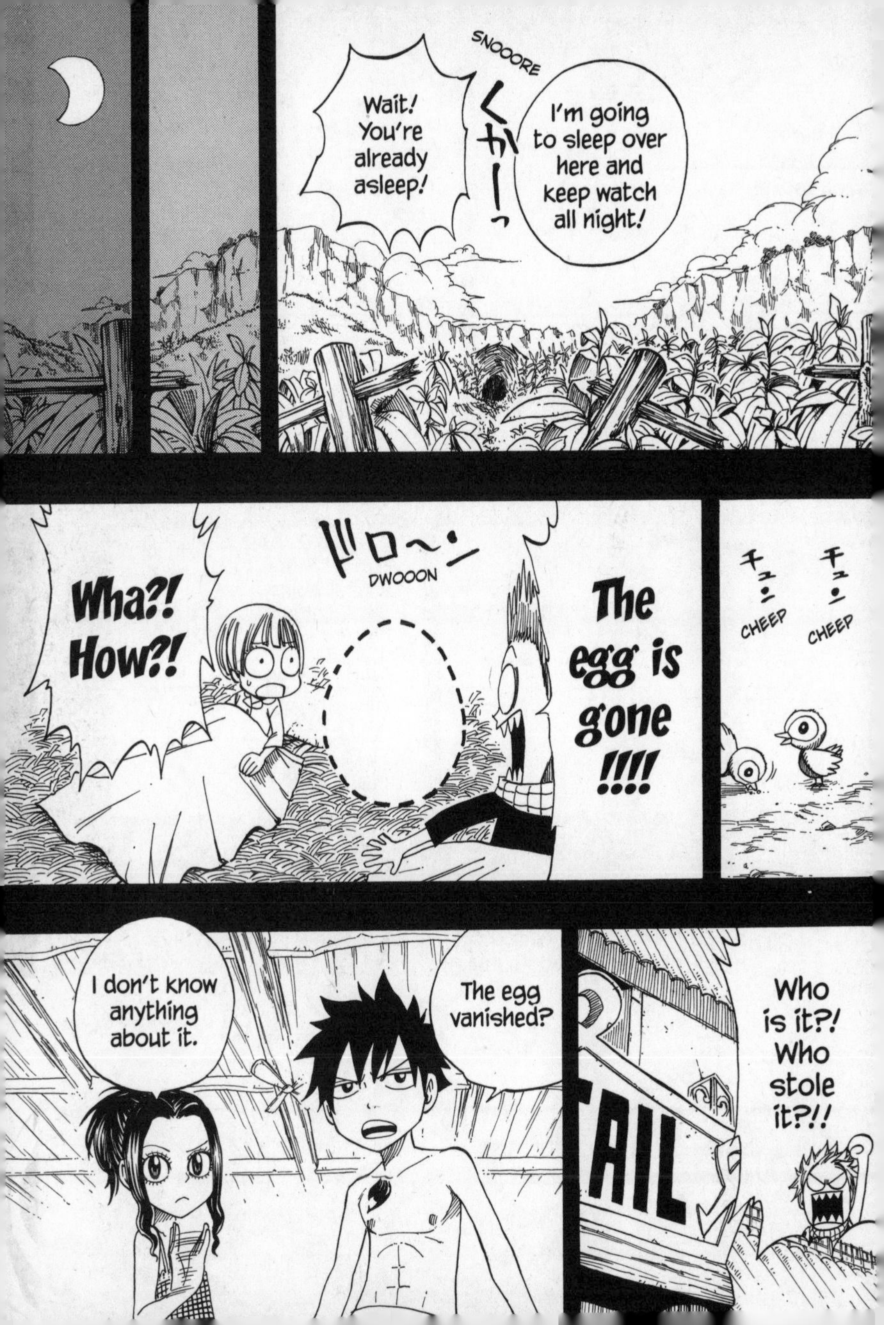
I'm going to sleep over here and keep watch all night!
SNOOORE
Wait! You're already asleep!
CHEEP
CHEEP
The egg is gone!!!!
DWOOON
Wha?! How?!
Who is it?! Who stole it?!!
FAIL
The egg vanished?
I don't know anything about it.

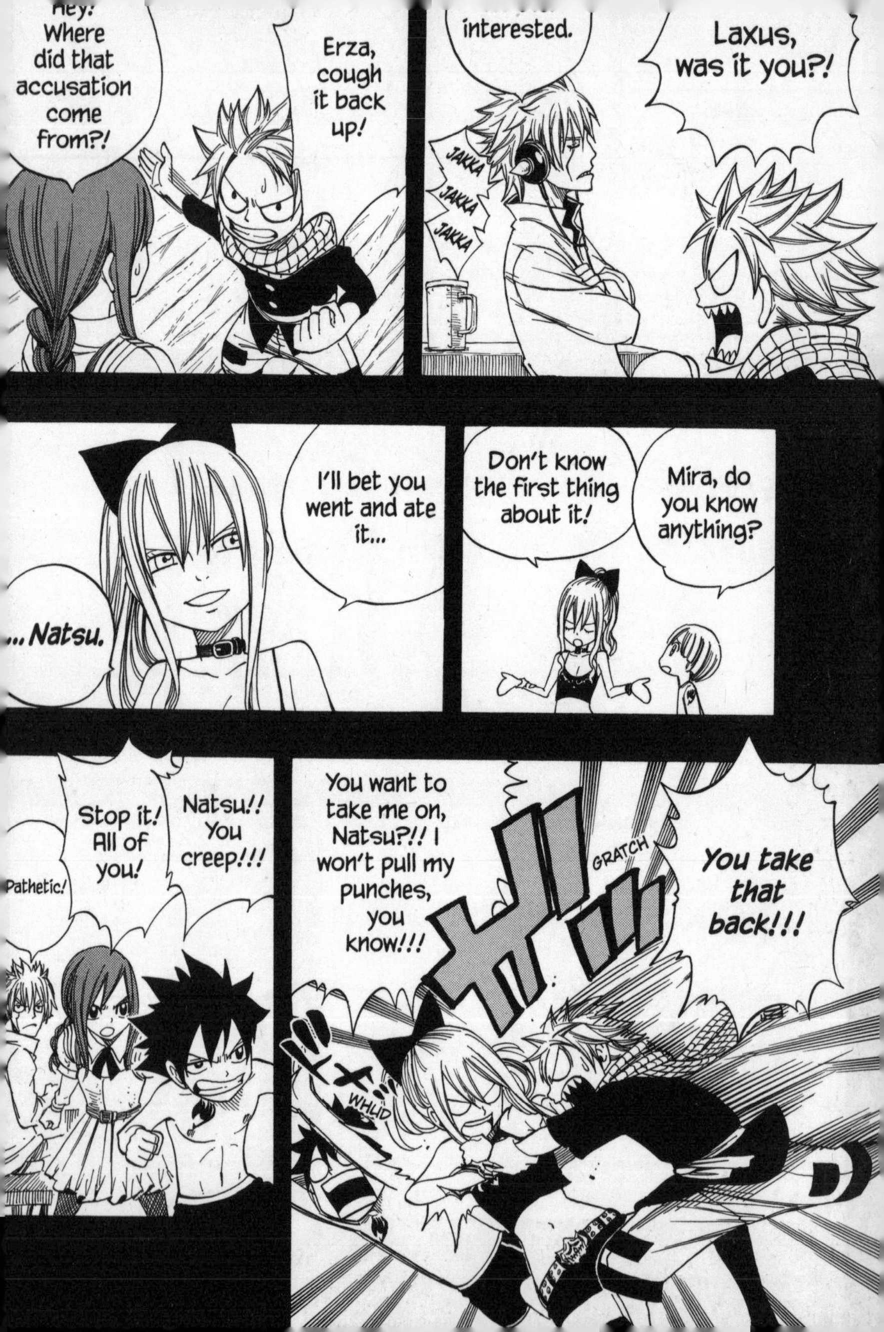
Laxus, was it you?!
interested.
JAKKA
JAKKA
JAKKA
Erza, cough it back up!
Hey! Where did that accusation come from?!
Mira, do you know anything?
Don't know the first thing about it!
I'll bet you went and ate it...
...Natsu.
You take that back!!!
GRATCH
You want to take me on, Natsu?!! I won't pull my punches, you know!!!
WHUD
Natsu!! You creep!!!
Stop it! All of you!
Pathetic!

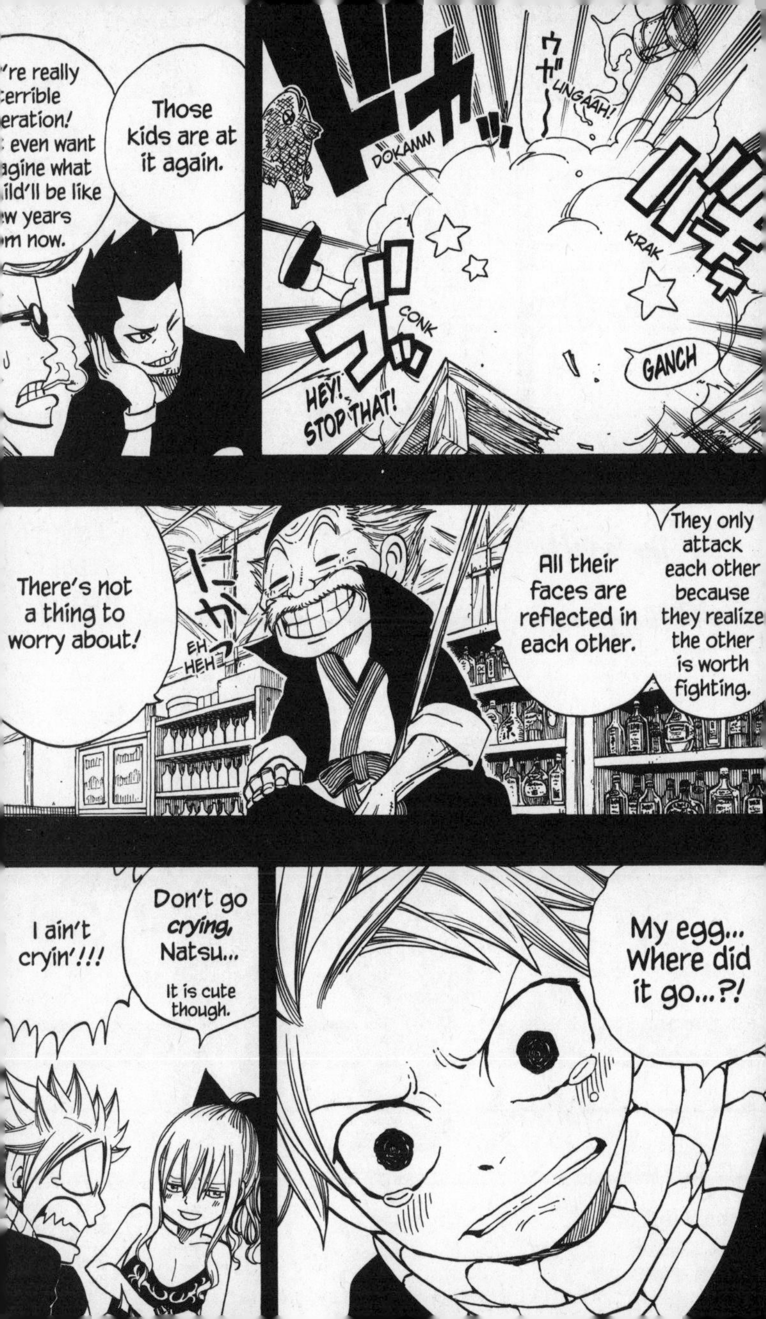
UNGAAH!
DOKAMM
KRAK
CONK
GANCH
HEY! STOP THAT!
Those kids are at it again.
're really terrible eration! even want agine what ild'll be like w years m now.
They only attack each other because they realize the other is worth fighting.
All their faces are reflected in each other.
EH HEH
There's not a thing to worry about!
My egg... Where did it go...?!
Don't go *crying,* Natsu...
It is cute though.
I ain't cryin'!!!

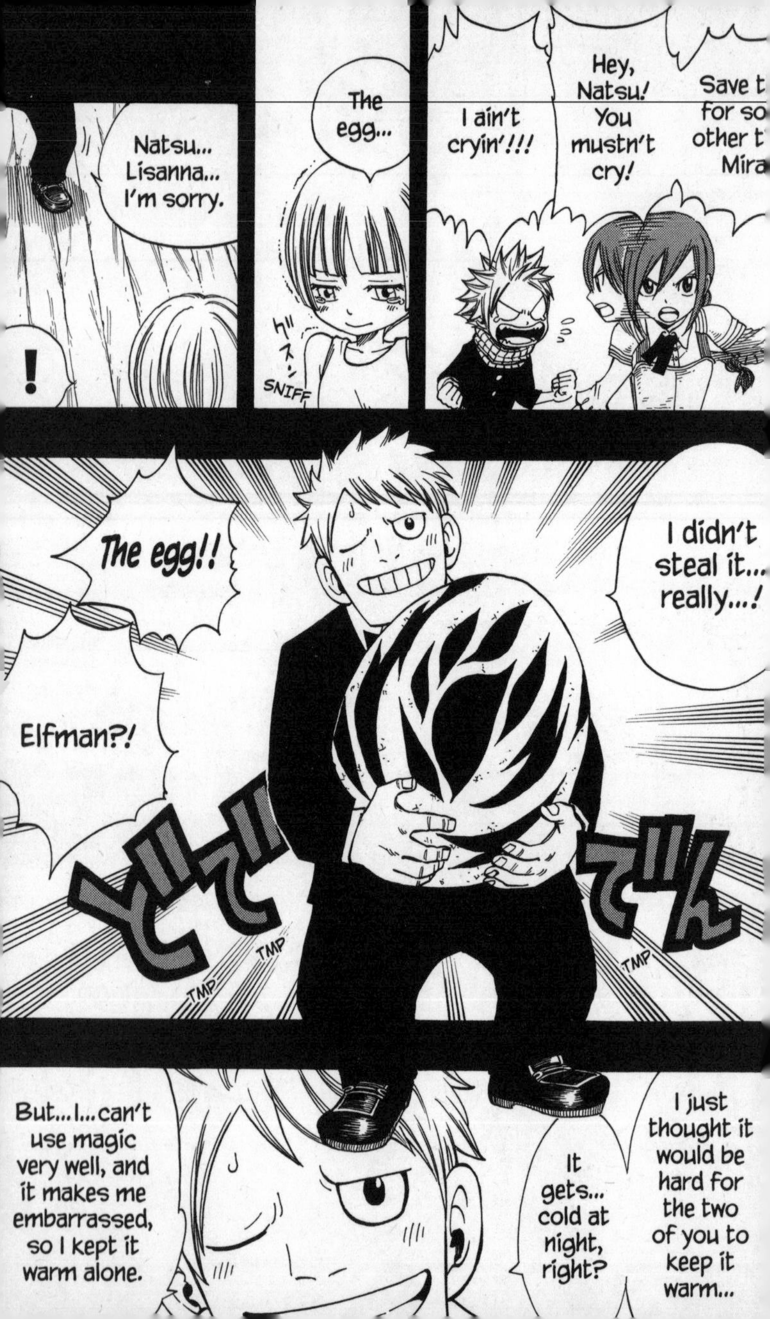

Save t
for so
other t
Mira
Hey, Natsu! You mustn't cry!
I ain't cryin'!!!
The egg...
SNIFF
Natsu... Lisanna... I'm sorry.
!
I didn't steal it... really...!
The egg!!
Elfman?!
TMP
TMP
TMP
I just thought it would be hard for the two of you to keep it warm...
It gets... cold at night, right?
But...I...can't use magic very well, and it makes me embarrassed, so I kept it warm alone.

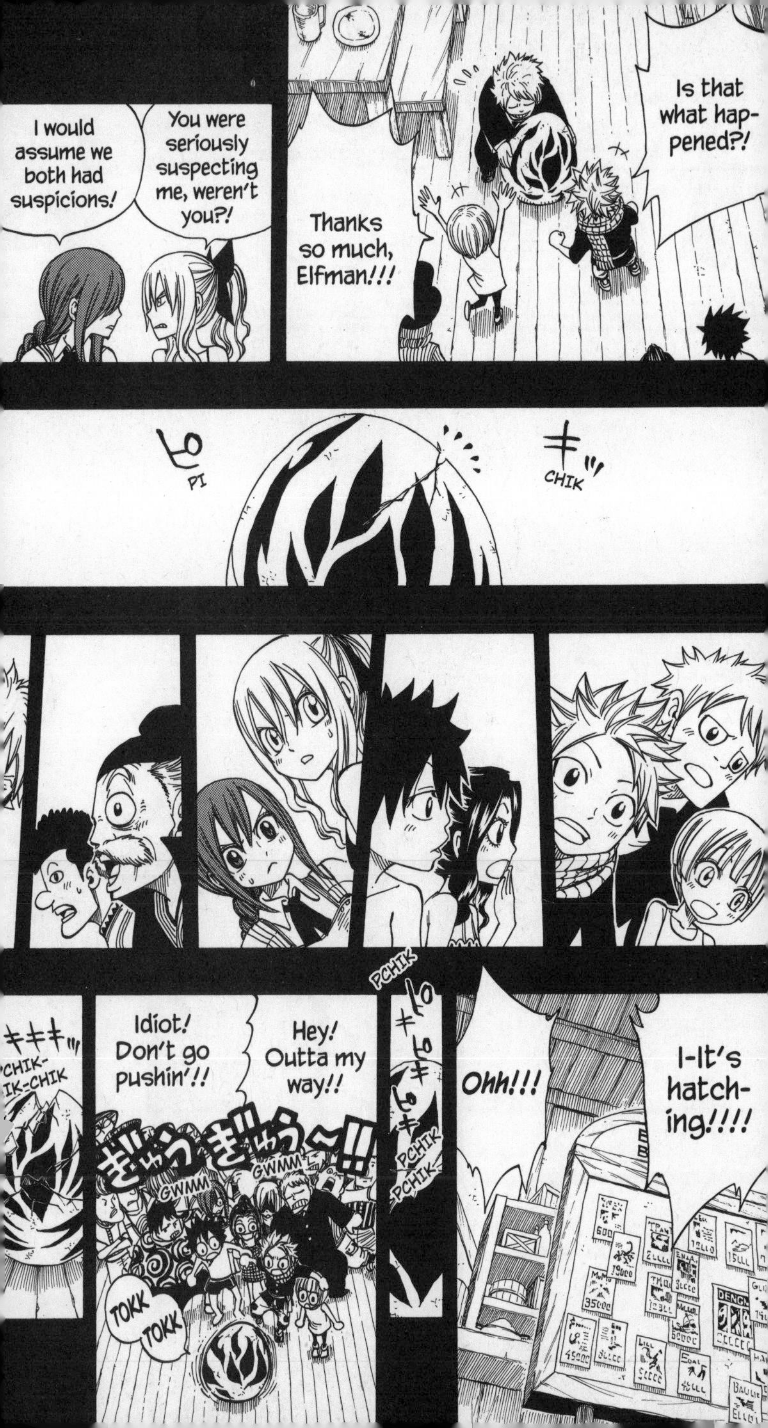

Is that what hap-pened?!
Thanks so much, Elfman!!!
You were seriously suspecting me, weren't you?!
I would assume we both had suspicions!
キ
CHIK
ピ
PI
I-It's hatching!!!!
Ohh!!!
PCHIK
ピキ
ピキ
PCHIK
PCHIK
Hey! Outta my way!!
Idiot! Don't go pushin'!!
ぎゅう ぎゅう〜!!
GWMM
GWMM
TOKK
TOKK
キキキ
PCHIK-
IK-CHIK

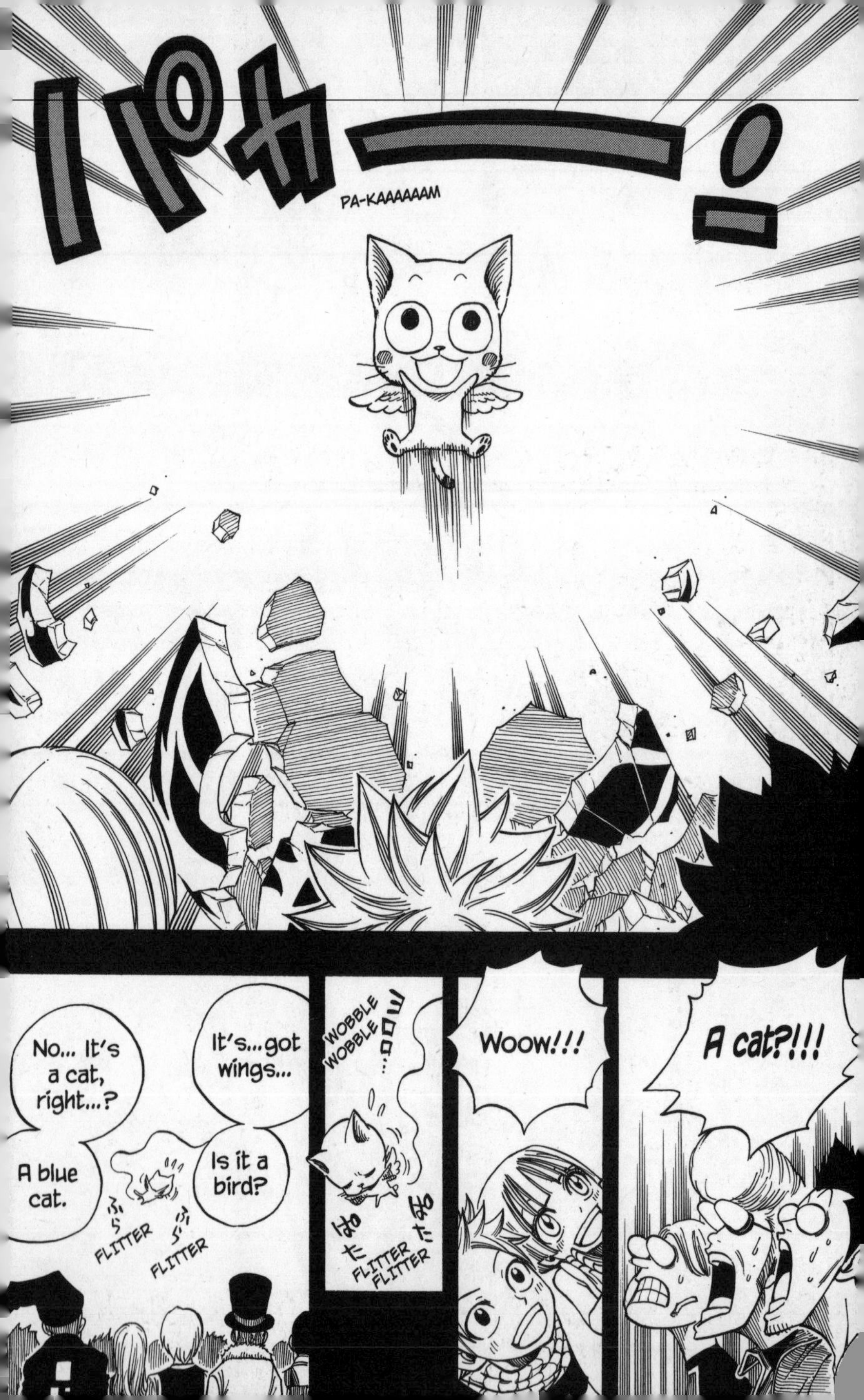
PA-KAAAAAAM
A cat?!!!
Woow!!!
WOBBLE WOBBLE
FLITTER FLITTER
It's...got wings...
No... It's a cat, right...?
Is it a bird?
A blue cat.
FLITTER
FLITTER

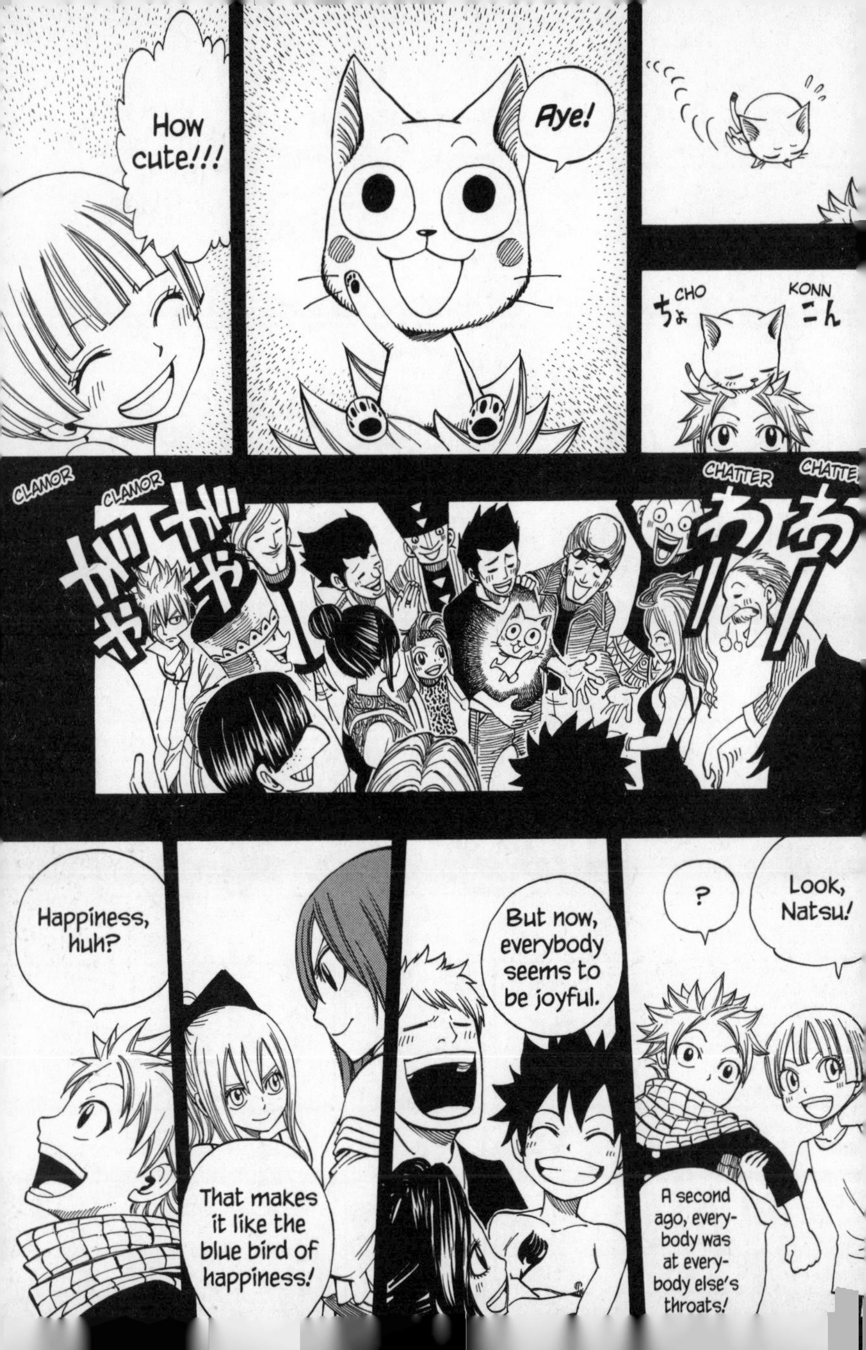

CHO
ちょ
KONN
こん
Aye!
How cute!!!
CHATTER
CHATTER
CLAMOR
CLAMOR
Look, Natsu!
?
A second ago, everybody was at everybody else's throats!
But now, everybody seems to be joyful.
That makes it like the blue bird of happiness!
Happiness, huh?

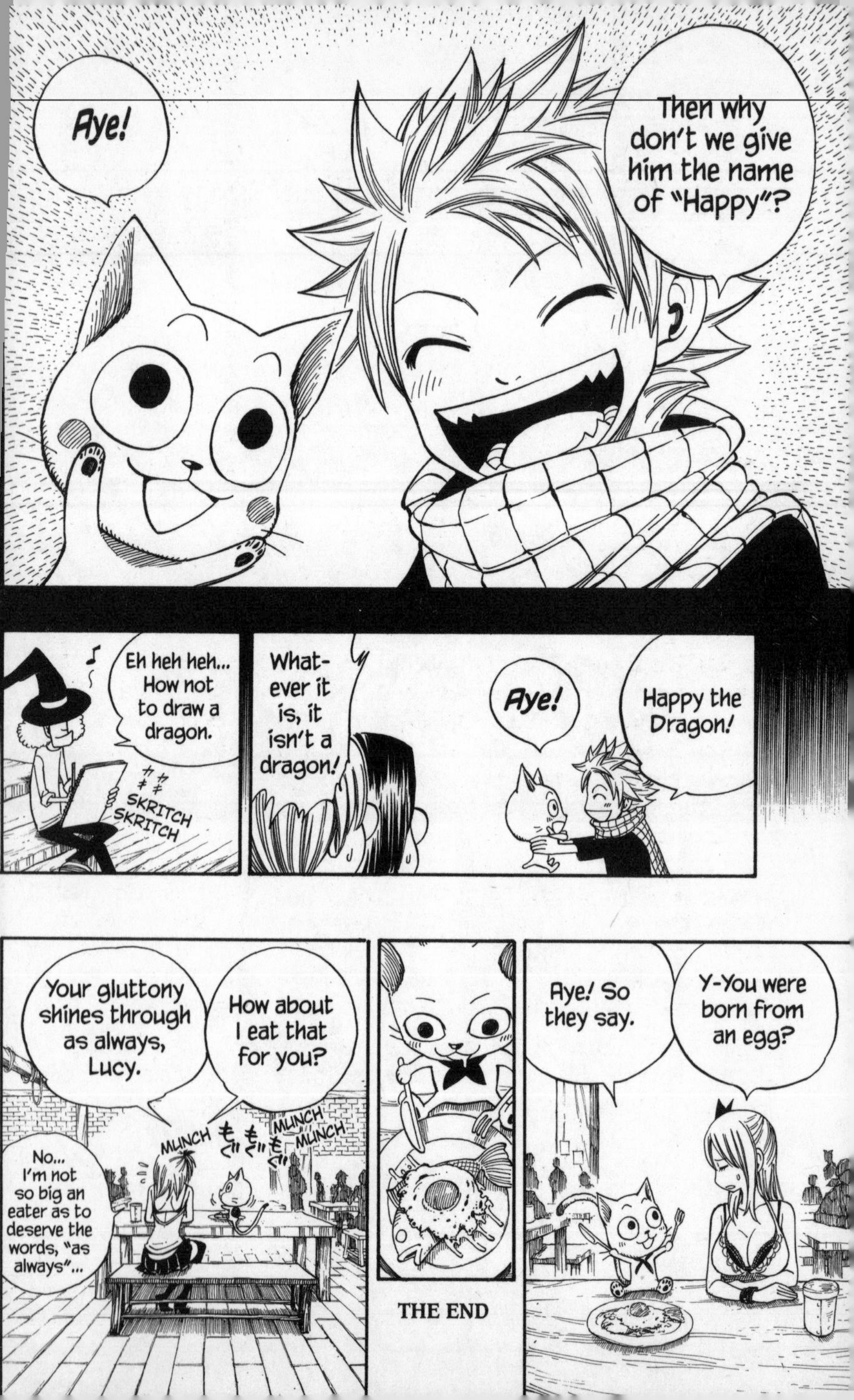
Then why don't we give him the name of "Happy"?
Aye!
Happy the Dragon!
Aye!
What-ever it is, it isn't a dragon!
Eh heh heh... How not to draw a dragon.
SKRITCH SKRITCH
Y-You were born from an egg?
Aye! So they say.
How about I eat that for you?
Your gluttony shines through as always, Lucy.
MUNCH MUNCH MUNCH
No... I'm not so big an eater as to deserve the words, "as always"...
THE END

AFTERWORD

This makes me really think hard about manga. Just kidding!! No, really, I went to signings in Taiwan and America, and I had also heard that they're really passionate about Fairy Tail in France too. And amid all this, I went to a party bringing together manga artists from both Sunday and Magazine, so I can say, I've had a good taste of manga events. I wrote a little about this in Volume 12, but Japan just doesn't seem to have any events that go beyond a particular publisher. If you're talking cars, you have the motor shows. Games have the Tokyo Game Show, and music has all of its festivals... There are loads of things like that. But there's none for manga. Of course, I think the rivalry between publishers is a good thing, but I also think that once a year, gathering all the publishers and having an event aimed at the fans would do some good. Sure, I know it'd cost a lot of money, and there are probably plenty of obstacles to it that I don't know about, but I think the days of being able to sell manga without lifting a finger are long over. It could be because of a change in consumer attitudes, or a change in the atmosphere surrounding manga, or the fact that we manga-ka have changed.... I'm sure there are many reasons, but you know, manga is Japanese culture. Isn't this the very time when the entire publishing industry should be gathering to go out and push it? At least, that's what I've been thinking lately. Huh... Here I go getting all serious, and now my shoulders have suddenly gotten stiff....

In the next Fairy Tail volume, we set a record, printing a chapter 128 that's very different than the magazine version!! It's an extended version where I've added some ten pages to it!! Look for it!!

Continued from the left-hand page

Then in comes the Master!

"Both of you! Well done!"

Lucy: And everybody is the best of friends!
Mira: And they lived happily ever after!

Hey, that may not be a bad idea.

Mira: Don't worry. "Those guys" will be back. In the next volume.

So why is it that Natsu and Gajeel couldn't get out of the Jutsu-shiki trap?

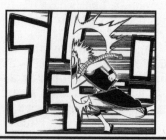

Lucy: Ohhh! So there's a mystery still left, huh?
Mira: It seems there is an actual reason for this.
Lucy: If I remember right, the rule went something like, "Stone statues and people over 80 years old may not leave." Or something like that, I think.
Mira: There was also a hint in Volume 4 and Volume 13 when it mentioned that Natsu's and Gajeel's ages were unknown.

Ehh?!! But that sort of gives the answer away, doesn't it? Are you sure it's okay to say that?!! That Natsu and Gajeel are both actually over 80 years old?!!

Sorry. Wrong.

Eh?

Mira: Beyond that would be revealing an important plot point, so I can't say any more.
Lucy: Nooo! Now you got me curious!!
Mira: On to the last question.

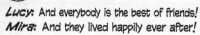

Hiro-kun is really just a big perv, right??

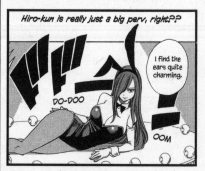

I find the ears quite charming.
DO-DOO
OOM

Lucy: I don't really think we need to answer that question.
Mira: True. He is always doing his very best for his male readers.
Lucy: That isn't what I mean! He isn't thinking of that at all! He's just a big perv!!
Mira: But he's doing his best for his female fans too! This volume, he had both Gray and Laxus strip down, didn't he?

I don't think just having everybody strip is "doing one's best"...

We are looking for questions about Fairy Tail! Send yours to:

Kodansha USA Publishing, LLC
451 Park Ave. South, 7th Fl.
New York, NY 10016

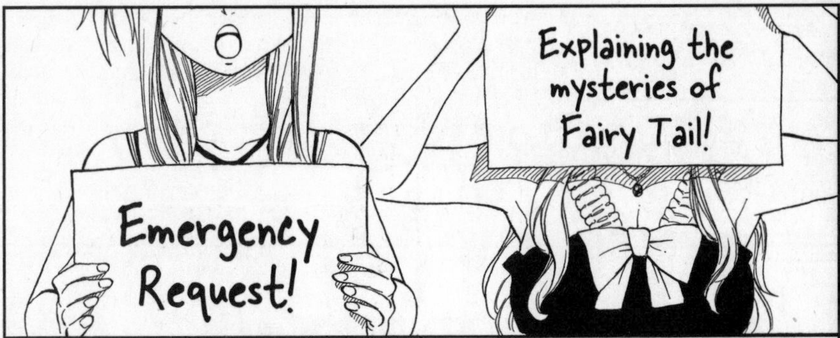
Explaining the mysteries of Fairy Tail!
Emergency Request!

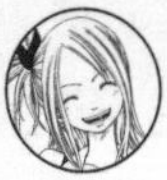 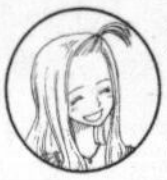

Moun•tain•li•on•pooooon!!!
Lucy: This time, we're going to have a great time answering your questions!

Mira: Woof, woof!
Lucy: ....
Mira: Woof!

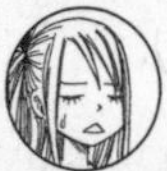

Okay. What's that for?

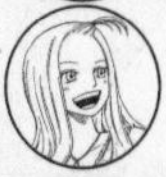

It's a mountainlion voice! Woof, woof!

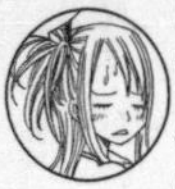

Mountain **LION**. It's one of the big cats!
Mira: So, on with the questions!

Don't you think Laxus is a little too macho with his shirt off?

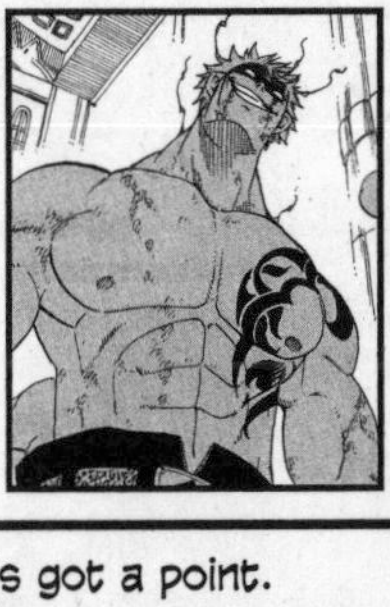

Lucy: The person's got a point.
Mira: I hear the manga artist thought a question like that would come along, and he was prepared.

Lucy: It isn't just Laxus. Whenever anybody is in a battle, they suddenly get all muscular.
Mira: Still, Dragon slayer magic is a type of magic that changes your body, so doesn't that explain it?

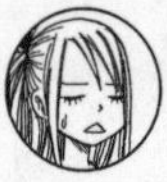

Isn't it just because he sucks at drawing people who are more delicate?
Mira: Next question!

Those guys... Who were they?

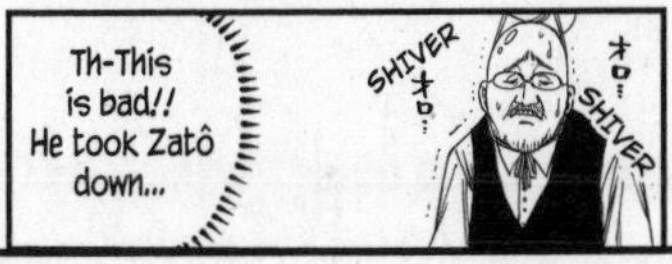
Th-This is bad!! He took Zatô down...
SHIVER
SHIVER

Lucy: Hey, you noticed the little bit of foreshadowing! Good for you!

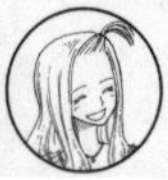

I hope the artist hasn't forgotten them himself.
Lucy: Maybe they were originally set to appear right in the middle of the Battle of Fairy Tail, right?
Mira: And it was up to Laxus and Natsu to defend the guild together!
Lucy: "You know I...really love Fairy Tail after all!" (Laxus's voice)
Mira: "Right! Then let's fight these bums together!" (Natsu's Voice)

Continued on the right-hand page

The *Fairy Tail* Guild d'Art is an explosion of fan art! Please send in your black-and-white art on large postcard stock!! Those chosen to be published will get a signed mini poster!♪ Make sure you write your real name and address on the back of your postcard!

d'ART

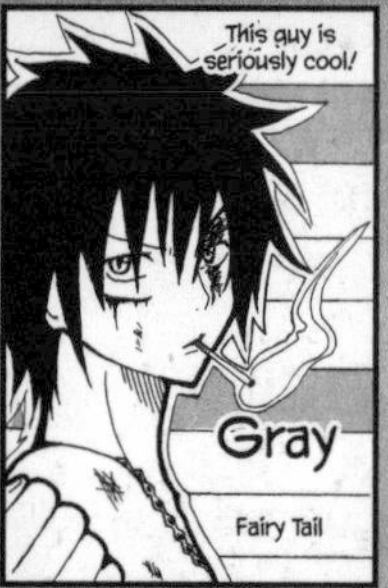
This guy is seriously cool!
Gray
Fairy Tail

▼Gray acting cool. But he's nude.

Okayama Prefecture, Ayaka Ikeda

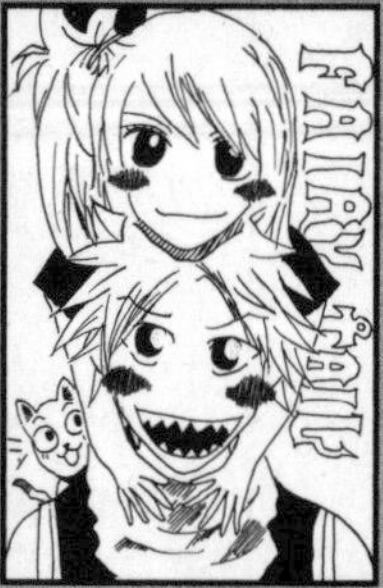
FAIRY TAIL

▼This is pretty cute. I like the combination.

Hokkaido, Hiroki Morimatsu

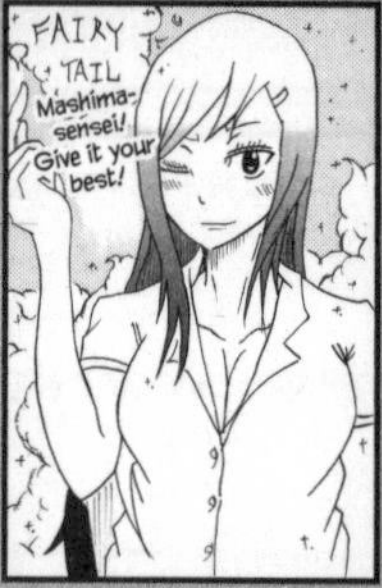
FAIRY TAIL
Mashima-sensei! Give it your best!

▼A refreshing Erza. Thank you! And thanks for the encouragement!

Tokyo, Ryo Hasegawa

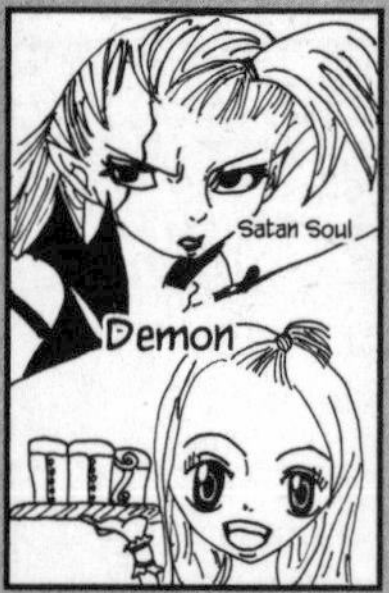
Satan Soul
Demon

▼The split personality of Mira-jane can be kind of scary, huh?

Kanagawa Prefecture, Fumio Koide

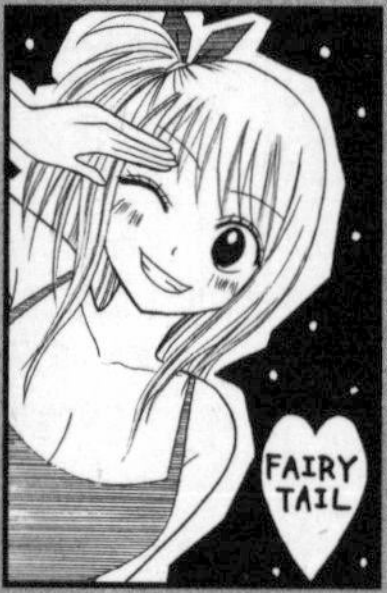
FAIRY TAIL

▼Hi there!! A cute pose for Lucy!

Hyogo Prefecture, Takobarada

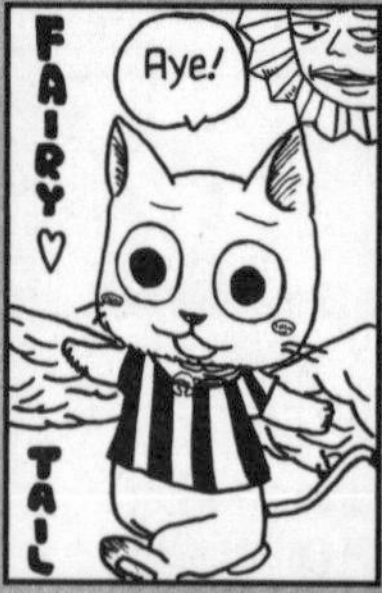
Aye!
FAIRY ♡
TAIL

▼Huh? What is that in the upper right?

Nagasaki Prefecture, Sayuri Hiraoka.

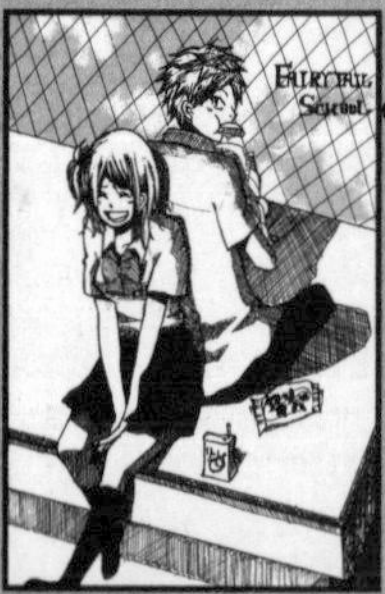
FAIRY TAIL School

▼Looks like the two of them during downtime at school.

Kanagawa Prefecture, Papiko

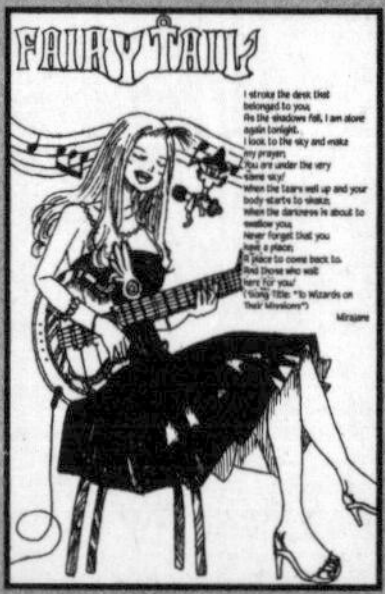
FAIRY TAIL

▼Lyrics by Hiro Mashima. Sorry.

Shizuoka Prefecture, Ryotty

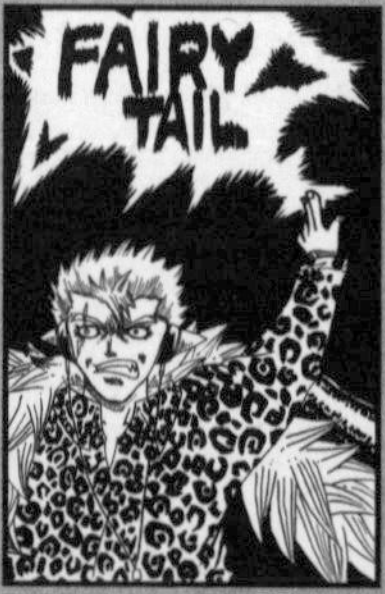
FAIRY TAIL

▼Laxus the strongest. It took the combined strength of Natsu and Gajeel together to take him down.

Osaka, Satoshi Senga

Kodansha USA Publishing, LLC
451 Park Ave. South, 7th Fl.
New York, NY 10016

GUILD

Rejection Corner

Tōyama Prefecture, Impact Abuzooba

It's already too late!!!
おくれだ!!
FAIRY TAIL

▲ Yeah, I have the feeling I drew something like this at some point, but I can't quite remember...

FARY TAIL
Gajeel

Iwate Prefecture, Yûya Abe

▼ It seems like he actually got into the fight with Laxus, maybe.

Nagano Prefecture, Chaahan

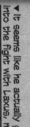

▼ That's an amazingly intelligent looking Natsu-kun.

Gifu Prefecture, Tomoka Yamashita

▼ Plue appearing on a checker pattern!!

My name is Ikaruga.
Ikaruga is so cute. I just love her!
Hiro Mashima-sensei, please take care and keep doing your best. I'm rooting for you!
FAIRY TAIL is the best!

Fukui Prefecture, Harukichi

▼ She was pretty good huh? Erza had a tough time fighting her

By sending in letters or postcards you give us permission to give your name, address, postal code and any other information you include to the author as is. Please keep that in mind.

▼ A really cute Juvia-san.

FAIRY TAIL

Ehime Prefecture, Ai Urushikawa

▼ Ohh! Natsu's turned into another Jason!

夢
Dream Collaboration
COOL!!

Osaka, Makoto Kihara

Translation Notes

Japanese is a tricky language for most Westerners, and translation is often more art than science. For your edification and reading pleasure, here are notes on some of the places where we could have gone in a different direction in our translation of the work, or where a Japanese cultural reference is used.

Names

Hiro Mashima has graciously agreed to provide official English spellings for just about all of the characters in Fairy Tail. Because this version of Fairy Tail is the first publication of most of these spellings, there will inevitably be differences between these spellings and some of the fan interpretations that may have spread throughout the web or in other fan circles. Rest assured that what is contained in this book are the spellings that Mashima-sensei wanted for *Fairy Tail*.

Wizard

In the original Japanese version of Fairy Tail, there are occasional images where the word "Wizard" is found. This translation has taken that as it's inspiration, and translated the word *madōshi* as wizard. But *madōshi*'s meaning is similar to certain Japanese words that have been borrowed into the English language such as judo (the soft way) and kendo (the way of the sword). *Madō* is the way of magic, and *madōshi* are those who follow the way of magic. So although the word "wizard" is used, the Japanese would think less of traditional western wizards such as Merlin or Gandalf, and more of martial artists.

Dance of Purgatory, page 16

The top two *kanji* on Mystogan's pants are the Japanese word for the Catholic religion's concept of purgatory -- a place to purge one's soul of sins before one can proceed to heaven. The bottom two, *kagura*, is a word for traditional music and dances of the Shinto religion.

Matenrō, page 25

In normal use, *matenrō* would mean a high-rise building, but obviously this particular magic has nothing to do with a building. The first *kanji* in the word means "to scrape," and the second means "the heavens." And considering what was awaiting Laxus up in the sky, "Sky Scraping" seems like a reasonable translation for the words.

Symbols on Chest, page 71

One of the passed-out wizards had a *kanji* and heart symbol either on a t-shirt or a tattoo on his chest. The first one is the *kanji* for *ai*, which means "love." So, although it would be pronounced the same as the "I heart" T-shirts, it basically means, "Love love."

Preview of Fairy Tail, volume 16

We're pleased to present you a preview from volume 16, now available from Kodansha Comics. Please check our Web site (www.kodanshacomics.com) for more information on Fairy Tail and our other great series!

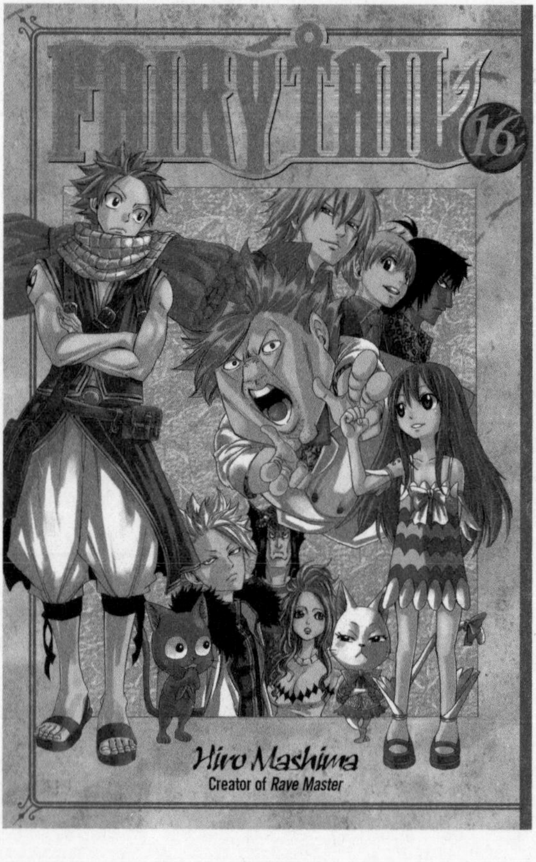
FAIRY TAIL
16
Hiro Mashima
Creator of Rave Master

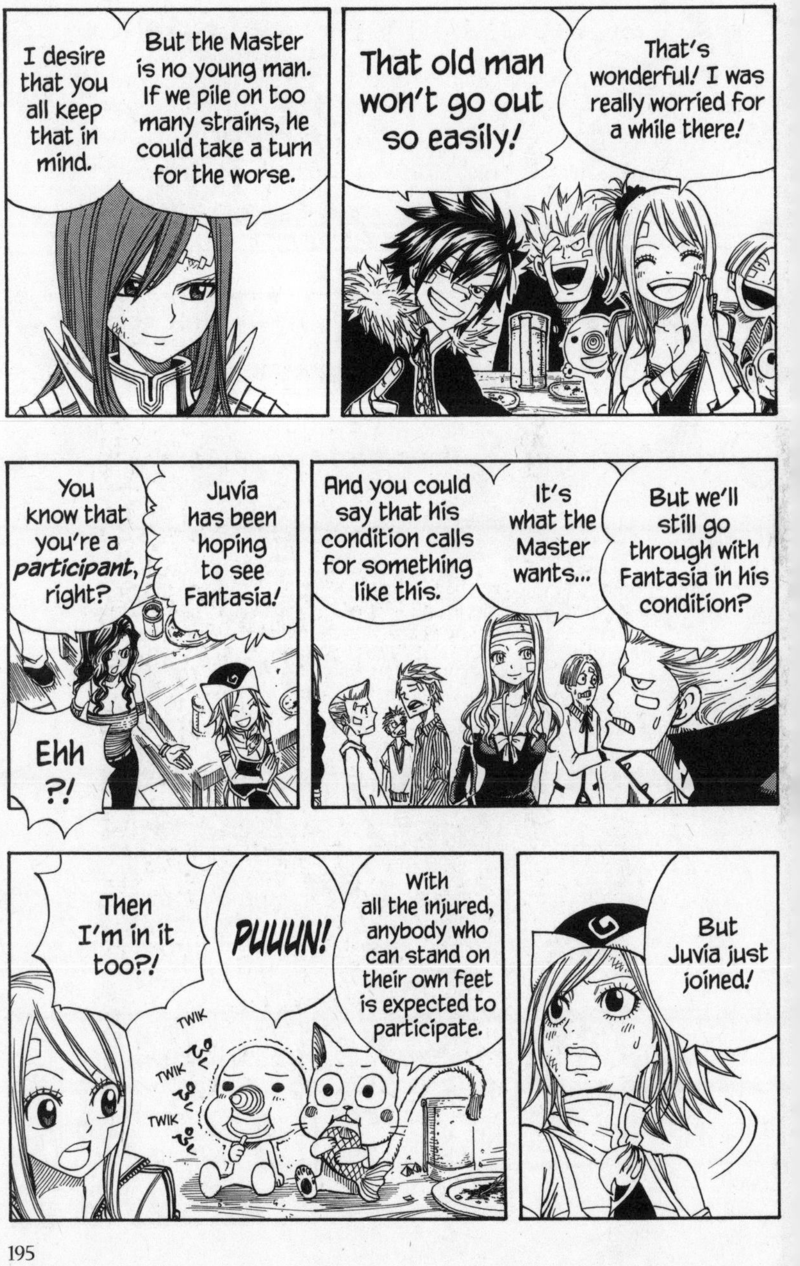
That's wonderful! I was really worried for a while there!
That old man won't go out so easily!
But the Master is no young man. If we pile on too many strains, he could take a turn for the worse.
I desire that you all keep that in mind.
But we'll still go through with Fantasia in his condition?
It's what the Master wants...
And you could say that his condition calls for something like this.
Juvia has been hoping to see Fantasia!
You know that you're a *participant*, right?
Ehh ?!
But Juvia just joined!
With all the injured, anybody who can stand on their own feet is expected to participate.
PUUUN!
Then I'm in it too?!
TWIK
TWIK
TWIK

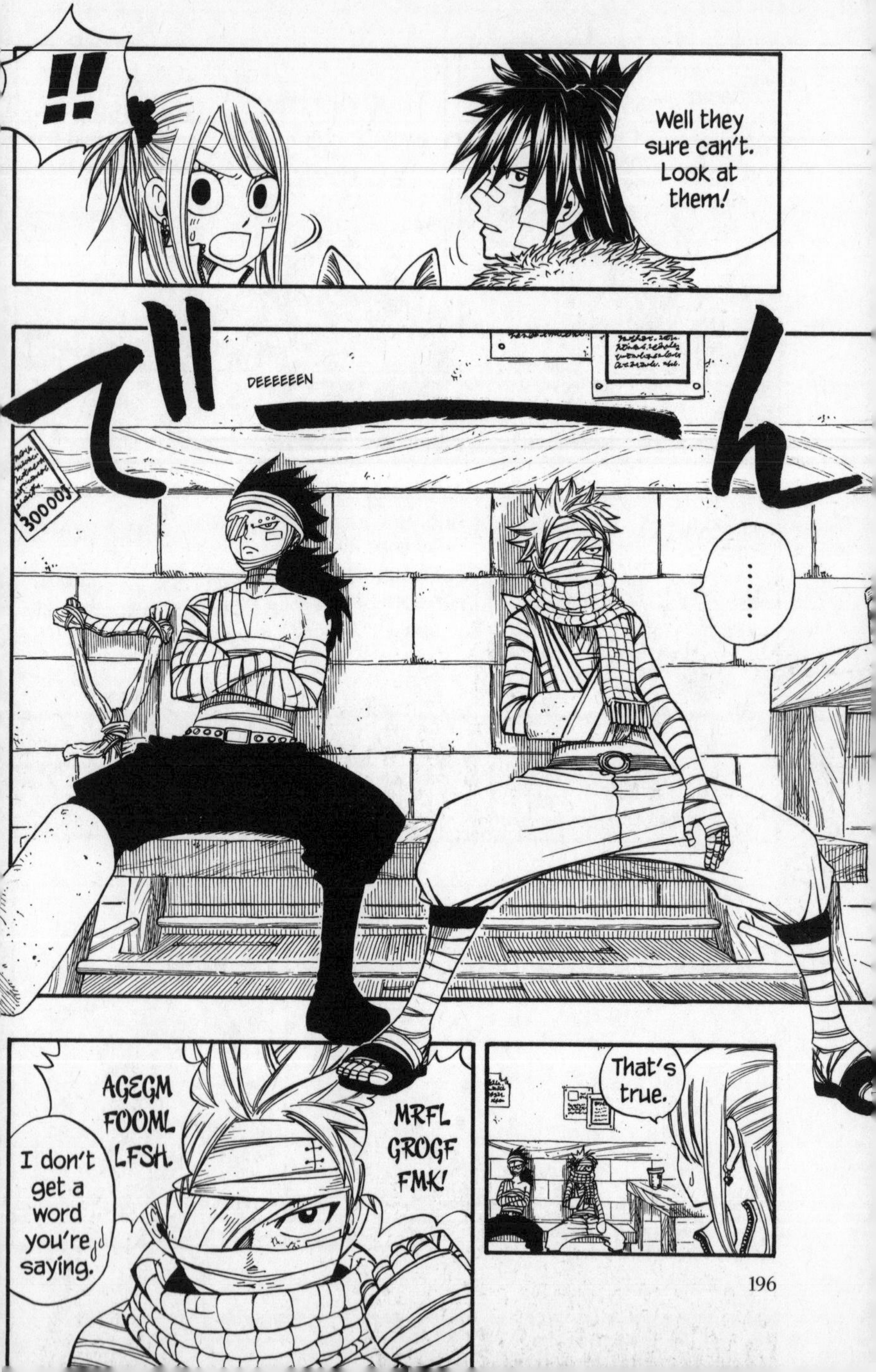
Well they sure can't. Look at them!
!!
でーん
DEEEEEEN
......
That's true.
MRFL GROGF FMK!
AGEGM FOOML LFSH.
I don't get a word you're saying.

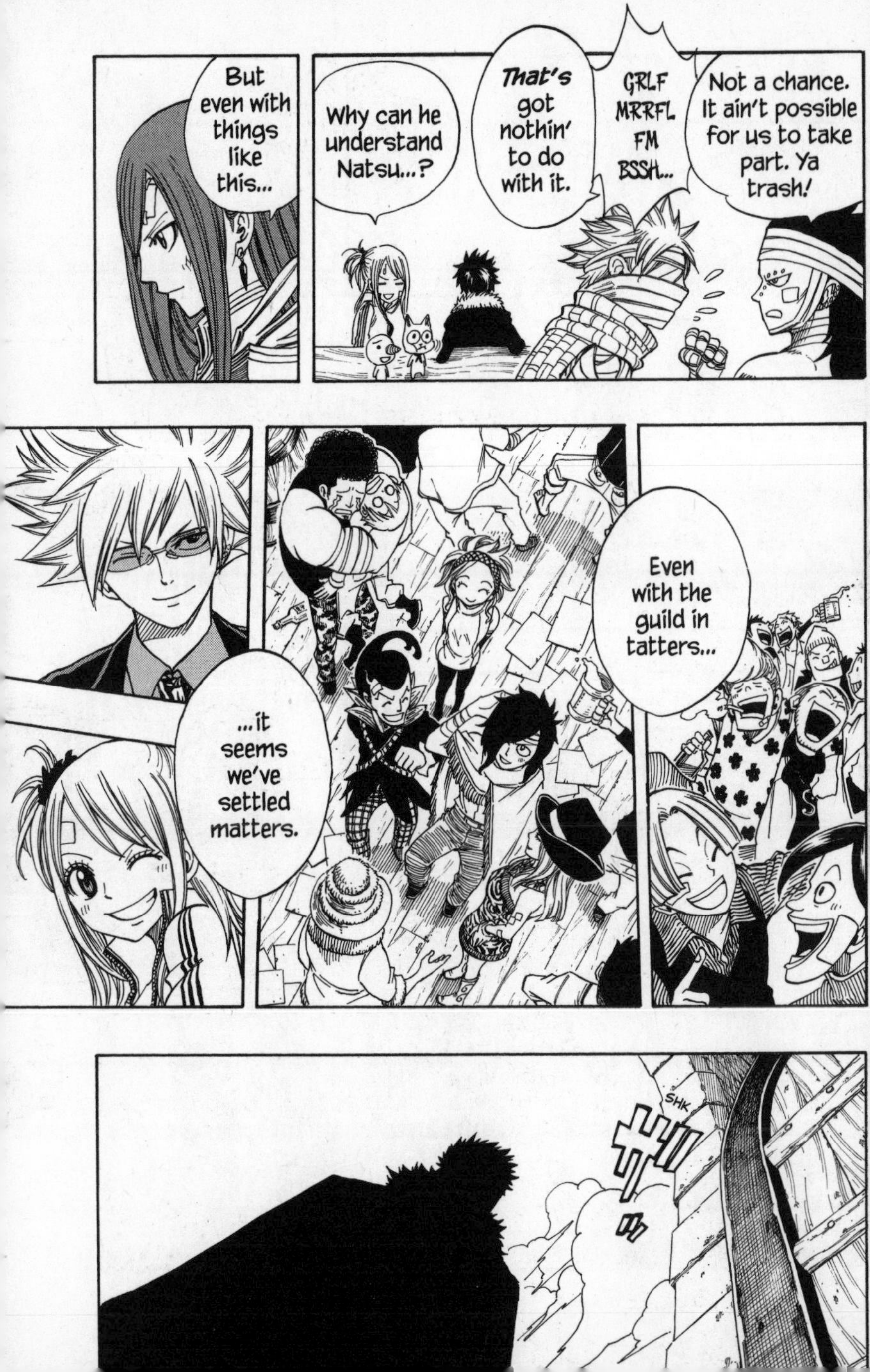
Not a chance. It ain't possible for us to take part. Ya trash!
GRLF MRRFL FM BSSH...
That's got nothin' to do with it.
Why can he understand Natsu...?
But even with things like this...
Even with the guild in tatters...
...it seems we've settled matters.
SHK

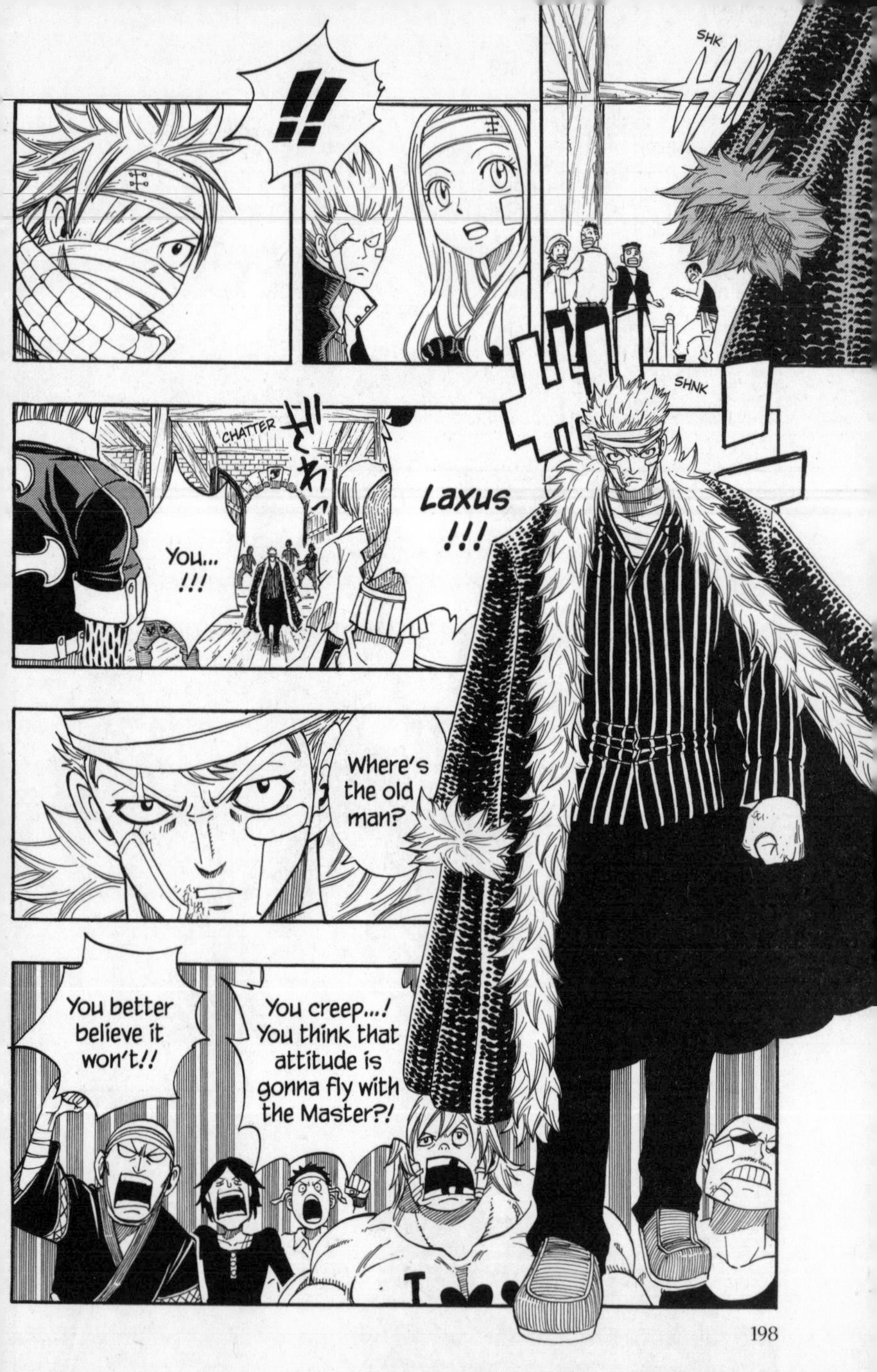
SHK
!!
SHNK
CHATTER
Laxus !!!
You... !!!
Where's the old man?
You creep...! You think that attitude is gonna fly with the Master?!
You better believe it won't!!

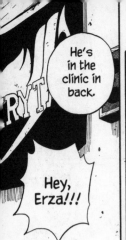

He's in the clinic in back.

Hey, Erza!!!

!!!

Leave him be.

WHOOSH

FML N MF FRIFLL !!!!

RAFFUZ !!!!

SHK SHK SHK

FAIRY TAIL

Natsu...

SKRRRCH

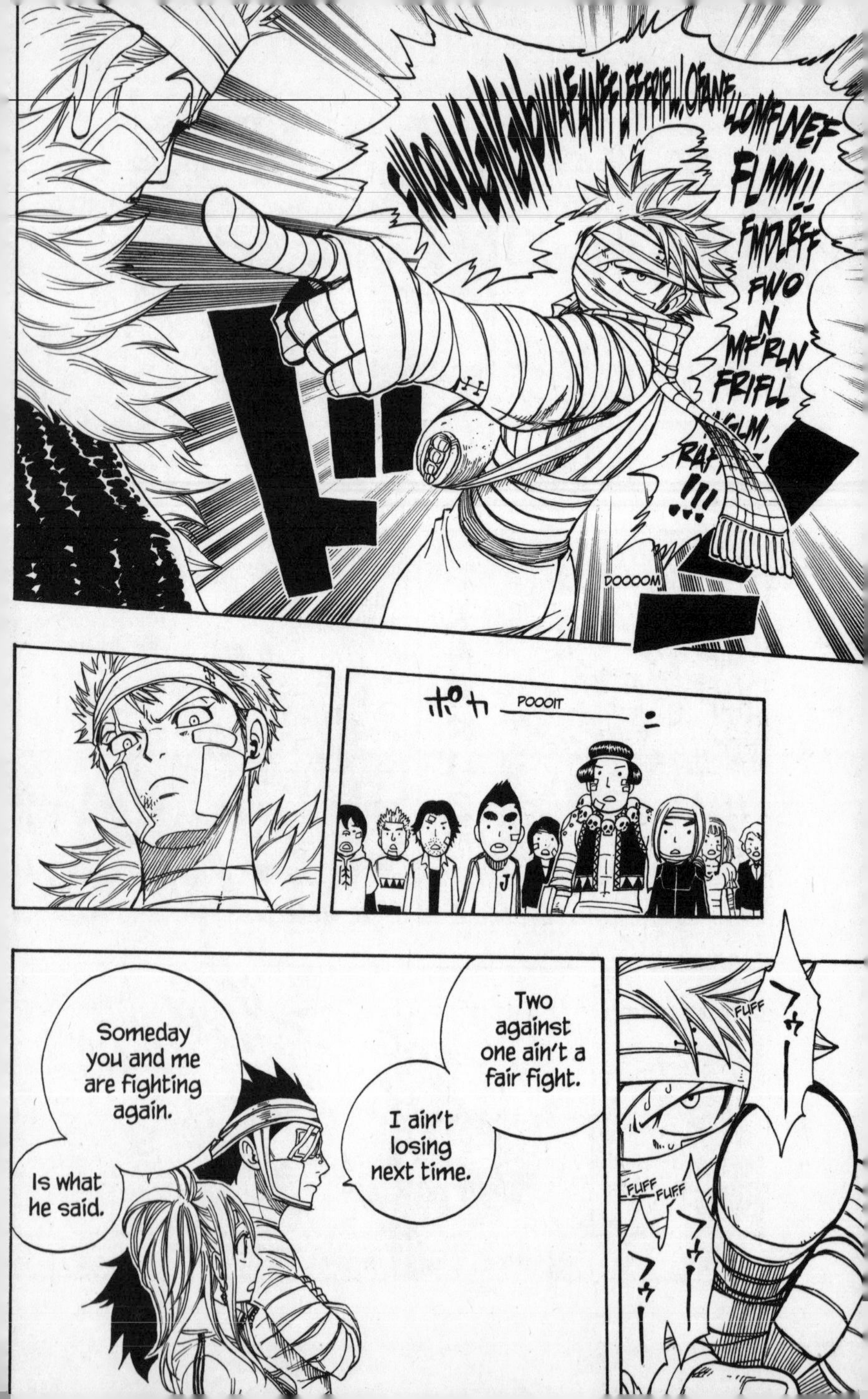
DOOOOM
ポカ
POOOIT
FUFF
FUFF FUFF
Two against one ain't a fair fight.
I ain't losing next time.
Someday you and me are fighting again.
Is what he said.

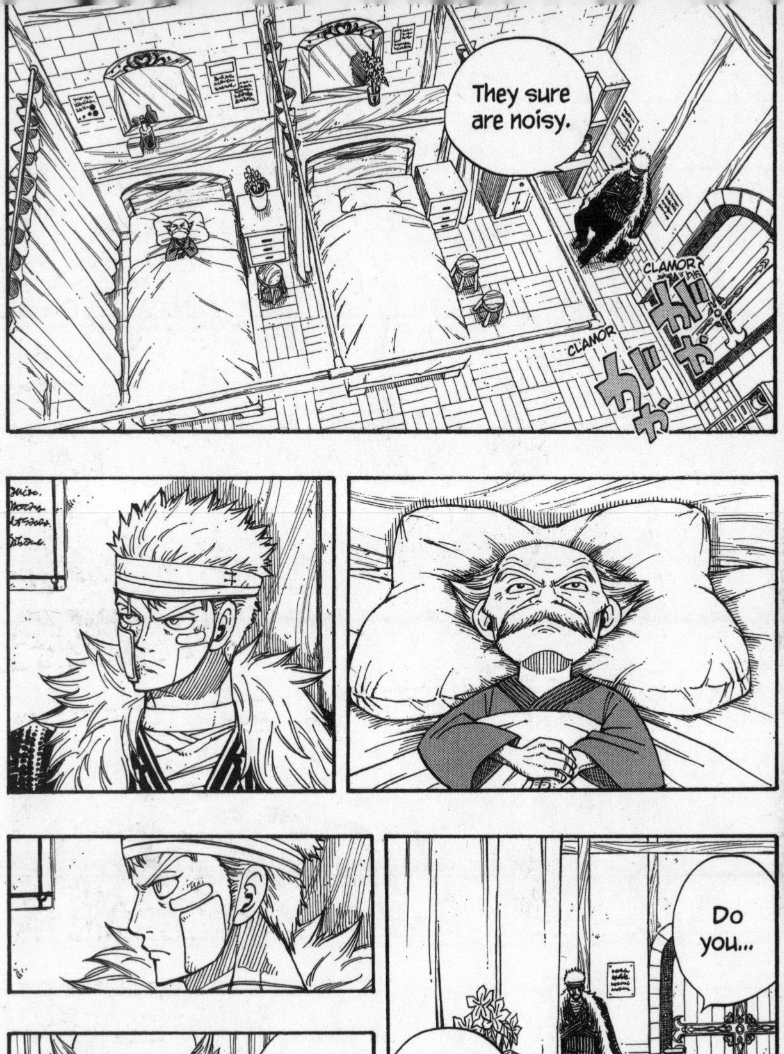
They sure are noisy.
CLAMOR
CLAMOR
Do you...
...have any idea of what you did?
GMPH
Look me in the eye!

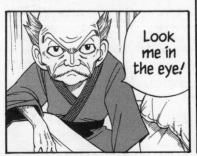

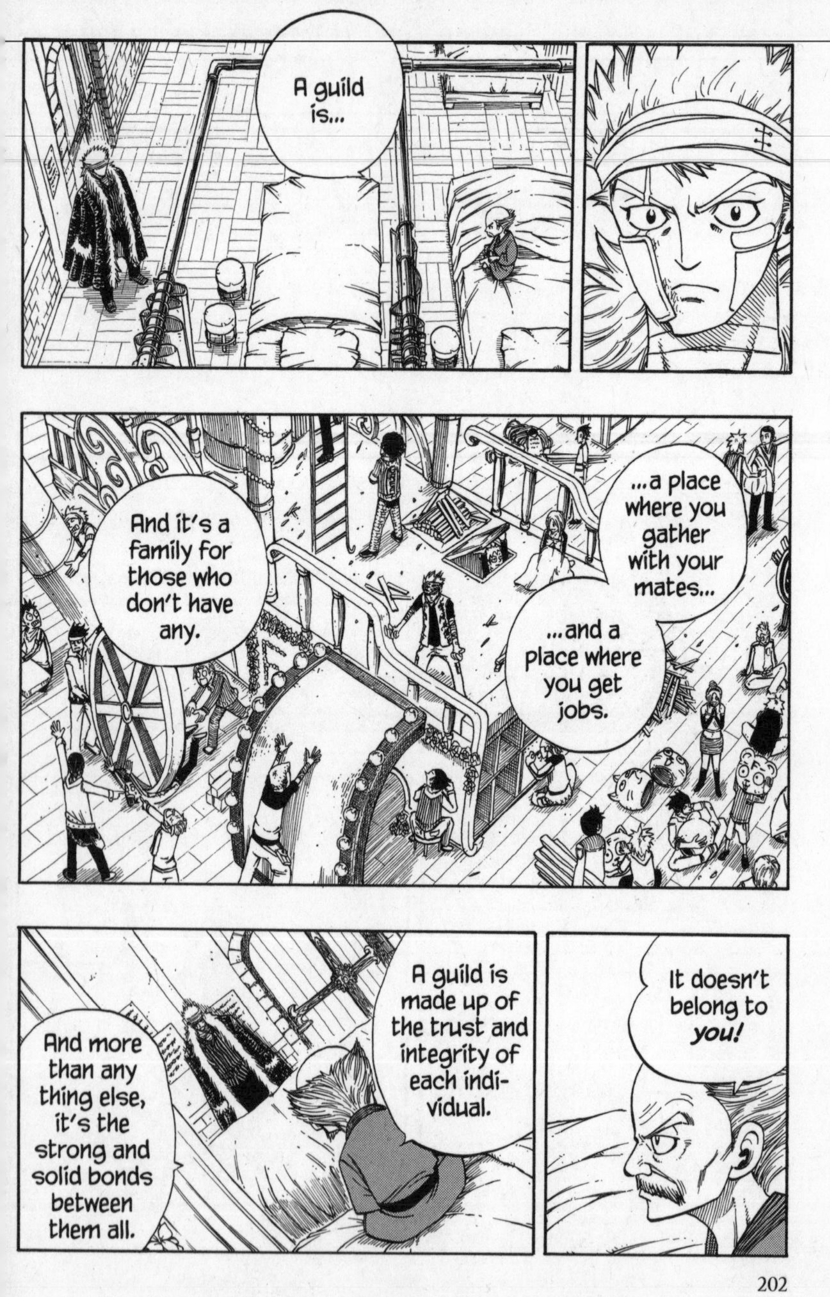
A guild is...
...a place where you gather with your mates...
...and a place where you get jobs.
And it's a family for those who don't have any.
It doesn't belong to *you!*
A guild is made up of the trust and integrity of each indi-vidual.
And more than any thing else, it's the strong and solid bonds between them all.

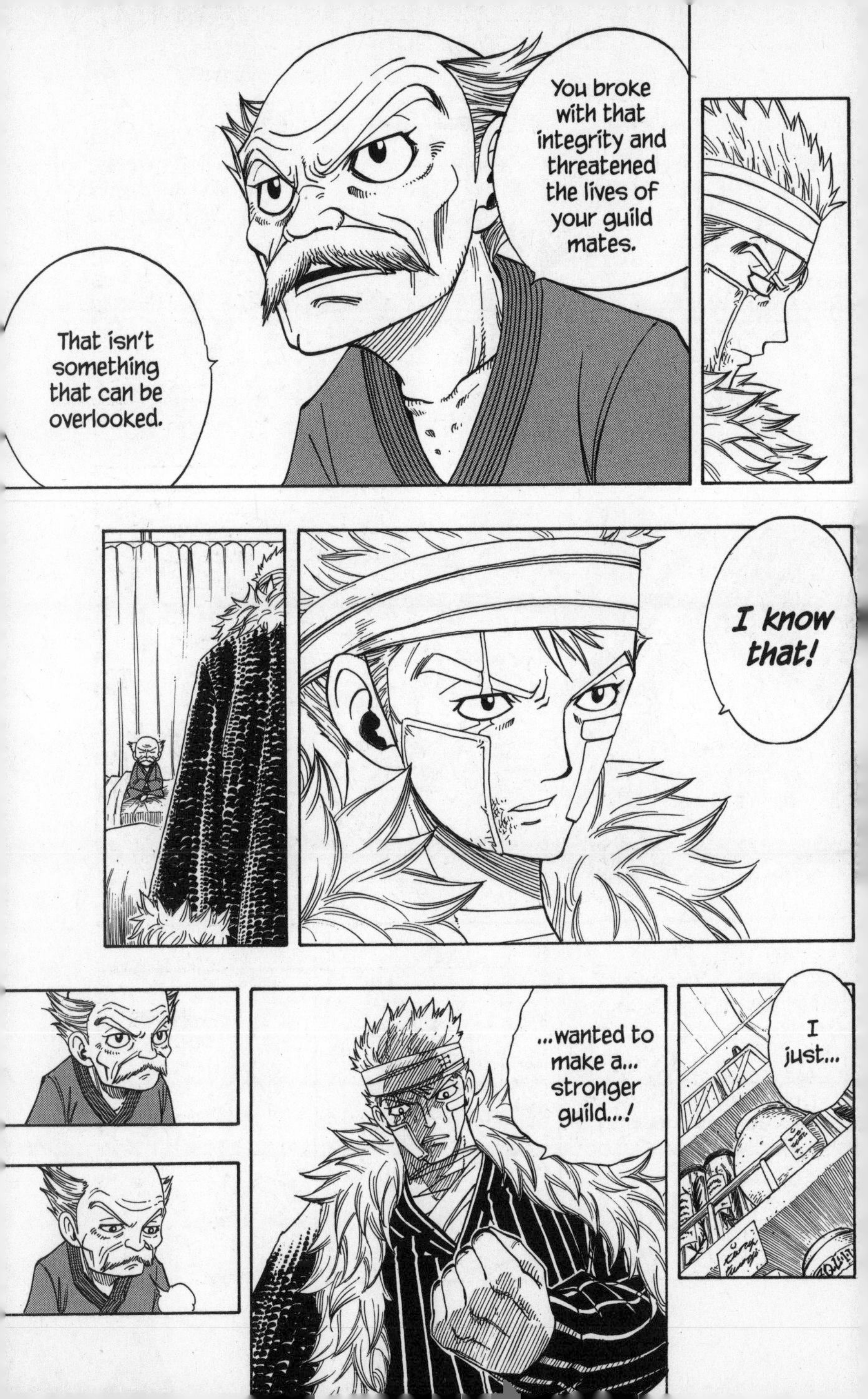
You broke with that integrity and threatened the lives of your guild mates.
That isn't something that can be overlooked.
I know that!
I just...
...wanted to make a... stronger guild...!

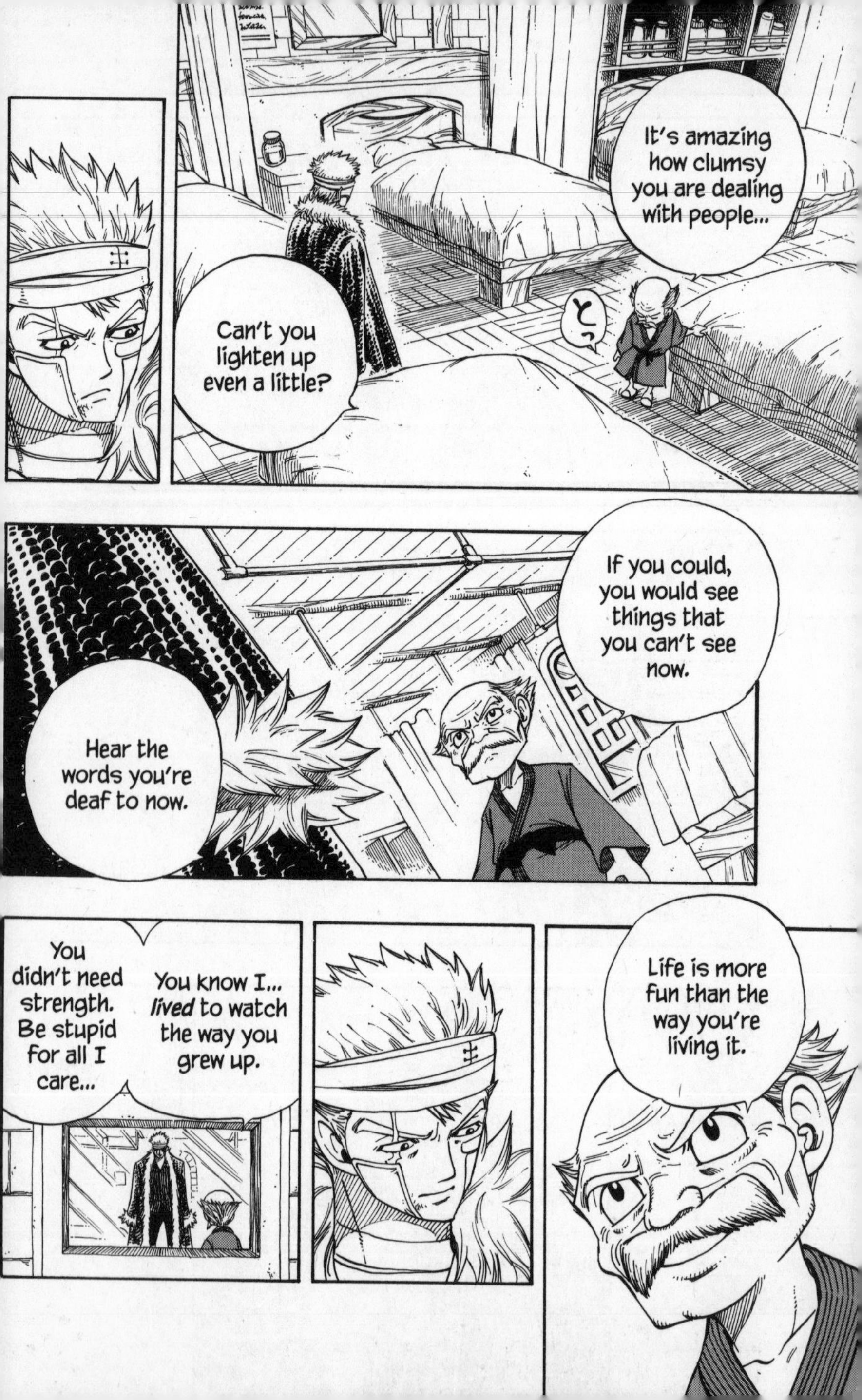
It's amazing how clumsy you are dealing with people...
とっ
Can't you lighten up even a little?
If you could, you would see things that you can't see now.
Hear the words you're deaf to now.
Life is more fun than the way you're living it.
You know I... *lived* to watch the way you grew up.
You didn't need strength. Be stupid for all I care...

But as long as you were full of energy ...

...that was all I was hoping for.

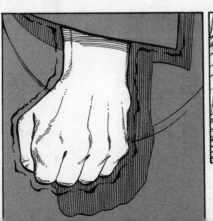

Laxus!

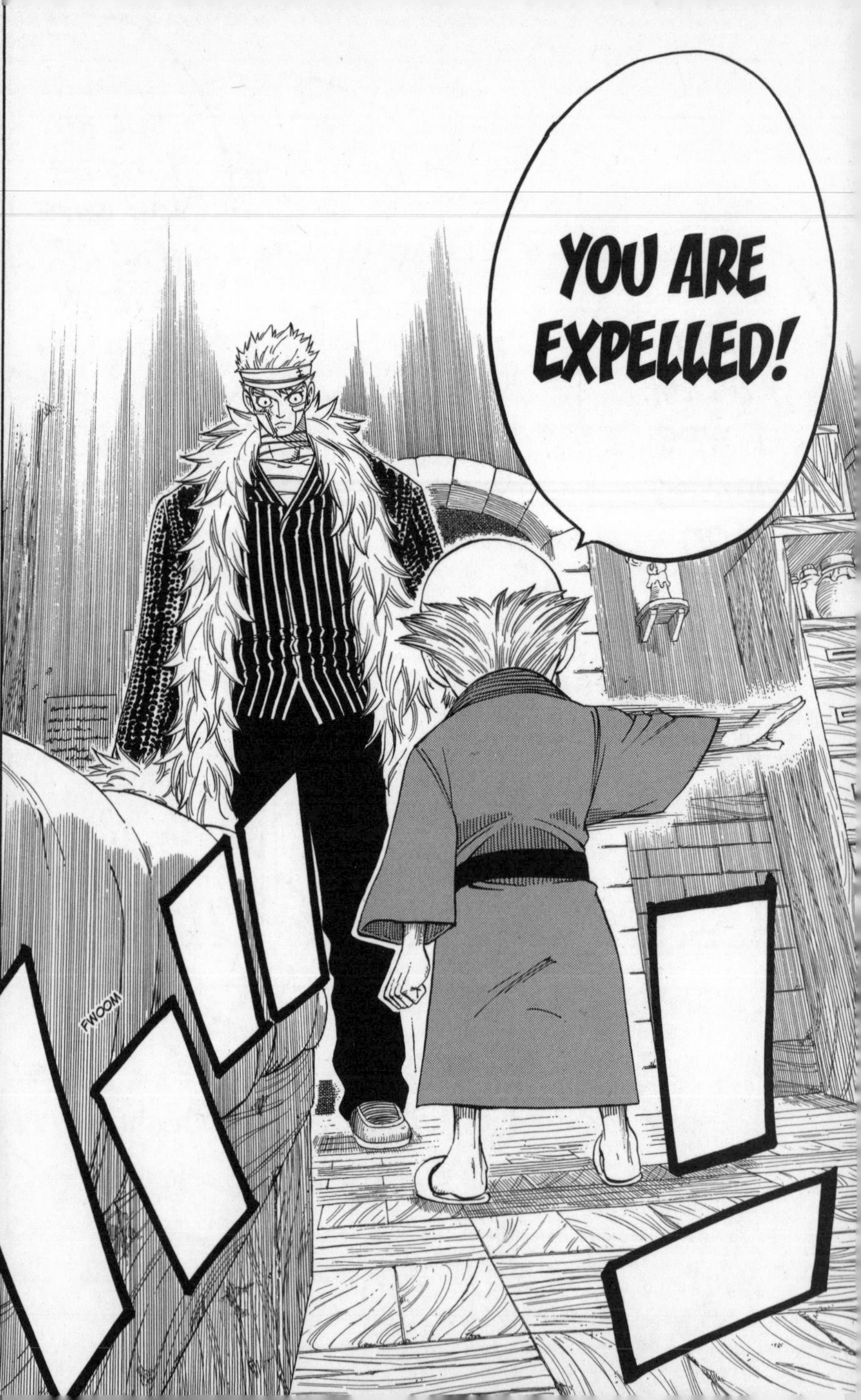
YOU ARE EXPELLED!
FWOOM

Fairy Tail volume 15 is a work of fiction. Names, characters, places, and incidents are the products of the author's imagination or are used fictitiously. Any resemblance to actual events, locales, or persons, living or dead, is entirely coincidental.

A Kodansha Comics Trade Paperback Original.

Published in the United States by Kodansha Comics, an imprint of Kodansha USA Publishing, LLC., New York.

Publication rights for this English edition arranged through Kodansha Ltd., Tokyo.

First published in Japan in 2009 by Kodansha Ltd., Tokyo.

ISBN 978-1-93542-934-0

Printed in the United States of America.

www.kodanshacomics.com

9 8 7

Translator/Adapter: William Flanagan
Lettering: North Market Street Graphics

TOMARE!

[STOP!]

You're going the wrong way!

Manga is a completely different type of reading experience.

To start at the *beginning*, go to the *end*!

That's right! Authentic manga is read the traditional Japanese way—from right to left, exactly the *opposite* of how American books are read. It's easy to follow: Just go to the other end of the book and read each page—and each panel—from right side to left side, starting at the top right. Now you're experiencing manga as it was meant to be!